# Microsoft
# Access 97
## Developer's Handbook

Solution
Developer
Series

Timothy M. O'Brien, Steven J. Pogge,
Geoffrey E. White

PUBLISHED BY
Microsoft Press
A Division of Microsoft Corporation
One Microsoft Way
Redmond, Washington 98052-6399

Library of Congress Cataloging-in-Publication Data
O'Brien, Timothy M.
    Microsoft Access 97 developer's handbook / Timothy M. O'Brien,
Steven J. Pogge, Geoffrey E. White.
        p.      cm.
    Includes index.
    ISBN 1-57231-358-7
    1. Microsoft Access.    2. Database management.      I. Pogge, Steven
J.    II. White, Geoffrey E.      III. Title.
QA76.9.D3O268  1997
005.75'65--dc21                                              97-1922
                                                              CIP

Printed and bound in the United States of America.

1 2 3 4 5 6 7 8 9  QMQM  2 1 0 9 8 7

Distributed to the book trade in Canada by Macmillan of Canada, a division of Canada Publishing Corporation.

A CIP catalogue record for this book is available from the British Library.

Microsoft Press books are available through booksellers and distributors worldwide. For further information about international editions, contact your local Microsoft Corporation office. Or contact Microsoft Press International directly at fax (206) 936-7329.

FoxPro, Microsoft, PowerPoint, Visual Basic, Visual C++, Windows, and Windows NT are registered trademarks and ActiveX, Developer Studio, and Visual FoxPro are trademarks of Microsoft Corporation. Other product and company names mentioned herein may be the trademarks of their respective owners.

**Acquisitions Editor:** Casey D. Doyle
**Project Editor:** Sally Stickney
**Technical Editors:** Dennis English, Kurt Meyer

# CONTENTS

## 3   Error Handling and Debugging ...................................... 85

## 4   The File Backup Application ...................................... 117

## PART TWO   Creating Professional Applications

## PART THREE   Working with Data

**PART FOUR   Using ActiveX and the Internet**

## PART FIVE   Appendixes

# ACKNOWLEDGMENTS

Aside from our families and those listed in our dedications, we want to thank the many people who have helped us write this book.

A special thank you goes to Malcolm Stewart for being Malcolm and for the authoritative voice on Jet issues. Malcolm is also responsible for much of the code in the sample database on the companion CD.

Thank you Matt Neerix, Jim Lucey, Steve Maslyk, Gary Yukish, Cathy Banks, and Kevin Mineweaser for your timely responses and technical assistance.

Thank you Rob Jacik, Steven Parsons, Dana McKittrick, Tabitha Barham, and Cary Russell for your work on the ErrTool97.MDA add-in included on the companion CD.

Thank you to our resource insiders: Kamran Iqbal, the subject matter expert for the Mastering Microsoft Access Programming CD; Lynn Shanklin, one of the leads responsible for the great product documentation; and Daniel Bien from Access Program Management.

Thanks to Tom Jebo, whose knowledge of ActiveX seems limitless.

Thanks to Katherine Krause for her insight and advice on writing styles and guidelines.

Thank you Lisa Nichols, Christi White, and Michael Patten for allowing us to moonlight to write this book and for your support.

Also a heartfelt "Thanks!" to Melvin for his entertaining tune and cocktail party information.

We also would like to extend a special thank you to the entire Microsoft Access product group unit and to everyone on the technical alias for the customer support and product knowledge that are invaluable to all of us. And thank you as well to all the extremely dedicated individuals we met at Microsoft's International Subsidiaries.

A special thank you also goes to Microsoft Marketing, to Scott Horn for his kind words, and to Christin Overton for getting us the betas.

Thanks to Sam Gill for reviewing the book and for his insightful comments.

And finally, many thanks to the folks at Microsoft Press: to Casey Doyle for giving us the opportunity and to Sally Stickney, Dennis English, and Kurt Meyer for all of their hard work.

# INTRODUCTION

It was Confucius who said, "What I hear I forget. What I see I remember. What I do I understand." This book was written with these ideas in mind. We've filled the book with examples, especially in the "solutions" chapters, so that you can see and understand how the theories and concepts presented apply to real-life business situations.

## Becoming a Solution Developer

This book is geared to those who want to become solution developers, not to those who are already solution developers or who are experienced Microsoft Access developers and want to learn advanced programming. To become a solution developer, you first need to learn the basics and to understand the concepts behind some of the advanced topics. You can consider this book a stepping-stone to advanced programming books. A good solution developer must have solid general knowledge about what features a product has and what functionality exists in the product: in this case, Microsoft Access 97.

In this book you'll learn to become a proficient solution developer and to take advantage of the powerful development features of Microsoft Access in order to build successful real-world business solutions. By "real-world business so-lutions" we mean the kinds of solutions that take into account the challenges programmers and developers encounter in their day-to-day work. Consider the following scenario.

A "Real-World Solution Developer"/ex-COBOL programmer has been working at a major corporation for the past 15 years doing COBOL programming. This developer is now told to build an application using Microsoft Access. He or she has the ability to get up to speed quickly by using all the powerful wizards and Automation tools provided in Microsoft Access. However, the application re-quires error handling or transaction processing. Things that were familiar and comfortable in COBOL can't be done with macros, wizards, or builders. And in many business environments, it would be unacceptable to produce an application that delivers an error message such as "Macro Failed" and then throws the user out of the application. So our developer is faced with two challenges: learning a new programming language and learning to make very user-friendly Microsoft Access applications. Finding out how to use Microsoft Access and VBA effectively and learning how to add proper error handling are examples of the many solutions covered in this book. You'll learn how to deal with the many requirements necessary to users with different security levels in real-world situations.

## Microsoft Access and You

Microsoft Access is a unique product that ships with Microsoft Office and is used by millions of people, both developers and users. This book was written for people of varying technical backgrounds. Although some people might never need to use the full potential of Access, others will explore its every nook and cranny. The purpose of this book is to focus on programming skills and concepts and to make complex topics such as Data Access Objects (DAO) and ActiveX easy to grasp for the novice yet detailed enough to answer the questions of an experienced developer. We also want to show you how you can use Visual Basic for Applications (VBA) with Microsoft Access to achieve tight integration among all the Microsoft Office applications.

## The Organization of This Book

This book has four parts. Each part is composed of "theory" chapters that provide you with a solid understanding of the programming concepts you will need to know about in order to create robust Microsoft Access applications. You'll further enhance your development skills by applying what you learned in these theory chapters to creating real-world solutions in the "solutions" chapters in each part.

Part One, The VBA Programming Environment, contains four chapters that introduce you to the world of VBA programming. This section is designed for novice programmers as well as for experienced developers coming from a different programming background. Beginners will learn how to create code from the ground up and use it right away. Experienced programmers will benefit from an overview of the programming functionality available, such as data types, built-in procedures, and structures. A unique aspect of Part One is that we have devoted an entire chapter to error handling, introducing this topic in the beginning of the book. Many books teach you how to use error handling after you have learned how to program or don't teach it to you at all. We want you to learn how to use error handling up front so that you can incorporate this critical aspect of creating successful applications early on, expediting your learning process.

Part Two, Creating Professional Applications, shows you how to make your applications and the elements within them conform to Windows application user-interface standards. You'll be introduced to the different controls and features developers can use to provide this consistent look and feel. You'll also learn everything you need to know to create forms, the objects most commonly used by Microsoft Access users. You'll also learn how to enhance your forms using VBA to take advantage of such functionality as event-driven programming, controls, and the Microsoft Access object model.

Part Three, Working with Data, concentrates on the heart of your database: the data itself and the database engine, Microsoft Jet. You'll learn about the DAO object model and how to use the objects within it. You'll discover how to perform common and useful tasks that you can apply to all your applications, such as relinking tables, coding for multiuser environments, building SQL (Structured Query Language) statements, creating custom search routines, and manipulating data. In addition, you'll find out how to effectively implement security in your applications.

Part Four, Using ActiveX and the Internet, shows you how to bring your applications up to date with the latest technological advancements. ActiveX encompasses OLE, Automation, COM (component object model), and ActiveX controls formerly known as OLE controls (OCXs). You'll learn about ActiveX technology so that you can take advantage of the functionality of other Microsoft Office products and of ActiveX controls. The last chapter will show you how to integrate your Microsoft Access application with the latest Internet technologies. You'll even learn how to add a custom Internet browser to your application.

The book also has two appendixes: Appendix A introduces you to DLLs, those versatile Windows procedures that allow you to extend your application beyond the functionality provided by the Microsoft Access programming environment. Appendix B covers most of the information you'll need to know to construct Help files for your application and includes many references to the more detailed Help information included on the companion CD.

## Using the Companion CD

The companion CD includes all of the sample applications presented in the book, including Internet solutions. It also contains much useful information and additional sample code: a utilities database that provides solutions from fellow developers, utility functions you can use with Microsoft Access, a DAO syntax builder, examples of DLLs, and instructions for creating Windows Help files, complete with samples.

To install the files on the companion CD, insert the disc in your CD drive. At the command prompt, enter D:\INSTALL. Follow the on-screen instructions. (You can also execute D:\INSTALL from the Windows Explorer.)

## Learn It from the Experts

Our (Tim's, Steve's, and Geoff's) backgrounds share common threads: training, development, and product support. In our careers we have not only supported Microsoft's customers but also traveled around the globe to teach Microsoft's Product Support Engineers. In June 1995, Geoff and Steve were developing training courses for Support Engineers, and Tim was involved in writing the Microsoft Access MES courseware for ATECs. We decided to pull together to write one of the best Microsoft Access VBA books in the industry. We are very familiar with the questions customers and engineers have about Microsoft Access. This book is a composition of our knowledge and experience in cities in just about every time zone and on every continent, including Charlotte, Boston, San Francisco, Minneapolis, Detroit, Chicago, Yardley, Orlando, Dallas, Tucson, Seattle, Toronto, London, Paris, Istanbul, Johannesburg, Mexico City, and São Paulo.

We hope you'll benefit from our real-world experiences and learn as much from reading it as we did from writing it.

# The VBA Programming Environment

# 1

# The ABCs of VBA

Since the introduction of Microsoft Access into the database market in October 1992, millions of users worldwide have embraced this flexible and easy-to-use product and made it one of the premiere database management systems. Microsoft Access 97 builds on the success of the earlier versions. In this book, we are going to assume that you thoroughly understand the fundamentals of Microsoft Access—including creating tables, relations, queries, forms, and macros—and want to expand your application development skills: learning to use Visual Basic for Applications (VBA) is a logical next step.

The VBA language enables you not only to use Microsoft Access to its full potential but also to develop applications for other Microsoft products that support VBA, such as Microsoft Visual Basic, Microsoft Excel, and Microsoft Project, to name a few. The goal of VBA is to provide programmers with a consistent language that they can use across multiple products, thereby streamlining their development time and costs. As a result, VBA is an excellent platform for rapid application development.

Speed and efficiency are not the only benefits of using VBA as a development platform. The following characteristics also make it invaluable:

- **Quick to edit, test, and debug** VBA has a full-featured development environment that includes extensive debugging tools.

- **Easy to learn** Because VBA is based on the BASIC language, one of the best-known languages available, the time required to learn it is minimal.

- **High-productivity development** With VBA, you can quickly draw an interface or a prototype of an application and write the code to respond to events or actions you want your application to perform.

- **Shared programming language** All Microsoft Office 97 applications support VBA, the development language used by Visual Basic. Because VBA is a shared language, you can apply the work you have done in it immediately to other applications.

- **ActiveX programmability support** With VBA, you can take advantage of the features found in other applications that use Automation.

- **International programmability** Applications written using the English version of VBA are easily distributed to other Microsoft Access users throughout the world.

This chapter is going to be a quick trip through the rudiments of VBA. You will learn how to do the following:

- Use the VBA interface in Microsoft Access

- Create your own VBA procedures

- Make your procedures more dynamic by using variables and constants

- Pass arguments to procedures

- Create decision structures and loop structures to increase the functionality of procedures

- Use arrays

You already understand and know how to use macros. In the following section, you'll see that VBA will let you accomplish tasks that are difficult or impossible with macros.

## VBA vs. Macros

When creating applications in Microsoft Access, you've probably come across situations in which macros are not the ideal solution for your problem. A VBA *procedure,* which contains statements that perform operations or calculate values, can often provide the answer you're looking for. The following sections describe some of the many ways in which VBA procedures can help you where macros cannot.

## Trapping for Errors During Execution

VBA gives you the ability to test for an error and to perform a specified operation if an error does occur. Say, for example, you create a macro that performs an action such as deleting a table but that in fact that table does not exist. You will find yourself confronted with the error message "Macro Action Halted." You don't want your user to encounter such messages. VBA lets you add error handling so that your applications can deal with errors gracefully.

## Reusing a Series of Expressions

Instead of typing expressions over and over as you do with macros, you can use VBA both to write a procedure that contains those expressions and to call that procedure from wherever you would normally enter the expressions. You can call custom procedures from many places in Microsoft Access (from form and control events, for example). We'll discuss custom procedures later in this chapter.

## Using Variables Within an Expression

You can use VBA to create highly flexible generic procedures by substituting variables for static values in the procedure. A variable stores values temporarily and dynamically, which allows you to change and retrieve the values as needed.

## Using Complex Logic for Decision-Making Routines

Visual Basic for Applications includes several flexible and logical decision-making structures. (If...Then...Else statements are an example.) Although simple logic routines can be performed using the condition column in macros, you might find it necessary to use the complex logic available in VBA procedures to check for all possible results.

## Using the Built-In Procedures of Microsoft Windows Operating Systems

With VBA, you can utilize and make calls to the Windows application programming interface (API) and Windows dynamic link libraries (DLLs). For example, you can return environment information not provided by VBA as well as information from communication and serial ports.

Macros are still useful for prototyping your application to create the initial navigational flow. However, nearly all tasks that can be done in macros can also be done in VBA.

**How to Convert Macros to VBA Code**

Using the Macro To VBA Conversion Wizard to convert macros to VBA code will automatically generate procedures with optional error trapping and macro comments. This wizard is a great feature in Microsoft Access.

To convert a macro to VBA code, follow these steps:

**1.** Open your macro in Design view, and from the File menu choose Save As/Export.

**2.** Select the Save As Visual Basic Module option in the Save As dialog box.

**3.** Click OK. You will then be prompted to add error trapping and the macro comments to the code.

This process will turn your macro into a real VBA procedure. You will learn more about how to create your own procedures later in this chapter.

## Before You Begin

The VBA programming language relies on the Windows operating system. To know how to use VBA, you must first understand the event-driven model used by Windows and, consequently, by all Windows-based programming languages.

### Event-Driven Programming

The term "event-driven programming" will come up frequently when you're programming in Microsoft Access. In *event-driven programming,* it is the user who decides how the program is executed; this type of programming differs from *batch programming,* in which a program executes from top to bottom.

What benefits does event-driven programming offer you as a developer and solution provider? First, it makes applications easier to create and debug, because you are developing only small pieces at a time. Second, it offers consistency, because it is used in all Windows programming environments, especially VBA applications. Throughout this book, we will present solutions that follow the event-driven programming approach—the best programming approach for creating Windows-based applications.

To better understand the difference between batch programming and event-driven programming, think of an application as a restaurant menu. The batch programming approach serves you each item on every page of the menu in sequence, one at a time, until you have been served everything on the menu. Event-driven programming allows you to choose only the "menu items" you want—that is, only the parts of the program you want to execute. This type of approach usually presents the user with a selection of command buttons, menu items, and toolbar buttons.

In event-driven programming, your application responds only to the user's actions. Later in this book, when we start to look at the objects within Microsoft Access (for example, forms and reports), you will see various events for each object. Each of the events for a particular object in Microsoft Access will cover almost any user action that can be applied to that object. For example, in the Windows environment the user can perform many events using just the mouse, as shown in the following table.

| Mouse Event | User Action |
| --- | --- |
| Click | The user clicks the left mouse button once. |
| DoubleClick | The user clicks the left mouse button twice in rapid succession. |
| MouseMove | The user moves the cursor while it is over an object. |
| MouseDown and MouseUp | The user presses or releases a mouse button. Microsoft Access can trap for the left mouse button or the right (secondary context) mouse button. |

**NOTE**  The mouse is typically configured for right-handed operation. In this configuration, the left button is the select mouse button and the right button is the secondary context mouse button. You can change the button orientation by using the Control Panel. Microsoft Access receives mouse properties from Windows. As a result, no special coding of the mouse events is necessary for right-handed or left-handed mouse users.

Most users in a Windows environment use the mouse to perform most actions. But to accommodate those who want to use the keyboard, Microsoft Access allows you to recognize, or *trap* for, keyboard events. The following table lists some common keyboard events.

| Keyboard Event | User Action |
| --- | --- |
| KeyPress | The user presses a key on the keyboard, and Microsoft Access can determine which key has been pressed. The KeyPress event will trap only for standard ANSI characters, such as the letters of the English alphabet. |
| KeyDown and KeyUp | The user presses or releases a key on the keyboard. These keyboard events can trap for keystrokes not trapped by the KeyPress event, such as the function and navigation keys. |

### The KeyPreview Property

The KeyPreview property is a useful feature in Microsoft Access. It allows you to determine whether a form's keyboard events will always take precedence over an individual object's (control's) keyboard events. This property is useful for trapping keystrokes in one location (the form) rather than having to place duplicate code in the keyboard events of all the objects (controls) on the form.

Notice that the names of the mouse and keyboard events are simple and truly descriptive of the event. This intuitiveness makes programming in the Microsoft Access event-driven programming environment logical and easy. The challenge is anticipating what events the user will be performing on a particular object.

In the Microsoft Access environment, you will be writing the majority of your event-driven code for forms and the controls they contain. The Click event is the most common event used by the command button object, but it is not the only one allowed. To discover the various events that are available for the command button object, you can do one of two things.

1. From Design view in a form, you can view the Event tab of the Property sheet for the Command Button object, as shown in Figure 1-1.

**NOTE**  You can also get to an object's code by using the Code Builder for a particular property. Say, for example, you want to set the Click event for a button. Simply select the On Click property of the button, click the Build button, and choose Code Builder. It will take you directly to the Form module, placing the cursor in the code for the Click event of the Command Button object.

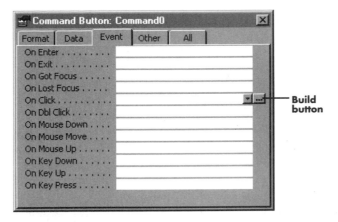

**Figure 1-1.** *The Click event on the Command Button object's property sheet.*

**2.** In Design view you can also see the list of events for a particular object by choosing Code from the View menu. This opens the form's Module window. In the Object combo box, select the object you want. When you click the down arrow in the Procedure combo box, you will see a list of events for that object, as shown in the following illustration:

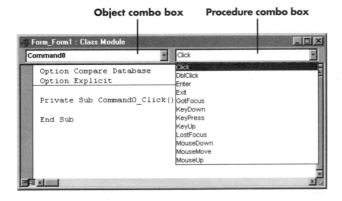

Now the challenge begins. From this list, which events do you use? For example, the illustration above lists events for a comm    tton object. If you write code for the DoubleClick event of a command button, the user might never trigger the event, because it is standard procedure to single-click a command button.

And how do you write code for multiple events? You must know the order in which these events occur. For example, if you have code in the Click event as well as in the DoubleClick event, when the user double-clicks the command button, the Click event will always occur before the DoubleClick event, because the first click of a double click is detected as a single click or a Click event. What if you now write additional code for the command button's MouseDown and MouseUp events? Which event gets triggered first? Knowing the order of the events is crucial in event-driven programming. If you do not know the order in which events occur, your code will return unpredictable results.

---

**Determining the Order of Events**

For a complete listing and explanation of the occurrence or order of events, search online VBA Help for "Order of events."

Another way to see the order of event execution is to open the ShowEvents form from within the Orders.MDB sample database that ships with Microsoft Access. Please take the time to open this form and to perform the actions specified. (For example, click in one control and tab to the next.) Notice that the order in which the events take place might not be the order you would assume.

---

## The VBA Interface in Microsoft Access

Microsoft Access provides you with an interface to develop your VBA code: the VBA Module window. In this window you can create VBA procedures to be used throughout your application. As with many Windows user interfaces, the VBA Module window also contains menu bars and toolbars. To create a new VBA module, click the Module tab of the Database window and then click the New button. A new Module window appears, with the associated Visual Basic toolbar and menu bar, as shown in Figure 1-2.

You'll find the following elements in the VBA Module window.

### Object combo box

The Object combo box identifies the object associated with the code you are editing. In a VBA Module window, this box always defaults to "(General)." In the VBA Module window of a form or report, this combo box can show the name of an object that exists on that form.

### Procedure combo box

The Procedure combo box identifies the name of the procedure you are editing. When you select a procedure from this drop-down list, the Module window will change to reflect the new procedure. In the VBA Module window of a form, the combo box will show the name of the event associated with the code you are editing.

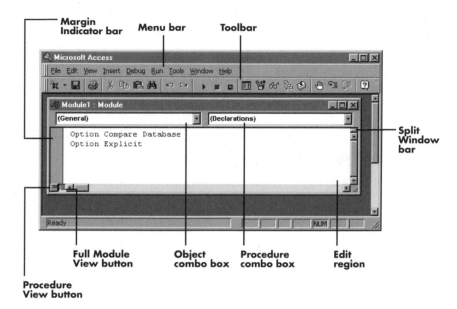

**Figure 1-2.** *VBA Module window.*

## Edit region

You will enter all of your code for functions and procedures in this area.

## Split Window bar

Use this to display two procedures or two different sections of the Module window at the same time.

**NOTE**    We will discuss the Module window's toolbar and menu bar further in this chapter and in Chapter 3.

## Procedure View button

This allows you to look at only one procedure at a time within the Module window.

## Full Module View button

You can see all procedures with or without separations. Checking the Full Module View option will show all sub procedures or functions within a module in the same window. This makes it very easy to scroll within the window and to edit all your functions. Figure 1-3 on the following page shows the Full Module View. Notice that both procedures appear in the same window.

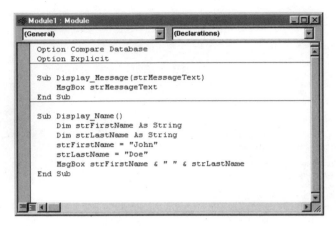

**Figure 1-3.** *Module window with Full Module View selected.*

### Margin Indicator bar

The gray vertical bar on the left-hand side of the Module window is the margin indicator bar. This bar is used to show breakpoints and bookmarks that you have defined. It also shows you the line of code to be executed when debugging your programs. (Breakpoints and debugging will be covered in Chapter 3.)

> **NOTE** A bookmark is simply a placeholder that you define so that you can quickly return to a line of code. To set a bookmark, place the cursor on the line of code you wish to mark. Choose Bookmarks from the Edit menu and select Toggle Bookmark.

## Enhancing Code Readability

When you're developing solutions, code can often become complex and can end up being quite lengthy. Long and involved code can be difficult to read if you need to debug your code or if you're returning to it after a long break. VBA has several features that enhance your ability to quickly comprehend and follow the actions your code is performing.

Although you have not written any VBA code up to this point, you should familiarize yourself with the VBA features that will enhance your code's readability. These features allow you to do the following:

- Customize the module (coding) interface from the Tools menu
- Add comments to your code
- Write multiple statements on a single line using a colon
- Use the line continuation character
- Indent and outdent code

## Customizing Your VBA Environment

To change the display features and functionality of the VBA environment, choose
Options from the Tools menu and then select the Module tab. The Options dialog
box, shown in Figure 1-4, allows you to customize the VBA editor and Module
window.

**Figure 1-4.** *User options for modules.*

### Code Colors

This area allows you to select the foreground, background, and indicator colors for each code element in a module. Some of the available code elements
in the Text area include Code Window Text, Selection Text, and Comment Text.

### Coding Options

This area contains eight options.

**Auto Indent**   When turned on, this feature causes a new line of code to be
indented the same amount as the previous line. By default, this option is on.

**Auto Syntax Check**   When turned on, VBA checks for correct syntax each time
a line of code is entered. By default, this option is on.

**Require Variable Declaration**   When turned on, this option forces explicit declaration of all variables for the project. Turning on this option does not mean that
all variables must be defined; it simply adds the statement Option Explicit to
any new modules you create. You can delete this statement from a particular
module so that you do not have to define all variables. By default, this option
is on.

## What Happens During Compile Time?

Traditional compiled languages, such as C, compile source code to machine-readable (and much faster) object code. To use these object programs, you then need to link them into an executable file.

Microsoft Access does not compile your code to an executable file or to an object file. When your code is compiled, two tasks are completed. First, Microsoft Access checks the syntax of your code. Second, Access creates the necessary interpreted code or p-code (short for pseudocode). *P-code* is an intermediate step between the high-level instructions in your program and the low-level native code your computer's processor executes.

**Compile On Demand**   When this option is turned on, Microsoft Access compiles a module only when code in the module changes or when a procedure in the module is called by a procedure in another module. When this option is turned off, Microsoft Access compiles all of the modules in the database (including form and report class modules) any time it compiles. By default, this option is on.

Turning on the Compile On Demand option has the same end result as choosing Compile Loaded Modules from the Run menu. When you choose Compile Loaded Modules from the Run menu, Microsoft Access immediately compiles all modules that are currently open. This includes form and report modules as well as standard and user-defined class modules. When Compile On Demand is turned on, modules are compiled only when a procedure in that module is executed.

When Compile On Demand is turned off, all modules in the database are compiled when the first procedure is called. Microsoft Access 97 loads modules on a need-only basis, so it is best to group procedures in modules with other procedures that they call. This can enhance your application's performance.

**Auto List Members**   When entering code into the Module window, having this option enabled will allow Microsoft Access to display a list of valid code elements from which you may select. You simply type the first part of the statement, and Microsoft Access figures out which type of element you're entering and allows you to select the specific element from a list.

**Auto Quick Info**   Enabling this option will give you the syntax for the function or statement you are currently typing in the Module window. This is a great feature to have enabled when you are first starting to program in Microsoft Access, because it displays the function arguments right in front of you.

**Auto Data Tips**   This option is useful when debugging your application. At run time, when stepping through your code, placing your mouse cursor over a variable will show the variable's value when this option is enabled.

**Tab Width**   This is the width of a tab stop specified in number of spaces. The minimum size is 1, and the maximum size is 40. The default for this option is 4.

### Font
This option determines the font to be used in the edit region and Debug window. The default font is Courier New. A sample of the selected font and size is displayed in the Sample text box.

### Size
This option determines the size of the font to be used in the edit region and Debug window. The default size is 10.

### Sample
This area displays text using the font and size you have selected.

### Window Settings
The five options listed in this section of the dialog box affect the appearance of the Module window.

**Full Module View**   Enabling this option performs the same task as selecting the Full Module View button within the Module window; you will be able to see more than one procedure at a time.

**Procedure Separator**   When Full Module View is selected, this option is enabled. Selecting this option will place a line above the function declaration so that you can see where the next function begins. Figure 1-3 (on page 12) shows the Full Module View and Procedure Separator options enabled.

**Drag-And-Drop Text Editing**   This option enables you to drag and drop code snippets within a function or between functions.

**Debug Window On Top**   Selecting this option will cause the Debug window to be placed on top of the Module window at all times.

**Margin Indicator Bar**   This gray vertical bar on the left-hand side of the Module window shows any breakpoints and bookmarks you have defined and the current line of execution during debugging.

### Current Database Only Section of the Advanced Tab
The Module tab on the Options dialog box is not the only place you will find useful information for coding. The Advanced tab also has some items of interest for Modules, which we will discuss next.

**Command-Line Arguments**   You can pass in a value to your application by using the /cmd command line switch at startup time. The built-in Command function will return the value that is supplied by the /cmd command line switch.
This option applies to the currently open database in the Microsoft Access user
interface.

**Conditional Compilation Arguments**   This box also applies to the currently open
database in the Microsoft Access user interface. This option allows you to compile sections of code based on the value of a variable.

**Project Name**   Entering a project name allows you to distinguish the application from the default filename of the database. This setting is displayed in the
Object Browser dialog box.

## Adding Comments to Your Code

All procedures and functions should begin with a brief comment describing what
they do. This description should not address *implementation details* (how they
do what they do), because these often change over time, resulting in unnecessary comment maintenance or even erroneous comments. Besides, the code
itself and any inline or local comments will describe the implementation. The
addition of comments increases your code's readability and makes it easier for
others to maintain your code. To create a comment within your VBA function
or procedure, use the apostrophe character (') at the beginning of each line, as
in the following example:

```
Sub Display_Greeting(strMessageText)
    ' This sub procedure will display a message box to the user.
    ' The parameter being accepted is displayed as the message
    ' text.
    MsgBox strMessageText
End Sub
```

Commenting your code will make debugging and code maintenance much easier
because you can comment on what a variable does or on why you did something a particular way within a function.

## Writing Multiple Statements on a Single Line of Code

With VBA you can use a colon ( : ) to place multiple statements on a single line
of code. The colon must be separated by a space preceding and following the
colon and cannot be part of a string. The following example demonstrates the
proper use of a colon to place multiple statements on a single line of code:

```
Dim intVar1 As Integer, intVar2 As Integer, intVar3 As Integer
intVar1 = 1 : intVar2 = 2 : intVar3 = 3
```

## Using the Line Continuation Character

In VBA an underscore ( _ ) serves as a line continuation character you can use when your code is too long to fit on a single line. The underscore must be preceded by a space and cannot be part of a string. An ampersand (&) is used to concatenate strings. The following example demonstrates how to concatenate a long structured query language (SQL) string and use the line continuation character:

```
strMySql = "SELECT DISTINCTROW Customers.CustomerID," & _
    "Customers.CompanyName FROM Customers;"
```

## Indenting and Spacing Your Code

You've probably noticed that in the coding examples you've seen so far, some of the code lines are indented—especially those in which decision and loop structures have been used. Indenting code makes your procedure more readable. If you have nested decision or loop structures, a lack of indention can make it extremely difficult to understand the flow of the procedure. It is also helpful to add blank lines between groupings of code that perform specific tasks. This separation improves readability and allows you to distinguish between the different aspects of your code. Indentions and extra blank lines do not affect the compilation or performance of your code.

Indenting a line of code in VBA works the same way as indenting a sentence in Microsoft Word. You can also outdent your code simply by "indenting" in the opposite direction. You can increase or decrease the indent of your code in the VBA Module window by using the keyboard, the menu bar, or the toolbar.

To indent your code using the keyboard, press the Tab key at the beginning of your line of code. To decrease the indent of your code, press the Shift and Tab keys together at the beginning of your line of code.

**TIP**  To increase or decrease the indent of more than one line of code at a time, select the lines of code with your mouse and then press Tab or Shift-Tab.

To increase or decrease the indent of your code using the menu bar, select the line or lines of code you wish to affect and then choose either Indent or Outdent from the Edit menu.

To indent or outdent your code using the Visual Basic toolbar, place your cursor on the line or lines of code you wish to affect and then click the Indent or the Outdent button.

TIPIf the Indent or Outdent buttons do not appear on your Visual Basic toolbar, choose Toolbars from the View menu and select Customize to open the Customize dialog box. Highlight Visual Basic under the Toolbars tab. Click the Commands tab and highlight Module Design under Categories. In the Commands list box, scroll down until you see the Indent and Outdent options. Then simply drag and drop the items onto the toolbar.

# Functions and Sub Procedures

Now that we have discussed the benefits of using VBA rather than macros and talked about event-driven programming and the VBA interface in Microsoft Access, we're ready to take a closer look at one of the fundamental parts of VBA: functions and sub procedures. These components provide the VBA backbone for applications you'll create in Microsoft Access.

## Differentiating Between Functions and Sub Procedures

In any programming language, *procedures* perform actions and tasks. Procedures are great for accomplishing repetitive routines or complicated routines that must be used more than once. Implementing procedures in your application saves the user from having to perform these repetitive or complicated actions. Microsoft Access has three types of procedures: function, sub, and property procedures.

For the time being, let's focus on functions and sub procedures, the two most common procedure types. We will discuss property procedures in more detail in Chapter 7.

Functions and sub procedures are similar in several ways:

- Both contain VBA statements that perform operations or calculate values.
- Both accept arguments.
- Both can be called from other functions or sub procedures.

But functions and sub procedures also differ in various aspects. A function can perform the following actions that a sub procedure cannot:

- Return a value
- Be executed from most event properties on forms and reports
- Be called from a macro

The main difference between functions and sub procedures is that a function can return a value whereas a sub procedure cannot.

## Microsoft Access built-in procedures

Like most programming languages, Microsoft Access provides built-in procedures for common tasks. The following table lists some of the more commonly used built-in procedures available with Microsoft Access.

**BUILT-IN PROCEDURES**

| Function | Description |
|---|---|
| **User Response/Input** | |
| MsgBox | Displays a Windows message box to notify the user of errors and other messages and to return the user's response to the message. |
| InputBox | Prompts the user to enter specific information, which is then returned by this function. |
| **Date/Time** | |
| Date | Returns the system date of your computer. |
| Time | Returns the system time of your computer. |
| Now | Returns the system date and time of your computer. |
| Day, Month, Year | Returns a number representing the day, month, and year of a given date. |
| Second, Minute, Hour | Returns a number representing the second, minute, and hour of a given time. |
| **String Manipulation** | |
| Left | Returns left portion of a string value. |
| Right | Returns right portion of a string value. |
| Mid | Returns middle portion of a string value. |
| Instr | Returns the position of a character or series of characters within a string value. |
| Trim | Removes leading and trailing spaces from a string value. |
| LTrim | Removes leading spaces from a string value. |
| RTrim | Removes trailing spaces from a string value. |
| **Domain (Data)** | |
| DLookup | Returns the value of a particular field from a specified set of records from a table or query. You can specify criteria to be applied to the table or query. |
| DSum, DCount, DAvg | Returns the calculated sum, count, or average, respectively, of a particular field from a specified set of records from a table or query. You can specify criteria to be applied to the table or query. |
| DMin, DMax | Returns the minimum or maximum value, respectively, of a particular field from a specified set of records from a table or query. You can specify criteria to be applied to the table or query. |

Microsoft Access offers many more built-in procedures than those shown above, including file input/output functions, financial functions, and statistical functions. For more information about built-in procedures, see *Microsoft Office Visual Basic Reference* and *Microsoft Access* and *Visual Basic for Applications Reference* in the Contents section of online VBA Help.

## Using the Microsoft Access built-in functions

You can use the built-in functions of Microsoft Access in the following common locations:

- Query By Example grid of the Query object

- Properties and events of forms and reports

- Properties and events of Form and Report controls

- Macro actions and conditions

- Custom code procedures (discussed later in this chapter)

**Using built-in functions in a query**   You can use the Eval and InputBox built-in functions in a query to create a more descriptive parameter box for the criteria section of the Query By Example (QBE) grid of the query, as shown in Figure 1-5.

> **NOTE**   The Eval function is required only with the InputBox function when used in query expressions. It is not necessary inside VBA procedures. In prior versions of Microsoft Access, the InputBox function could be used by itself in a query expression.

Using the Eval and InputBox functions in the QBE grid as shown in Figure 1-5 results in the dialog box shown in Figure 1-6 when the query is executed.

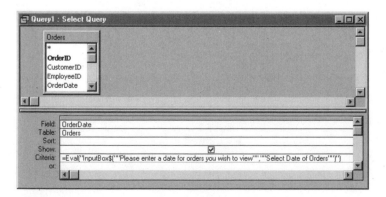

**Figure 1-5.** *Using the built-in InputBox function in a query.*

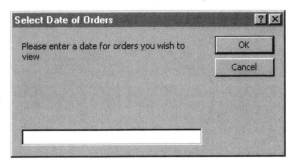

**Figure 1-6.** *Example of an InputBox invoked from a query.*

**Using built-in functions in a form**   You can call a built-in function from the ControlSource property of a control such as a text box. Use the DCount function to display in a text box the total number of customer orders taken by a particular employee, as shown here:

You can also call built-in functions from other properties. For example, you might want to store the date and time whenever the user adds a new record through your form. To accomplish this, use the Now function as the default value for a text box bound to a Date/Time field, as shown here:

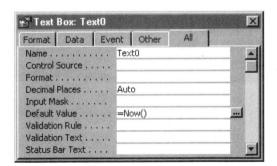

You can also use the Date function in a validation rule for a Birthdate field, for example. This way, a user cannot enter a birth date that is greater than the current date, as shown at the top of the following page.

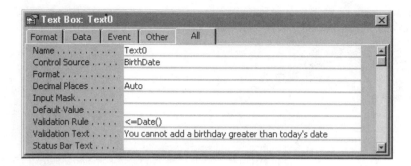

These are just some of the many ways in which you can use the Microsoft Access built-in functions. However, because you cannot make changes to built-in functions, you might also want to create custom functions to meet more specific requirements.

### Methods

A method is a special kind of procedure. Methods operate in the same manner as procedures, but they are components of specific objects. To call a method, you place the object name and the method name, separated by a period, in your sub procedure. We will discuss methods in more detail in Chapter 7.

## Locating and Viewing Functions and Sub Procedures

Once you begin to create multiple functions and sub procedures in several code modules, it can become difficult to locate the code you need. In Microsoft Access you can locate and view code by using the Object Browser and the Expression Builder.

### The Object Browser

The Object Browser, shown in Figure 1-7, is a dialog box that allows you to browse all the procedures, methods, and properties available to the current database. The Object Browser is available from the View menu of a module in Design view, from the Visual Basic toolbar, and by pressing the F2 key. You can use the Object Browser for the following purposes:

- Learn about the different objects available in Microsoft Access 97, VBA, and other libraries

- View the procedures and properties available in objects or libraries

- Select procedures, methods, and properties, and paste the text directly into a code module

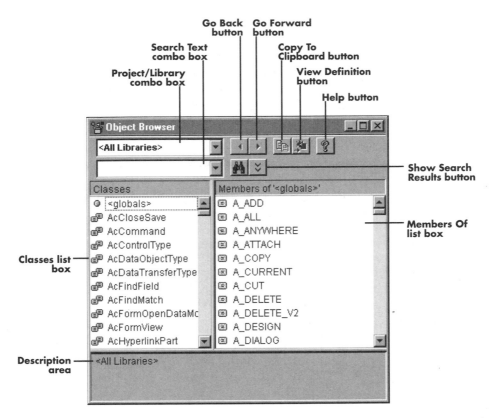

**Figure 1-7.** *The Object Browser.*

The following sections describe the controls on the Object Browser.

**Project/Library**    This combo box displays a list of all the libraries and databases directly referenced by the current project (database). This list includes the current database, the Microsoft Access application, and the VBA-type libraries, as well as any libraries added by the user. You can locate and view both built-in procedures and custom procedures by selecting the appropriate library or database.

To locate and view your custom procedures, select your database name from the Project/Library combo box. To locate and view built-in VBA procedures, select "VBA"; to locate and view built-in procedures specific to Microsoft Access, select "Access." The built-in procedures stored in the VBA library can be used by any application that uses VBA. Those stored in the Microsoft Access library are specific to Access applications.

**Search Text combo box** If you want to look for a specific method, property, constant, or event, you can enter the name in the Search Text combo box. Clicking the Search button will expand the Object Browser to include a Search Results pane. This pane allows you to see all the items that meet the criteria you entered in the combo box. The library, class, and member to which the search string belongs are all displayed in the Search Results list box. The button next to Search, Show Search Results, will change to reflect whether or not the Search Results list box is currently visible. For example, it will have the ScreenTip text of "Hide Search Results" and clicking the button will hide the Search Results list box. If the Search Results list box is currently not visible, then clicking the button again displays the Search Results list box.

**Classes** The Classes list box displays an alphabetical list of all the modules and classes defined in the type library and specified in the Project/Library combo box. Secured modules (modules the user does not have access to) in the object library are not displayed in this list.

**Members Of list box** The Members Of list box displays an alphabetical list of all the methods, properties, and data members available from the item selected in the Modules/Classes list. Module-level variables, constants, and user-defined types are not displayed.

**Help button** When clicked, the Help button (the question mark in the upper right corner of the dialog box) activates the Help screen for the currently selected class, method, property, or function. When the Help button is pressed, a reference dialog box is opened. The item selected in the Members Of list box will be the subject of the Help text. The Help text displays the procedure, method, or property definition that can be copied to the clipboard when the Copy To Clipboard button is pressed. The Help button text includes remarks and examples, and lists all necessary arguments. If no Help file is available, this button will be grayed out. A specific Help file is created for each Microsoft Access library.

**Description area** The remainder of the area inside the area frame is the description area. As the user highlights different classes, modules, or methods, the Help string will change to describe the one currently selected. Because this string comes from the type library attached to the project, the string contains the language of the type library, not necessarily the current user's language. This area supports three lines of approximately 60 characters each. If the procedure definition and comment contain more than three lines, the comment will be cut off. As long as the combined number of lines in the procedure definition and the comment do not exceed three, all text will be displayed.

**View Definition button**   The View Definition button opens the appropriate module and displays the procedure selected in the Object Browser. You can use this button to find the name of a procedure you want to see while you are viewing a database.

**Copy To Clipboard button**   You can use the Copy To Clipboard button to copy selected items in the Object Browser so that you can paste them into a code module.

**Navigation buttons**   The Go Back and Go Forward buttons allow you to return to items in the Object Browser you have already visited.

## The Expression Builder

You can use the Expression Builder to locate and view built-in and custom procedures. You can call the Expression Builder from most locations from which you can enter an expression or call a function. Using the Build button, you can call the Expression Builder from the following locations:

- Property sheets
- Query By Example (QBE) or Design grid
- Macro window

The Expression Builder is shown in Figure 1-8 on the next page.

From the Functions folder, you can choose from different categories of built-in functions or choose the database from which you'd like to select your custom procedures. If you click the OK button, your code will be pasted into the area from which the Expression Builder was called.

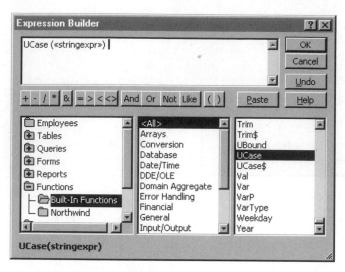

**Figure 1-8.** *The Expression Builder.*

# Custom Procedures

Built-in procedures are a great resource because they easily perform common tasks for you. For example, the Now( ) procedure returns the system's date and time information. Without this procedure, you would have to make Windows application programming interface (API) calls, which would entail more work on your part. Sometimes, however, no built-in procedure will meet your needs.

Whenever the built-in functions and sub procedures of Microsoft Access do not provide all the functionality you require, you can create your own. VBA allows you to create custom functions and sub procedures to tailor your application to meet your user's specific needs. You can call your custom procedures from the same locations as you call the built-in procedures.

## Creating a New Procedure

Each function or sub procedure you create will reside in a VBA module. To create a new function using the VBA interface, switch to Module Design view and then follow these steps:

1. Choose Procedure from the Insert menu. Microsoft Access displays the Insert Procedure dialog box, as shown in Figure 1-9.

2. Select Function from the Type options, and then type a valid name for the function in the Name text box.

3. Choose OK.

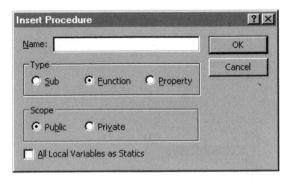

**Figure 1-9.** *The Insert Procedure dialog box.*

## Procedure naming guidelines

You can give your functions and sub procedures any name that follows these simple rules:

- The name must be less than 255 characters in length.

- The name must begin with a letter.

- The name can contain only letters, numbers, and the underscore character. Punctuation characters and spaces are not allowed.

- The name cannot be a reserved word. A *reserved word* is a word that is already being used by Microsoft Access. To determine whether a word is reserved, search for the word in online Help.

These naming conventions apply to all the names you create in VBA, including variables, constants, and arguments. (We will discuss variables, constants, and arguments later in this chapter.) You should use names that quickly identify the purpose of your procedure. For example, if you are creating a procedure to convert Fahrenheit temperatures to Celsius, you might name the procedure "FahrenToCel" rather than the longer "ConvertingFahrenheitToTheCelsiusTemperatureScale."

**NOTE**  A database's procedures are stored in a name table that is inaccessible to the user. The number of names in the table cannot exceed 32,768.

In the Insert Procedure dialog box, you can choose to create a sub procedure, a function, or a property procedure. (As mentioned earlier, we will discuss property procedures in Chapter 7.) Figure 1-10 on the next page shows you the anatomy of a procedure.

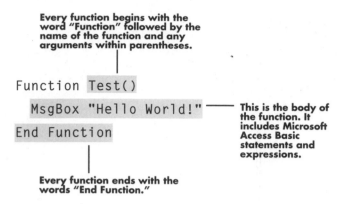

Every function begins with the word "Function" followed by the name of the function and any arguments within parentheses.

```
Function Test()
    MsgBox "Hello World!"
End Function
```

This is the body of the function. It includes Microsoft Access Basic statements and expressions.

Every function ends with the words "End Function."

**Figure 1-10.** *The anatomy of a procedure.*

## Executing Functions and Sub Procedures

You can execute the procedures in your application in several ways. The easiest way is to use the Debug window. (Note that the Debug window is useful only for testing code.) To open the Debug window, from Module Design mode, choose Debug Window from the View menu. Type in the name of the function or sub procedure, and press Enter. The function or sub procedure is executed.

> **TIP**　You may also execute your functions or sub procedures by placing your cursor within the procedure and clicking the Go/Continue button on the Visual Basic toolbar or by selecting Go/Continue from the Run menu.

You can also call functions (but not sub procedures) from an Event property in a form or report. To call a function from an Event property, beside the name of the Event property type an equal (=) sign followed by the name of the function, as shown in Figure 1-11. Sub procedures can be called only from another function or sub procedure; they cannot be called from an Event property.

### Typing a Procedure Directly into a Module

You can create a new function or sub procedure without using the Insert Procedure dialog box; simply type the procedure directly into a module.

1. Open a new or existing module.

2. On an empty line, type *Function* or *Sub*, followed by a space and the name you want to give the procedure.

3. Press Enter.

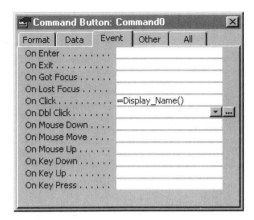

**Figure 1-11.** *Executing a function from an Event property.*

The syntax used to call both custom and built-in functions differs slightly from that used to call custom and built-in sub procedures. To call the built-in sub procedure MsgBox, for example, you can use one of the following two forms:

```
MsgBox "Hello World!"

Call MsgBox("Hello World!")
```

Both of these statements display a message box.

> **NOTE** The MsgBox function is actually a function because it can return a value representing the user's response to the message in the message box.

When you use the Call command to execute a sub procedure or a function, the arguments being passed must be enclosed in parentheses. Because functions typically return a value, when you execute a function its results may be assigned to a variable, but when using the Call statement to execute a function the return value is ignored. Using the Call statement for a sub procedure is optional, but it can enhance your code's readability. The following example demonstrates how to call the MsgBox function, which returns a value that indicates the button pressed by the user:

```
intResponse = MsgBox("Are you ready?", vbYesNo)
```

In this example, the message box will display "Are you ready?" and return the value of Yes or No, depending on which button the user presses. That value is then assigned to the variable intResponse. (We will discuss variables in more detail later in this chapter.)

## Understanding Procedure Scope

All procedures are created and stored in modules. In fact, you could store all the procedures you create in one module. That being the case, why would you want to use more than one module? There are two reasons to separate procedures into different modules: to logically group procedures that have the same types of functionality, and to determine the scope of your procedures.

Logical separation allows you to place procedures in groupings or categories of common functionality. For example, if you create a collection of financial functions, you will probably want to store them in one module. If you create a collection of statistical functions, you will want to store them in another module. Using separate modules allows you to easily export a specific category of functions to another database without having to export extra, unnecessary procedures.

All functions and sub procedures created within Microsoft Access have scope. *Scope* refers to the visibility and accessibility of one procedure from other procedures. Procedures can be declared as either Public or Private. (Later in this chapter you'll see these terms used again in reference to variables.) A *Public* function is a function that can be called from any module, event procedure, or macro within the database application. A *Private* function, however, is one that can be called only from another function or sub procedure within the same module. To declare a procedure as either Public or Private, insert the Public or Private keyword before the word "Function" or "Sub" in the first line of the procedure. By default, all procedures are Public, even if the Public keyword is not explicitly used in front of the procedure name. The following example creates a Public procedure called "Test":

```
Public Sub Test()
    MsgBox "Hello World!"
End Sub
```

Now that you've learned how to change the scope of your procedures, you might be wondering why you would want to make some procedures Public and others Private. If you are separating procedures into logical groups by storing them in their own distinct modules, you might have developed utility sub procedures and functions that are used only by that specific category of procedures. Since only those procedures will need these utility sub procedures or functions, you should declare all your utility procedures in that module Private. Doing so will save on the global space needed for the procedure and is therefore a more efficient use of memory. Public procedures require much more global space. Also, if you want to use these Private procedures in other databases, you will eliminate the risk of creating and calling a procedure name that already exists in another module. If you want all procedures in all modules to have access to your procedure, however, you must declare it as Public.

TIP
As you will see in later chapters, other Microsoft Access data-bases and applications using VBA will be able to access your database's code if it is declared Public. However, if you want your procedures and variables to be available only to other modules in your database, you can use the Option Private Module statement in the Declarations section of your module.

## Variables

VBA gives you the ability to store values temporarily in memory. Microsoft Access stores these values in variables. For example, let's say you want to add two values and use the result in another calculation. To do this without vari-ables, you would have to do the following:

```
1 + 1 = 2
2 * 10 = 20
```

The disadvantage of this method is that you must manually obtain the result of the first calculation before you can create and use the second calculation. By using variables, you can greatly simplify the process and make it more generic:

```
intVar1 = 1 + 1
intResult = intVar1 * 10
```

(When using variables in Microsoft Access, the variable names must meet the same criteria as must procedure names.)

You can inform Microsoft Access about, or *declare,* a variable in two ways: implicit declaration and explicit declaration. In *implicit declaration* you don't need to declare a variable before using it, as shown in the following example:

```
Function intTest() as Integer
    intValue = 1 + 1
    intTest = intValue
End Function
```

*Explicit declaration* requires that you declare a variable before using it. For times when you forget to declare a variable before you use it, you can force Microsoft Access to generate an error message by placing the following statement in the Declarations section of the module:

```
Option Explicit
```

When Option Explicit is set for a module, all variables must be defined before they can be referenced within a procedure. What advantage is there to using Option Explicit to force variable declaration? When writing complex procedures, you will probably use many variables. If you misspell a variable name, it can cause errors in your procedure that might go unnoticed because no run-time or system error is generated even though the results of the function might be invalid. For example, the following procedure forces the intResult variable to return a value of 0 instead of 20 because the variable intVar1 was misspelled as "intVvar1" in the second line of the code:

```
Sub GetResult()
    intVar1 = 1 + 1
    intResult = intVvar1 * 10
End Sub
```

The Option Explicit statement forces you to declare all variables. Using the Option Explicit statement will eliminate the possibility of misspelling a variable that's used throughout one or more of your procedures. For example, if you declare a variable as "strResponse" and then accidentally refer to it as "strResponsee" (with an extra "e"), the code will not run because the variable "strResponsee" is not explicitly declared.

Although variables are typically defined at the beginning of a function or sub procedure, they can be declared at any point as long as they are declared before being referenced, as shown in the following example:

```
Sub Test()
    Dim intValue As Integer
    intValue = 1 + 1
End Sub
```

> **TIP**
>
> To ensure that the Option Explicit statement is included every time you create a code module, you can set this option through the interface. To do so, while in Module Design view in the module, select Tools from the menu bar and then choose Options. Select the Module tab, and select the Require Variable Declarations coding option.

The Dim keyword in this example informs the compiler that what follows will be the name of a variable. Including the As keyword allows you to specify the variable as a specific data type.

## Variable Data Types

All variables, whether explicitly or implicitly defined, are of a specific data type. As you learned earlier, a variable is used to store values temporarily. Think of a variable as a kind of container, or glass. The type of glass you use depends on what you intend to put in it. (You'd use a different size glass for milk than for whiskey, for example.) When you declare a variable to be of a specific data type, you are telling Microsoft Access what kind of values will be stored in that variable and how much memory space to allocate for it. The following table summarizes the data types, the amount of memory required to hold each variable, and which values or ranges are accepted by the data type.

**VARIABLE DATA TYPES**

| Data Type | Memory Required | Acceptable Values |
|---|---|---|
| Byte | 1 byte | A number from 0 through 255 |
| Boolean | 2 bytes | True or False |
| Integer | 2 bytes | A number from −32,768 through 32,767 |
| Long (long integer) | 4 bytes | A number from −2,147,483,648 through 2,147,483,647 |
| Single (single-precision floating-point) | 4 bytes | A number from −3.402823E38 through −1.401298E-45 for negative values; a number from 1.401298E-45 through 3.402823E38 for positive values; and 0 |
| Double (double-precision floating-point) | 8 bytes | A number from -1.79769313486232E308 through -4.94065645841247E-324 for negative values; a number from 4.94065645841247E-324 through 1.79769313486232E308 for positive values; and 0 |
| Currency (scaled integer) | 8 bytes | A number from −922,337,203,685,477.5808 to 922,337,203,685,477.5807 |
| Date | 8 bytes | A date from January 1, 100, through December 31, 9999 |
| Object | 4 bytes | Any object reference |
| String (variable-length) | 10 bytes + string length | A value from 0 through approximately 2 billion characters (or approximately 65,400 for Windows version 3.1 and earlier) |
| String (fixed-length) | Length of string | A value from 1 through approximately 65,400 characters |
| Variant (numeric) | 16 bytes | Any numeric value in the range of a Double |
| Variant (character) | 22 bytes + string length | A value from 0 through approximately 2 billion characters (or approximately 65,400 for Windows version 3.1 and earlier) |
| User-defined (using the Type keyword) | Number required by elements | Range of each element must be the same as the range of its data type |

To use any data type except Variant, you must use the Dim, Public, DefType, Private, or Static keyword to declare a variable as the desired data type. These declaration statements also determine the scope of the variable, which we will discuss in the "Variable Scope" section beginning on page 37.

## Variant data type

The Variant data type can store any kind of data except fixed-length string data and user-defined data. If no data type is defined for a variable, the Variant data type is assigned by default. VBA automatically performs any necessary conversions. Although you may be tempted to code your functions using the Variant data type, be aware of the big drawback to using it: the increased amount of memory it requires.

Think back to the glasses example. Let's say you have several glasses of different sizes: a 2-ounce shot glass, a 12-ounce glass, and a 20-ounce glass. The 20-ounce glass will certainly hold a shot, but the unused 18 ounces are going to waste. The Variant data type is like a 20-ounce glass—it takes more memory than any other data type. To make the most efficient use of your system's memory, you should define each variable as a specific data type, if possible.

Although any operation can be performed using a Variant type variable, it might be necessary for you to determine the data type the variable represents. Microsoft Access provides several functions to determine the type of data contained within a Variant variable, including IsNumeric, IsDate, and IsNull. You might also have to explicitly state the data type by using the conversion functions CStr, Cint, and CLng. These conversion functions will be demonstrated in examples in Chapter 2.

Just because a variable is not declared explicitly does not always mean that it will be of type Variant. The DefType statement can be used to define a variable beginning with certain letters to be of a particular data type, as in the following example:

```
DefStr s-z
strMyVar = "Hello World!"
```

The above example will define all implicitly declared variables that begin with the letters "s" through "z" to be of type String. You can use the DefType statement wherever you declare variables.

## User-defined data type

Microsoft Access gives you the ability to define a data type of your own, called a *user-defined data type* (UDT). You can use a UDT when the VBA variables do not meet the needs of your application. For example, say that you want to store information about an automobile, such as color, engine size, model, and year. No Automobile data type exists, but you can create one. A UDT usually consists of multiple parts based on existing data types. For your automobile UDT, the color could be a Long data type, the engine size an Integer, the model a String, and the year a Date. You can also think of a UDT as a table in which you are defining the fields. You use the Type statement to create a UDT. A UDT can be defined only in the General declarations section of a module. The following example creates a UDT called "Automobile" in the General declarations section of a module. The sub procedure then declares a variable as the UDT and sets its values.

```
Type Automobile
    strModel as String
    dtmYear as Date
    intEngineSize as Integer
    lngColor as Long
End Type

Sub UserTypes ()
    Dim udtMyAutomobile as Automobile
    udtMyAutomobile.strModel = "Beetle"
    udtMyAutomobile.dtmYear = 1979
    udtMyAutomobile.intEngineSize = 1800
    udtMyAutomobile.lngColor = 215873
End Sub
```

**NOTE**    User-defined data types can also be used when calling Windows API functions. These functions are typically within dynamic link libraries (DLLs), which accept a UDT as a parameter.

## Variable Naming Conventions

Establishing naming conventions for your VBA code is a good idea. Naming conventions can help you easily identify the data type or object type of a variable. They are also useful for the following reasons:

■ They standardize the structure, coding style, and logic of an application.

■ They allow you to create precise, readable, and unambiguous source code.

■ They help you comply with programming language conventions (notably, the Visual Basic *Programmer's Guide* and standard Windows Hungarian notation).

■ They add to your efficiency from a string size and labor standpoint, thus allowing a greater opportunity for longer (more specific) object names.

To use the naming conventions within Microsoft Access efficiently, you first need to make sure that all the variables you are using are defined. Using the Option Explicit setting and declaring all variables will save programming time by reducing the number of bugs caused by typographical errors.

Variable and procedure names have the following structure: prefix, body, and qualifier. For example, assume three variables are used to contain the name of the first, next, and last record values: intGetRecordFirst, intGetRecordNext, and intGetRecordLast. This example can be broken down as follows:

| Part | Description | Example |
|------|-------------|---------|
| <prefix> | Describes the use and scope of the variable | int |
| <body> | Describes the variable | GetRecord |
| <qualifier> | Denotes a derivative of the variable | First, Next, Last |

The following table defines variable name prefixes that are based on Hungarian notation for Windows. Use these prefixes with all variable names.

## VARIABLE NAMING CONVENTIONS

| Prefix | Extended Prefix | Data Type |
|--------|-----------------|-----------|
| a | ary | Array |
| f | bln | Boolean |
| c | cur | Currency |
| d | dbl | Double |
| dt | dtm | Date and Time |
| l | lng | Long |
| i | int | Number/Counter/Integer |
| s | str | String |
| udt | udt | User-defined type |
| vnt | vnt | Variant |

**NOTE**  The values in the Extended Prefix column represent efforts to standardize the naming standards for Visual Basic, Visual Basic for Applications, and Microsoft Access Basic.

Each variable name tells a programmer something very different. The extended prefix indicates the data type, and the body is a word that represents the contents or usage of the variable.

## Variable Scope

Whenever you define a variable, you are also defining the variable's scope. The scope of a variable can be thought of as its life span. Once the variable goes out of scope, you cannot refer to its contents. Like procedure scope, variable scope is determined by its declaration in a module. Variable scope is also determined by its location in a module. You can use four different scopes of variables to declare a variable: Public, Private, Static, and Dim.

### Declaring variables

Earlier in this chapter, you learned how to declare procedures as either Public or Private. Similarly, defining a variable using the Public keyword allows that variable to be referenced from any module anywhere within your database application. You can declare a variable to be Public only in the General Declarations section of a module. The following example defines a Public variable:

```
Public strName As String
```

The Private keyword can be used only in the General Declarations section of a module as well. When a variable is Private, it can be referenced only by another function or sub procedure that resides in the same module. The following example defines a Private variable:

```
Private strName As String
```

The Dim keyword can be used within a function or a sub procedure or in the General Declarations section of a module. When you use the Dim keyword in the General Declarations section of a module, it has the same effect as defining that variable as Private.

When you use the Dim keyword within a procedure, the variable exists only when that procedure is running. When the procedure is finished executing, the variable is removed from memory. The following example uses the Dim keyword to define a variable within a procedure:

```
Sub Calculate_It()
    Dim intValue As Integer
    intValue = intValue + 1
    MsgBox intValue
End Sub
```

When the procedure above is called for the first time, the numeral "1" is displayed in a message box. The second time this procedure is executed, a "1" is displayed again. The value of intValue is not incremented to "2" because when the procedure finishes executing, the variable is removed from memory.

The Static keyword can be used only within a function or a sub procedure. A Static variable can be referred to only inside the procedure it is defined in. Unlike the Dim statement, when a procedure ends, a Static variable retains its value so that the next time the procedure is executed you can refer to the previous value of the variable, as in the following example:

```
Sub Calculate_It()
    Static intValue As Integer
    intValue = intValue + 1
    MsgBox intValue
End Sub
```

When the procedure above is called for the first time, a "1" is displayed in a message box. The second time the procedure is executed, a "2" is displayed. The number changes because when the procedure finishes executing, the variable is not removed from memory. The next time the procedure is executed, the variable still has its value from the last time the procedure was called.

To force all the variables within a procedure to become Static, you can declare a procedure itself using the Static keyword, as in the following example:

```
Static Sub Calculate_It()
    Dim intValue As Integer, intValue2 As Integer
    intValue = intValue + 1
    intValue2 = intValue2 + 1
    MsgBox intValue
    MsgBox intValue2
End Sub
```

When this procedure is called for the first time, a "1" is displayed in both message boxes. The second time the procedure is executed, a "2" is displayed in both message boxes. Without the Static keyword in front of the procedure name, the variables would lose their values when the procedure finished executing.

**TIP** To reset all the variables to their initial state, choose the Reset command from the Run menu in the Design view of the Module window.

# Constants

A *constant,* as you might guess, always has the same value. Constants are useful because you define their value only one time, and thereafter you can refer to them from anywhere else in your code. If later you want to change the value of a constant, you need change it in only one place in your program because you assigned it in one place instead of in multiple functions and sub procedures. When defining constants, you can define them in the General Declarations section of a module or within a procedure. Following is an example of defining a constant and using the value of the constant in a function:

```
Const dblPi As Double = 3.14

Sub Times_Pi()
    Dim dblValue As Double
    dblValue = 5
    dblValue = dblValue * dblPi
    MsgBox dblValue
End Sub
```

The preceding code multiplies the value of the variable dblValue by the constant dblPi. The value will then be displayed in a message box.

VBA includes three types of constants: symbolic, intrinsic, and system-defined.

## Symbolic Constants

These are constants that you create for your custom procedures by using a Const statement.

## Intrinsic Constants

These constants are part of Microsoft Access or VBA and are defined in the Microsoft Access or VBA type library.

Microsoft Access and VBA contain a number of predefined intrinsic constants. All of these constants are contained within the type library; however, they are not loaded into memory until you make a reference to the constant. To view or refer to these constants, you can use the Object Browser in Microsoft Access.

## System-Defined Constants

Most programming languages use system-defined constants to evaluate procedures, variables, and other values. In Microsoft Access these are True, False, and Null.

NOTE You can use the Object Browser to learn about the different objects available in Microsoft Access 97, VBA, and other libraries. In the Object Browser, you can view the procedures and properties available in objects or libraries; you can also select procedures, methods, and properties and paste the text directly into a code module.

## Viewing Intrinsic Constants with the Object Browser

As mentioned earlier in the chapter, the Object Browser is a dialog box that allows you to browse all the procedures, methods (actions for objects), and properties available to the current database. To view intrinsic constants, follow these steps:

1. Open a code module in Design view.

2. Choose Object Browser from the View menu.

3. Select the "Access" type library in the Project/Library combo box.

4. Select "Constants" in the Classes list box.

5. In the Members Of list box you will see the list of Microsoft Access intrinsic constants. You can use the Copy To Clipboard command button to copy the constant onto the clipboard, allowing you to switch to your code and paste the constant at the appropriate syntax location.

TIP To view or use the Microsoft Access version 2 constants, select "OldConstants" in the Modules/Classes list box. Microsoft Access 97 and Microsoft Access 95 share the same constants.

# VBA Operators

*Operators* allow you to evaluate and make comparisons between variables and data. When writing code, you will often need to evaluate and compare different values, so it is important to be familiar with the different kinds of operators that you can use.

Although up to this point we have used only the equal sign (=), plus sign (+), and multiplication sign (*) operators, VBA contains several types of operators. All VBA operators fall into one of three categories: relational operators, mathematical operators, or logical operators. The following table describes the operators available in VBA.

## VBA OPERATORS

| Category of Operator | Meaning |
| --- | --- |
| **Relational** | |
| = | Is equal to |
| <> | Is not equal to |
| < | Is less than |
| <= | Is less than or equal to |
| > | Is greater than |
| >= | Is greater than or equal to |
| **Mathematical** | |
| * | Multiplication |
| + | Addition |
| - | Subtraction |
| / | Division |
| \ | Integer result of the division of two values; does not return any decimals |
| ^ | Result of the preceding value raised to the power of the following value |
| Mod | Remainder of the result of the preceding value divided by the following value |
| **Logical** | |
| And | Condition1 And Condition2 (both conditions must be met for the result to be True) |
| Or | Condition1 Or Condition2 (either condition1 or condition2 or both must be met for the result to be True) |
| Not | Logically negates an expression |

## Concatenating Strings

When you want to concatenate two string values, you should always use an ampersand (&) rather than a plus sign (+). For example, if you have one variable that contains a first name and one that contains a last name, you might want to concatenate the two to show the full name, as in the following example:

```
Sub Display_Name()
    Dim strFirstName As String, strLastName As String
    strFirstName = "John"
    strLastName = "Smith"
    MsgBox strFirstName & " " & strLastName
End Sub
```

**NOTE** Use the plus sign only to add two variables together to achieve an arithmetic sum.

In addition to concatenating strings contained in variables, you can concatenate them to the following objects, data types, and values:

- Constants
- Literal values
- References to the values of form or report properties and controls
- Function return values

Notice how various elements are concatenated in the following code example:

```
Const strMyForm As String = "form: "
Function Test()
    Dim strMyDate As String, strReturnValue As String

    DoCmd.OpenForm ("MyForm")
    strMyDate = "Today's Date is "
    strReturnValue = strMyDate & Date & " on the following " & _
        strMyForm & Forms!MyForm.Name
    Test = strReturnValue
End Function
```

The Test function, when executed from the Debug window using the ?Test() syntax, will print the following string:

```
Today's Date is 2/14/97 on the following form: MyForm
```

Note that concatenated values don't have to be String data types.

## Arguments

You can declare arguments along with a procedure so that you can supply information to the procedure when you call it. Most of the built-in procedures available in Microsoft Access accept arguments. You can also define arguments within functions and sub procedures that you create so that you can pass values to your custom procedures. You can then manipulate these values within the procedure so that they are returned or displayed in the application if necessary.

Figure 1-12 shows how to write a function that accepts two arguments.

**Length and width are your
procedure's arguments.**

```
Function intSqrFoot (intLength As Integer, _
                     intWidth As Integer) As Integer
  intSqrFoot = intLength * intWidth
End Function
```

**Figure 1-12.** *Declaring arguments for a procedure.*

## Passing Parameters to Procedures

To pass a parameter to a function, place the values the application is passing to the function within parentheses. For example, to call the intSqrFoot function (shown above), the following syntax can be used:

```
=intSqrFoot(4,5)
```

The numbers 4 and 5 are parameters that are passed to the function. Be sure to pass the parameters in the order in which they are defined by the procedure's arguments. For example, the built-in MsgBox function has these arguments:

MsgBox(prompt [, buttons] [, title] [, helpfile, context])

### Prompt
This argument is the message to be displayed.

### Buttons
This argument is used to determine the types of command buttons that will be displayed in the message box (for example, the Yes, No, and Cancel buttons).

### Title
This argument is used to determine the title of the message box.

### Helpfile
This argument can be used to associate a help file to the message box.

### Context
This argument must be used with the help file argument as the context identifier of the help topic to be used.

NOTE    An argument enclosed in square brackets [ ] indicates that the argument is optional.

The following example demonstrates how to call the MsgBox function:

```
intResponse = MsgBox("Hello World!", vbYesNo, "My Application")
```

In this example, the first parameter is the message to be displayed in the box. The second parameter is the number of buttons and type of icon to be displayed. (Here, the constant vbYesNo was used to indicate that the Yes and No buttons should appear.) For a list of valid values for this parameter, search the Microsoft Access online Help under "MsgBox Function." The third parameter is the title that will appear in the title bar of the message box. Because the MsgBox function is being used, a value will be returned. The value represents the button clicked by the user. The variable, intResponse, will store this value.

When passing an argument to a sub procedure, you can pass the argument after the sub procedure name or, if the sub procedure is executed using the Call statement, you can pass the argument within parentheses. For example:

```
MsgBox "Hello World!"
```

or

```
Call MsgBox ("Hello World!")
```

It's often difficult to remember the order in which arguments are defined. In Microsoft Access 97, you can also create named arguments. *Named arguments* allow you to pass arguments in any order, without having to worry about the order in which they were defined. You can assign a value to the name of an argument at the time you call the function or sub procedure. Arguments are named in the function or procedure definition. For example:

```
Sub MySub (strFirstName As String, strLastName As String)
    MsgBox "First Name: " & strFirstName
    MsgBox "Last Name: " & strLastName
End Sub
```

The code above lists two arguments, strFirstName and strLastName. When calling this procedure, you can refer to the name of the argument and assign it a value. For example, to execute the procedure MySub, enter the following in the Debug window:

```
MySub strLastName:= "Leverling", strFirstName:= "Janice"
```

The above sub procedure will execute and display the proper values for the arguments passed to it even though they are not in order, because named arguments are used when you call the sub procedure. To the left of the ":=" is the name of the argument as defined in the sub procedure; to its right is the value passed to the sub procedure. Named arguments can be used for any function or sub procedure that exists in Microsoft Access or that you create.

Passing arguments to procedures enables you to create dynamic procedures to which you can pass different pieces of information to be processed each time the procedure is called. VBA also allows you to define your argument as optional, which makes your code flexible in terms of the number of arguments it can accept. VBA offers two keywords to help you define your arguments: Optional and ParamArray.

■ **Optional keyword** This keyword allows you to declare arguments as optional. This functionality is the same as some of the built-in procedures that accept optional arguments, such as the MsgBox function.

■ **ParamArray keyword** This keyword allows you to pass multiple values into a single procedure argument.

## Using Optional Arguments

If you know that from one situation to another your VBA procedure may or may not need a particular argument, VBA provides a mechanism to make that argument optional. Of course, you can always make an optional argument part of a ParamArray if it's possible that no value can be passed to a particular procedure. (ParamArray is discussed in more detail in the next section.) However, by making arguments optional you can keep unique names for them when they are passed. Optional arguments must be of the Variant data type. To make an argument optional, simply enter the keyword Optional in the procedure definition. When you declare an argument to be optional, all the arguments to the right of it must be optional too. For example, the following procedure defines vntParam1 as optional and must therefore also define vntParam2 as optional:

```
Sub OptParameter(Optional vntParam1, Optional vntParam2)
End Sub
```

To determine whether an argument has been passed, the IsMissing function can be used, as follows:

```
Sub OptParameter(Optional vntParam1, Optional vntParam2)
    If IsMissing(vntParam1) Then
        MsgBox "The first parameter was not passed."
    End If
End Sub
```

If the first argument in the example above had not been passed, the If state-ment would be True. In that case you might need to assign it a default value. For example, this default value might be necessary if you were to use one of the optional arguments in string concatenation or in a calculation.

Procedures that you create will require that you provide all arguments unless you use the Optional keyword; if you don't use the Optional keyword, you will get an Argument Count Mismatch error. You might find that you want to make some arguments optional. Let's take a look at a built-in function, DSum, as an example of how to do this. DSum gives you the ability to add a particular col-umn in a table or query. The arguments are

DSum (*expr, domain*[, *criteria*])

In this example the first argument is the field name, the second is the table or query name, and the third is the criteria. If you do not want to pass any crite-ria, this argument is optional.

## Using ParamArray

Using ParamArray as an argument, you can dynamically change all your argu-ments, thereby changing the number of values passed to the procedure. The arguments must be passed as an array of Variants. The following example uses the ParamArray argument so that any number of arguments can be passed to the procedure. Each argument is then displayed in a message box.

```
Sub MultiArgTest(ParamArray aVarArgs())
    Dim vntMyArg
    For Each vntMyArg In aVarArgs
        MsgBox vntMyArg
    Next
End Sub
```

To call the MultiArgTest sub procedure above, you can use the following sub procedure, MultiArgCaller:

```
Sub MultiArgCaller()
    MultiArgTest 2, 3, 4
End Sub
```

The MultiArgCaller sub procedure passes three arguments to MultiArgTest: 2, 3, and 4. These numbers are all displayed, in the order they were passed, in a message box.

# Decision Structures

You will often need to test for specific conditions in your procedures. VBA provides you with many ways to test for specific values using decision structures, as you'll see in the sections that follow.

## If...Then...Else

When using a macro, you can set up conditions that will perform the macro action if the condition evaluates to a True condition. In VBA you can do the same thing using the If...Then...Else statement. For example, if you want to apply a discount of 10 percent to quantities of over 100, the syntax in VBA would be:

```
If intQuantity > 100 Then
    dblDiscount = .10
Else
    dblDiscount = 0
End If
```

If you are testing for just one condition to be True, you can do this using a single line of code, as shown here:

```
If intQuantity > 100 Then dblDiscount = .10
```

## ElseIf

Your branching may be more complex than testing for one condition. By using the If...Then...Else[If] structure, you can test for multiple conditions. The following example outlines the order in which Microsoft Access evaluates the conditions:

```
If condition1 Then
    [statement block 1]
ElseIf condition2 Then
    [statement block 2]
Else
    [statement block 3]
End If
```

Microsoft Access will first evaluate condition1. If condition1 evaluates to a True condition, then statement block 1 is executed and execution is directed to any code following the End If statement. If condition1 evaluates to a False condition, Microsoft Access proceeds to condition2, and so on, until a True condition is met or until it reaches the Else clause.

When you are testing for more than one value, your If...Then...Else decision structure can become rather complex, as in this example:

```
Sub Case_Select()
    Dim intResponse As Integer
    intResponse = InputBox("Enter a number between 1 and 3")
    If intResponse = 1 Then
        ' Code to execute if intResponse is 1
    ElseIf intResponse = 2 Then
        ' Code to execute if intResponse is 2
    ElseIf intResponse = 3 Then
        ' Code to execute if intResponse is 3
    Else
        ' Code to execute if intResponse is not 1, 2, or 3
    End If
End Sub
```

In such cases you can use another decision structure in VBA to improve the readability of your code. This structure is the Select Case statement, which can be very useful when you are testing for a variable that can contain different values. This construct provides functionality similar to the If...Then...Else statement, but the code is easier to read. The performance is also better with the Select Case statement, because when it is used only one statement, rather than multiple If...Then...Else statements, is evaluated.

## Select Case

The Select Case statement will evaluate one expression and then execute a block of code associated with the case that has a True condition, as shown in the following example:

```
Sub Case_Select()
    Dim intResponse As Integer
    intResponse = InputBox("Enter a number between 1 and 3")
    Select Case intResponse
        Case 1
            ' Code to execute if intResponse is 1
        Case 2
            ' Code to execute if intResponse is 2
        Case 3
            ' Code to execute if intResponse is 3
        Case Else
            ' Code to execute if intResponse is not 1, 2, or 3
    End Select
End Sub
```

Each Case statement tests for the value of the variable intResponse. If you are testing for more than one value in the same line, the values must be separated by a comma, as shown here:

```
Sub Case_Select()
    Dim intResponse As Integer
    intResponse = InputBox("Enter a number between 1 and 3")
    Select Case intResponse
        Case 1, 2
            ' Code to execute if intResponse is 1 or 2
        Case 3
            ' Code to execute if intResponse is 3
        Case Else
            ' Code to execute if intResponse is not 1, 2, or 3
    End Select
End Sub
```

The function above will execute the same code statements whether the value of intResponse is 1 or 2.

**TIP**  If you know that one case is likely to be selected more than the others, move it to the top of the Select Case structure. Doing this will provide you with the best performance, because the minimum number of conditions will be tested within the Select Case structure.

# Loop Structures

Sometimes you need to execute certain lines of a program multiple times. Rather than hard-coding each line over and over, you can write the code to be executed inside a loop.

Microsoft Access uses two main loop structures: Do...Loop and For...Next.

## Do...Loop

The Do...Loop executes the statements contained within it until a condition is True. You can use the Do...Loop in two ways. The first is to execute the statements in the loop at least one time, regardless of whether the condition is True. The second way is to execute statements in the loop only if the condition is True. The following code demonstrates both these approaches:

```
Sub DoUntil()
    Dim intVar1 As Integer, intVar2 As Integer
    intVar1 = 1
    intVar2 = 0

    Do
        Debug.Print "Hello"
        intVar1 = intVar1 - 1
    Loop Until intVar1 = 0
```

*(continued)*

```
    Do Until intVar2 = 0
        Debug.Print "Goodbye"
    Loop
End Sub
```

In this example the first loop is executed one time and the word "Hello" is printed in the Debug window. Because the variable intVar1 becomes 0 the first time through the loop, the loop is exited. The variable comparison for the second Do...Loop is made before the loop is executed. This condition is True; therefore, no code in the second loop is executed.

To exit a Do...Loop structure before completion, you can use the Exit Do statement anywhere inside the loop.

There is a third Do...Loop structure called the DoWhile...Loop. You can read about it in Help.

## For...Next Loop

Unlike the Do...Loop, the For...Next loop will execute statements of code a specified number of times. The reason for this difference is that in the For...Next statement you know how many times the loop will be executed, whereas in a Do...Loop you do not. The For...Next loop uses a counter to keep track of how many times the code has been executed. The following example demonstrates how a For...Next loop can be used:

```
Sub Looping
    ' Declare variable used in For...Next loop.
    Dim intCounter As Integer

    For intCounter = 0 To 9
        Debug.Print intCounter
    Next intCounter
End Sub
```

The variable, intCounter, is automatically incremented by 1 when the Next statement is encountered. When intCounter reaches a value greater than or equal to 10, the loop is exited. The value of intCounter is printed in the Debug window each time the loop is executed.

By default, the counter value is incremented by 1. You can, however, increment the counter by a value other than 1 by using the Step statement:

```
For intCounter = 0 To 10 Step 5
    Debug.Print intCounter 'Prints the value of intCounter
Next intCounter
```

The variable, intCounter, is automatically incremented by 5 when the Next statement is encountered. When intCounter reaches a value greater than 10, the loop is exited. In the example above, the loop will be executed only three times and the value of intCounter is printed in the Debug window three times with the values of 0, 5, and 10.

---

### Decrementing the Counter Variable

You can also decrement the counter variable by using the Step statement with a negative number. This is useful when you're deleting objects from the database or closing opened objects, as demonstrated in Chapter 9. For example:

```
For intCounter = 10 To 0 Step - 5
    Debug.Print intCounter
Next iCounter
```

---

To exit a For…Next statement before completion, you can use the Exit For statement anywhere inside the loop.

## Arrays

An *array* is a series of variables of the same data type, arranged contiguously in memory. Each variable within an array is called an *element*. Arrays can be useful for storing a series of values, such as an entire record, to one variable. This arrangement of elements is known as a one-dimensional array. Imagine, for example, a post office that has five mailboxes. The boxes are always in the post office, even if their owners don't receive mail.

**Post Office**

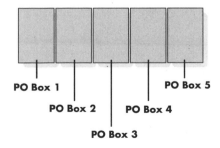

**Figure 1-13.** *Post office mailboxes exemplifying a one-dimensional array.*

In Figure 1-13 on the previous page, "Post Office" represents the name of the array. With VBA, creating a one-dimensional array is an easy and logical process when you use the built-in Array function. The Array function returns a Variant value containing the array. Our post office example would translate into the Array function as follows:

```
Dim aPostOffice(4) As String
Sub FillArray()
    aPostOffice = Array("PO Box 1", "PO Box 2", "PO Box 3", _
        "PO Box 4", "PO Box 5")
End Sub
```

Below is another way to create an array in VBA code using the example of a post office:

```
Dim aPostOffice(4) As String
Sub FillArray()
    aPostOffice(0) = "PO Box 1"
    aPostOffice(1) = "PO Box 2"
    aPostOffice(2) = "PO Box 3"
    aPostOffice(3) = "PO Box 4"
    aPostOffice(4) = "PO Box 5"
End Sub
```

Notice that the number in the declaration of the aPostOffice array variable is one less than the number of elements the array will have. To refer to each element individually, you give the array name followed by the number of the element in parentheses. In the example above, the first element in the array is zero (0). All arrays in Microsoft Access are zero-based by default. If you want the first element in the array to be 1, you can use the command Option Base 1 in the General declarations section of the module.

You may be asking yourself, "Why should I use an array when I could achieve the same result by declaring five different variables?" It's true that you could accomplish the same task by declaring a variable each time you need one, but doing so would require that you know at run time how many variables you will need. When using an array, you can redimension it to take up only the amount of memory it requires, as you'll see in the next section. One of the most important benefits of using arrays is their use in loop structures. As you will see in the "Retrieving Information from Arrays" section beginning on page 54, the loop structure is a very quick and easy method of filling an array.

**TIP** To determine through code whether a variable has been declared as an array, you can pass the variable into the built-in
IsArray() function. If the variable is an array, the IsArray()
function will return True; it will return False if the variable is not
an array.

## Multidimensional Arrays

VBA allows you to create arrays of up to 60 dimensions. In most cases you will
not need an array of more than two dimensions. A two-dimensional array is
similar to a table in a database. When you specify the second element in an array,
it's like defining the number of fields within the table. When filling the array,
you need to fill the fields in the table for a particular record. An example of a
two-dimensional array follows:

```
Dim aPostOffice(1,1) As String
Sub MultiArray()
    aPostOffice(0,0) = "Building 1, Apartment 1"
    aPostOffice(0,1) = "Building 1, Apartment 2"
    aPostOffice(1,0) = "Building 2, Apartment 1"
    aPostOffice(1,1) = "Building 2, Apartment 2"
End Sub
```

This example assigns a value to each element of the array. As mentioned above,
you can think of this as assigning a value to a field in a table, or as delivering
mail to two apartments in the same building. The following table shows what
the array, aPostOffice, looks like in memory.

| Row | Column 0 | Column 1 |
|-----|----------|----------|
| 0 | Building 1, Apartment 1 | Building 1, Apartment 2 |
| 1 | Building 2, Apartment 1 | Building 2, Apartment 2 |

## Dynamic arrays

Occasionally, you won't know the specific size of an array and will want the
capability of changing its size at run time. In VBA you can create a *dynamic*
array, which allows you to change the number of elements contained in the array
at run time. You use the ReDim statement to change the number of elements
in an array, as in the following example:

```
Dim aDynArr() As String
ReDim aDynArr(5)
```

You'll notice that the declaration of the array aDynArr does not specify the number of elements it contains. The ReDim statement allows you to specify the appropriate number of elements. Using dynamic arrays, you can be sure that you are taking up as little memory as possible, wasting none. When an array is redimensioned, all the elements in it are removed by default. If you want to keep the current values in the array, you can use the Preserved keyword with the ReDim statement, as shown here:

```
Sub Dynamic_Array()
    Static aMyArray As String
    ReDim aMyArray(3)
    aMyArray(0) = "apple"
    aMyArray(1) = "banana"
    aMyArray(2) = "mango"
    aMyArray(3) = "kiwi"
    ReDim Preserve aMyArray(4)
    aMyArray(4) = "pineapple"
End Sub
```

The example above maintains all the values in the array because the Preserve keyword is used the second time it is redimensioned. If the Preserve keyword had not been used, the only element in the array to have a value at the end of the procedure would be the last element, aMyArray(4).

> **TIP**
>
> You can use the Erase statement to reinitialize the elements of fixed-size arrays. For example, the contents of an array dimensioned as *Dim aMyArray(4) As Integer* can be reinitialized to 0 with *Erase aMyArray*. You can also use the Erase statement to free the memory used by dynamic arrays. For example, *ReDim aMyArray(5)* dynamically allocates storage space in memory. You can reclaim the allocated memory with *Erase aMyArray*.

## Retrieving Information from Arrays

Now that you are able to declare and fill an array, you need to be able to retrieve the information stored in it. You can retrieve information with any of the following structures:

- For...Next loop
- For...Next loop using the LBound and UBound built-in functions
- For...Each loop

To return the values stored in an array, you must know how many elements the array contains. If you know how many elements are in the array, you can use the For...Next loop to return those values. (The For...Next loop was covered in greater detail earlier in this chapter.) For example, the following code will fill an array and print the values to the Debug window:

```
Sub FillandPrintArray()
    Dim aMyArray() As String
    ' Dynamically dimension an array.
    ReDim aMyArray(3)
    Dim intCounter As Integer

    ' Fill the array with a For...Next Loop.
    For intCounter = 0 To 3
        aMyArray(intCounter) = "A" & intCounter
    Next intCounter
    ' Retrieve the values stored in the array.
    For intCounter = 0 To 3
        Debug.Print aMyArray(intCounter)
    Next intCounter
End Sub
```

The Array function could also be used to fill the array above, as in this example:

```
aMyArray = Array("A1", "A2", "A3", "A4")
```

The problem with literally using the bounds in the For...Next loop is that if the array is redimensioned to a different size, the For...Next loop will not work properly. To be able to determine the size of an array at any time, you can use the LBound and UBound functions. The LBound function will give you the lower limit of an array dimension; the UBound function will give you its upper limit. The following example uses the same For...Next loop as above, but with the LBound and UBound functions:

```
' Retrieve the values stored in the array.
For intCounter = LBound(aMyArray) To UBound(aMyArray)
    Debug.Print aMyArray(intCounter)
Next intCounter
```

You can also use the For...Each loop to retrieve the values stored in an array. The For...Each loop structure repeats a group of statements for each element in an array. The For...Each block is executed if the group has at least one element. When you use the For...Each loop with arrays, you must declare the variable used to access each element as a Variant data type. The advantage of For...Each loops over For...Next loops is that with a For...Each loop it is not necessary to determine the number of elements in an array. The following example prints all the elements in an array:

```
' Retrieve the values stored in the array.
Dim vntElement As Variant
For Each vntContent In aMyArray
    Debug.Print vntContent
Next
```

**TIP**  To exit a For...Each loop structure before completion, you can use the Exit For statement between the For...Each statement and the Next statement.

Although the For...Each loop syntax is simple to use, it does have limitations. One is that you will retrieve all elements in the array. (Using the For...Next loop, you can begin and end with any element within the array.) Another limitation is that you cannot use a For...Each loop to fill an array, whereas you could fill it using a For...Next loop.

For multidimensional arrays you can use nested For...Next loops in conjunction with LBound and UBound functions. However, if all the elements in an array need to be retrieved, the For...Each loop is the easiest method to use to accomplish this goal. The following example uses a nested For...Next loop to fill a multidimensional array and then uses a For...Each loop to retrieve the values and print them in the Debug window:

```
Sub NestedForandArray()
    ' Dimension a multidimensional array.
    Dim aMyArray(2, 2) As String
    ' Declare variables to be used to fill array.
    Dim iRN As Integer, iFN As Integer
    ' Declare variables to be used to retrieve array elements.
    Dim vntElement

    ' Filling the array
    For iRN = 0 To 2
        For iFN = 0 To 2
        aMyArray(iRN, iFN) = "Record " & iRN & " Field " & iFN
        Next iFN
    Next iRN

    ' Retrieve the values stored in the array.
    For Each vntElement In aMyArray
        Debug.Print vntElement
    Next vntElement
End Sub
```

This procedure prints the following values to the Debug window:

```
Record 0 Field 0
Record 1 Field 0
Record 2 Field 0
Record 0 Field 1
Record 1 Field 1
Record 2 Field 1
Record 0 Field 2
Record 1 Field 2
Record 2 Field 2
```

You may sometimes want to extract the contents of only one element of an array rather than enumerate all its elements. You can easily extract single elements by having the function accept an argument whose value corresponds to the desired array element.

## PREVIEW of the next chapter

In this chapter you learned what VBA is, and you saw the basic tools for using it. In the next chapter, you will create custom procedures to solve a business problem.

# 2

# Creating Solutions Using Custom Procedures

Developing your programming skills is a little like building a house: if you begin with a strong foundation and increase your understanding gradually, you'll avoid many problems in the long run. Think of Chapter 1 of this book as work on a foundation. In this chapter you will learn how to build a small solution to add to your solid understanding of fundamental programming concepts.

You can create procedures in many different ways to complete the same task. Some ways are better than others, however. In this chapter we explain, step by step, the best way to create a procedure. The benefit of learning in steps is that you can see why certain tasks are performed in a particular order and understand how all the individual parts of a procedure fit together and affect the whole. We could just give you the function and say "Here is the solution," but that wouldn't help you much in the long run. There is an ancient proverb: "Give a man a fish and you feed him for a day; teach a man to fish and you feed him for a lifetime." We want to show you how to fish.

In the first chapter you learned the basics of Visual Basic for Applications programming. Here you will see how to put some of those skills to work.

## Defining Your Task

A formula does not necessarily have to be difficult to justify creating a procedure for it; you might want to create a procedure simply because the formula is hard to remember, as is the case with converting degrees Fahrenheit to degrees Celsius. You can look up the formula and hard code the calculation, but it's easier to include this routine in a module or a database library of procedures.

The procedures you create in this chapter will be for a floor-tile company that wants to help its customers correctly calculate the number of tiles they will need.

West Coast Sales is a large floor-tile distribution center in Nowhere, USA. It is a large-volume retailer that keeps its prices low by carrying only a limited number of products and selling only by the case. The owners have approached you to assist them in developing a solution that will help their customers purchase the appropriate amount of floor tiles. Using your application, the customer will enter the dimensions of the room that needs tiling and the size of the floor tile desired. The system will then return the number of cases the customer will need to purchase, as shown in Figure 2-1.

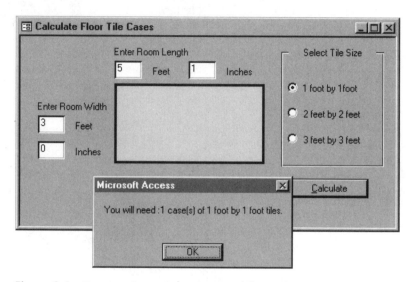

**Figure 2-1.** *Buying the right amount of floor tiles.*

## Creating Your First Procedure

The first step in developing this solution is to create a procedure that calculates a room's dimensions. Start by determining whether Microsoft Access has a built-in function that will perform this task by using the Expression Builder (see Chapter 1). In this case it does not, so you will have to create one.

Your next step, then, is to create a new module and save it as "Tile Calculations." Because this procedure is going to return the result of the formula, you must create it as a function since sub procedures cannot return values. In the module window, type the following code:

```
Function intSqrFt(intLength As Integer, intWidth As Integer) _
    As Integer
End Function
```

Here, intSqrFt is the name of the function. The prefix "int" signifies that this function will return an integer value. The body, "SqrFt," signifies that it will calculate square footage. Notice that this function has been defined to accept two arguments, intLength and intWidth, as Integer data types so you can pass in varying room lengths and widths.

Now that we have defined the function's structure, it's time to create its body. The formula to determine square footage is length times width. Because the function has already been defined to accept the length and width of a room, the only line of code it needs is one for evaluating length times width. The VBA syntax for this is shown in bold below:

```
Function intSqrFt(intLength As Integer, intWidth As Integer) _
    As Integer
    intSqrFt = intLength * intWidth
End Function
```

Because you set the function name equal to the expression (length times width), the function now returns that value.

> **NOTE** From this point on, bold text in code shows new additions and changes.

## Testing Your Function

You can execute a function to confirm that it's working properly in several different ways. One way is to use the Debug window, which was introduced in Chapter 1. (The Debug window is explained in detail in Chapter 3.) To open the Debug window, first open a module in Design view. Now choose Debug Window from the View menu. Type a question mark followed by the function name in the Debug window. Functions return a value, and the question mark instructs VBA to display that returned value in the Debug window. To execute the intSqrFt function, type the following into the Debug window and then press the enter key:

```
?intSqrFt(8,10)
```

The example above passes the room dimensions of length 8 and width 10 to intSqrFt. The function will return a value of 80 when executed in the Debug window.

## Using Correct Data Types

Now that the function executes properly, try passing in different values to it, such as a length of 20 and a width of 16. The result should be 320 square feet. Try to execute the function by passing in a length of 9999 and a width of 9999. Instead of returning a value (99980001), the function displays an overflow error. This error occurs because the value of the two integers multiplied is greater than what is allowed by the Integer data type. An integer is a 2-byte value; therefore, the largest number you can pass in is 32,767. When you multiply this figure by a second integer of the same value (32,767 × 32,767), your result is 1,073,676,289, which is too large for the Integer data type. However, this number is smaller than the maximum value allowed for the Long data type.

To work around the limitations of the Integer data type, you will have to convert the integer values to Long so that the procedure will return a Long value. To do this, use the built-in CLng function to modify your procedure. Since the function will now return a Long data type, you need to change the prefix to reflect this. The following code shows how the function will look after you've changed it to return a Long value:

```
Function lngSqrFt(intLength As Integer, intWidth As Integer) _
    As Long
    ' Convert integer arguments to a Long data type.
    lngSqrFt = CLng(intLength) * CLng(intWidth)
End Function
```

Now execute the procedure a few more times, passing in values less than or equal to 32,767 as the parameters.

## Dealing with Challenges

When developing solutions, you are bound to encounter more issues than you had anticipated. For example, in the West Coast Sales project, what are you going to do if a customer requests 1-foot-by-1-foot tiles for a room that measures 10.5 feet by 10.5 feet? You need to remember that although floor tiles come in fixed sizes, rooms do not. In your formula you're going to have to adjust for odd measurements, for those cases in which the tile size and the room size do not allow for a "perfect fit."

Let's look at a couple of simple examples to figure out how to calculate the remaining portions of floor tile needed. As you're writing your function, you might find it useful to work out the formulas manually on paper so you have a way of judging your results.

In the following example, the room is 3 square feet. Assuming that the customer has chosen tiles that are 1 foot by 1 foot, only 9 tiles would be needed to complete the job.

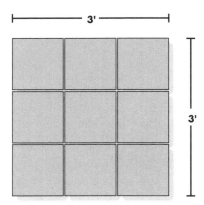

Now consider a different scenario.

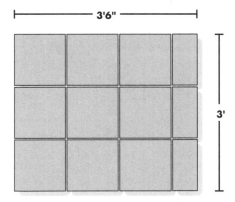

The room shown above is 10.5 square feet. To allow for the additional half-foot, you could simply purchase 11 tiles and cut the tenth and eleventh pieces in half, leaving only one-half tile unused. However, you are not always going to be that lucky with room measurements. The next example poses a more difficult challenge.

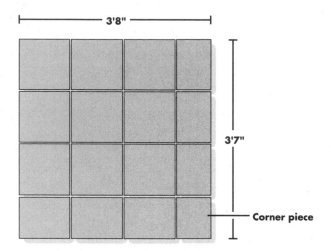

The configuration above is 13.14 square feet (3.58 × 3.67). You might think that the customer will need to purchase 14 1-foot-square tiles. But the room length is 3 feet 7 inches and the width is 3 feet 8 inches, so the "leftover" dimensions of 7 and 8 inches, respectively, combine to be more than 12 inches. If the sum of the two dimensions were less than 12 inches, one 12-by-12-inch tile could be divided to cover both leftovers. Because the sum of the leftovers in this case is more than 12 inches, however, you will not be able to split the tiles to cover the leftover 15 inches. Instead, you will need nine whole tiles (12 x 12 inches), three 12-by-7-inch tiles, three 12-by-8-inch tiles, and one corner 7-by-8-inch tile, for a total of 16 tiles, to have enough tile to cover the room. You will learn how to calculate partial tiles later in this chapter.

You have already created a function to calculate the overall square footage of a room. Now you need to calculate the number of tiles needed based on their size. To make this problem even more interesting, you must also factor in the fact that the customer can purchase tiles only by the case. (Remember, in order for West Coast Sales to keep its prices low, it has to operate with reduced overhead, that is, by selling tiles only by the case.)

Your solution will have a simple user interface because in this example, for your application to be a success, it is more important that you focus on how your procedures work rather than on how your application looks. (User interface design is covered in greater detail in Chapter 5.)

## Building Your Application

You will build this application step by step, one piece of the puzzle at a time, instead of implementing all functionality at once. Your interface will start out with a very simple form, Calculate Floor Tile Cases, in which you will enter room dimensions based on feet. You will then use the length and width values to calculate the number of tile cases the customer will need to purchase. When you have finished, your form will look similar to the one shown in Figure 2-2.

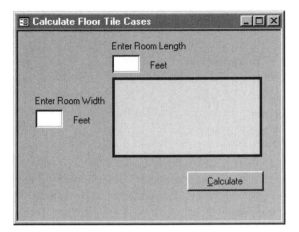

**Figure 2-2.** *The Calculate Floor Tile Cases form.*

## Creating the Form

The Calculate Floor Tile Cases form is the entire user interface because the application has only one responsibility to the user: to calculate cases of floor tiles needed. To create the form, follow these steps:

**1.** In a new database, create a new blank form that is unbound.

**2.** To view the Form properties, choose Select Form from the Edit menu. If the Properties window is not displayed, select Properties from the View menu.

**3.** Select the Control Wizard button on the toolbar to turn off the Control Wizard.

**4.** Set the following Form properties:

| Property Name | Value |
| --- | --- |
| Caption | Calculate Floor Tile Cases |
| Scroll Bars | Neither |
| Record Selectors | No |
| Navigation Buttons | No |
| Auto Center | Yes |

**5.** Add a rectangle to visually represent a room. (This addition is for visual appeal only and does not affect the outcome of the application.)

**6.** Add a text box to enter the measured length of the room in feet. Change the Name property to txtLengthFeet. Change the Caption property of the text box's label to Feet.

**7.** Add a text box to enter the measured width of the room in feet. Change the Name property to txtWidthFeet. Change the Caption property of the text box's label to Feet.

**8.** Add a label with the caption "Enter Room Width," as shown in Figure 2-2.

**9.** Add another label with the caption "Enter Room Length," as shown in Figure 2-2.

**10.** Add a command button to the form and set the following properties:

| Property Name | Value |
| --- | --- |
| Name | cmdCalculate |
| Caption | &Calculate<br>(The ampersand allows you to use the letter "C" in "Calculate" as a hot key. In the future, you can execute the function used to calculate by pressing Alt + C instead of clicking the command button with the mouse.) |

**11.** Save the form as frmFloorTiles.

The Calculate Floor Tile Cases form now consists of one command button, two labels, two text boxes, and a rectangle, as shown in Figure 2-2 on page 65.

## Creating the DisplayTiles Function

Now you need to create a new function that will pass the room dimensions to the lngSqrFt function. This new function must also display the result in a message box. To do this, create the following procedure in the Tile Calculations module:

```
Function DisplayTiles()
    ' Use a message box to display
    ' the room dimensions.
    MsgBox lngSqrFt(8, 9)
End Function
```

Notice that "DisplayTiles" does not have a data type prefix. This function will not be used to return a value, but since you need to call this procedure from a form, you must nevertheless use a function because you cannot call a sub procedure from the property sheet.

To call this function by using a command button, you must place the name of the function in the On Click event of the control. To do this, open the frmFloorTiles form in Design view. Click the Calculate button. The Properties window will now reflect the properties of this object. Click the Events tab in the Properties window and place your cursor in the On Click event. Enter the name of the function you created, preceded by an equal sign (="DisplayTiles( )"). Your screen should look similar to the one shown in Figure 2-3.

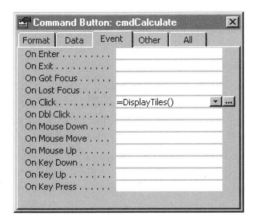

**Figure 2-3.** *The On Click event property for the cmdCalculate command button.*

To test your work, open the form in Form view. Click the Calculate button. You will see the message box shown in Figure 2-4.

**Figure 2-4.** *Result of DisplayTiles function.*

## Passing the Values to the Function

Next you need to pass the values to the function through the user interface. To do this, you will retrieve the values from the text boxes on the form. You can reference the form in the same way you would reference a form in a macro. As shown in the code below, the syntax you will use is Forms!*form-name!Text box-name*. The following code declares two variables as type Variant and assigns the variables with the values of text boxes on the frmFloorTiles form. You declare the variables as variants so the user interface can accept any value entered in the text boxes. (The purpose for this is discussed later in this chapter.)

```
Function DisplayTiles()
    Dim vntLength As Variant
    Dim vntWidth As Variant

    ' Assign the values entered in the form
    ' to variables.
    vntLength = Forms!frmFloorTiles!txtLengthFeet
    vntWidth = Forms!frmFloorTiles!txtWidthFeet

    ' Use a message box to display
    ' the room dimensions.
    MsgBox lngSqrFt(vntLength, vntWidth)
End Function
```

Because you could replace the variable references in the lngSqrFt procedure with the actual references to the text boxes, declaring the new vntLength and vntWidth variables is not necessary at this time; it does, however, make the code easier to read.

Compile the procedure to make sure it is syntactically correct. To do this, select Compile Loaded Modules from the Debug menu. You will receive an error message indicating that incorrect parameter data types are being passed, as shown in Figure 2-5.

**Figure 2-5.** *Error message for incorrect parameter data types.*

In the lngSqrFt function, the data types of the arguments were defined as integers, but you need to declare the variables in DisplayTiles as Variant data types in case a user enters alphabetical information into the text boxes by accident. To do this, you need to convert the Variant data types into integers before passing the values to the lngSqrFt function by using the built-in CInt function. Now the data type of the variables being passed to the lngSqrFt function is of the same data type as the lngSqrFt function's arguments. Make the following changes to the MsgBox line of your code in the DisplayTiles function:

```
MsgBox lngSqrFt(CInt(vntLength), _
    CInt(vntWidth))
```

Compile the procedure again to make sure it is syntactically correct. Open the form in Form view and add values to the two text boxes. Next, click the command button. A message box will appear showing the square feet for the room dimensions you entered. You are now retrieving the values from the form. Enter other numeric values in the text boxes and click the Calculate button. Try this a few times to see different results.

## Concatenating Values

The number displayed in the message box would be more meaningful if you included text describing what the number represents. To do this, you can concatenate text to the beginning and end of the message. Make the following changes to the MsgBox line of your code in the DisplayTiles function so that the message box will look like the one shown in Figure 2-6.

```
MsgBox "The room is " & lngSqrFt(CInt(vntLength), _
    CInt(vntWidth)) & " square feet."
```

**Figure 2-6.** *Displaying the results of your square footage function.*

## Testing the DisplayTiles Function

Now let's break the code! Experiment by entering values that are not numeric. Try a text string of alpha characters before executing the procedure. When you click the Calculate button, you will encounter a type mismatch error. To avoid a similar error in your application, you can test the values of the text boxes to ensure that numeric values have been entered.

You can use the IsNumeric function to test whether the value is a Numeric data type. If it is, you can process the procedure; if it is not, you can have the procedure display an informative message to the user. The following example uses the IsNumeric function to test the values of the text boxes. If alphabetic characters have been entered, the user is prompted with a message box indicating the correct type of data to be entered.

```
Function DisplayTiles()
    Dim vntLength As Variant
    Dim vntWidth As Variant

    ' Assign the values entered in the form
    ' to variables.
    vntLength = Forms!frmFloorTiles!txtLengthFeet
    vntWidth = Forms!frmFloorTiles!txtWidthFeet
    ' Check the variables to see whether they are numeric.
    If IsNumeric(vntLength) And IsNumeric(vntWidth) Then
        ' Use a message box to display
        ' the room dimensions.
        MsgBox "The room is " & lngSqrFt(CInt(vntLength), _
            CInt(vntWidth)) & " square feet."
    Else
        MsgBox "Measurements must contain numeric data."
    End If
End Function
```

Compile the function, and then test it by using the frmFloorTiles form.

The next step would be to add the logic to ensure that the user does not enter a value greater than the range allowed for an integer.

```
Function DisplayTiles()
    Dim vntLength As Variant
    Dim vntWidth As Variant

    ' Assign the values entered in the form
    ' to variables.
    vntLength = Forms!frmFloorTiles!txtLengthFeet
    vntWidth = Forms!frmFloorTiles!txtWidthFeet
    ' Check the variables to see whether they are numeric.
    If IsNumeric(vntLength) And IsNumeric(vntWidth) Then
        ' Check the variables to see whether they are integer values.
        If (vntLength >= 0 And vntLength < 32768) And _
            (vntWidth >= 0 And vntWidth < 32768) Then
        ' Use a message box to display
        ' the room dimensions.
        MsgBox "The room is " & lngSqrFt(CInt(vntLength), _
            CInt(vntWidth)) & " square feet."
        Else
            MsgBox "Please enter a number between 0 and 32,767."
        End If
    Else
        MsgBox "Measurements must contain numeric data."
    End If
End Function
```

**NOTE** Notice that the If statements are nested so that the procedure checks to see whether the numbers are in the appropriate range only if the entries are numeric.

Compile and test the procedure via the frmFloorTiles form by entering both numeric and character data. As it stands now, the function accommodates a room's dimension in feet only. The form and the function must now be modified to accommodate for inches also, as shown in Figure 2-7.

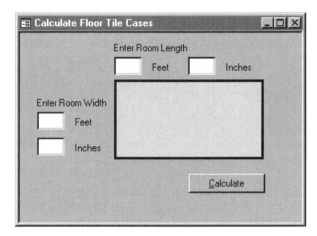

**Figure 2-7.** *Entering inches for room dimensions.*

To modify the frmFloorTiles form, open it in Design view and perform the following steps:

**1.** Add a text box to enter the length of the room in inches measurement. Change the Name property to txtLengthInch. Change the Caption property of the text box's label to Inches.

**2.** Add a text box to enter the width of the room in inches measurement. Change the Name property to txtWidthInch. Change the Caption property of the text box's label to Inches.

All of the capabilities your function has for handling measurements in feet must also exist for handling measurements in inches. For example, you will need to test to see whether the data entered is numeric and to make sure the values do not exceed the maximum value of an Integer data type. In addition, you will need to modify the code so that if a user enters a number in inches the function can convert that to feet. For example, 12 feet 1 inch is a valid number. But if the user enters 10 feet 12 inches as the room's dimensions, the text boxes should display the value of 11 feet 0 inches. If 60 inches is entered, the function should convert it to 5 feet 0 inches. You will also want to test that a valid integer value is entered in each of the text boxes. A blank or *null* is not a valid integer value. You should substitute a zero for null values.

To build this functionality into your DisplayTiles function, add the following lines of code:

```
Function DisplayTiles()
    Dim vntLength As Variant
    Dim vntWidth As Variant
    Dim vntLengthIn As Variant
    Dim vntWidthIn As Variant

    ' Assign the values entered in the form
    ' to variables.
    vntLength = Forms!frmFloorTiles!txtLengthFeet
    vntWidth = Forms!frmFloorTiles!txtWidthFeet
    vntLengthIn = Forms!frmFloorTiles!txtLengthInch
    vntWidthIn = Forms!frmFloorTiles!txtWidthInch

    ' Check the variables to see whether they are numeric.
    If IsNumeric(vntLength) And IsNumeric(vntWidth) And _
        IsNumeric(vntLengthIn) And IsNumeric(vntWidthIn) Then
        ' Check the variables to see whether they are integer values.
        If (vntLength >= 0 And vntLength < 32768) And _
            (vntWidth >= 0 And vntWidth < 32768) And _
            (vntLengthIn >= 0 And vntLengthIn < 32768) And _
            (vntWidthIn >= 0 And vntWidthIn < 32768) Then
            ' Convert inches > 11 for the length to feet.
            If vntLengthIn > 11 Then
                vntLength = vntLength + Int(vntLengthIn / 12)
                vntLengthIn = vntLengthIn Mod 12
                ' Change the text boxes on the form to reflect
                ' the new measurement.
                Forms!frmFloorTiles!txtLengthFeet = vntLength
                Forms!frmFloorTiles!txtLengthInch = vntLengthIn
            End If
            ' Convert inches > 11 for the width to feet.
            If vntWidthIn > 11 Then
                vntWidth = vntWidth + Int(vntWidthIn / 12)
                vntWidthIn = vntWidthIn Mod 12
                ' Change the text boxes on the form to reflect
                ' the new measurement.
                Forms!frmFloorTiles!txtWidthFeet = vntWidth
                Forms!frmFloorTiles!txtWidthInch = vntWidthIn
            End If
            ' Use a message box to display
            ' the room dimensions.
```

```
            MsgBox "The room is " & lngSqrFt(CInt(vntLength), _
                CInt(vntWidth)) & " square feet."
        Else
            MsgBox "Please Enter a Number Between 0 and 32,767."
        End If
    Else
        MsgBox "Measurements must contain numeric data."
    End If
End Function
```

**NOTE**  At this point, the example still assumes that the tiles are 1 foot wide by 1 foot long.

The function above determines the square footage based solely on the number of feet entered in the form. For example, if the user enters a length of 5 feet 14 inches and a width of 2 feet 1 inch, the function will convert the dimensions to 6 feet 2 inches by 2 feet 1 inch. However, the square footage returned will be 10. The extra 2 inches in length and the extra 1 inch in width are ignored at this point so that you can determine the total number of whole tiles needed before having to "break them up" to accommodate the extra inches. In the next section you will learn how to deal with extra inches.

## Creating the Formulas

In the steps that follow, you will create the formulas to properly convert the square footage of a room into the number of tiles needed and then to convert that information into the number of cases necessary to complete the job.

### Determining number of tiles to square feet

Now that you know the room's square footage without the extra inches, you need to determine the number of tiles the customer must purchase. This number must be enough to cover both the square footage calculated in the previous section and any additional inches for which tiles must be broken up. After the total number of 1-foot-square tiles is determined, your application will display a message box that displays that number.

```
Function DisplayTiles()
    Dim vntLength As Variant
    Dim vntWidth As Variant
    Dim vntLengthIn As Variant
    Dim vntWidthIn As Variant
    Dim lngTotalTiles As Long
    ' Assign the values entered in the form
    ' to variables.
```

*(continued)*

```
vntLength = Forms!frmFloorTiles!txtLengthFeet
vntWidth = Forms!frmFloorTiles!txtWidthFeet
vntLengthIn = Forms!frmFloorTiles!txtLengthInch
vntWidthIn = Forms!frmFloorTiles!txtWidthInch

' Check the variables to see whether they are numeric.
If IsNumeric(vntLength) And IsNumeric(vntWidth) And _
    IsNumeric(vntLengthIn) And IsNumeric(vntWidthIn) Then
    ' Check the variables to see whether they are integer values.
    If (vntLength >= 0 And vntLength < 32768) And _
        (vntWidth >= 0 And vntWidth < 32768) And _
        (vntLengthIn >= 0 And vntLengthIn < 32768) And _
        (vntWidthIn >= 0 And vntWidthIn < 32768) Then
        ' Convert inches > 11 for the length to feet.
        If vntLengthIn > 11 Then
            vntLength = vntLength + Int(vntLengthIn / 12)
            vntLengthIn = vntLengthIn Mod 12
            ' Change the text boxes on the form to reflect
            ' the new measurement.
            Forms!frmFloorTiles!txtLengthFeet = vntLength
            Forms!frmFloorTiles!txtLengthInch = vntLengthIn
        End If
        ' Convert inches > 11 for the width to feet.
        If vntWidthIn > 11 Then
            vntWidth = vntWidth + Int(vntWidthIn / 12)
            vntWidthIn = vntWidthIn Mod 12
            ' Change the text boxes on the form to reflect
            ' the new measurement.
            Forms!frmFloorTiles!txtWidthFeet = vntWidth
            Forms!frmFloorTiles!txtWidthInch = vntWidthIn
        End If
        ' Because the inch value might have changed to zero,
        ' it needs to be tested again.
        lngTotalTiles = lngSqrFt(CInt(vntLength), _
            CInt(vntWidth))
        If vntLengthIn > 0 Then
            lngTotalTiles = lngTotalTiles + _
                CLng(Forms!frmFloorTiles!txtWidthFeet)
        End If
        If vntWidthIn > 0 Then
            lngTotalTiles = lngTotalTiles + _
                CLng(Forms!frmFloorTiles!txtLengthFeet)
        End If
        If vntLengthIn > 0 And vntWidthIn > 0 Then
            ' The corner piece
            lngTotalTiles = lngTotalTiles + 1
        End If
```

```
            MsgBox "You will need " & lngTotalTiles & " tiles."
        Else
            MsgBox "Please enter a number between 0 and 32,767."
        End If
    Else
        MsgBox "Measurements must contain numeric data."
    End If
End Function
```

## Calculating for number of tiles to cases

At this point you are able to calculate the total number of 1-foot-square tiles the customer will need to tile a room. One possibility we will not consider in our sample application is that you could split tiles and use both pieces to cover odd areas. We will assume that split tiles will have only one usable piece. You now have one more calculation to make. Since West Coast Sales sells tiles only by the case, you must also determine the number of *cases* the customer must buy. (Unfortunately, the customer will usually have to purchase more tiles than necessary if the number of tiles needed doesn't match the number of tiles per case.)

For your solution, assume that one case contains 24 individual tiles. Since the number of tiles per case will remain static for long periods of time, you can use a constant to represent this ratio in your code. (If the number of tiles per case changes in the future, you will need to change the value of the constant.) Add the following line of code to the beginning of your DisplayTiles function:

```
Const intTilesPerCase As Integer = 24
```

To determine the number of cases the customer will need, use the following expression:

```
lngTotalTiles = lngTotalTiles / intTilesPerCase
```

Unfortunately, if you use this expression and a fractional portion of the number remains, the customer will be short one case of tiles. If his or her total number of tiles is 100, the expression evaluates to 4.17, which will round down to four cases. Because you want the program to return five cases of 1-foot-square tiles, you need to test for this condition.

You will not be able to accomplish this by using the expression above because the data type for TotalTiles is Long, which does not support fractions—therefore, the expression would return a value of 4. You can get around this by changing the lngTotalTiles variable to a Double data type and then changing the Dim statement in your code to the following:

```
Dim dblTotalTiles As Double
```

Notice the change in the first three letters of the variable name to represent its new data type. By default, whenever you create a new module, the Option Explicit statement is inserted at the top of the module. One great advantage of using the Option Explicit statement in your modules is that it forces you to define all variables in your procedures.

Change all uses of the variable lngTotalTiles to represent the new name (dblTotalTiles). Add the following expression in the line above the message box that shows the total tiles needed:

```
dblTotalTiles = dblTotalTiles / intTilesPerCase
```

Now compile, save, and try entering various combinations of parameters until you get an expression that returns a fraction—for example, 20 feet 1 inch for length and 28 feet 1 inch for width. The message box will inform you that 25.375 tiles are needed. The function needs to be modified so that the correct whole number amount can be returned. You can do this by adding another expression to the function. The expression should test to see whether there is a remainder, and if so, it should add the number 1 to the result after it removes the remainder. Using the previous example, the message box would now display "26 tiles are needed." You can use the following code to do this, placed after the expression above:

```
If CLng(dblTotalTiles) < dblTotalTiles Then
    dblTotalTiles = CLng(dblTotalTiles) + 1
Else
    dblTotalTiles = CLng(dblTotalTiles)
End If
```

You will also need to change the MsgBox line of code below the code you've just entered to reflect the number of cases needed instead of the number of tiles. The MsgBox line should look like the following:

```
MsgBox "You will need " & dblTotalTiles & " case(s) of tiles."
```

## Working with Select Case Statements

You now have an application that allows customers to enter the dimensions of a room and then determine how many cases of tiles will be required to cover their floor. However, at this point it will only calculate the number of cases based on a tile size of 1 foot by 1 foot, and West Coast Sales also offers tiles that are 2 feet by 2 feet and 3 feet by 3 feet. To allow the customer to select any of the three tile sizes, you need to modify the form by adding an Option Group control with three option buttons, as shown in Figure 2-8.

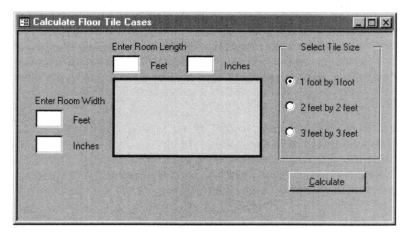

**Figure 2-8.** *Selecting tile sizes.*

1. Add an option group to the form by opening the form in Design view, selecting the Option Group button, and placing the option group on the form. Verify that the Controls Wizards button on the Toolbox is deselected.

| Property Name | Value |
|---------------|-------|
| Name | optSelectSize |
| DefaultValue | 1 <br> (This will be the default tile size. 1 foot by 1 foot = 1 square foot) |

2. Change the caption of the option group control (optSelectSize) to Select Tile Size.

3. To add three option buttons to the option group, select the Option Button Tool from the Toolbox and place an Option Button within the optSelectSize option group. Repeat this step two more times to get three Option Buttons.

4. Change the optSelectSize1 label's caption to 1 foot by 1 foot.

| Property Name | Value |
|---------------|-------|
| Name | optSelectSize1 |
| OptionValue | 1 <br> (This will be the default tile size. 1 foot by 1 foot = 1 square foot) |

**5.** Change the optSelectSize2 label's caption to 2 feet by 2 feet.

| Property Name | Value |
| --- | --- |
| Name | optSelectSize2 |
| OptionValue | 4 |
| | (2 feet by 2 feet = 4 square feet) |

**6.** Change the optSelectSize3 label's caption to 3 feet by 3 feet.

| Property Name | Value |
| --- | --- |
| Name | optSelectSize3 |
| OptionValue | 9 |
| | (3 feet by 3 feet = 9 square feet) |

You will use the value of the option group to determine the number of cases the customer needs based on tile size. To do this, change one line of code in the DisplayTiles function from

```
dblTotalTiles = dblTotalTiles / intTilesPerCase
```

to

```
dblTotalTiles = (dblTotalTiles / _
    Forms!frmFloorTiles!optSelectSize) / intTilesPerCase
```

To include the tile size in your message to the user, create the following new function, which returns a string value indicating the tile size selected:

```
Function strGetTileSize(intSelectedSize As Integer) As String
    If intSelectedSize = 1 Then
        strGetTileSize = "1 foot by 1 foot"
    End If
    If intSelectedSize = 4 Then
        strGetTileSize = "2 feet by 2 feet"
    End If
    If intSelectedSize = 9 Then
        strGetTileSize = "3 feet by 3 feet"
    End If
End Function
```

Every If statement in this function gets evaluated, even if the first one is True. With extremely long conditions, this can drastically decrease the performance of your code. Change the function so that it uses the Select Case statement:

```
Function strGetTileSize(intSelectedSize As Integer) As String
    Select Case intSelectedSize
```

```
        Case 1
            strGetTileSize = "1 foot by 1 foot"
        Case 4
            strGetTileSize = "2 feet by 2 feet"
        Case 9
            strGetTileSize = "3 feet by 3 feet"
    End Select
End Function
```

Once the value is found, only one Case statement is executed. This type of decision structure offers the best performance in this scenario.

In the DisplayTiles function you will use the strGetTileSize function to return the string to be displayed in your message box. Modify the message box line of code as shown here:

```
MsgBox "You will need: " & dblTotalTiles & " case(s) of " & _
    strGetTileSize(Forms!frmFloorTiles!optSelectSize) & " tiles."
```

Now open the form in Form view and test your application.

Congratulations! You have created a fully functional application. The previous program is a good example of a practical application and a fine introduction to VBA programming. It is intended to be simple and to provide a close approximation of the number of cases of tiles a customer needs. If you are satisfied with what you have achieved by creating this example, then you can move on to the next chapter. If you are not content with this example and you want to refine it, complete the following exercise.

As you become more experienced with programming, and as you progress through this book, you will learn the importance of testing your programs thoroughly. You will learn to test your programs not only with valid or good data, but also with invalid data, data at break points or transitions, and data at the extremes.

Try entering a few examples and look at the results. Everything appears to work properly. Although this program has probably returned the correct number of cases for the few examples you have tried, it contains an error. The problem is a *logic error*. This particular logic error is in the algorithm to calculate the number of tiles used to cover the square footage. As an example, enter a length of 42 feet and 0 inches in length, 5 feet and 0 inches in width, and select the 3 feet by 3 feet tiles option. When you click the Calculate button, the message box should return a value of 1 case. If you analyze this differently, you will see that you need 28 tiles, or 2 cases. Look at the example on the following page, which illustrates the dimensions you just entered.

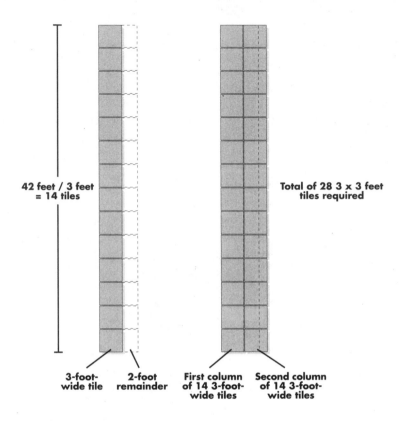

**42 feet / 3 feet = 14 tiles**

**Total of 28 3 x 3 feet tiles required**

**3-foot-wide tile**   **2-foot remainder**   **First column of 14 3-foot-wide tiles**   **Second column of 14 3-foot-wide tiles**

First, you can see that it will take 14 of the 3-feet-by-3-feet tiles to cover the 42-foot-long column. The problem lies in the 5-foot width. Because we used one 3-foot-square tile to cover the first column, we now have a remaining area of 42 feet by 2 feet. It will take 14 more tiles to cover this area. That is a total of 28 tiles, or 2 cases (one full case and one partial case) of tiles. This could have been a significant problem if your customer arrived home with only one case of tiles.

To change the code to compensate for this error, remove the following block of code from the DisplayTiles function:

```
' Because the inch value might have changed to zero,
' it needs to be tested again.
dblTotalTiles = lngSqrFt(CInt(vntLength), _
    CInt(vntWidth))
    If vntLengthIn > 0 Then
        dblTotalTiles = dblTotalTiles + _
            CLng(Forms!frmFloorTiles!txtWidthFeet)
    End If
```

```
        If vntWidthIn > 0 Then
            dblTotalTiles = dblTotalTiles + _
                CLng(Forms!frmFloorTiles!txtLengthFeet)
        End If
        If vntWidthIn > 0 And vntLengthIn > 0 Then
            ' The corner piece
            dblTotalTiles = dblTotalTiles + 1
        End If
```

Insert three new blocks of code in the proper locations so the DisplayTiles function is the same as shown here:

```
Function DisplayTiles()
    Dim vntLength As Variant
    Dim vntWidth As Variant
    Dim vntLengthIn As Variant
    Dim vntWidthIn As Variant
    Dim dblTotalTiles As Double
    Const intTilesPerCase As Integer = 24
    Dim TileSize
    Dim intTilesLong As Integer
    Dim intTilesWide As Integer

    ' Check to make sure an entry has been made
    ' to each text box or insert a zero.
    If IsNull(Forms!frmFloorTiles!txtLengthFeet) Then
        Forms!frmFloorTiles!txtLengthFeet = 0
    End If
    If IsNull(Forms!frmFloorTiles!txtWidthFeet) Then
        Forms!frmFloorTiles!txtWidthFeet = 0
    End If
    If IsNull(Forms!frmFloorTiles!txtLengthInch) Then
        Forms!frmFloorTiles!txtLengthInch = 0
    End If
    If IsNull(Forms!frmFloorTiles!txtWidthInch) Then
        Forms!frmFloorTiles!txtWidthInch = 0
    End If

    ' Assign the values entered in the form
    ' to variables.
    vntLength = Forms!frmFloorTiles!txtLengthFeet
    vntWidth = Forms!frmFloorTiles!txtWidthFeet
    vntLengthIn = Forms!frmFloorTiles!txtLengthInch
    vntWidthIn = Forms!frmFloorTiles!txtWidthInch
    TileSize = Forms!frmFloorTiles!optSelectSize
```

*(continued)*

```vba
' Check the variables to see whether they are numeric.
If IsNumeric(vntLength) And IsNumeric(vntWidth) And _
    IsNumeric(vntLengthIn) And IsNumeric(vntWidthIn) Then
    ' Check the variables to see whether they are
    ' integer values.
    If (vntLength >= 0 And vntLength < 32768) And _
        (vntWidth >= 0 And vntWidth < 32768) And _
        (vntLengthIn >= 0 And vntLengthIn < 32768) And _
        (vntWidthIn >= 0 And vntWidthIn < 32768) Then
        ' Convert inches > 11 for the length to feet.
        If vntLengthIn > 11 Then
            vntLength = vntLength + Int(vntLengthIn / 12)
            vntLengthIn = vntLengthIn Mod 12
            ' Change the text boxes on the form to reflect
            ' the new measurement.
            Forms!frmFloorTiles!txtLengthFeet = vntLength
            Forms!frmFloorTiles!txtLengthInch = vntLengthIn
        End If
        ' Convert inches > 11 for the width to feet.
        If vntWidthIn > 11 Then
            vntWidth = vntWidth + Int(vntWidthIn / 12)
            vntWidthIn = vntWidthIn Mod 12
            ' Change the text boxes on the form to reflect
            ' the new measurement.
            Forms!frmFloorTiles!txtWidthFeet = vntWidth
            Forms!frmFloorTiles!txtWidthInch = vntWidthIn
        End If

        ' To perform calculations in
        ' inches rather than square feet,
        ' convert length and width to inches
        ' and determine the number of tiles
        ' needed to cover the length, then the width.

        vntLengthIn = (vntLength * 12) + vntLengthIn
        intTilesLong = CInt(vntLengthIn / TileSize)
        If (vntLengthIn Mod TileSize) > 0 Then
            intTilesLong = intTilesLong + 1
        End If
        vntWidthIn = (vntWidth * 12) + vntWidthIn
        intTilesWide = CInt(vntWidthIn / TileSize)
        If (vntWidthIn Mod TileSize) > 0 Then
            intTilesWide = intTilesWide + 1
        End If
```

```
    dblTotalTiles = lngSqrFt(intTilesLong, intTilesWide) / _
        intTilesPerCase

    If CLng(dblTotalTiles) < dblTotalTiles Then
        dblTotalTiles = CLng(dblTotalTiles) + 1
    Else
        dblTotalTiles = CLng(dblTotalTiles)
    End If
    ' Use a message box to display
    ' the number of tiles.
    MsgBox "You will need: " & dblTotalTiles & " case(s) of " _
        & strGetTileSize(Forms!frmFloorTiles!optSelectSize) _
        & " tiles."
    Else
        MsgBox "Please enter a number between 0 and 32767."
    End If
    Else
        MsgBox "Measurements must contain numeric data."
    End If
End Function
```

Next you need to open frmFloorTiles in Design view to change the Option Value properties of the Option group and Option buttons as follows:

**1.** Change the optSelectSize Option group Default Value from 1 to 12.

**2.** Change the optSelectSize1 button Option Value from 1 to 12.

**3.** Change the optSelectSize2 button Option Value from 4 to 24.

**4.** Change the optSelectSize3 button Option Value from 9 to 36.

Also, change the SelectCase statement in the strGetTileSize function to match these new values.

Carefully examine the changes you have just made and determine for yourself how the calculations are different and why the changes were necessary. Compile all modules, save the database, and execute your program again. Use the 42-feet-by-5-feet example and 3-feet-by-3-feet tiles option again. You should get the message "You will need 2 case(s) of 3 feet by 3 feet tiles" displayed in the message box. Try several other examples and see if you can cause a wrong answer. Remember to test your code thoroughly by using good data, bad data, and data at the extremes. The completed application can be found in the CHAP02 subfolder of the folder in which you installed the companion CD files.

## PREVIEW of the next chapter

You have just created your first application using VBA. Although this application was relatively easy to build and test, you will find that not all applications are so uncomplicated. The next chapter introduces the tools you will need to debug your applications and implement error handling.

# 3

# Error Handling and Debugging

To create robust and user-friendly applications, you want to avoid situations in which the user sees an error message or finds that the application has terminated abruptly. Error messages can diminish your application's usability and credibility.

Unfortunately, you cannot account for every contingency in your application. This is why you need to learn about error handling. *Error handling* is the process of *trapping* errors that occur at run time. Let's say, for example, that a user creates a Microsoft Access application with a custom Visual Basic for Applications (VBA) file save procedure and tries to save a file to floppy disk through the application. An example of an error might be trying to save a file to floppy disk via your VBA code when no disk is in the drive. Without an error handling routine, this type of error would cause the application to terminate. It's easy to see why efficient error handling techniques are critical to any successful Microsoft Access solution.

*Debugging* is the process of stepping through your code at design time to check for logic errors that might prevent the code from running as you expect. While error handling techniques can enhance your application by gracefully handling errors that occur, debugging techniques can improve your productivity by allowing you to test and check your code for logic errors.

This chapter will focus on both error handling and debugging concepts. You will learn about different types of errors and how to trap for anticipated errors as well as unexpected ones.

Macros are great for producing prototype applications: they allow you to develop the flow and navigation of your application with relative ease and without too much development time. However, error handling is a feature of VBA; it is not available in macros. When it comes time to deploy your solution, you will want to use VBA to handle unexpected errors in your application. And because VBA is a shared language, the techniques used here are also applicable for any other VBA-aware applications, such as Microsoft Excel and Microsoft Visual Basic.

In many books you might find a chapter on error handling and debugging closer to the back of the book. We've positioned this chapter early in the book because we think it's important for you to learn the proper way to avoid errors as well as to deal with them once they happen. Think of this chapter as "preventive medicine" for programmers—it's better to take measures to avoid getting sick than to suffer through an illness (buggy code in this case)!

# Types of Errors

Programming errors fit into three general categories:

- Language
- Run-time
- Logic

## Language Errors

*Language errors* are errors that result from incorrect syntax. Typing a keyword incorrectly (such as "MsdBox" instead of "MsgBox"), omitting necessary punctuation, and using a Next statement without a corresponding For statement are all examples of language errors. This error type is most common when you are entering code in a module window. VBA can automatically detect language and syntax errors when you enter code or move the cursor from the line of code, or immediately before it runs the code. Before the procedure you've created can be executed, all language errors must be corrected. If you are not sure what the correct syntax is, look up the function in the Microsoft Access online Help.

> **TIP** To ensure that VBA is checking for language errors as you type your code, choose Options from the Tools menu. Then select the Auto Syntax Check check box in the Coding Options section of the Module tab.

## Run-Time Errors

During run time (while the application is running), if the user attempts an operation the system can't perform, what is known as a *run-time error* occurs. Say, for example, that you are going to have your application back up some data to a floppy disk, or even to another hard drive. What types of errors would you anticipate? Such a drive might not exist, the disk could be full, or the disk might not be formatted. You might also write code that references a form and then rename the form without updating your code: although your syntax is correct, the object does not exist, and a run-time error will result. When Microsoft Access encounters a run-time error during program execution, it selects the line of code that caused the error and prompts you with a dialog box. The dialog box contains command buttons labeled Debug that opens the Debug window in which you can attempt to fix the problem line of code; End, which immediately terminates the procedure; and Help. See Figure 3-1 for an example of a run-time error dialog box.

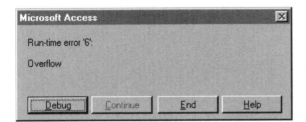

**Figure 3-1.** *A sample run-time error dialog box in Microsoft Access.*

Run-time errors are generally more difficult to fix than language errors simply because run-time errors can be caused by multiple scenarios. In addition, the sources of run-time errors are not always obvious; often you'll have to do some testing to find them. For instance, although an application runs well under normal circumstances, it might not if a user accidentally enters the wrong type of data. You need to be able to create error handling routines to trap such run-time errors and take specific action on them, depending on their type.

### Trapping run-time errors

By trapping run-time errors, you will make your application more tolerant of the errors it encounters. You can then deal with those errors using error handling routines, thus making your application more robust and allowing for graceful exits when the unexpected happens.

Applications that trap run-time errors can handle common user errors without stopping the application. The more skill you have at anticipating common errors (such as your application requiring the user to enter a number and the user entering a character instead) and protecting against them, the less likely your application is to crash. For example, in a situation in which your application is waiting for the user to enter a number, you could use an error handling routine that prompts the user to insert a number rather than an alpha character.

### Exiting gracefully

On those occasions when an error handling routine cannot resolve a run-time error, it can still perform important actions, such as closing any open data files (and potentially saving considerable amounts of data that would otherwise be lost). In the example on the preceding page, if the user does not enter a number when prompted, the application can be terminated so that it doesn't continually ask the user to enter a number. Be sure to keep graceful exits in mind as you create your error handling routine.

## Logic Errors

Logic errors occur when code doesn't perform the way you intended. Your code might be syntactically valid (no language errors) and run without performing any invalid operations (no run-time errors) and yet produce incorrect results. Most likely, the cause is a *logic error*—meaning something is wrong with the logic or formula of the executing code.

The following formula, which converts feet into yards, demonstrates a logic error:

```
Function intFeetToYards(intNumberOfFeet As Integer) As Integer
    intFeetToYards = intNumberOfFeet * 3
End Function
```

If you call this procedure and pass the number 3, you want it to return the number 1, because 3 feet equals 1 yard. However, this procedure incorrectly returns the number 9. Such logic errors are very common; they are also the most difficult to detect because they do not invoke a language or run-time error. One way to detect a logic error is to hard-code values into the procedure to test the formula. For example, by modifying the function above to use specific values (3 * 3), you can quickly determine whether the formula is logically correct:

```
Function intFeetToYards(intNumberOfFeet As Integer) As Integer
    intFeetToYards = 3 * 3
End Function
```

As you can see, with a small procedure such as this one, the error is quite easy to discover. Unfortunately, not all errors will be as simple to track down; but through various techniques introduced later in this chapter, you will learn how to use some VBA features to assist you in finding less obvious errors. You will also learn how to halt execution and step through your code line by line to troubleshoot logic errors.

# Debugging

When you create a procedure, you should consider yourself lucky if your code executes flawlessly the first time. A good programmer not only must write code quickly and accurately but must also be able to find and fix code that doesn't work. When your code does not execute properly, you must discover why and resolve the problem. In the following section, you'll learn how to debug your code in the Microsoft Access VBA programming environment.

## Using VBA Tools to Debug Code

Now that you are familiar with the most common types of errors that can occur in your application, you need to learn how to correct them in your code. In the days of punch card programs, programmers had to make sure their applications had no bugs before they even ran them. If the code had problems, programmers had to redo the punch cards and try again. Microsoft Access provides you with tools that allow you to debug your code as you write it.

Some of the most common debugging functions on the Visual Basic toolbar are shown in Figure 3-2. The Visual Basic toolbar is available whenever a Module window has the focus in the Microsoft Access environment.

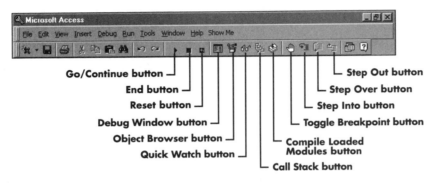

**Figure 3-2.** *The Visual Basic toolbar.*

**NOTE**　　　All the commands available on the Visual Basic toolbar are also accessible through the menu bar in Module Design view or via the keyboard.

### Go/Continue

*Break mode* is the state in which code execution is temporarily paused. You can enter break mode in one of three ways: by setting a breakpoint, by causing a run-time error, or by executing the Stop statement. Once you are in break mode, clicking the Go/Continue button will allow program execution to proceed. You can also press the F5 key or choose Go/Continue from the Run menu. Go/Continue can also be used to execute a procedure from the Module window. To do this, place your cursor in the procedure you want to execute and select Go/Continue.

### End

The End button terminates program execution immediately and brings you back to Design view in your module. The End button does not reset global variables, whereas the Reset button does. Global variables are accessed by all parts of the program. You can end program execution by choosing End from the Run menu.

### Reset

If you do not want to continue program execution or step through your code, you can click the Reset button. This button terminates the program and clears all variables. Reset can also be activated by pressing Shift-F5 or choosing Reset from the Run menu.

### Debug Window

Clicking the Debug Window toolbar button, choosing Debug Window from the View menu, or pressing Ctrl-G on the keyboard will open the Debug window. The Debug window is one of the most useful tools for debugging and testing code. We will discuss how to use the Debug window in the next section.

### Object Browser

The Object Browser toolbar button is used to open the Object Browser dialog box. You can also open this by choosing Object Browser from the View menu or by pressing the F2 button. Using this tool allows you to browse different libraries and select built-in and custom classes and members. The Object Browser and its uses were discussed in detail in Chapter 1.

### Quick Watch

The Quick Watch button brings up the Quick Watch dialog box, which displays the current value of a selected expression or variable. If you want to continue evaluating the expression or variable, however, you can add it to your Watch pane, which will track its value as the code continues to execute. (See the "Watch pane" section beginning on page 96 for details.) Imagine a Watch pane as a surveillance camera in a department store. If someone is suspected of shoplifting, the camera can follow that person from department to department. Quick Watch tracks your code like this. Often when you are writing code, you will use a variable or an expression several times in one or more procedures. If the value of the variable or expression is changed frequently, an unexpected or incorrect outcome could result in your code. It can be very difficult to monitor a variable or an expression as it is used from procedure to procedure. With Quick Watch, you can select a variable or an entire coding expression and track its value as it changes. Quick Watch is a great tool for determining which part of code is not functioning properly and helping you to locate your logic errors. Pressing Shift-F9 will also initiate a Quick Watch.

### Call Stack

The Call Stack button brings up the Call Stack dialog box, which displays the chain of procedure calls. This chain is useful for determining whether certain procedures that are making calls to other procedures are causing an error. This feature is discussed later in "The Calling Chain" section beginning on page 111.

## Compile Loaded Modules

The Compile Loaded Modules toolbar button is used to compile the modules that are currently open; this includes form and report modules. After making additions and deletions to your code, you can compile the loaded module or compile all modules before execution. If you don't compile before executing a procedure, Microsoft Access does this for you prior to executing the procedure.

## Toggle Breakpoint

This toolbar button creates or removes a *breakpoint* in your code. In Microsoft Access, a breakpoint enables you to voluntarily stop the flow of executing code so you can evaluate your code at that specific point. Breakpoints are handy for discovering and fixing logic errors. For example, you could use a breakpoint in the intFeetToYards function to discover that you should be dividing by 3 instead of multiplying by 3. To set a breakpoint, select a line of code, click the Toggle Breakpoint button, and the line will be highlighted or toggled on. Click the button again, and Access will deselect or toggle off that line as a breakpoint. The F9 key performs the same action.

## Step Into

The Step Into button allows you to execute your code one line at a time. If the code calls another procedure, you will continue to execute line by line, one procedure to the next, until you encounter the final line of code. Step Into is like the frame advance button on a VCR. After you pause on a scene in a movie (the equivalent of setting a breakpoint), you can move ahead frame by frame until you find the frame you're looking for. Step Into does the same thing in code. After you've set a breakpoint on a line of code, you can press the Step Into button or F8 key to execute one line at a time until you find the piece of code that is causing the problem.

## Step Over

The Step Over button allows you to execute your code an entire procedure at a time rather than line by line. If your procedure calls other procedures, you can use the Step Over button or Shift-F8 key to execute those procedures without having to "step into" the procedure one line of code at a time. Step Over is like a VCR's fast-forward button: you can skip scenes that don't interest you. When you see an area in the movie that you want to focus on, you can use the frame advance button (the Step Into button) to get more detail. In Microsoft Access, you might know that when procedure 1 calls procedure 2, procedure 2 functions perfectly. If procedure 2 has 100 lines of code, there is no need to use the Step Into button to evaluate each line. It would be more efficient to use the Step Over button to execute those lines of code in procedure 2 and then to stop on the next line of code in procedure 1.

### Step Out

The Step Out button is used to execute all lines of code and nested procedures while in break mode. Execution starts at the current line of code and returns to the next executable statement in the calling procedure. This button is used to avoid stepping through each line of code in nested procedures. This feature can also be initiated by choosing Step Out from the Debug menu or by pressing Ctrl-Shift-F8.

## Using the Debug Window

You can use the Debug window to call your code or your procedures for testing purposes. You can open the Debug window when your Module window has the focus. Choose Debug Window from the View menu, or press Ctrl-G at any point in your application. You can use the Debug window to monitor the values of expressions and variables while stepping through the statements in your code. You can also use the Debug window to change the values of variables in break mode to see how different values affect your code.

Think of the Debug window as a movie director. By the time the movie is released in a theater, all the audience sees is the finished product, ideally without any rough edges. But prior to the movie's release, the director goes through many takes for each scene, trying out different camera angles, stunts, and sets to make sure everything worked according to plan. Your application should be like the final cut of a movie: by the time the user runs your application, it will be fine-tuned and flowing smoothly. The user will not see your code executing, nor will he or she see the values as they change in your code unless your code displays them in a form or report. Before your application gets to the user, you need to make sure that every variable is storing the correct values and every procedure is being called properly when needed.

The Debug window allows you to initiate, monitor, and evaluate the flow of code execution in your application. As shown in Figure 3-3, the Debug window is made up of the following parts:

- Immediate pane
- Code State text box
- Call Stack button
- Locals pane
- Watch pane

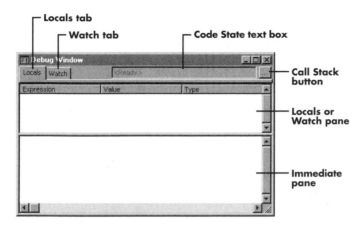

**Figure 3-3.** *The Debug window.*

## Using the Immediate pane

With the Immediate pane, you display information that results from Print statements in your code or that you request by typing commands directly into it. For example, if you are debugging or experimenting with code, you might want to test procedures, evaluate expressions, or assign new values to variables or properties. You can do that in the Immediate pane.

To execute a function in the Immediate pane, you can type the function name preceded by either the Print statement or a question mark, which is a shorthand method for representing the Print statement. For example, Microsoft Access has a built-in Date function that returns the date from your system clock. To execute or call the Date function, type *Print Date( )* or *?Date( )* in the Immediate pane, and then press the Enter key.

After you press the Enter key, the cursor in the Immediate pane will drop down a line and the date will be displayed, as shown in Figure 3-4 on the next page.

**TIP** To execute a sub procedure, you can use the Call statement or just the name of the sub procedure in the Immediate pane. With functions, you can use the Print statement because functions typically return a value, but you cannot use the Print statement with sub procedures because a sub procedure cannot return a value. If you want to execute a function and disregard its return value, enter the name of the function in the Immediate pane.

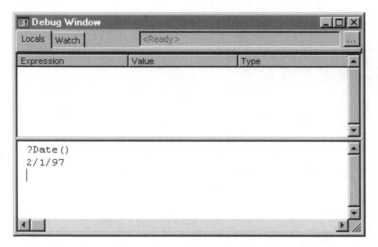

**Figure 3-4.** *Current date displayed in the Immediate pane.*

To set and return values for variables, type the following in the Immediate pane and then press the Enter key:

```
intVar1 = 50
```

The cursor will drop down to the next line in the Immediate pane, but nothing will be displayed. The above statement assigned the value 50 to the variable intVar1. To retrieve the value of the variable intVar1, you must use the Print statement or question mark and then press the Enter key, as shown here:

```
Print intVar1
```

or

```
?intVar1
```

The cursor will drop down to the next line in the Immediate pane and display the value 50.

## Determining the state of executing code

The text box next to the Call Stack button displays the following information, depending on the state of execution your code is in:

- **Wait mode** Displays <Ready>. No code is running that is initiated from the Immediate pane. You are in this mode when working on your modules in Design view.

- **Run mode** Displays <Running>. Code is currently executing.

- **Break mode** Displays the code module and procedure that contain the point at which code execution is halted or suspended.

The Debug window's Call Stack button invokes the Call Stack window, as does the Call Stack button on the Visual Basic toolbar. This button is discussed in more detail in "The Calling Chain" section beginning on page 111.

## Using the Locals pane

When your code is suspended (in break mode), you can view the current value of all the variables and objects within the current procedure. In other words, the current value of any variable or object that is within the scope of the procedure currently suspended is displayed in the Locals pane of the Debug window. To suspend execution of a procedure, you can use the Stop statement or set a breakpoint. Setting breakpoints and looking at the variables of a procedure are discussed in more detail later in this chapter.

Let's use a hypothetical example to explain. When running the following code example from within Module2 of the CHAP03.MDB file in the CHAP03 subfolder of the folder in which you installed the Companion CD files, it would be suspended at the Stop statement:

```
Function Test() As Integer
    Dim intNum1 As Integer, intNum2 As Integer
    intNum1 = 10
    intNum2 = 20
    Test = intNum1 + intNum2
    Stop
End Function
```

Once the code had been suspended, the Locals pane of the Debug window would look like the one shown in Figure 3-5.

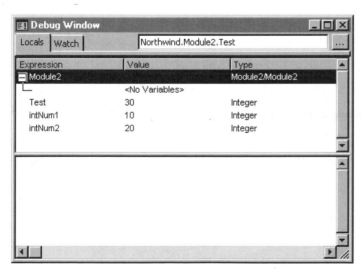

**Figure 3-5.** *The Locals pane of the Debug window when code is suspended.*

Notice that the values of intNum1 and intNum2 are displayed as 10 and 20, their respective values. The return value of the Test function is also displayed. If the Stop statement were placed before the Test = intNum1 + intNum2, a value of 0 would be displayed. (Remember that the initial value of an integer is 0.) You will also notice that under Module2 you see <No Variables>. If there were any Public variables, their values would also be displayed because their scope would allow them to be available to the Test procedure.

### The Watch pane

The Watch pane allows you to monitor the values of your variables, expressions, and control references within your code over the course of its execution. You will find more detailed information on using the Watch pane in the "Using the Watch Pane of the Debug Window" section beginning on page 99.

## Using the Debug.Print Statement to Debug Code

In the previous section, you used the Debug window to run a procedure, set variable values, and display those values. You can also call a method of the Debug window to display values from within a procedure. To do this, you can use the Debug.Print statement inside the procedure. Previously, the variable intVar1 was assigned a value in the Immediate pane, and then the value of intVar1 was printed. To do the same thing from within a procedure, you can use the following code:

```
Sub PrintVar()
    Dim intVar1 As Integer
    ' Assign a value to the variable.
    intVar1 = 50
    ' Print the value of the variable to the Debug window.
    Debug.Print intVar1
End Sub
```

The main advantage of Debug.Print is that it allows variable tracking at full-speed execution. You do not have to set a breakpoint and print out the values of variables one at a time. In addition, it creates a history in the Immediate pane. For example, the following segment of code will print five different values in the Debug window on separate lines:

```
Sub TestImmediatePane()
    Dim intCounter As Integer
    For intCounter = 1 to 5
        Debug.Print "Line: " & intCounter
    Next
End Sub
```

To execute this procedure from the Immediate pane, simply type the name of the procedure and then press Enter:

```
TestImmediatePane
```

Executing this procedure displays the following in the Debug window:

```
Line: 1
Line: 2
Line: 3
Line: 4
Line: 5
```

As previously described, you can use the Print method of the Debug window within your code to send output to the Debug window. An *object* is just what it sounds like—something tangible that can receive your actions. Your computer monitor is one type of object: it's tangible, and you can turn it on and off. An object has properties and methods that you can use to manipulate it. Print is a method of the Debug object that will write information to the Debug window, creating a history of the value of a variable or property. When the execution of your code pauses or completes, you can review the displayed values to ensure that your procedure is functioning properly.

This technique works best when there is a particular place in your code at which the variable (in this case, intCounter) is known to change. In our example, we put the statement in a loop that repeatedly alters intCounter.

## Using Break Mode to Debug Code

As mentioned earlier, break mode pauses code execution and gives you a picture of the state of your code at that moment. VBA enters break mode when any of the following occurs:

- Execution reaches a line that contains a breakpoint.

- Execution reaches a Stop statement.

- A statement in a line of code generates a run-time error that has not been trapped by the error handler.

- You press Ctrl-Break on the keyboard to break execution of your code.

- A break expression defined in the Add Watch dialog box changes or becomes true, depending on how you defined it.

In break mode, variable and property settings are preserved, so you can watch the values of variables, properties, and expressions and make changes to these values for testing purposes.

## Setting a breakpoint

When you set a breakpoint in your code, it means that you want to enter break mode at that point to check values being generated or manipulated by your code. For example, you might pass in a wholesale price as a parameter to a CalculateMarkUp procedure, which returns the full retail price a store should charge its customers. You feel that the markup is incorrect, however, so you decide to work your way through the procedure to make sure every line of code is executing and calculating properly.

To use a breakpoint, open your module in Design view and select the procedure you want to evaluate. Place your cursor on the line of code you think might be causing the problem. Click the Toggle Breakpoint button on the Visual Basic toolbar, or press F9 on your keyboard. The line of code is now highlighted, indicating that execution will pause when that line of code is executed.

| TIP | You can also use the Stop statement in your code to enter break mode. The execution of the code will pause when it reaches the Stop statement. Breakpoints are cleared when the database is closed. Therefore, use them instead of Stop statements to avoid leaving them in by mistake. |
| --- | --- |

If your code causes an unexpected run-time error, a dialog box similar to the one shown in Figure 3-6 will appear, giving you an option to enter break mode.

**Figure 3-6.** *Dialog box showing a run-time error.*

The command buttons in this dialog box and the actions they perform are listed below.

**Debug**   You click this button to enter break mode; the Debug window and the current execution point will be displayed.

**Continue**   You click this button to continue execution from the current execution point.

**End**   You click this button to reset the code; no further actions will occur unless you execute the code again.

**Help**   Click this button if you want online Help for the given error.

## Using the Watch Pane of the Debug Window

When debugging code, you sometimes need to check the values of the variables or expressions within a procedure to make sure the code is operating correctly. The Watch pane in the Debug window displays the current watch expressions (expressions whose values you decide to monitor as the code runs). Figure 3-7 shows the Debug window with the Watch pane in the top half of the window.

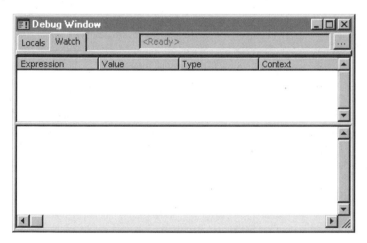

**Figure 3-7.** *The Debug window's Watch pane.*

In the Watch pane, the Context column indicates the procedure, module, or modules in which each watch expression is evaluated. The Watch pane can display a value for a watch expression only if the expression is in the current context. Otherwise, the Value column displays a message indicating that the expression is not in context. For example, if you have not executed your code, the variable or expression cannot yet be evaluated in the Watch pane and is therefore out of context.

The Expression column displays the variable or expression you select in the code. The text displayed in the Type column is the object type of the selected expression.

## Adding a watch expression

While in break mode, you can add watch expressions before running procedures. Watch expressions let you observe the value of a variable, property, or other expression. The Add Watch dialog box is illustrated in Figure 3-8.

To add a watch expression, use the following steps:

**1.** Select Add Watch from the Debug menu.

**2.** In the Expression box, type the expression you want to evaluate.

**3.** To set the scope of the expression to be watched, select the appropriate procedure and module name in the Context frame.

**4.** To determine how you want VBA to respond to the watch expression, select an option under Watch Type.

**5.** Choose OK.

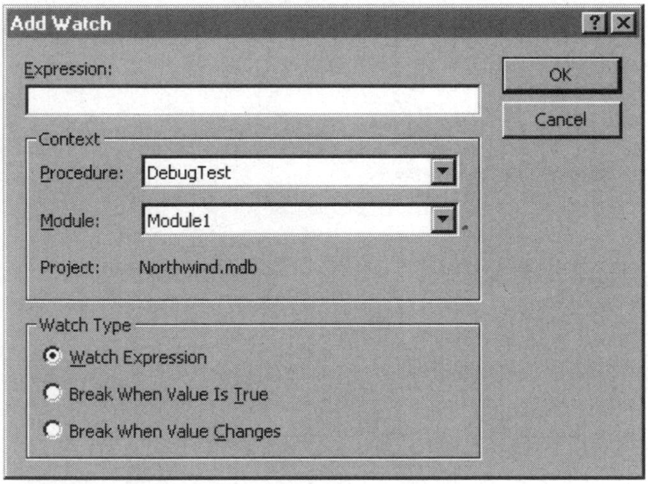

**Figure 3-8.** *The Add Watch dialog box.*

Add Watch dialog box controls and their functions are listed below.

**Expression**  If an expression is already selected in the Module window, it is automatically displayed in the dialog box. If no expression is displayed, enter the expression you want to evaluate. This expression can be a variable, a property, a function call, or any other valid expression.

**Context**  The Context drop-down list boxes display sorted lists of all the procedures within the selected module in the current project and of all the modules in the current project. Select a procedure or module context in the Context frame to specify the range for which the expression will be evaluated. Keep in mind the following things about the Context options:

- For ease and speed of execution, select the narrowest range possible.

- When the watch expression is added to the Watch pane, it will be sorted by context.

- It is not possible to set the context to a project other than the current project.

**Watch Type**    In the Watch Type frame, you specify what type of watch should be added to the Watch pane. You have three choices:

- **Watch Expression** If this Option button is selected, the value of the watch expression is displayed.

- **Break When Value Is True** The value of the watch expression is displayed; if the expression evaluates to True, execution stops.

- **Break When Values Change** The value of the watch expression is displayed; if the value of the expression changes, execution stops.

### Changing or deleting a watch expression

To change or delete a watch expression, select the expression in the Watch pane and then select Edit Watch from the Debug menu. In the Edit Watch dialog box, you can change or delete a watch expression. The Edit Watch dialog box is similar to the Add Watch dialog box. You can also edit the expression in place from the Watch pane or right-click on the expression and choose Edit Watch from the pop-up menu.

You can delete the watch expression by selecting the watch expression in the Watch pane of the Debug window and pressing the Delete key on the keyboard.

### Creating a Quick Watch

You'll sometimes want to look at a value in your code on the spur of the moment while the code is executing. To do this, you can perform a Quick Watch. A Quick Watch differs from a watch expression in that no expression is added to the Watch pane of the Debug window. To create a Quick Watch, use the following steps:

1. Suspend execution of the code (for example, using breakpoints or the Stop statement).

2. Select the expression whose value you want to observe.

3. Select Quick Watch from the Debug menu (or press Shift-F9 on the keyboard).

Microsoft Access displays the Quick Watch dialog box, shown in Figure 3-9, in which you can view the value of the expression. From here you can add the expression to the Watch pane.

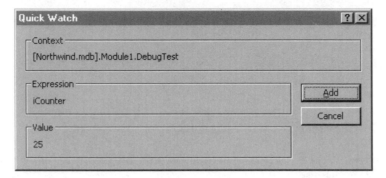

**Figure 3-9.** *The Quick Watch dialog box.*

Below is a list of the controls available in the Quick Watch dialog box, followed by their functions.

**Context** This displays the scope of the expression selected in the module. For example, the context (scope) for an expression might be the database name, the form name, and the control object and its event.

**Expression** This displays the text that is currently selected in the module window that has the focus. If the selected text is not a valid expression, an error will be displayed.

**Value** This displays the result of the expression within the current context.

**Add button** This adds the expression to the list of watch expressions. The context of the selected expression is used when the expression is added. If these default values are not what you want, edit the watch expression using the Edit Watch dialog box.

## Trapping Errors at Run Time

When you are within a procedure, you can enable error handling by using the On Error statement. The error trap will be enabled until an Exit Sub, Exit Function, End Sub, or End Function command is reached. Most error handlers use the same general logic.

When VBA encounters a run-time error, it searches for an On Error statement indicating the presence of an error handling routine. If it finds one, the error is handled and execution is resumed either at the statement that caused the error or at a different statement (depending on how the error handler is enabled). If VBA cannot find an On Error statement, execution halts and a run-time error message is displayed, which might be confusing to your application's user.

There are three standard error handling statements, objects, and functions:

- On Error statement
- Err object
- Error function

## On Error GoTo Statement

The On Error GoTo statement is one of three On Error statements, and it enables an error handling routine and specifies the location of the routine within a procedure.

> **TIP**
>
> The On Error GoTo statement can also be used to disable an error handling routine. Disabling error handling can help you be sure that you are trapping for all possible errors when you are debugging your application. As stated previously, you will encounter run-time error messages if error handling is disabled as you encounter errors. This will indicate to you the kinds of error trapping to put into your code. To disable error handling, use the following syntax:
>
> ```
> On Error GoTo 0
> ```

## Err Object

The Err object contains information about an error that has just occurred. Using its properties and methods, you can identify which error occurred, clear an error value, or display an error dialog box.

## Error Function

This function returns a descriptive error message that corresponds to a given error number. Because of the enhancements made to the Err object since Microsoft Access version 2.0, the Error function can be used only for backward compatibility. You should now use the Raise method of the Err object, which has the same functionality as the Error function, because it can be used to display more than just an error description.

## Creating an Error Handling Routine

Creating a successful error handling routine involves three basic steps:

- Setting an error trap
- Writing the error handling routine
- Creating an exit from the routine

### Setting an error trap

Each sub procedure or function that uses error trapping must include an On Error statement that tells VBA where to look for error handling instructions. *Line labels* are labels you use to identify a line of code within a procedure. Line labels are used most frequently in procedures that use error trapping. Although the On Error GoTo statement must reference a line label or line number within the same procedure, the statements following the label can call another procedure. All line labels must begin with an alpha character and end with a colon.

In the illustration below, *CheckError* is a line label that is used to identify the code to execute when an error occurs within the current procedure.

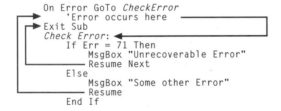

```
  On Error GoTo CheckError
     'Error occurs here
  Exit Sub
  Check Error:
     If Err = 71 Then
        MsgBox "Unrecoverable Error"
        Resume Next
     Else
        MsgBox "Some other Error"
        Resume
     End If
```

### Writing an error handling routine

An error handling routine usually consists of a decision-making statement (for example, the Select Case statement) that identifies different error numbers and then handles (resolves) that specific error.

As mentioned earlier, the Err object is an object that contains information about an error that has just occurred. It has properties and methods that allow you to identify the error, clear an error value, or display an error dialog box. Before jumping into using properties and methods of the Err object, let's review what those properties and methods are as they apply to errors.

A *property* is an attribute of an object—for example, its color, size, shape, and font. The Err object has six properties: Number, Description, Source, HelpFile, HelpContext, and LastDLLError. Properties of an object are referred to by using the syntax ObjectName.Property. For example, to refer to the Number property of the Err object, type *Err.Number*.

**Err.Number**    The Number property is an integer value that indicates the last error that occurred. You can use this property in error handling routines to determine what error occurred. Each individual error has a unique number; by default, the Err object's Number property is set to zero (0) to indicate that no error has occurred.

**Err.Description**    The Description property is a string that contains a description of the error. The Description property contains only the Microsoft Access error message. Once an error is trapped, however, you can present the user with a custom message by using the MsgBox function.

**Err.Source**    The Source property contains the name of the object application that generated the error. This property is helpful when you are using Automation or other COM-based technologies to work with Access and another application. For example, if you access Microsoft Excel from Microsoft Access and Excel generates an error, Excel sets the Err.Source property to "Excel.Application."

**Err.HelpFile**    You can use the HelpFile property to specify the path and filename of a VBA help file. This property is useful for displaying user-friendly information about a particular error. By default, the HelpFile property displays more information on a particular error by returning the default help file that Microsoft Access uses.

**Err.HelpContext**    You can use the HelpContext property to specify context-sensitive help. This property must be used in conjunction with the HelpFile property before a particular help topic can be displayed to the user. By default, the HelpContext property displays more information on a particular error by returning the default context ID that refers to the appropriate topic in Microsoft Access Help.

**Err.LastDLLError**    The LastDLLError property contains the system error code for the success or failure of the last call to a dynamic link library (DLL).

A *method* describes an action performed by or on an object. For example, when pressing the power button on your monitor, you could be invoking the OnOff method, if one existed. The Err object supports two methods: Clear and Raise.

**Err.Clear**    The Clear method clears an error by setting the value of the Err.Number property back to 0. You use this method after you have handled the error so the rest of your code remains unaffected by the error. VBA calls the Clear method automatically whenever any of the following statements are executed:

- Any type of Resume statement.
- An Exit Sub, Exit Function, or Exit Property statement.

- Any On Error statement. Since you might have multiple On Error statements within a procedure, when this statement is encountered, the
  Err.Number property is set to 0.

**Err.Raise**    The Raise method causes an error. This technique is good for creating your own custom errors so that you can display more meaningful error
messages to the users. (For further information on the Raise method, see the
"Centralizing Your Error Handling" section beginning on page 114.) VBA does
not use all available numbers for its own errors.

The Raise method uses the following syntax, in which all of the arguments are
optional except for Number. (These arguments are the same as the properties
of the Err object.)

```
Err.Raise (Number, Source, Description, HelpFile, HelpContext)
```

If you want to generate and trap your own errors, begin your numbering scheme
with 65535 and work your way down. This approach is effective because 65535
is the highest error number there is and Microsoft Access does not have the
highest error numbers predefined. For example,

```
Err.Raise Number := 65535, Description := "My Custom Error"
```

would invoke your error handling code and pass the error number 65535 to the
error handling procedure in effect.

> **NOTE**    You can also pass in your own source information and custom
> help file reference when using the Raise method.

### Exiting an error handling routine
Three statements can be used to exit an error handling routine:

- Resume

- Resume Next

- Resume *line* or Resume *line label*

**Resume**    The Resume statement will return to the statement that caused an error.
The Resume statement is very useful because it lets you repeat an operation after
correcting the error. The function below is an example of how to use the Resume
statement to re-execute the line of code that caused an error. In this example,
you are attempting to copy a file. If the file does not exist, the error routine
creates the file. Once the file exists, a backup copy of the file is created. (This
routine can be found in Module1 of the CHAP03.MDB file.)

```
Sub CopyFile1()
    ' Set Error handling on.
    On Error GoTo ErrHand
    Dim SourceFile As String, DestinationFile As String
    SourceFile = "C:\ACCSOL\TEST.TXT"
    DestinationFile = "C:\ACCSOL\Copy of TEST.TXT"
    ' If SourceFile does not exist, an error occurs on the next line.
    FileCopy SourceFile, DestinationFile
    MsgBox "File Copied"
    Exit Sub    ' Exit procedure so error routine is not executed
                ' if an error does not occur.

ErrHand:
    If Err.Number = 53 Then    ' The SourceFile was not found.
        Dim intFile As Integer
        intFile = FreeFile    ' Get a Free File Number.
        ' Create the SourceFile next.
        Open SourceFile For Output As #intFile
        Close #intFile
        Resume    ' Now execute the FileCopy statement again.
    Else
        ' Force Microsoft Access to display the errors
        ' other than the ones you are trapping for.
        Err.Raise Err.Number
    End If
End Sub
```

In the example above, if an error other than number 53 occurs, Microsoft Access will display the Break Mode dialog box with the error number and message. This way, you can see other errors that are occurring within the procedure, and you can add the appropriate Select Case statements to trap for them.

**Resume Next**    The Resume Next statement will return to the statement that immediately follows the one that caused the error. You can use this statement in conjunction with the On Error statement or in an error handling routine. When the On Error Resume Next statement is used, any error that occurs within the procedure is ignored and the line following the error is executed. The following example modifies the previous procedure and ignores the FileCopy line if an error occurs. (You can use the Err.Number property to see whether an error really did occur.)

```
Sub CopyFile2(SourceFile As String, DestinationFile As String)
    On Error Resume Next        ' Ignore any errors that occur.
    FileCopy SourceFile, DestinationFile
```

*(continued)*

```
        If Err.Number = 53 Then
            ' Check to see whether an error occurred.
            MsgBox SourceFile & " does not exist.  No file was copied."
        ElseIf Err.Number <> 0 Then
            ' Force Microsoft Access to display the errors
            ' other than the ones you are trapping for.
            Err.Raise Err.Number
        Else
            MsgBox "File was copied."
        End If
End Sub
```

When Resume Next is used within an error handling procedure, the line following the line that caused the error is executed.

The following example traps specifically for Error Number 53 ("File does not exist"), and if the file is not found, it displays a message box to the user. Then the line following the line that caused the error executes.

```
Sub CopyFile3(SourceFile As String, DestinationFile As String)
    On Error GoTo ErrHand
    FileCopy SourceFile, DestinationFile
    Exit Sub

ErrHand:                        ' Line label
    If Err.Number = 53 Then    ' The SourceFile was not found.
        MsgBox SourceFile & " does not exist.  No file was copied."
        Resume Next   ' Execute line of code following line that
                      ' caused the error.
    Else
        ' Force Microsoft Access to display the errors
        ' other than the ones you are trapping for.
        Err.Raise Err.Number
    End If
End Sub
```

| NOTE | When using the On Error Resume Next technique, you cannot trap and resolve a specific error that occurs other than by checking Err.Number after every line of code. |
|------|---|

**Resume *line* or Resume *line label***   The Resume statement allows you to specify a line or a line label in the procedure to continue program execution. The following example modifies the previous program to demonstrate that different sections of the program can be executed if an error occurs.

```
Sub CopyFile4(SourceFile As String, DestinationFile As String)
    On Error GoTo ErrHand
    FileCopy SourceFile, DestinationFile
    MsgBox "File was copied."  ' Executed only if FileCopy line
                               ' executes without error.
ExitProc:                      ' Line label.
    Exit Sub

ErrHand:
    If Err.Number = 53 Then
        MsgBox SourceFile & " does not exist.  No file was copied."
        Resume ExitProc
    Else
        ' Force Microsoft Access to display the errors
        ' other than the ones you are trapping for.
        Err.Raise Err.Number
    End If
End Sub
```

This procedure will resume execution on the specified line label (ExitProc) if the error number 53 occurs. If any other error occurs, Access will display the Break Mode dialog box with the error number and message.

## Error Handling Alternatives

At times you might want to disable or limit error handling, such as during prototyping, when you know that your error handling is not yet fully developed. Disabling or limiting error handling allows you to make sure that your application does not terminate because of unexpected errors.

You can use the following techniques to defeat or limit any error handling capabilities in a procedure:

- On Error GoTo 0 statement
- Break On All Errors setting
- Inline error handling

**WARNING** If you use any of these techniques, be certain that you remove them before you release your application.

### On Error GoTo 0 statement

Inserting the following statement in a procedure disables any currently enabled error handler in that procedure:

```
On Error GoTo 0
```

This way, if an error occurs, Microsoft Access will go into break mode, causing the procedure to halt. You should use this statement only when you are testing your code. Do not use it for the distributed version of your application.

### Break On All Errors setting

In the Module tab of the Options dialog box, you can turn the Break On All Errors setting on or off. If a run-time error occurs when this option is on, VBA ignores any On Error statement and enters break mode. This is a useful tool for debugging when you are in the Microsoft Access or VBA design environment.

---

### Disabling the Break On All Errors Setting

If you want to be certain that the Microsoft Access environment does not have Break On All Errors enabled, using the following line of code will disable this feature within any procedure:

```
Application.SetOption "Break On All Errors", False
```

Using the above line of code at the top of a procedure will ensure that the Break On All Errors setting is always disabled when the procedure is executed. Disabling this setting prevents you from having to worry about changing the value of this option in the Options dialog box.

---

### Inline error handling

Rather than setting up an error handler that you branch to, you might want to establish an error handler to ignore an error if one occurs. If an error occurs on any line of your code, you can instruct VBA to skip that line and proceed to the next one. To do this, insert this line at the beginning of the procedure:

```
On Error Resume Next
```

The following code is an example of inline error handling. Notice that after the line that could possibly cause an error (line 4), a Select Case statement is used to determine whether Err.Number contains a value other than 0.

```
Sub cmdOpenFile_Click ()
    Dim temperr As Integer
    On Error Resume Next
    Open "C:\NEWORDER.TXT" For Input As #1
    Select Case Err.Number
        Case 0:
            ' Nothing to do.
```

```
        Case 53:
            ' File not found.
            ' Code to prompt for file.
        Case 55:
            ' File already open.
            ' Code to correct.
        Case Else
            temperr = Err.Number
            On Error GoTo 0
            Err.Raise temperr
    End Select
    Err.Clear      ' Reset the error number.
    Open "C:\NEWORDER.TXT " For Input As #2
End Sub
```

**NOTE**  When using inline error handling, be sure to reset the error number by using the Clear method. If you do not, the error number still exists in the Number property and any subsequent checks of this property could produce inconsistent results.

## The Calling Chain

When VBA encounters a run-time error, it searches the following for an active error handler in this sequence:

■ The current procedure

■ The procedures listed in the Calls list (beginning with the most recently called procedure)

The following illustration shows how an error is handled in the order that the procedures are called (calling chain).

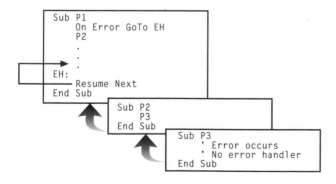

Suppose that P1 is the only procedure containing any error handling code. P1 calls P2, and P2 calls P3. If an error occurs in P3, Microsoft Access looks for an active error handler within that procedure. Because it does not find one, it goes back to P2. Access then looks for an active error handler within P2, but again, it does not find one, so it goes back to P1 where it handles the error.

Wherever the error handler is encountered, the error handling code is executed. If the error handling code includes a Resume statement, the application resumes at the level at which the error handler is located (not necessarily the level at which the error occurred).

The Call Stack dialog box helps you trace the flow of code through multiple procedures. For example, one procedure can call a second procedure, which can call a third procedure—all before the first procedure is completed. Such nested procedure calls can be difficult to follow. The Call Stack dialog box shows this flow. The flow of procedure calls is important information to have if you do not place error handling code within each of your procedures.

To display the Call Stack dialog box from the Debug window, click the Build button to the right of the Status box (the box containing the name of the current procedure) in the Debug window. Your screen should look similar to the one shown in Figure 3-10.

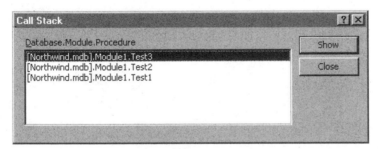

**Figure 3-10.** *The Call Stack dialog box.*

The first procedure listed in the Call Stack dialog box executed most recently. The last procedure in the list was the first one to execute in the chain.

**TIP** You can also open the Call Stack dialog box via the Call Stack toolbar button or by choosing Call from the View menu. The Call Stack dialog box can be enabled only when you are in break mode.

If a run-time error occurs within an error handler, the error is passed up to the calling procedure. If there is no calling procedure, the application displays a message allowing you to enter break mode.

You should keep your error handling code simple to prevent other errors from occurring. From your error handling routine, you can also invoke other procedures that contain their own error handling code.

## Resolving Logical Errors Using CVErr and IsError

You can use the CVErr and IsError functions to create user-defined errors and to evaluate them in user-defined procedures. *User-defined errors* are logical errors that can occur in code but do not invoke or cause actual run-time errors.

User-defined errors do not invoke a run-time error message box, and they cannot be trapped by traditional error handling routines. They simply provide a clean method of evaluating code.

### CVErr

Using the CVErr function, you can create user-defined errors in your custom procedures. For example, if a function accepts several arguments, it can evaluate the input arguments to ensure that they are within the acceptable range. If they are not, it is likely that the function will not return what is expected. In this event, CVErr can return a user-defined error number that tells the procedure what action to take. CVErr returns a Variant data type defined as type Error containing an error number specified by the procedure. In the following syntax, the error number argument is any valid error number that is a whole number from 0 through 65,535:

```
CVErr(errornumber)
```

In the following example, a Variant type variable is assigned an error by the CVErr function:

```
vntMyError = CVErr(4321)
```

The vntMyError variable is assigned the following value:

```
Error 4321
```

To extract the number from the string Error 4321, use the CLng function. It returns the integer value 4321, as shown here:

```
lngMyErrorNumber = CLng(CVErr(4321))
```

### IsError

Error values are created by converting numbers to error values using the CVErr function. The IsError function is used to determine whether a numeric expression represents an error. IsError returns a Boolean value indicating whether an expression is an error value. It returns True if the expression argument indicates an error; otherwise, it returns False. The following syntax requires the expression argument to be a Variant data type defined as type Error:

```
IsError(expression)
```

The following code uses the CVErr and IsError functions to test whether the number 56515 is a valid user-defined error number. This number could also be passed to the Raise method of the Err object, where an error handling routine could trap for the error number.

```
Sub ValidateName(strUName As String)
    Dim vntReturnvalue As Variant
    If strUName = CurrentUser Then
        vntReturnvalue = "You Are the Current User"
    Else
        vntReturnvalue = CVErr(56515)
    End If
    ' Check to see if error is valid.
    If IsError(vntReturnvalue) Then
        Debug.Print "vntReturnvalue: " & CStr(vntReturnvalue)
        Debug.Print "VarType: " & VarType(vntReturnvalue)
        Debug.Print "User-Defined Error Number: " & _
            CLng(vntReturnvalue)
        Debug.Print "Custom Message: Not a Valid Name"
    Else
        MsgBox vntReturnvalue
    End If
End Sub
```

**NOTE**    The value returned by the VarType function is equal to the value of the internal VBA constant vbError.

IsError can also be useful in trapping errors generated by Automation objects used in code. Automation is discussed in Chapter 14.

## Centralizing Your Error Handling

In large applications, error handling routines can become quite complex. There are a couple of techniques you can use to simplify your error handlers.

First, remember that you can put a Raise method in all error handling routines for cases in which no code in the error handling routine deals with a specific type of error. Doing so ensures that an error message will be displayed for errors that your code does not handle. When you test your code, use of the Raise method helps you uncover the errors you are not handling adequately.

If you choose not to use the Raise method, you can use *centralized error handling,* a generic error handling procedure that all of your error handlers can call as a last resort.

To centralize your application's primary error handling, you create a main error handling function that tells a procedure how to process an error. There is no way to create a global error handling function in VBA; therefore, you still need an On Error statement in all of your procedures. What this means is that rather than creating redundant code within each procedure, you should have the error handling routine within each procedure execute a main error handling function. This main error handling function should trap for every possible error your application might encounter and handle them appropriately.

The main error handling function should return a value—for example, True or False—so that the calling procedure will "know" how to proceed. (The calling procedure might execute a Resume statement if the function returns True or it might execute a Resume Next statement if the function returns False.) Boolean values (True and False) might not meet all of your requirements, so the error handling function can return any value that is handled in the form of a Select Case statement, as demonstrated in the following example:

```
Sub CodeWithErrorHandling()
    On Error GoTo ErrHndr
    ' ... Procedure code ...
ErrHndr:
    iErrorType = Error_Handler(Err) ' Call centralized error handler.
    Select Case iErrorType
        Case 1
            ' Code to resume on the line that caused error.
            Resume
        Case 2
            ' Code to resume on line following error.
            Resume Next
        Case 3
            ' Code to resume at a specific label.
            Resume LineLabel
            ' Assume a label named "LineLabel".
        Case 4
            ' Code to exit application gracefully.
    End Select
End Sub
```

*(continued)*

```
Function Error_Handler(iError_Num) As Integer
    Select Case iError_Num
        Case 11   ' Division by zero
            ' Any code needed to resolve this condition.
            Error_Handler = 1
        Case 53   ' File not found
            ' Any code needed to resolve this condition.
            Error_Handler = 2
        Case 71   ' Disk not ready
            ' Any code needed to resolve this condition.
            Error_Handler = 3
        Case Else ' All other errors
            ' Any code needed to resolve this condition.
            Error_Handler = 4
    End Select
End Function
```

Resume statements tell a procedure how to recover from an error. However, because Resume statements can appear only within a procedure that contains an On Error statement, some error handling code must remain within each procedure that requires error handling capabilities.

Taking the centralized approach to error handling also allows your error handling function to be more complex and handle other errors that might occur. In the code example above, the function Error_Handler could have its own On Error statement to handle any errors that occur within that procedure.

## PREVIEW of the next chapter

In this chapter, you learned how to utilize debugging and how to implement error handling in your code. In the next chapter, you'll create an application to back up a file. Don't let the simplicity of this task fool you—surprisingly, you will need to use every topic discussed in this chapter to properly implement a backup application.

# 4

# The File Backup Application

In the first three chapters you learned how to use Visual Basic for Applications (VBA) to create custom procedures that are more powerful than the standard Microsoft Access macros because of their increased functionality and error handling. In this chapter you will learn how to implement error handling solutions while creating an application that allows the user to back up a file to a floppy disk.

As a solution provider, you often have to create applications for users who are not completely comfortable with computers or are not familiar with your particular application. You can create utilities within your application to reduce the need for the user to search other programs and folders for similar utilities. For example, you can use Microsoft Access to create a simple file backup utility. For this application to be a successful solution, it must do the following:

- Allow the user to specify a file to back up

- Allow the user to select a floppy disk drive as a destination for the backup file

- Notify the user when the floppy disk is full

- Notify the user if there is no disk in the floppy drive

- Notify the user of unexpected errors during the backup process

To accomplish these tasks, you will create a solution by using custom procedures, error handling, and some of the built-in VBA procedures in Microsoft Access. Be aware that the utility you are creating has several but not all of the features of similar utilities in other applications and Microsoft Windows 95. This utility is just fine for demonstrating error handling, but it requires additional features to become a "successful solution." Features such as wildcard character handling have been left out intentionally. The completed application can be found in the CHAP04.MDB file in the \CHAP04 subfolder of the folder in which you installed the Companion CD files.

## Back Up File To Floppy Form

Your first step in creating a backup application will be to design a Back Up File To Floppy form, as shown in Figure 4-1. (You'll see how to create this form in the following pages.) This is the form in which the user will enter the name of the file to be backed up and select a destination drive.

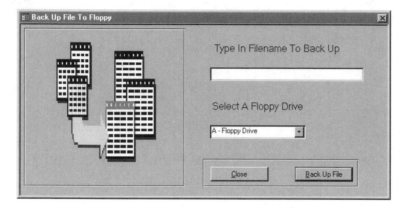

**Figure 4-1.** *Back Up File To Floppy form.*

As you can see, the Back Up File To Floppy form consists of a text box, a combo box, two command buttons, two labels, and an image.

**Type In Filename To Back Up text box**   This is the box in which the user will type the name and location of the file to be backed up.

**Select A Floppy Drive combo box**   The user will select a floppy drive from this combo box as the destination for the file specified in the filename text box. Only available floppy drives will be listed in the combo box.

**Close command button**   Clicking this command button closes the Back Up File To Floppy form.

**Back Up File command button**   When the user clicks this command button, a function will validate the filename entered in the filename text box, and if the filename is valid, the file will be copied to the floppy drive displayed in the Select A Floppy Drive combo box.

**Labels**  In this example the labels are static and provide the user instructions for the data to be entered in the text and combo boxes just below them.

**Image**  This is an area that displays a graphical image. In this example the image suggests movement of files.

## Creating the Form

The Back Up File To Floppy form is this application's entire user interface, since the application serves only one function for the user. To create the Back Up File To Floppy form, follow these steps:

**1.** In a new database, create an unbound blank form, and set the following form properties:

| Property Name | Value |
|---|---|
| Caption | Back Up File To Floppy |
| Scroll Bars | Neither |
| Record Selectors | No |
| Navigation Buttons | No |
| Dividing Lines | No |
| Auto Center | Yes |
| Min Max Buttons | None |
| On Open | =On_Form_Open( ) |

The code for this form will be added when you create the On_Form_Open function on page 124.

**2.** Add an image control to the form, and set the following properties:

| Property Name | Value |
|---|---|
| Name | imgFileCopy |
| Picture | C:\ACCSOL\CHAP04\T-IMPORT.BMP |
| Size Mode | Stretch |

**3.** Add a label to the form, and set the following properties:

| Property Name | Value |
|---|---|
| Name | lblFileName |
| Caption | Type In Filename To Back Up |
| Font Size | 10 |

**4.** Add a text box to the form, and set the following property:

| Property Name | Value |
|---|---|
| Name | txtFileName |

**5.** Add another label to the form, and set the following properties:

| Property Name | Value |
|---|---|
| Name | lblFloppyDrive |
| Caption | Select A Floppy Drive |
| Font Size | 10 |

**6.** Add a combo box to the form, and set the following properties:

| Property Name | Value |
|---|---|
| Name | cboSelectFloppy |
| Row Source Type | Value List |
| Column Count | 2 |
| Column Widths | 1";0" |
| Bound Column | 2 |

Notice that you will be using two columns in the combo box, even though you'll display only the unbound column. (The bound column is the one that gets its contents from the underlying control source.) This allows the combo box to show a description of the floppy drive but to return just a drive letter. For example, the first column will display "A-Floppy Drive," but the second column (the bound column that returns the value selected in the combo box) will be "A:\," to be used by your application to refer to the location to which the file will be backed up.

**7.** Add a command button to the form, and set the following properties:

| Property Name | Value |
|---|---|
| Name | cmdClose |
| Caption | &Close |
| Cancel | Yes |
| On Click | =Close_Form() |

The code for this button will be added when you create the Close_Form function on page 128.

**8.** Add another command button to the form, and set the following properties:

| Property Name | Value |
| --- | --- |
| Name | cmdBackUpFile |
| Caption | &Back Up File |
| Default | Yes |
| On Click | =BackUpFile( ) |

The code for this button will be added when you create the BackUpFile function on page 126.

**9.** Draw a frame around the two command buttons and another around the image, as shown in Figure 4-1 on page 118.

**10.** Select Save from the File menu, and save the form as frmBackUpFile.

So that this form will open when the database is opened, make the form the Startup form of the database by doing the following:

**1.** Select Startup from the Tools menu.

**2.** In the Startup dialog box, set the Application Title to "Back Up File To Floppy" to replace the default title ("Microsoft Access").

**3.** Select frmBackUpFile from the Display Form combo box.

**4.** Click the OK button.

**5.** Close the database, and then re-open it to test the new Startup form.

## Creating the Application

When a file is being backed up to a floppy, several problems can occur:

- The filename entered might be invalid.

- There might be no available floppy drive.

- The floppy disk might become full during the backup process.

- The floppy disk might not have been inserted in the floppy drive.

- The file might be open while the user is trying to back up the file to the floppy drive.

The illustration on the following page shows a conceptual layout and flow of the application.

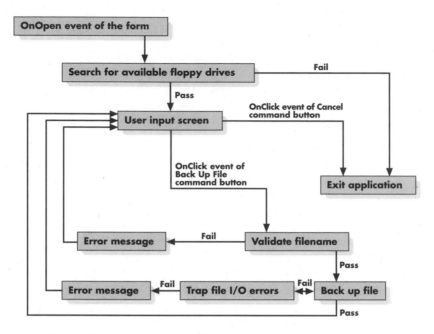

## Checking for Available Floppy Drives

When you open the Back Up File To Floppy form, your application will call a function to determine whether any floppy drives are available on the computer. If at least one floppy drive is available, the code will create a valid Row source for the cboSelectFloppy combo box. The user will use the cboSelectFloppy combo box to select a floppy drive as the backup destination for the file. If no floppy drives are available, the user will be notified and the frmBackUpFile form will not open. Without a floppy drive, the user cannot back up a file.

To determine whether a floppy drive exists, you will use the built-in function GetAttr to test for a valid A:\ or B:\ directory. If the floppy drive does not exist, your application will trap the error "Error 68 - Device unavailable (Floppy drive does not exist)."

If the floppy drive does exist but no floppy is inserted, your application will trap the error "Error 71 - Disk not ready (Floppy drive exists but a floppy is not inserted)." Create a new module called BackUpFiles. In the Declarations section of the BackUpFiles module, add the following line of code:

```
Const DidNotPass = 65535
```

This constant will be used to create a user-defined error you can use when a procedure does not return a passing result.

GetAttr() is a built-in function that returns an integer value for the attributes of the specific file, folder, or disk drive for the explicit path or filename contained within the parentheses.

To determine whether a valid floppy drive exists, add the following function to the BackUpFiles module:

```
Function vntFindDrives() As Variant
    On Error GoTo Err_strFindDrives
    Dim intDummyA As Integer, intDummyB As Integer
    Dim strRowSource As String, strMsg As String

    ' Determine whether floppy drive A exists (device available).
    intDummyA = GetAttr("a:\")
    ' vbDirectory is a VBA constant that represents a value
    ' returned by the GetAttr built-in function if a directory
    ' exists. GetAttr returns a number representing the attributes
    ' of a directory (folder) in this case and also for individual
    ' files.
    If intDummyA = vbDirectory Then
        strRowSource = "A - Floppy Drive;A:\"
    End If
    ' Determine whether floppy drive B exists (device available).
    intDummyB = GetAttr("b:\")
    If intDummyB = vbDirectory Then
        ' If both floppy drives A and B exist.
        If strRowSource <> "" Then
            strRowSource = strRowSource & ";"
        End If
        ' If floppy drive B exists.
        strRowSource = strRowSource & "B - Floppy Drive;B:\"
    End If
    If strRowSource = "" Then
        strMsg = "No Floppy Drives Available on This Computer."
        MsgBox strMsg
        ' Return user-defined error.
        vntFindDrives = CVErr(DidNotPass)
    Else
        ' Display available floppy drives in cboSelectFloppy.
        Forms!frmBackUpFile!cboSelectFloppy.RowSource = _
            strRowSource
        ' Select first available floppy drive in
        ' cboSelectFloppy.
        Forms!frmBackUpFile!cboSelectFloppy = _
            Forms!frmBackUpFile!cboSelectFloppy.ItemData(0)
```

*(continued)*

```
        ' At least one floppy drive is found.
        vntFindDrives = "Pass"
    End If
    Exit Function

Err_strFindDrives:
    Select Case Err.Number
        Case 68
            ' Device (floppy drive) unavailable; try another.
            Resume Next
        Case 71
            ' Floppy drive found, but no disk inserted.
            ' Set the combo box RowSource property
            ' to the values of the floppy drives found.
            If strRowSource = "" Then
                strRowSource = "A - Floppy Drive;A:\"
            Else
                strRowSource = _
                    strRowSource & ";B - Floppy Drive;B:\"
            End If
            Resume Next
        Case Else
            ' Trap for any unexpected errors.
            Err.Raise Number:=Err.Number, _
                Description:=Err.Description
            Err.Clear
            Exit Function
    End Select
End Function
```

In the BackUpFiles module add the function shown below. You will call this function from the OnOpen event of the frmBackUpFile form. This code will cancel the opening of the form if no floppy drive is available; if a floppy drive is available, it will add the existing floppy drive or drives to the cboSelectFloppy combo box.

```
Function On_Form_Open()
    On Error GoTo Err_On_Form_Open
    ' If no floppy drive is available,
    ' close the form.
    If IsError(vntFindDrives) Then
        DoCmd.CancelEvent
    End If
    Exit Function

Err_On_Form_Open:
    ' Trap for any unexpected errors.
    Err.Raise Number:=Err.Number, Description:=Err.Description
```

```
        Err.Clear
        Exit Function
End Function
```

## Determining Whether the User Has Entered a Filename

To determine whether a filename has been entered in the txtFileName text box, add the following procedure to the BackUpFiles module.

```
Function vntCheckForFileName() As Variant
    ' Check txtFileName for a null value.
    Dim strMsg As String
    strMsg = "Please Enter a Filename"
    If IsNull(Forms!frmBackUpFile!txtFileName) Then
        ' txtFileName is null.
        MsgBox strMsg
        Forms!frmBackUpFile!txtFileName.SetFocus
        ' Return user-defined error.
        vntCheckForFileName = CVErr(DidNotPass)
    Else
        ' txtFileName is not null.
        vntCheckForFileName = "Pass"
    End If
End Function
```

## Validating the Filename

To validate the filename entered by the user, add the following code to the BackUpFiles module.

```
Function vntValidFileName() As Variant
    ' Validate the filename stored in txtFileName.
    Dim strFile As String, strMsg As String
    ' vbCrLf is a VBA constant that creates a
    ' carriage return and line feed so as to create
    ' an additional line for the MsgBox prompt argument.
    strMsg = "Please Enter a Valid Filename" & vbCrLf & _
        "Include File Path and Extension"
    strFile = Dir(Forms!frmBackUpFile!txtFileName)
    If strFile = "" Then
        ' Filename entered in txtFileName is not valid.
        MsgBox strMsg
        Forms!frmBackUpFile!txtFileName.SetFocus
        ' Return user-defined error.
        vntValidFileName = CVErr(DidNotPass)
    Else
        ' Return valid filename entered in txtFileName.
        vntValidFileName = strFile
    End If
End Function
```

## Validating the Floppy Drive Selection

To determine whether the user has selected a floppy drive that is available, add the following procedure to the BackUpFiles module:

```
Function vntCheckForProperFloppy() As Variant
    ' Determine whether floppy drive is selected.
    Dim strMsg As String
    strMsg = "Please Select Floppy Drive"

    If IsNull(Forms!frmBackUpFile!cboSelectFloppy) Then
        ' cboSelectFloppy is null.
        MsgBox strMsg
        ' Return user-defined error.
        vntCheckForProperFloppy = CVErr(DidNotPass)
    Else
        ' cboSelectFloppy contains valid floppy drive.
        vntCheckForProperFloppy = "Pass"
    End If
End Function
```

Even though you check for valid floppy drives in the OnOpen event of the form, you need to make sure that they are still available—that is, functioning properly—at the time the file is actually being backed up. This will be performed in the BackUpFile function.

## Completing the Process

To complete the file backup process, add the procedure below to the BackUpFiles module and call it from the OnClick event of the cmdBackUpFile command button. This code uses the built-in FileCopy procedure. If one of the procedures used in the OnClick event of the cmdBackUpFile command button returns a user-defined error, the backup process should not occur. Once the filename and the floppy drive destination have been validated, the backup process should proceed.

```
Function BackUpFile()
    On Error GoTo Err_cmdBackUpFile_Click
    Dim strMsg As String, strErr_Msg As String
    Dim strBackupFileName As String

    ' Check txtFileName for a null value.
    If IsError(vntCheckForFileName()) Then Exit Function

    ' Validate the filename stored in txtFileName.
    If IsError(vntValidFileName()) Then Exit Function
```

```
' Determine whether floppy drive is selected.
If IsError(vntCheckForProperFloppy()) Then Exit Function

' Ready to back up valid file.
strBackupFileName = _
    Forms!frmBackUpFile!cboSelectFloppy & _
        Dir(Forms!frmBackUpFile!txtFileName)
strMsg = "Overwrite File: " & strBackupFileName & "?"

' Determine whether valid file to back up exists on floppy
' selected.
If Dir(strBackupFileName) <> "" Then
    If MsgBox(prompt:=strMsg, buttons:=vbYesNo) = vbNo Then
        Exit Function
    End If
End If

' Back up file to selected floppy.
' If error occurs, Err_cmdBackUpFile_Click will handle the
' error and exit sub.
FileCopy Forms!frmBackUpFile!txtFileName, strBackupFileName

' File backup completed with no errors.
strMsg = "File backup completed"
MsgBox strMsg
Forms!frmBackUpFile!cmdClose.SetFocus
Exit Function

Err_cmdBackUpFile_Click:
    Select Case Err.Number
        Case 61
            ' Not enough space on floppy disk to copy file.
            strErr_Msg = "Floppy Disk Is Full" & vbCrLf & _
                "Cannot Back Up File"
            MsgBox strErr_Msg
            ' Use the Kill built-in sub procedure to
            ' delete the partial file on the floppy disk
            ' because it cannot fit.
            Kill strBackupFileName
            Err.Clear
            Exit Function
        Case 70
            ' File is open; cannot back up (permission denied).
            strErr_Msg = "File is open" & _
                vbCrLf & "Cannot Back Up File"
```

*(continued)*

```
            MsgBox strErr_Msg
            Err.Clear
            Exit Function
        Case 71
            ' Floppy drive exists, but there is
            ' no floppy disk in the floppy drive.
            ' Prompt user to insert a floppy disk.
            strErr_Msg = "Please Insert A Floppy Disk"
            MsgBox strErr_Msg
            Err.Clear
            Exit Function
        Case Else
            ' Trap for any unexpected errors.
            Err.Raise Number:=Err.Number, _
                Description:=Err.Description
            Err.Clear
            Exit Function
    End Select
End Function
```

## Closing the Form

After the user has completed the file backup process, he or she can close the frmBackUpFile form and exit the application. To allow the user to exit the Back Up File To Floppy application, add the following procedure to the BackUpFiles module, and call it from the OnClick event of the cmdClose command button:

```
Function Close_Form()
    ' Called from the OnClick event of the command button
    ' cmdClose in the form frmBackUpFile.
    ' Close the form frmBackUpFile.
    On Error GoTo Err_Close_Form
    DoCmd.Close A_FORM, "frmBackUpFile"

Exit_Close_Form:
    Exit Function

Err_Close_Form:
    ' Trap for any unexpected errors.
    Err.Raise Number:=Err.Number, Description:=Err.Description
    Resume Exit_Close_Form
End Function
```

## PREVIEW of the next chapter

In the next chapter we will introduce you to application and user interface design guidelines that will help make your applications more robust. We'll discuss forms and their components and operations; various kinds of menus; and controls, which are the tools of the trade for Microsoft Access developers. We'll also touch on design issues such as layout, MDI windows, and user assistance. Then we'll talk about how you pull all these elements together to create great looking, easy-to-use applications.

# PART

# TWO

## Creating Professional
## Applications

# 5

# User Interface and Application Design

In this chapter you will learn about some of the key components of user interface design (including forms, menus, and toolbars) and application design (fitting various forms and controls together into a coherent application). How you design the user interface and the application itself is crucial to an application's success. Your applications should be consistent with other Microsoft Windows–compliant applications so you can take advantage of the user's familiarity with these products. For example, if the user is accustomed to seeing a ScreenTip when the mouse pointer is placed over an object, he or she will expect this functionality in your application, too. Or if you have provided a button on a form to complete a particular task, you should also have a menu command that carries out the same task.

A user interacts with your application mostly through forms, which are actually windows. Whether you are an experienced Windows user or a former mainframe programmer, this chapter will provide you with the essential information to thoroughly understand how forms operate. In this chapter you will also learn the Windows terminology that will be used in the remainder of this book.

## How Does Windows Work?

Imagine trying to design a car if you didn't know how engines functioned or if you didn't know how to drive. You would be hard-pressed to build a car that worked at all, much less one that worked effectively and efficiently. You won't need to know quite as much about Windows as an automobile engineer needs to know about how an engine's components fit together and what the car's drivers will be expecting, but an application designer needs to know some basics about how the Windows operating system works in order to create applications that users will find useful and easy to work with.

In the underlying code of a window, you might see several windows without realizing what they are. If you were to create a program using the Microsoft Windows Software Development Kit (SDK) and the C programming language (which is how Microsoft Access 97 was created), each object you'd see within a window, from command buttons to scroll bars, would be an individual window. Creating windows in Microsoft Access involves a much simpler process: you simply drag controls to a form to create the user interface.

Think of an air traffic control center: it receives messages from and dispatches messages to surrounding air traffic. An airport's air traffic control center handles two types of traffic: planes in the air and planes on the ground. The Windows operating system also deals with two types of traffic and all of their interactions in complex situations: the applications and the hardware. This capability of dealing with complexity is the biggest advantage to writing applications in Windows. You can write your application without having to worry about what type of printer or keyboard the user has because the Windows operating system can accommodate a wide variety of these devices. Imagine this scenario: you've written a report in Microsoft Access; you developed your application for a dot matrix printer but plan to distribute it to someone who has a laser printer. Are you faced with a programming nightmare? No! You do not have to write a single line of code to allow for these differences. The flexibility and versatility of the Windows operating system will save you thousands of development hours trying to test and write for the many hardware devices that currently exist.

So, just how does Windows work? The Windows operating system communicates with active applications by sending and receiving messages. When any activity is happening on the system, Windows immediately begins to send and receive messages. Windows applications receive these messages and process them accordingly. If you have or know someone who has Spy or Spy++, an application that ships with Microsoft Developer Studio, you can watch these messages get dispatched. You might be amazed by how many messages Windows sends. Spy is an application that permits a developer to see what messages get dispatched during a Windows session. You can specify different Windows or application messages to watch. For more detailed information on Spy, consult the Developer Studio documentation. Figure 5-1 shows Spy displaying the messages that are sent as a result of a mouse moving across a window and of a click of the left mouse button.

Microsoft Access 97 simplifies the task of having to know the specific message names and how to process them by providing event properties. You can imagine how time-consuming it would be to have to create a Select Case statement and process every message as it takes place. Instead, a form in Microsoft Access has an On Click property. Looking at the Spy output in Figure 5-1, you can

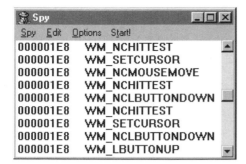

**Figure 5-1.** *Windows messages resulting from a simple mouse move and click.*

see that the Microsoft Access application intercepts the WM_NCLBUTTONDOWN message and triggers the form's On Click property, or the Click event. This process is completely transparent to the Microsoft Access developer—another example of how easy it is to program in the Microsoft Windows environment.

**NOTE** You can "decipher" the WM_NCLBUTTONDOWN message by separating its parts: WM stands for Windows message, NC means nonclient, L is left, and BUTTONDOWN is button down.

The Windows operating system dispatches thousands of messages to an application as it runs. Messages may also be sent in a different order each time. Messages also have different priorities. Recall the air traffic control center example. Say, for example, that two planes have requested clearance to land: one plane has plenty of fuel left and the other is low on fuel. As you can predict, the plane that is low on fuel is going to be given permission to land before the plane that has plenty of fuel. Windows messages are assigned priorities in a similar way. For example, the WM_PAINT message, which redraws a window, is always processed last; you might have noticed that a portion of your window sometimes does not get redrawn immediately after you uncover part of the window that was hidden by another window. The Windows operating system controls the message priority, and you cannot change it. You can, however, design your applications to, for example, prevent other forms from opening on top of a form that contains a large graphic.

So now you have a general idea of how Windows works. An in-depth explanation of the details of the Windows operating system would be a book in itself and beyond the scope of our discussion here. If you would like additional information about the Windows operating system, please refer to Charles Petzold's book *Writing Windows Applications*.

# Forms

In Microsoft Access, forms provide the fundamental way by which a user views and interacts with data. Forms are really just windows; think of a form as a window through which the user views underlying data. Whether it be a table or a query, a form allows the user to interact with the data easily. You can design forms to create various message boxes, dialog boxes, and navigation menus that provide access to different types of information.

## Components of a Form

In Microsoft Access 97, a default form, which is a new form that you create, consists of the following items:

- Border
- Title bar
- Title bar icon
- Title bar command buttons
- Record selector
- Scroll bars
- Navigation buttons

The following sections discuss each component. When executed, a default form looks like Figure 5-2.

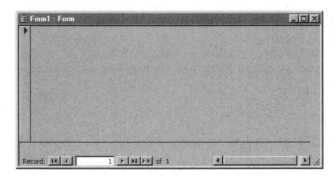

**Figure 5-2.** *Microsoft Access default form.*

## Form border

Every form has a border that defines its area. The form Border Style property offers four choices: None, Thin, Sizable, and Dialog. A form with a sizeable border is the default. If a form has a sizeable border, the user can resize the window using the mouse at the control points.

Sometimes, however, as in a message box, you will want a form to have a border that the user cannot resize. You could use the MsgBox function to create such a standard message box. If you want to add features that are not built into MsgBox, however, you can create your own message boxes using a form. The standard guideline is to make the form's border a fixed size. You can do this by setting the form's Border Style property to Thin. Look at Figure 5-3. You won't notice a major difference between this fixed border and the default sizeable border shown in Figure 5-2 except that in this one you will not get the sizing tool when the cursor is placed immediately over the edge of the form.

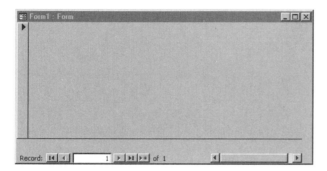

**Figure 5-3.** *Form with a fixed border.*

Be careful when creating fixed-size forms. Whenever you set the Border Style property to None, Thin, or Dialog, remember that it is impossible for the user to change the form's size. To avoid creating a form that is only partially visible to your users, develop your application using a monitor resolution of 640 × 480. This resolution is the smallest size available in Windows 95 or Windows NT. As long as you can see the entire form on your development machine, you can be assured that the users will also be able to, regardless of their screen resolution. If you developed an application using a 1024 × 768 monitor resolution and made the form full screen without a sizeable border, a user running a 640 × 480 resolution would not be able to get to the controls in the lower right portion of the form.

The None border type will remove the border and the title bar. The most common use for this type of form is for a splash, or startup, screen. To see the Microsoft Access 97 splash screen shown in Figure 5-4 on the following page, simply start Microsoft Access.

The startup screen for your application should always display a logo and an application name at the very least. The Solutions database (a sample database provided with Microsoft Access) contains step-by-step instructions for creating such a form under the Show Me help topic "Create a Startup Form."

**Figure 5-4.** *Microsoft Access splash screen.*

The final border type is Dialog. This option gives the form a thick border, and the form itself can include only a title bar and a Control menu. The form cannot be maximized, minimized, or resized. (The Maximize, Minimize, and Size commands are not available on the Control menu.) You often use this setting for custom dialog boxes. You could create this type of form by setting the Border Style property to Thin and removing the Min and Max buttons, but you don't need to do all that extra work if you use the Dialog option because Microsoft Access will do it for you.

The next properties you need to set in conjunction with Border Style to change the window type are the Modal and Pop Up properties.

**Modal** When a form is modal, you cannot click outside the form or set focus to another form.

**Pop Up** The Pop Up property simply places the form on top of all other windows. Although you can select other windows in the background and allow them to have focus, they will not come to the foreground. The pop-up form will always remain on top.

Dialog boxes and startup screens are typically both modal and pop-up windows.

### Disabling the Menu Bar

Setting both Modal and Pop Up properties to True will completely disable the menu bar and the toolbars for the particular form. You would want this combination for a dialog box or message box. When such a message box is active, you cannot click outside it to select a menu or toolbar item.

## Form title bar

The title bar, which is located at the top of the window immediately inside the form's border, helps identify the form. It typically displays text that describes the form. The text in a title bar is referred to as the form's *caption*. The title bar extends across the width of the window; its size and appearance cannot be modified. By default, the caption will be the name of the form. You can change this by setting the Caption property of the form in Microsoft Access.

The title bar is also used to move the form around the screen. For this reason, you will want to remove the title bar of a startup screen but provide one for a dialog box. A user does not need to be able to move a startup screen, but he or she must have the capability to move dialog and message boxes. For example, a user sometimes needs information on an underlying form to complete answers in a dialog box.

## Form title bar icon

The icon of the form appears in the left corner of the title bar. The title bar icon allows the user to invoke the Control menu for that particular form. The Control menu includes commands to restore, move, size, minimize, maximize, or close the form. Maximize, of course, makes the form full screen, and Restore returns the form to the size it was just before maximizing. Figure 5-5 shows the items available on a form's Control menu.

**Figure 5-5.** *Form Control menu.*

The title bar icon also visually indicates to the user what type of object is currently being worked with.

> **NOTE**   You cannot modify a form's Control menu, nor can you change the title bar icons for individual forms, tables, queries, and so on.

## Form title bar command buttons

Command buttons appear on the right side of the title bar. They are shortcuts to specific form commands.

The following buttons appear on a form's title bar:

▪ Minimizes the form

▯ Restores the form

▢ Maximizes the form

✕ Closes the form

You can disable the Minimize, Restore, and Maximize buttons by setting the Min Max Buttons property to None; you can disable the Close button by setting the Close Button property.

The Restore button will appear only if a form is currently maximized. The Close button will close the application. In the main form of your application, you will want to set the On Close property to close the entire application by executing a Quit statement.

### Record selector
The area just inside the left border of the form is the record selector. If you have multiple records on the form, the record selector gives you the ability to select one record. It also indicates the current record.

### Scroll bars
If a form is sized smaller than its defined boundaries, scroll bars will appear. These allow the user to move the visible region of the form.

A form can have a horizontal scroll bar, a vertical scroll bar, both, or neither. The scroll bar aligns with the edge of the form for the respective orientation it supports. It is very easy to add horizontal and vertical scroll bars to your form or to disable them by setting the Scroll Bars property. If a form's content is never scrollable in a particular direction, do not include a scroll bar for that direction.

### Navigation buttons
Immediately inside the bottom left border are the navigation buttons. These buttons permit a user to move to certain records. Inside the navigation buttons is an indicator of the total number of records in the form's recordset.

## Basic Form Operations
Forms in Microsoft Access have some basic operations built into them so that when you develop an application, your forms are capable of carrying out the following operations:

- Activating and deactivating a form
- Opening and closing forms
- Moving and sizing forms
- Scrolling forms

The following sections describe these operations.

### Activating and deactivating a form

Although Microsoft Access supports displaying multiple forms simultaneously, the user generally works within a single form at a time. The form the user is working in is called the *active form*. It is visually distinguished by its title bar, which is displayed in the active window title bar color. All other forms are inactive, and their title bar color will differ from that of the active form. While inactive forms may have ongoing background processes, only the active form can receive the user's input. The title bar of an inactive form displays the system inactive window title bar color.

### Opening and closing forms

When you open a form for the first time in Form view, it will be the same size it was the last time it was opened in Design view. As you continue to use that form in Form view, you might change the size of a form. When you close the form, Windows will remember its size and shape. The next time you open the form, it will open to the size and shape that it was when last closed. To make a form a specific size, just set the appropriate Width and Height properties in the form's On Open event.

If any transactions are pending after a user attempts to close a form, a message asking the user whether to save any changes, discard any changes, or cancel the close operation is displayed. If no transactions are pending, the form simply closes.

### Moving and sizing forms

The user can move a form either by dragging its title bar or by choosing the Move command on the form's shortcut menu.

**Resizing forms**   The user can change the size of a form by dragging the sizing border at the edge of the form with the mouse or by choosing the Size command on the form's menu. If you do not want your users to have the ability to resize the forms within your application, simply set the Border Style property to Thin.

**Maximizing forms**   Maximizing a form makes it the largest possible size. Because screen resolution and orientation vary, your software should not assume a fixed screen size but should adapt to the shape and size defined by the system.

**Minimizing forms**   To minimize a form, or reduce it to its smallest size, the user can choose the Minimize command on the form's shortcut menu or the title bar Minimize command button. You may want to add an entry in the Window menu to restore the minimized form. Because the form will not appear in Task Manager, a user may lose the minimized form. The ways to restore the form are via either shortcut keys or the menu command.

**Restoring forms**   After maximizing or minimizing a form, you can use the Restore command to restore it to its previous size.

### Scrolling forms

When a form contains more content than will fit into the window, the user can scroll vertically or horizontally unless you disable the scroll bar in the Scroll Bars property. Scrolling enables the user to view portions of the object that are not currently visible in a window.

**Keyboard scrolling**   Navigation keys support scrolling with the keyboard. When using a navigation key, the cursor moves to the appropriate location. For example, pressing arrow keys at the edge of a scrollable area scrolls in the corresponding direction and moves the cursor. Similarly, Page Up and Page Down keys scroll comparably to clicking in the scroll bar shaft and also move the cursor. Page Up and Page Down are also affected by the page-break control in your forms, so you may not scroll proportionately.

# Command Bars

In Microsoft Access 97 as well as in the rest of the Microsoft Office 97 applications, you use command bars to create menu bars, toolbars, and shortcut menus for your own applications. You don't need to create different objects for menu bars, toolbars, and shortcut menus anymore: these are now all CommandBar objects. Besides being easier to use and more efficient, command bars also give you more flexibility; you can create functional command bars that have the characteristics of both traditional menu bars and toolbars. Another great feature of command bars is that once you learn how to create and manipulate them in Microsoft Access, you'll be able to apply your knowledge throughout the rest of the Microsoft Office applications: all the Office 97 applications use command bars in the same way.

## Why Use Command Bars?

So now you can create flexible and powerful menu bars, toolbars, and shortcut menus for your applications using just one process. Often, the default menu bars and toolbars give the user more control over the application than you would like. For example, you may want a toolbar and menu bar for a form that will not allow the user to go into Design view and change the contents of the form. To limit what the user can do or to give the user additional power beyond what the default menu bars and toolbars provide, you can create a custom menu bar, toolbar, and shortcut menu bar for any form or report object. You can also create custom command bars that apply to your entire application rather than to a specific form or report.

## Where Can You Use Command Bars?

Custom command bars can be displayed automatically when a form or report is opened or when your database application is first opened. Once you close your form or report or even the database, the default menu bars and toolbars will be displayed unless you have specified custom ones.

The following table lists the three types of command bars you can create and points out where you might use them in a Microsoft Access application.

| Command Bar Type | Location | Property |
|---|---|---|
| Menu bar | Startup properties | Menu Bar |
| | Form properties | Menu Bar |
| | Report properties | Menu Bar |
| Toolbar | Form properties | Toolbar |
| | Report properties | Toolbar |
| Shortcut menu bar | Startup properties | Shortcut Menu Bar |
| | Form properties | Shortcut Menu Bar |
| | Report properties | Shortcut Menu Bar |

**TIP**

To enter the Startup dialog box, choose Startup from the Tools menu. To turn off the default command bars for your application, uncheck the following Startup options: Allow Full Menus, Allow Default Shortcut Menus, Allow Built-in Toolbars, and Allow Toolbar/Menu Changes. (Figure 5-15 on page 164 shows the Startup dialog box.)

To turn off shortcut menus for a specific form, change the value of the Shortcut Menu property to No.

To turn off a menu bar for just a single form or report, create a blank macro and set the Menu Bar property to the name of the blank macro.

## Creating Command Bars Through the User Interface

To create a command bar for your application, you must first be in Database view. Choose Toolbars from the View menu, and then select Customize. You will see the Customize dialog box shown in Figure 5-6.

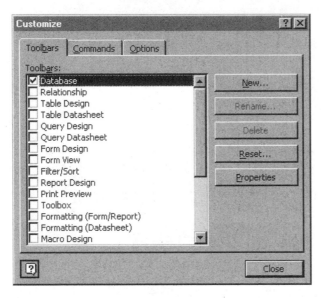

**Figure 5-6.** *Customize dialog box.*

Click New on the Toolbars tab. You will then be prompted for a name for your new command bar in the New Toolbar dialog box. Enter a name and click OK.

| TIP | If you are going to create multiple command bars, you might want to include in the name of the command bar the object it is to be used with as well as its type. For example, if you are creating a menu bar for your Employees form, you could use the name Employees Form Menu Bar. |
|---|---|

You will notice in the Toolbars tab that the command bar you just created is checked, meaning that it is visible. To determine the type of command bar you want this to be, click Properties from the Toolbars tab. You will see the Toolbar Properties dialog box shown in Figure 5-7.

**Figure 5-7.** *Toolbar Properties dialog box.*

In this dialog box, you can set the following properties for your command bar:

| Property | Description |
|---|---|
| Selected Toolbar | Contains a list of all available command bars. Use this to change the properties of a specific command bar. |
| Toolbar Name | Changes the name of the selected custom command bar. The names of built-in command bars cannot be changed. |
| Type | Can be Menu Bar, Toolbar, or Popup |
| | Menu Bar creates a menu bar–type command bar. Only command bars of type Menu Bar can be used in the Menu Bar properties of forms and reports or in the startup Menu Bar property. Toolbar creates a toolbar-type command bar and is the default. Only command bars of type Toolbar can be used in the Toolbar properties of forms and reports. Popup is used to create shortcut menus. Only command bars of type Popup can be used in the Shortcut Menu Bar properties of forms and reports or in the startup Shortcut Menu Bar property. The type of a built-in command bar cannot be changed. |

*(continued)*

| Property | Description |
| --- | --- |
| Docking | Can be Allow Any, Can't Change, No Vertical, or No Horizontal. |
| | You can determine the type of docking that is allowed for custom command bars as well as for built-in command bars. |
| Show On Toolbars Menu | When you right-click the mouse over a command bar, you will see a list of all available and visible command bars. If you do not want your command bar to appear on this list (for example, if you want to prevent users from hiding it), uncheck this property. |
| Allow Customizing | To prevent users from changing your command bar when the Customize dialog box is invoked, uncheck this option. The user will still be able to go into the property sheet of the toolbar and check this property. To prevent that from happening, uncheck the Allow Toolbar/Menu Changes option in the Startup properties. |
| Allow Resizing | You can prevent users from resizing a particular floating toolbar or menu bar by checking this check box. |
| Allow Moving | You can prevent users from moving a floating or docked command bar by checking this check box. |
| Allow Showing/Hiding | You can prevent a user from closing a command bar that you have open by checking this check box. If the command bar is closed, it shows up in the list of command bars that are available by right-clicking on a command bar; but the command bar name is grayed out. |
| Restore Defaults | Applies only to built-in command bars. If you make changes to a built-in command bar and you want to return it to its original state when you installed Microsoft Access, click this button. You can also select a command bar and then click the Reset button on the Toolbars tab of the Customize dialog box. |

## Creating Menu Bar Command Bars

As mentioned earlier, the menu bar–type command bar is used in the Menu Bar properties of forms and reports and in the startup Menu Bar property. To create a menu bar–type command bar, select View from the Database menu bar and choose Toolbars. From the Toolbars cascading menu, select Customize. On the Toolbars tab, click New. In the Toolbar Name box, type the name you want, and then click OK. Then click Properties on the Toolbars tab. From the Toolbar Properties dialog box, select Menu Bar from the Type list.

Now click the Close button to go back to the Customize dialog box and select the Commands tab. You will see a list of commands that can be found on the built-in command bars in Microsoft Access. To avoid confusing the user, create a menu bar that includes File, Edit, Window, and Help menus in addition to your custom menus. Such menu bars are recommended in all Windows applications. To create these menus, select New Menu, the last category in the Categories list box, as shown in Figure 5-8.

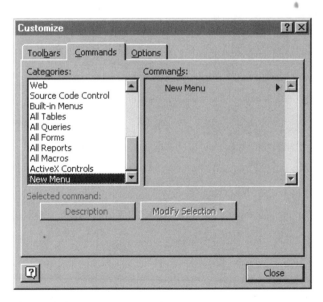

**Figure 5-8.** *Creating a new menu.*

From the Commands list box, drag and drop New Menu to your newly created Menu Bar command bar. To change the properties of this particular control, right-click on that item on the command bar and select Properties. You can also change the control's properties by clicking the Modify Selection button in the Commands tab of the Customize dialog box and selecting Properties. The Form Menu control properties sheet appears in Figure 5-9 on the following page.

**Figure 5-9.** *Employees Form Menu Bar Control Properties dialog box.*

In this dialog box, you can set the following properties for each individual control on your command bars of all types.

| Property | Description |
|----------|-------------|
| Selected Control | Lists all the controls that are currently on a command bar. Select the command bar control whose properties you would like to change. |
| Caption | For command bar controls that contain text, use this property. For example, &File would display on the command bar control as File. |
| Shortcut Text | If you want to assign hot keys to that particular command bar control, use this property. These are not truly hot keys, however, just the text next to the option. You will need to create an AutoKeys macro for the hot key effect to work with this command bar control. This property can be set only for command bar controls that have On Action set. |
| ToolTip | Provides a ScreenTip for the command bar control when the user passes the cursor over it. |
| On Action | When a user selects this command bar control, you can call a macro or a function (but not a sub procedure). You can call functions that accept parameters, such as hard-coded values, other functions, or even values from controls on forms. |

| Property | Description |
|---|---|
| Style | Default Style, Text Only (Always), Text Only (In Menus), Image And Text |
| | The Default Style setting displays both an image and a caption on a menu command; Text Only (Always) displays a caption on a menu command or on a button; Text Only (In Menus) displays only a caption on a menu command and only an image on a button; Image And Text displays an image and caption on both a menu command and a button. |
| Help File | Assigns a Help file to a particular command bar control. |
| Help ContextID | Use this number to select a mapped Help topic to be displayed. Entering 0 into this property will display the Help file's Contents page. |
| Parameter and Tag | Think of these properties as extra custom properties in which you can store string or numeric information. This could be useful to determine if this command bar control should be available for a particular form if the command bar applies to several forms. (You would check this using a VBA procedure and enable or disable the control appropriately.) |
| Begin A Group | Places a grouping line right before the control. You can use this to group similar controls. When resizing the command bar, those in a group stay together. |

To create additional items under the top-level command bar controls, just drag and drop the New Menu item or other commands from other categories underneath the appropriate command bar controls. (As you drag the cursor over an existing item, Access will show you all the places where you can drop the new item.) To create cascading menus, just drag and drop the appropriate commands to the right of the selected command bar control.

Remember that assigning a macro or a function to each custom command bar control is what makes selecting that control perform an action. If you select a command from the built-in categories, it will perform the same action as on the built-in menu or toolbar.

## Creating Shortcut Menu Command Bars

Shortcut menus appear when you right-click an item on the screen. You create a Popup shortcut menu–type command bar the same way you create a Menu Bar command bar, except you change the Type property of the command bar to Popup. Shortcut menus can have only one top-level command bar control, and this will not be displayed—only the command bar controls placed underneath it will show.

When you create a Popup type command bar, it is displayed in the Toolbars tab as a menu item under the Custom menu of the Shortcut Menus command bar. So if you want to modify it, double-click Shortcut Menus on the Toolbars tab of the Customize dialog box, and then select Custom on the menu that appears.

## Creating Toolbar Command Bars

Toolbar-type command bars may be used as toolbars to accompany your Microsoft Access forms or reports. You create a Toolbar command bar in the same way you create the other types of command bars, except you change the Type property of the command bar to Toolbar.

# Controls: Tools of the Trade

Controls are the tools of the trade for a Microsoft Access developer. These controls are grouped together and displayed as graphical objects in the Toolbox. You can choose one of the controls in the Toolbox, drag it to a form, and start building your application. The built-in controls of Microsoft Access give you the fundamental objects, or building blocks, you need to create professional looking, fully functional, and robust Windows applications. But why stop there? With the implementation of ActiveX controls, you have the ability to add custom controls to your applications.

Think of an ActiveX control as a third-party custom control. If you want your application to include a feature that the built-in controls of Microsoft Access do not support or that would take hours to build from scratch, you can use ActiveX controls to save you both time and effort. For example, you could create a calendar in a form by including a series of text boxes that contain all the logic needed to display the correct months, days of the week, dates, and so on. An easier and less time-consuming way to add a calendar to your form is to use the Calendar control included with Microsoft Access. Simply by dragging and dropping this control into your form, you have added a calendar that would have taken you hours to build "by hand."

Controls provide feedback to the user that indicates when they have the focus and when they are activated. For example, when a text box has the focus, a cursor blinks in it.

With Microsoft Access you can include shortcut menus for controls. Shortcut menus are time-savers because they give the user access to the most common tasks for a particular control without having to move the cursor to the form's menu bar. With a single mouse click, the user can access the most common tasks for a particular object. For example, you can provide a Help menu for every control on your form.

A shortcut menu for a control is contextual to what the control represents rather than to the control itself. Therefore, do not include commands, such as Check or Uncheck, for a check box control. Instead, provide a shortcut key combination to activate the control.

So just what built-in tools of the trade does Microsoft Access provide to help you design the forms for your user interface? In the following sections we will describe each control and discuss when to use it.

## The Toolbox

When you display the Design view of a form or report, Microsoft Access displays the Toolbox shown in Figure 5-10. The Toolbox groups the controls you can add to a form or report. To select a control, click the tool you want. Move the cursor to your form; the cursor changes to the picture on the tool. Click the form or report in the location that you want to place the control.

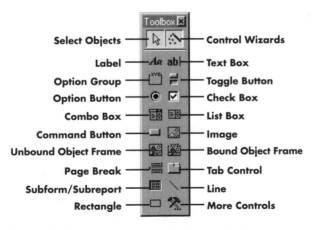

**Figure 5-10.** *Microsoft Access forms Toolbox.*

To show or hide the Toolbox, click the Toolbox button on the toolbar or choose Toolbox from the View menu or the Toolbar Shortcut menu.

Because the Toolbox is a type of toolbar, you can perform the following actions with it:

- Move it to a different location

- Display information about it or its buttons while you're working in Microsoft Access

- Modify it, including moving buttons, adding or removing buttons, and creating buttons that run a macro

Now let's take a look at the individual controls on the Toolbox. Keep in mind that you can create custom toolbars that are used only in the database in which you create them.

### Select Objects control

You must use this tool in order to select existing controls on a form or report.

### Control Wizards control

The Control Wizards tool determines whether Microsoft Access displays a Control Wizard when you place certain types of controls on a form or report. You can turn Control Wizards on or off by selecting the Control Wizards tool before placing controls.

### Label control

You use labels on a form or report to display descriptive text such as titles, captions, or brief instructions. Labels do not display values from fields or expressions; they are always unbound and do not change as you move from record to record.

Usually a label is attached to another control. When you create a text box, for example, a label that displays a caption for that text box is attached. When you create a label using the Label tool, however, the label stands on its own—it is not attached to any other control.

Microsoft Access automatically adds a label when you create most controls. You can omit the label by changing a control's default for the AutoLabel property.

After choosing the Label tool, you can add a label to a form by clicking the form and typing. The label expands as you type each letter. Press Ctrl-Enter to create a new line in the label. Pressing the Enter key at the end of the first line defines the label's width.

## Text Box control

Text boxes are used to display and accept a variety of data—names, addresses, phone numbers, descriptions, and so on. Depending on how much data you want the text box to hold, you can create either a single-line or a multiple-line text box.

Single-line text boxes display one line of data. When viewing data, you can use the arrow keys to scroll to the right if the text box isn't big enough to show all the data in the field.

### Access Keys

You can assign an access key (shortcut or accelerator key) to a label or button. When you assign an access key to a label, button, or menu item, you can press Alt+ the underlined character to move the focus to the control attached to that label, to the button, or to the menu item. To set an access key for a label or button, select the Caption property box in the property sheet and type an ampersand (&) immediately before the character you want to use as the access key.

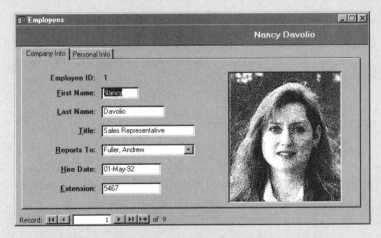

**Figure 5-11.** *Employees form redesigned with access keys.*

Figure 5-11 shows the Employees form from the Northwind example redesigned using access keys. Currently the focus is in the First Name field. If a user wanted to go to the Extension field, he or she would need either to take his or her hands off the keyboard and move the mouse pointer to the Extension field or to press the Tab key five times. In a high-speed data entry facility this would not be productive or practical. By adding access keys, the data entry person could press Alt+E to go to the field.

Multiple-line text boxes wrap data onto successive lines. You create a multiple-line text box by sizing it. If the text box isn't tall enough to display all the data, you can use the arrow keys to scroll down to view the rest of the data. You can also provide a vertical scroll bar by setting the text box's Scroll Bars property to Vertical.

You can limit the number of characters accepted as input for a text box if the text box is bound to a field. In addition, bound text boxes can be defined to support auto-exit; that is, as soon as the last character is typed in the text box, the focus moves to the next control.

### Option Group control

An option group is a control that displays a group frame to which you add check boxes, option buttons, or toggle buttons that represent choices on a form. Option groups generally do not directly process any input; they simply group a set of other controls. For example, you could use an option group to identify whether an order should be shipped by air, sea, or land.

Use an option group when the data is limited to a fixed set of only a few choices and the records will be viewed primarily in Form view. However, because option group data is stored as a number (specified by the Option Value property setting), consider using a list box or combo box if you'll be adding or editing the records in Datasheet view. With a list box or combo box, your choices are displayed as full text and options are available from a drop-down list and not limited to a fixed set. The group frame can be bound to a field in the table, set to an expression, or null. You assign to each option a numeric value that is stored in the underlying table or query when the option is chosen.

You can make the label for controls that you place in a group box relative to the group box's label. In our previous example our group had option buttons labeled Land, Sea, or Air. The group can have a separate label "Ship By."

**TIP** If you have Control Wizards on before you select the Option Group tool, you can create an option group using the wizard. To turn Control Wizards on or off, click the Control Wizards tool. (Control Wizards is on when the button appears sunken.)

### Toggle Button control

A toggle button is a control that you "push down" (select) to indicate that a situation is true (for example, that an order is paid). When not selected, it indicates that the situation is false.

Toggle buttons have the same purpose as option buttons and check boxes. The three controls differ only in appearance and in the format in which you use them:

toggle buttons are used only in forms; option buttons and check boxes can be used in both forms and reports.

These controls are most useful when bound to fields with a Yes/No data type; however, you can bind them to fields with other data types as well.

You can use toggle buttons in an option group to select one option from a group. A good example of this is a toolbar; when you select one option from the toolbar by pressing it, the previously selected toolbar button rises.

To display text or pictures on the faces of toggle buttons—for example, to illustrate the choices in the option group—set the Caption or Picture property.

## Option Button control

An option button (also known as a radio button) represents a single choice within a limited set of mutually exclusive choices; that is, in any group of option buttons, only one option in the group can be set. Although the Option Group Wizard permits you to use check boxes in an option group and have them be mutually exclusive, you do not want to deviate from the standard user interface design. Option buttons would be the best format for mutually exclusive choices.

Option buttons appear as a set of small circles. When an option button choice is set, a dot appears in the middle of the circle. When the option button is not set, the circle is empty. Avoid using option buttons to initiate an action other than setting a particular option or value represented by the option button.

Limit use of option buttons for small sets of options (typically seven or less, but always at least two). If you need more choices, consider using another control, such as a list box or combo list box.

Option buttons include a textual label. If you need graphical labels, consider using toggle buttons instead. Define the label to best represent the value or effect for that choice. You also use the label to indicate when the choice is unavailable.

Assign access keys to option button labels to provide a keyboard interface to the buttons.

## Check Box control

A check box is a control that indicates whether a situation is true or false (for example, whether an address has changed).

Like option buttons, check boxes support options that are either on or off. Check boxes differ from option buttons, however, in that they are used for nonexclusive choices. A check box appears as a square box with an accompanying label.

When the choice is set, a check mark appears in the box. Figure 5-12 shows the different styles of check boxes available in Microsoft Access. To change the appearance of the check box, set the Special Effect property.

**Figure 5-12.** *Different appearances for Check Box controls.*

A check box's label is typically textual. You can make a graphical label by deleting the label and adding a Picture Box control next to the check box. However, you should use toggle buttons when you need a graphical label. Define the label to appropriately express the value or effect of the choice. You can also use the label to indicate when the control is unavailable. You might have seen this represented by a label that is grayed out. Whenever you disable a control or make it unavailable, you should clearly define for the user how to enable it again.

Grouping check boxes does not prevent the user from setting the check boxes on or off in any combination. Although each check box's setting is typically not mutually exclusive and is independent of the others, you can use a check box's setting to affect other controls. For example, you can use the state of a check box to filter the content of a list. If you have many choices or if the number of choices may vary, consider using a multiple selection list box instead of check boxes.

Define access keys for check box labels to provide a keyboard interface for navigating to and choosing a check box. In addition, the Spacebar toggles a check box when the input focus is on the check box (as in a dialog box).

## Combo Box control

In a combo box you can either type a value in the text box or select a value from the list. The list of a list box or combo box consists of a number of rows of data. Each row can have one or more columns, which can appear with or without headings. For combo boxes, you can also control whether the user can enter new values. When you use a list box or combo box to view or modify data, you can scroll through the list to see all the possible values.

In Form view, Microsoft Access does not display the combo box list until you click its down arrow.

TIP If you have Control Wizards turned on before you select the combo box tool, you can create a combo box using the wizard.

The interface for the combo box follows the conventions supported for each of its components (the list and text box), except that the Up Arrow and Down Arrow keys move only in the list box.

Combo boxes are an effective way to conserve real estate and reduce clutter on your forms. However, the design tradeoff is that they require more user interaction for browsing and selecting an item than does a single selection list box.

## List Box control

A list box is a control that displays a list of values from which you can choose one value. Use a list box when you want to limit the value of a control to the values in the list.

Unlike a combo box list, which appears only when you click its down arrow, the contents of a list box list are always displayed when you are in Form view. The list can have one or many columns, and the columns can appear with or without headings.

You can display the most meaningful value in a list (such as an employee name) but have Microsoft Access store a different value (say, the employee's ID number) in the underlying table when a name is selected. You define the source for the rows in the list by setting the Row Source and Row Source Type properties. You can update a list box's list after its values have changed in the source where they are stored by using the Requery action in a macro. Both the list box and combo box controls have this ability.

TIP If you have Control Wizards on before you select the List Box tool, you can create a list box using the wizard.

List boxes are best for displaying large numbers of choices that vary in number or content. If a particular choice is not available, omit the choice from the list.

Order the entries in a list in a way that is most appropriate for the list's content and that facilitates easy user browsing. For example, alphabetize a list of file names, but put a list of dates in chronological order. If there is no natural or logical ordering for the content, alphabetize the list.

List box controls include their own labels. Make certain that you add support for keyboard access by adding an access key to the label. The user will then be able to set the focus to the list box by pressing Alt+ this key.

When a list box is disabled, its label is typically grayed out or blank. In addition, all of the list entries will be unavailable to avoid confusing the user about whether the control is enabled or not. If you are disabling the control because a user may not have security privileges to view the data within the control—such as social security numbers or credit card information—you might want to also change the Visible property so the list appears only when it is enabled.

The width of the list box should be sufficient to display the average width of a list entry. If that width is not practical because of space limitations or the variability of the information the list items include, you should consider making the list box wide enough to allow the list entries to be sufficiently distinguished.

You can classify the list boxes by mode of display (or by type of selection they support). There are two types of list boxes: single selection and multiple selection. The following paragraphs describe each type.

**Single selection list boxes**    A single selection list box is designed for the selection of only one item in a list. Therefore, the control provides a mutually exclusive operation similar to a group of option buttons, except that a list box can more efficiently handle a large number of items. Define a single selection list box to be tall enough to show at least three but no more than eight choices. The currently selected item in a single selection list box is highlighted.

The keyboard interface uses navigation keys, such as the arrow keys, Home, End, Page Up, and Page Down keys, as well as alphanumeric keys (for example, pressing M scrolls the entry beginning with M to the top of the list). These keys not only navigate to an entry in the list but also select it.

**Multiple selection list boxes**    Although most list boxes are single selection lists, some contexts require the user to choose more than one item. Microsoft Access 97 gives you the ability to incorporate multiple selection list boxes into your application.

Extended and simple multiple selection list boxes follow the same conventions for height and width as do single selection list boxes. Base the width of the box on the average width of the list entries. The height should be able to display no less than three items and generally no more than eight, unless the size of the list varies with the size of the window.

Extended selection list boxes support the selection interface for contiguous and disjoint selection; that is, they are optimized for a single item selection or for a single range, while still providing for disjoint selections. The user can select contiguous items by holding the Shift key and selecting the first and last items. Disjoint selections are made by holding the Ctrl key and selecting individual items.

When you want to support user selection of several entries from a list but the grouping of the entries does not make extended selection efficient, you can define a simple multiple selection list box. Whereas extended selection list boxes are optimized for individual item or range selection, simple multiple selection list boxes are optimized for independent selection.

## Command Button control

The Command Button control runs a macro or calls a VBA event procedure when the button is pressed (clicked on).

The macro or event procedure executes an action or a series of actions. For example, you can use a Command button to open one form from within another form.

You display a picture on the Command button by setting the Picture property, or you display text on the button by setting the Caption property. Figure 5-13 shows both types of Command buttons.

**Figure 5-13.** *Command buttons.*

You designate a Command button as the default button or as the cancel button on a form or report by setting the button's Default or Cancel properties.

> **TIP**   If you have Control Wizards on before you select the Command Button tool, you can create a Command button using the wizard.

You can define access keys for command buttons. In addition, the Spacebar activates a Command button if the user moves the input focus to the button.

If the control is unavailable (disabled), the label of the button is grayed out.

Include an ellipsis (…) as a visual cue for buttons associated with commands that require additional information, such as ones that invoke a dialog box. As on menu items, the use of ellipses on command buttons indicates that further information is needed.

## Image control

The Image control is used for displaying images that require no changes by the user. This control is useful for displaying static images such as business logos. The image then becomes part of the .MDB file and is not stored within a table in the database.

## Unbound Object Frame control

The Unbound Object Frame control displays a picture, a graph, or any OLE object not stored in a table in a Microsoft Access database. For example, you could use an unbound object frame to display a picture that you created and stored in Microsoft Paint. This control allows you to create or edit the object from within a Microsoft Access form or report by using the application in which the object was originally created. An unbound object frame can display linked or embedded objects.

### Bound Object Frame control

This control can display a picture, graph, or any OLE object stored in a table in a Microsoft Access database. For example, if you store pictures of your employees in a table in Microsoft Access, you can use a bound object frame to display these pictures on a form or report. This control allows you to create or edit the object from within the form by using another OLE application.

A bound object frame is bound to a field in an underlying table. To display objects not stored in an underlying table, use the Unbound Object Frame control. The field in the underlying table to which the bound object frame is bound must use the OLE Object data type.

The object in a bound object frame changes for every record. The bound object frame can display linked or embedded objects.

### Page Break control

The Page Break control is used to mark the start of a new screen or printed page on a form. In a form, a page break is active only when you set the form's Default View property to Single Form. Page breaks do not affect a form's datasheet.

In Form view, press Page Up or Page Down to move to the previous or next page break.

Position page breaks above or below other controls. Placing a page break on the same line as another control will split the control's data.

### Tab control

The Tab control is used to store groups of information in a limited area of space using only a single form. For example, if you have a large data entry screen, instead of making a multipage form with page breaks you can add a Tab control. To see an example of this, refer to the Employees form in the Northwind Traders database.

You can easily get to the grouping of information you want by using the Tab control. Whenever a tab on the Tab control is selected, it comes to the foreground and you immediately see that particular group of information.

Here's how to use the control: when you're in Design view, select the tab you want to add controls to and add the controls the same as you would for a form. Repeat this step for the rest of the tabs.

### Subform/Subreport control

The Subform/Subreport control displays an embedded form on a form or report or an embedded report on a report.

For example, you can use a form with a subform to present one-to-many relationships, such as one product category with the items that fall into that category. In this case, the main form could display the category ID, name, and description; the subform could display the ID numbers of all available products in that category.

Instead of creating the main form and then drawing the Subform control on it, you can simultaneously create the main form and subform with a wizard. You can also create a subform by dragging an existing form from the Database window to the main form. You can create subforms to avoid the clutter of having multiple forms open at the same time.

### Line control

The Line control is used to display a horizontal, vertical, or diagonal line on a form. Lines can be used for the following purposes:

- Group related information

- Draw attention to important information

- Make the form or report look like a printed document

### Rectangle control

The Rectangle control is used to display a rectangle on a form. Rectangles can be used for the following purposes:

- Group related information

- Make the form or report look like a printed document

- Emphasize key areas on a form or report

- Create a shadow effect by placing rectangles under other controls

Rectangles drawn over other controls (except list boxes and subforms) hide those controls. You can place the rectangle behind other controls by choosing Send To Back from the Format menu or make it transparent by setting the BackStyle property to Clear.

### More Controls control

This button gives you the ability to add ActiveX controls to your form. There are literally hundreds of ActiveX controls, many by third-party vendors, some of which already complete a task you are trying to accomplish. Not all ActiveX controls are compatible with Microsoft Access, however. You will need to refer to the vendor's documentation for a particular control. You should also check Microsoft's Web site for the latest information on what controls are available. Several controls that work with the Internet are part of the Office Developer's Edition and will be covered in Chapter 15.

## Layout

You should orient the controls in your forms to the way people read information. In countries in which roman alphabets are used, this orientation is from left to right and top to bottom. Locate the primary field the user interacts with as close to the upper-left corner as possible. The same rules apply for orienting controls within groups in a dialog box.

Lay out the major command buttons either stacked along the upper-right border of the dialog box or lined up across the bottom of the dialog box. The most important button—typically the default command—should be the first button in the set. If you use the OK and Cancel buttons, group them together. If you include a Help button, make it the last button in the set. You can use other arrangements if you have a compelling reason, such as a natural mapping relationship. For example, it makes sense to place buttons labeled North, South, East, and West in a compasslike layout.

## MDI Windows

Multiple Document Interface (MDI) allows you to have a parent form and a child form. The child form is displayed only when the parent form is open. To illustrate the difference between a single document interface and a multiple document interface, we'll look at the Wordpad applet and Microsoft Word. The Wordpad applet that ships with Windows 95 does not support MDI; Microsoft Word does. MDI gives Word the capability to have several documents open at the same time. You can tile the windows and switch between them.

Although you might want to create an MDI-style interface for your application, you cannot do it in Microsoft Access. Microsoft Access itself is the primary, or parent, window, and since all forms are child windows, you cannot create a child window within a form in your application. (If you want to make such an application, you will need to use either Microsoft Visual Basic or Microsoft Visual C++.) Although you cannot create grandchild windows, you can simulate a parent-child window in Access by making your startup form a maximized form that has the Minimize, Maximize, and Restore buttons disabled. Then in the Close event of the form you can simply close the entire application, including Microsoft Access.

# User Assistance

User assistance is an important part of a product's design. A well-designed Help interface provides the user with assistance on demand; but the assistance must be simple, efficient, and relevant so a user can obtain it without becoming lost in the Help interface. A user wants to accomplish a specific task—a Help interface design should assist in that objective without being intrusive.

The following types of user assistance are available in Microsoft Access:

- Context-sensitive help
- What's This
- ScreenTips
- Status bar help
- Office Assistant

For instructions on creating and adding help in your applications, please refer to Appendix B.

# Putting It All Together

An application is made up of the same objects as a Microsoft Access database—tables, queries, forms, reports, macros, and modules. The objects are stored in one or more Microsoft Access database (.MDB) files.

The goal of application design is to create an application that is easy to use and structured around the real-world tasks the users need to perform. The controls you put in your application should have the look, feel, and function of other Windows programs the user may be familiar with. This will make the use of your program intuitive to the user. In addition, your application can be designed to protect the underlying database structure from being inadvertently modified.

## Creating a Main Form

When designing a main form, consider what the user's primary task is. Position the form related to that task as close as possible to the surface of the application. For example, if the application focuses on one task, such as taking orders, the order entry form can be used as the main form. When the user opens the application, the form he or she needs to use should be presented right away.

## Creating a Main Menu or Switchboard

If an application contains numerous forms and reports and the order in which they are used cannot be predicted, the application can be started by displaying a main form that acts as a switchboard. This type of form often uses command buttons to group related objects and tasks. Refer to the Main Switchboard in Northwind, shown in Figure 5-14, to see what kinds of objects and tasks can be included on such a form.

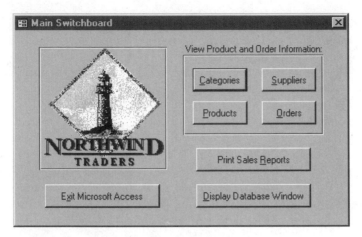

**Figure 5-14.** *Northwind Main Switchboard.*

## Controlling the Application Startup

When it comes time for you to distribute your application to users, you will want to change the application's title bar and icon. You can do so by modifying the Startup properties. To view the Startup options, choose Startup from the Tools menu. The dialog box in Figure 5-15 appears.

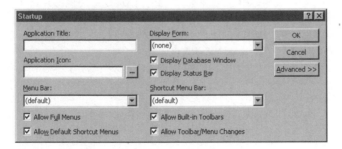

**Figure 5-15.** *Dialog box showing Startup options.*

The Startup options apply only to the current database. When you specify a setting in the Startup dialog box, you automatically set the database property associated with that setting. To bypass these settings when opening a database, hold down the Shift key until the database is opened.

## Application title

The application title appears in the title bar of the application window. After choosing the OK button in the Startup dialog box, the caption in the title bar of the application window will change to the value you entered in the Application Title text box.

## Application icon

The application icon will contain the icon to appear when the application is minimized; when Alt-Tab, which toggles from application to application, is pressed; or when the taskbar of Windows 95 is viewed.

## Display Form

The Display Form combo box allows you to specify any form in the database that is to be opened when the database is opened.

## Menu Bar and Shortcut Menu Bar

The Menu Bar and Shortcut Menu Bar properties in the Startup dialog box do not override the property settings for specific forms or reports that have a custom menu bar or shortcut menu. These options allow you to specify a menu that you have created to be the default menu bar. Forms or reports in Microsoft Access that display their own custom menu bar will still work. These options affect only the default menu bar and shortcut menu bar.

The check boxes listed in the Startup dialog box will toggle properties to True or False. For example, Display Database Window will hide or show the window depending on how it is set.

You can use the Startup dialog box instead of or in addition to an AutoExec macro. An AutoExec macro runs after the Startup options have taken effect; therefore, you should avoid any actions in an AutoExec macro that change the effect of the Startup option settings. The table on the following page lists the properties that you can set in the Startup dialog box.

### Hiding Forms at Startup

If an application contains many forms, its performance can be improved by displaying the Startup screen and at the same time opening and hiding all the forms. In the OpenForm action that is used to open the forms, set the Window Mode to Hidden. Then instead of having the application open each form when the user needs it, the form's Visible property is set to True. When the user finishes with a form, its Visible property is set to False. Using this technique, the application takes longer to start, since it opens all its forms at startup, but its performance after startup can be greatly improved.

**DATABASE PROPERTIES SET BY STARTUP OPTIONS**

| Property Name in Startup Dialog Box | Property Name in VBA |
|---|---|
| Application Title | AppTitle |
| Application Icon | AppIcon |
| Display Form | StartupForm |
| Display Database Window | StartupShowDBWindow |
| Display Status Bar | StartupShowStatusBar |
| Menu Bar | StartupMenuBar |
| Shortcut Menu Bar | StartupShortcutMenuBar |
| Allow Full Menus | AllowFullMenus |
| Allow Default Shortcut Menus | AllowShortcutMenus |
| Allow Built-in Toolbars | AllowBuiltInToolbars |
| Allow Toolbar Changes | AllowToolbarChanges |
| Allow Viewing Code After Error | AllowBreakIntoCode |
| Use Access Special Keys | AllowSpecialKeys |

## Distributing Upgraded Versions of an Application

At some time during your application's life cycle, you will need to distribute upgraded versions. Splitting an application into two .MDB files can help to facilitate this process.

If an application is distributed to any number of users or if data is located on a server, you might find it convenient to use one database to hold the application's data (tables) and another to hold its queries, forms, reports, macros, and modules. All objects can be attached to tables from the database that contains the data.

When the application's data is separated from its forms and other objects, it is easy to distribute upgraded versions of the application. Upgraded queries, forms, reports, macros, and modules can be distributed without disturbing the application's data. And if the data is located on a server, the network load can be reduced by having users run the application from their workstations rather than from the server.

If you know from the beginning that you intend to split your application into two database files, you can develop it with this in mind. Another design option is to keep tables and objects together in the same file and split them only when you are finished and ready to distribute the application.

Users open and use the application database (APP.MDB). Because the objects in the application database are based on attached tables, changes that users make to the data using these objects change the data in the data database (DATA.MDB). Security can be implemented on all the objects in this application, including both the tables in the data database and the objects in the application database.

Splitting the database has certain advantages. However, if your application is not used primarily for data entry, you have an alternative for application distribution—the replication feature. Replication is used not only for replicating data but also for replicating your development changes to other users. For more information on replication, refer to the Microsoft Access documentation.

## P R E V I E W of the next chapter

In the next chapter you will take a slightly different approach to implementing user interface design. You will modify an existing application, applying the concepts you learned in this chapter.

# 6

# Enhancing Your Applications

In Chapter 5 we discussed the components of user interface and application design and examined some of the rules you need to follow when creating an application that uses the Microsoft Windows user interface. For example, we described forms, menus, and Toolbox controls and provided some guidelines governing their use. In this chapter you will learn how to implement those guidelines. Since you are past the stage of creating an application from scratch and have had some exposure to designing forms, we will take a slightly different approach here to implementing user interface design. Instead of asking you to create an entire application in Microsoft Access and apply the user interface design guidelines up front, we will have you modify an existing Microsoft Access 97 sample application, Northwind Traders, to adhere to the guidelines given in the preceding chapter. This experience will provide you with valuable practice in modifying applications—experience you can then use to modify some of your own existing applications.

## Before You Begin

To be certain that you are referring to the Northwind Traders sample application discussed in this chapter, make sure you are working with the NWIND.MDB file in the CHAP06 subfolder of the folder in which you installed the files from this book's companion CD. This copy of the Northwind Traders application is provided in case you have already modified the NORTHWIND.MDB file that comes with Microsoft Access.

When you start the Northwind application for the very first time, the dialog box shown in Figure 6-1 appears.

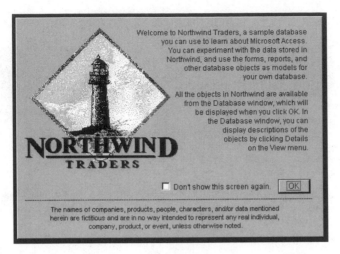

**Figure 6-1.** *Startup screen of the Northwind Traders application.*

After you choose OK, click the Forms tab in the Database window and change the name of the form from Startup to OldStartup. To rename the Startup form, click the Startup form icon, choose Rename from the Edit menu, and edit the form name. If you close and reopen the database, you will get an error message. Ignore this error for now. We will address it in the "Creating a Startup Form" and "Setting Startup Properties" sections beginning on pages 184 and 186, respectively.

## A Preview of Northwind Traders

The Northwind Traders sample application gives you great examples for learning Microsoft Access. You will find that many of the Help file and documentation examples for Microsoft Access refer to the Northwind Traders database. It is not a finished application, however. By dissecting it, you will be able to see the design enhancements required to make it robust and learn how to enhance your own applications with such modifications.

At this point you might want to take some time to familiarize yourself with the Northwind Traders application. Open some of the forms, preview the reports, check out the various queries, and so on. This application is rather complex in that it contains many tables, queries, forms, and other objects. For illustration purposes in this chapter, we will narrow our focus to the following forms from the Northwind database:

- Main Switchboard

- Products

- Orders

- Startup

Once these forms are introduced and we have discussed their strong points and their weaknesses, you will be shown how to modify them to make them more user-friendly.

## Main Switchboard

The Northwind Traders application already contains a Main Switchboard form. Do not confuse the Main Switchboard form with a startup or splash screen. As discussed in Chapter 5, a startup form displays your application's title, logo, and perhaps some copyright information. The Main Switchboard form, on the other hand, is a navigation mechanism for the user. Figure 6-2 shows you what the Main Switchboard form looks like.

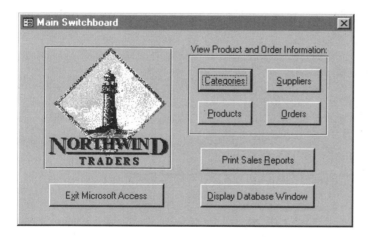

**Figure 6-2.** *Main Switchboard form of the Northwind Traders application.*

This form exemplifies good user interface design. The tasks are grouped together, the objects are balanced, and all the command buttons have shortcut keys so a user does not have to move his or her hands from the keyboard. To complete this form, however, you need to add a custom menu. You will learn how to customize menus in several ways in the "Creating Custom Menu Bars" section beginning on page 181 of this chapter.

## Products

The Products form in the Northwind Traders application, shown in Figure 6-3, allows a user to update product information.

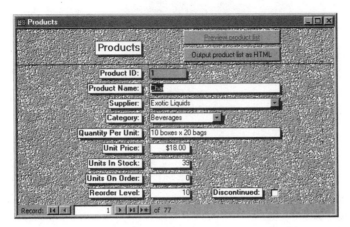

**Figure 6-3.** *Products form of the Northwind Traders application.*

At first glance this form might look complete. But imagine that you are a user whose cursor is positioned in the Product Name field and that you want to go directly to the Reorder Level field without using the mouse. You would have to press the Tab key seven times. You could make your user's life easier by providing a key combination that would take him or her directly to the Reorder Level field.

Also notice that there isn't a button to return the user to the Main Switchboard form after he or she is done with this Products form. To close this form, the user would have to use the mouse. Not all users have a mouse. For example, your application might track sales for a retail store, but when was the last time you saw a mouse next to a cash register?

When designing forms, remember to provide multiple methods for the user to move through your application.

## Orders

The user can enter new orders into the system on the Orders form, shown in Figure 6-4.

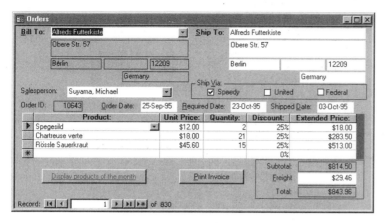

**Figure 6-4.** *Orders form of the Northwind Traders application.*

This interface is very intuitive because it looks like a standard business invoice. It capitalizes on the fact that many users have likely used paper or electronic forms similar to this one. The tab order of this form takes the user from field to field in a logical progression. (Tab order will be discussed in more detail later in this chapter.) Notice the Ship Via option group, however. From looking at the check boxes, you might assume that you could choose multiple methods to ship the product—for example, both Speedy and United—if the order were too large for just one shipper to handle. Your assumption would be wrong. The form has mutually exclusive check boxes. To indicate to the user that only one box can be selected at a time, you will need to change the check boxes to option buttons, which is the standard way of indicating mutually exclusive choices.

## Increasing an Application's Usability

Your task will be to tie these forms together into a complete application. The application should display a startup form for seven seconds and then load a switchboard. The user should not be able to get into Design view but should be able to use the keyboard or the mouse to move through the application. You should revise the Main Switchboard, Products, and Orders forms, implementing what you have learned about making user interface designs robust, in order to create a complete application that users will find convenient and simple to use. A copy of the sample application with all the changes suggested in this chapter is included in the CHAP06.MDB file in the CHAP06 subfolder of the folder in which you installed the companion CD files.

Now let's look at some things that you'll need to modify in these forms to make them more user-friendly:

■ When you open the database, the Microsoft Access toolbar is visible, allowing the users to get into Design view.

■ *All* Microsoft Access menu items are always available to the users, not just ones specific to the currently active form.

■ Not all of the items on the forms have shortcut keys.

Although these changes are perhaps most obvious in the order listed above, you will want to implement them in the opposite order. Keep in mind that you will need access to the standard menus and toolbars for development, so make changes involving them last. In general, start with the user interface changes on individual forms before you make global Microsoft Access changes; then create custom menus and, finally, custom toolbars.

We will discuss the following user interface and application enhancements you can make:

■ Creating shortcut keys

■ Defining tab order

■ Supplying ScreenTips

■ Morphing controls

■ Creating custom menus

■ Creating a Startup form

■ Setting Startup properties

## Creating Shortcut Keys

You can make your application more user-friendly by providing the user with more than one way to accomplish a particular task. For example, if you create an application that is going to be used primarily for data entry and you require the users to click the mouse to carry out a particular task, you are forcing them to take their hands off the keyboard. Doing so can be inconvenient and might decrease their productivity. Therefore, you will want to provide methods for controlling the application that use the keyboard only. On the other hand, some users prefer to use the mouse. To make your application more robust, provide both methods.

Shortcut keys should be available for all the controls on the form. A shortcut key is a letter or number that the user presses in combination with the Alt key to invoke a particular command. For example, Alt-R could let the user choose a command that opens a switchboard allowing him or her to print the application's reports. Shortcut keys appear underlined in the user interface.

Begin by adding shortcut keys to the Products form. Open the Products form in Design view. Recall from Chapter 5 that to create a shortcut key you simply add an ampersand (&) before the letter that will appear underlined and act as the shortcut key. This process is simple, but it does require some planning. You do not want two items to use the same letter as their shortcut key. For example, if your label were First Name and you inserted the & in front of the "F" in First, you would create a conflict with the shortcut key for the File menu; the user would not be able to invoke the File menu from the menu bar using the Alt-F shortcut. This does not mean, however, that you can use a letter only once for a shortcut key of a label. For example, you could use a common letter to cycle through common fields. For that to work, the user would have to cycle through the shortcuts by pressing the key combination a second time. We will take this approach on the Products form.

**TIP**  Keep in mind other common shortcut keys. For example, Alt-X (eXit), Alt-E (Exit), and Alt-Q (Quit) are all common shortcut keys for closing a window; Alt-P (Print) is a standard shortcut for printing a form. Try to avoid using these common letters as your shortcut keys.

The following table lists some shortcuts you can use for the Products form.

**SHORTCUT KEYS FOR PRODUCTS FORM**

| Label Name | Label Caption with Shortcut Key |
|---|---|
| ProductNameLabel | Product &Name |
| SupplierLabel | &Supplier |
| CategoryLabel | &Category |
| QuantityPerUnitLabel | Qu&antity Per Unit |
| UnitPriceLabel | &Unit Price |
| UnitsInStockLabel | &Units In Stock |
| UnitsOnOrderLabel | &Units On Order |
| ReorderLevelLabel | &Reorder Level |
| DiscontinuedLabel | &Discontinued |

To set up a shortcut, select the label you want to change, click the Properties button on the toolbar, and on the Format tab, add an ampersand (&) to the Caption property in front of whichever letter you want to act as the shortcut key. Figure 6-5 shows how the Products form labels look after the shortcut keys are assigned as indicated in the table above.

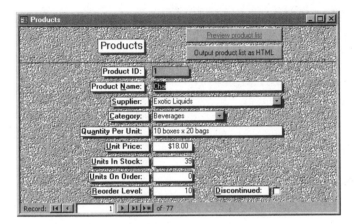

**Figure 6-5.** *Shortcut keys for the Products form.*

Now open the form in Form view, and test the shortcut keys. Press Alt-U several times, and notice how the cursor cycles through the controls that use the letter "U" as their shortcut key. Also note that Alt-D not only takes you to the Discontinued field but also checks or unchecks the check box, as if you had clicked it with the mouse or set the focus to it and then pressed the Spacebar.

For practice, implement appropriate shortcut keys in the Suppliers form as well.

## Defining Tab Order

The next step in designing user-friendly interfaces is to figure out the best tab order, which is the order in which the cursor moves from field to field when the user presses the Tab key. Even though you have defined shortcut keys, a user might want to move to the next field on the form simply by pressing the Tab key. If the tab order is not properly defined, however, the user might end up in a field several fields away from the one he or she anticipates. This causes confusion and the extra work of pressing a set of key combinations or using the mouse in order to get to the proper field.

To demonstrate this, open the Products form in Design view and make the following changes: select and move all the fields below the Product ID field down far enough to insert a field; move the Discontinued field to the top of the form, placing it just below the Product ID field. Your form should look like the one shown in Figure 6-6.

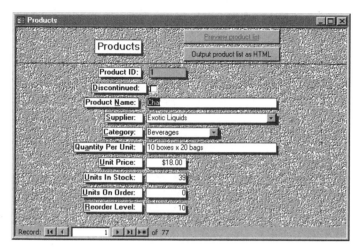

**Figure 6-6.** *Rearranged Products form to demonstrate tab order.*

Save and close the form. Open the form to test the tab order. The Discontinued field is still the last field in the tab order. Return to Design view, and choose Tab Order from the View menu. You will see the Tab Order dialog box shown in Figure 6-7.

**Figure 6-7.** *Tab Order dialog box.*

Choose the Auto Order button. Microsoft Access will automatically reorder the tab order of the fields to match their location on the form, from top to bottom and left to right. But what if you want to change the tab order differently? You can modify the existing tab order so your users can tab through the fields in a different order. For example, click the box to the left of the Discontinued field in the Tab Order dialog box to select the field, and then drag it to just below the ProductID field. Now choose the OK button, change back to Form view, and note the changed functionality of the tab order.

You might also want to change what happens when the user presses the Tab key on the last field of a record. Currently in the Products form, you will cycle back to the first field of the current record on the form. Take the following steps to change the tab behavior for the last field in a record on a form:

1. In Form Design view, double-click the form selector to open the form's property sheet. (The form selector is the square box in the upper left corner of the form where the vertical and horizontal rules intersect.)

2. Click the Other tab, place the cursor in the Cycle property, and then select one of the following settings:

| Cycle Property Setting | Description |
| --- | --- |
| All Records | When you press Tab in the last field of the record, the focus moves to the first field of the next record. |
| Current Record | When you press Tab in the last field of the record, the focus moves back to the first field of the current record. |
| Current Page | On a multipage form, when you press Tab in the last field of a form page, the focus moves back to the first field in the same page. The Employees form uses this setting. |

3. Save and close the form.

## Supplying ScreenTips

ScreenTips are another great way to give quick instructions or briefly describe the functionality of a particular object without requiring the user to initiate a What's This command or enter Help. ScreenTips are invoked when a user positions the cursor over an object and pauses for a moment. This functionality is built into the Main Switchboard form in Northwind Traders. Open that form, then position your cursor over the Products button and pause for a moment. Notice the label that appears below your mouse cursor; this is a ScreenTip.

NOTE The tip will appear only if the button has the focus.

Figure 6-8 shows the ScreenTips for the Products button on the Main Switchboard form.

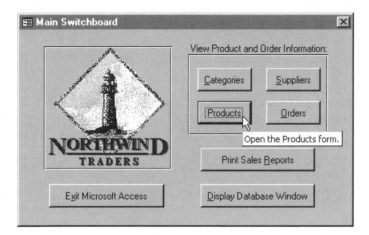

**Figure 6-8.** *Using ScreenTips.*

To add ScreenTips throughout your application, simply follow these two steps:

**1.** In Form Design view, double-click the control you want to create a tip for. (Double-click the control itself, not the control's label.)

**2.** Click the Other tab on the Properties sheet, place the cursor in the ControlTipText property in the Property sheet, and type the message you want to display for the control. The message can contain up to 255 characters.

You can also create custom Help files or custom What's This tips for your form. For more information on these topics, search the Microsoft Access Online Help for What's This.

You can add online assistance to Microsoft Access controls, forms, or reports in several ways. If you want to display a tip that pops up when the user moves the cursor over a particular control, use the ControlTipText property. You could also use the StatusBarText property to display information about a form or control in the status bar. You can also create tips for toolbar buttons you create.

If you want to include more extensive Help or have an appropriate Help topic for the control that has the focus pop up when you press F1, you can use a text editor or word processing program to create a Help file (the program must be able to save documents in Rich Text Format). Then you can compile the Help file with the Windows Help Compiler and attach it to a form, report, or control using the HelpFile and HelpContextID properties.

> **NOTE**  The Windows Help Compiler is included with the Microsoft Office Developer Edition, Microsoft Visual Basic, Microsoft Visual C++, and the Microsoft Windows Software Development Kit (SDK).

## Morphing Controls

Microsoft Access 97 also provides you with the ability to change a control's type while in Design view of your form. The ability to change a control from one type to another is called *morphing*. You might need to morph controls to adhere to user interface guidelines. For example, if you need to present two choices, of which the user can select only one or the other, you would use option buttons in an option group. If you want to allow the user to select one, both, or none of the options, you should use check boxes.

When you morph a control, Microsoft Access copies the appropriate property settings from the original control to the new control. If a property exists for the original control but not for the new control, Microsoft Access does not copy it. If a property exists for the new control but not for the original control, Microsoft Access sets the property to the default value for that type of control.

To morph a control, follow these steps:

1. In Design view, click the control you want to change.

2. Choose the Change To command from the Format menu, and then view the list of types that the selected control can be changed to. If a type of control appears dimmed on the menu, you cannot change the selected control to that type.

3. Click the type of control you want to change to.

Open the Orders form in the Northwind Traders application, and look at the Ship Via field. As you can see in Figure 6-9, check boxes are currently in this field even though the user can enter only one shipper. Select the three check boxes, one at a time, and morph them into option buttons to improve the intuitiveness of the user interface.

**Figure 6-9.** *Ship Via check boxes.*

Keep in mind that you are not allowed to morph at will. There are limits set so you do not morph, for example, an image into a text box, and lose many of the property settings. The following table lists each control and the control types it can be morphed to.

### MORPHING CONTROL TYPES

| Control Type | Can Be Morphed to |
|---|---|
| Bound Object Frame | \<nothing\> |
| Check Box | Toggle Button, Radio Button |
| Combo Box | Text Box, List Box |
| Command Button | \<nothing\> |
| Custom Control | \<nothing\> |
| Image | \<nothing\> |
| Label | Text Box |
| Line | \<nothing\> |
| List Box | Text Box, Combo Box |
| Option Group Frame | Text Box |
| Page Break | \<nothing\> |
| Radio Button | Check Box, Toggle Button |
| Rectangle | \<nothing\> |
| SubForm/SubReport | \<nothing\> |
| Tab | \<nothing\> |
| Text Box | Label, List Box, Combo Box |
| Toggle Button | Check Box, Option Button |
| Unbound Object Frame | Image |

# Creating Custom Menu Bars

The next user interface enhancement will be to create application-specific menu bars. Menu bars are most commonly used with forms but can also be applied to the Print Preview view of reports. Designing your menu bars on paper before building them in Microsoft Access will save you a lot of time.

One of the main reasons for having custom menu bars in your application is to prevent users from getting into Design view and modifying the application. But if your *only* reason for creating custom menu bars is to keep users out of Design view, you can accomplish this more easily by setting certain startup properties, a topic we'll discuss in the "Setting Startup Properties" section.

In this section, we'll create a custom menu bar for the Products form that looks like this:

To create this custom menu bar, do the following:

1. Choose Toolbars from the View menu.

2. Select Customize to open the Customize dialog box.

3. Select the Toolbars tab.

4. Click the New button to create the menu bar.

5. Change the Toolbar Name to Products Menu Bar, and click OK. The new menu bar will appear on the screen. Drag it out of the way of the Customize dialog box if necessary.

6. Click the Properties button on the Toolbars tab of the Customize dialog box.

7. In the Type combo box, select Menu Bar.

8. Click the Close button.

9. Select the Commands tab on the Customize dialog box.

10. In the Categories list box, select New Menu.

11. From the Commands list box, drag and drop the New Menu item into the newly created menu bar, as shown on the facing page.

12. Right-click on the New Menu item on the Products Menu Bar, and change the Name property to &File.

Follow steps 11 through 12 to create the &Records menu.

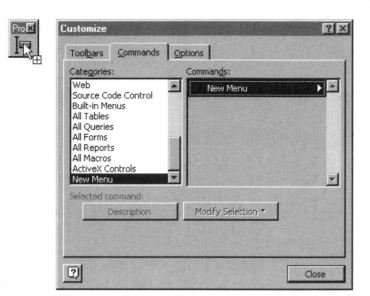

Now place a command named &Close on the &File menu as follows:

1. From the Commands tab, select View from the Categories list box.

2. Scroll down to see the Close command in the Commands list box.

3. From the Commands list box, drag and drop the Close command beneath the File menu, as shown here:

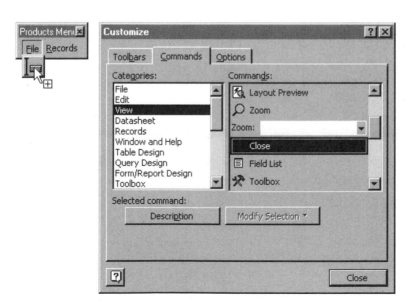

**4.** Follow steps 1 through 3 to create the First and Next commands for the Records menu. (The First and Next commands are in the Records category.)

**5.** Close the Customize dialog box, and open the Products form in Form view. View the contents of the various menus. You will see that the default menu bar is still being used. Switch to Design view.

**6.** Set the Menu Bar property of the Products form to Products Menu Bar.

**7.** Switch to Form view. Look at the menu bar displayed at the top of the screen. You should see the custom menu you just built. Try selecting a menu command. Notice that the commands you added to the custom menu bar are fully functional.

**8.** Save the changes, and close the form.

## Modifying Existing Menu Bars

You can also drag an entire menu or a single menu command from an existing menu bar to a custom menu bar. Simply open the Customize dialog box, and display both the existing menu bar and your custom menu bar. Hold down the Ctrl key as you drag and drop any menu item from one menu bar to the other. If you drag a menu, the menu and all its commands are copied to your custom toolbar. Make sure you hold down the Ctrl key, though, or you will remove the menu or the command from the original menu bar.

TIP     To remove a menu or a command, drag it off the menu bar.

# Creating a Startup Form

When your application starts, you might want to display its name, copyright information, and logo for a brief time. To create a Startup form in the sample database you've been working with, create an unbound form to display some appropriate information about your application. In the detail section, create labels that display your application's name and copyright information. Also, create an unbound object frame that displays your application's logo, and use the Picture property to display a colorful background. Set the form properties listed in the following table:

| Property | Setting |
|---|---|
| DefaultView | Single Form |
| ViewsAllowed | Form |
| ScrollBars | Neither |
| RecordSelectors | No |
| NavigationButtons | No |
| AutoCenter | Yes |
| BorderStyle | None |
| ShortcutMenu | No |

Save the form as Startup. (If you save the form with another name, you must change the Display Form property in the Startup dialog box by choosing Startup from the Tools menu of the Database window.) On the Modules tab of the Database Window, create a new module. Then create the following function, which you will use to set the TimerInterval property of the Startup form:

```
Function SetTimer()
' Set the timer for 7 seconds.
    Forms![Startup].TimerInterval = 7000
End Function
```

Next add the following function to the same module to open the Main Switchboard form, and close the Startup form:

```
Function CloseNewStartupForm()
    Reset the TimerInterval property.
    If Forms![Startup].TimerInterval <> 0 Then
        Forms![Startup].TimerInterval = 0
    End If

    ' Close the Startup form, and open the Main Switchboard form.
    DoCmd.OpenForm "Main switchboard"
    DoCmd.Close acForm, "Startup"
End Function
```

Save the module as Close New Startup Form. Next open the Startup form in Design view. Change the On Open event property to =*SetTimer()*, and change the On Timer event property to =*CloseNewStartupForm()* so that the timer will be set when the form is opened and the CloseStartupForm function will be called when the TimerInterval has elapsed.

Close and reopen the database to see how your new Startup form works.

## Setting Startup Properties

To display your startup form when the database is opened, set the Startup properties as shown in Figure 6-10. (Choose Startup from the Tools menu in the Database window to display this dialog box.) In the Display Form box, select Startup. Through the Startup properties dialog box, you can also hide the database window, hide built-in toolbars, create a title for your application, and so on. The Startup options apply only to the current database or application. To make the changes take effect, close and reopen the database.

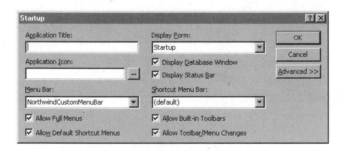

**Figure 6-10.** *Startup properties dialog box.*

> **TIP** Selecting the Advanced button on the Startup dialog box will display the Allow Viewing Code After Error and Use Access Special Keys check boxes.

## Standard Properties

The following properties are displayed in the Startup dialog box.

### Application Title

The Application Title property will change the application title from the default Microsoft Access title to the name of your application. Enter *My Northwind* in the Application Title text box.

NOTE The Application Title property can also be set using VBA code. For more information, search in Microsoft Access Online Help for "Set Startup Properties from Visual Basic."

## Application Icon

This icon will appear when the application is minimized. The default is the Microsoft Access icon.

## Menu Bar

The Menu Bar property contains the name of the custom menu to be used as the default menu when a custom menu is not specified for a form.

TIP To disable a menu for an application or a form, create and save a macro without any actions. Call this macro in your form's Menu Bar property or from the Menu Bar startup property.

## Allow Full Menus

This check box enables or disables the default menus. By unchecking this box, you will disable all menu items that will permit a user to modify the application. The user will be able to modify data in the forms but not the forms themselves.

## Display Form

The Display Form property allows you to select a form that will open automatically when the database is opened.

## Display Database Window

Unchecking the Display Database Window property automatically hides the Database window when the user opens the database. The user does not need to view the list of objects in your database application.

## Display Status Bar

The Display Status Bar property hides or shows the status bar.

## Shortcut Menu Bar

The Shortcut Menu Bar property allows you to specify a custom shortcut menu for the default shortcut menu bar for any form that does not have a custom shortcut menu bar defined.

### Allow Built-In Toolbars

The Allow Built-In Toolbars property hides or shows the default toolbars. Since the user can get to Design mode from the toolbars, it's a good idea to disable them.

### Allow Toolbar/Menu Changes

You can use this property to specify whether your database allows the user to customize the command bars. For example, you can prevent the user from deleting a command bar button or an entire command bar from your application.

### Allow Default Shortcut Menus

You might also want to disable the default shortcut menus. These menus are displayed when you click the right mouse button when the cursor is on an object. You can disable the default shortcut menus by unchecking the Allow Default Shortcut Menus property. Some shortcut menus allow a user to get into design views and modify objects, so it might be a good idea to implement your own shortcut menus and disable the default ones entirely.

## Advanced Properties

After selecting the Advanced button you will see the following two properties: Allow Viewing Code After Error and Use Special Access Keys. With both of these options checked, the user can use the Ctrl+Break key combination to halt the execution of code and view it in the Module window. For the release version of your application, you can prevent this by unchecking both options.

## PREVIEW of the next chapter

In Chapter 7 we will continue to work with forms by implementing features and functionality using VBA. You can do wonders with forms and their controls by adding some code to your application—much more than you can do with macros.

# 7

# Coding with Forms and Reports

All forms and reports in Microsoft Access consist of properties, events, and controls. You can use properties to change the characteristics of an object. For example, you can set the Caption property of a form or toggle its Visible property. Events are actions that occur as a result of user or system intervention. For example, when you click a command button, the Click event is triggered; or when the Interval property of a Timer elapses, the Timer event occurs. Knowing the order in which these events occur is very important when you are writing an application. Controls are the objects on forms and reports with which users interact. For example, the user types his or her name into a text box control. Properties and events of forms, reports, and controls can be used to call functions and procedures.

In chapters 5 and 6 we discussed how to use properties, events, and controls to design forms and make them user-friendly. In this chapter we will focus on how you can use functions with forms, reports, and controls.

## Calling Functions from Forms and Reports

In chapters 2 and 3 you saw how to write functions using modules and then how to call these functions from the Debug window and from other procedures. You can also call functions from a form or report by using event properties, such as On Click and On Open, or any other properties that call macros and functions.

### Using Event Properties to Call Functions

To call any function from an event property in Microsoft Access, you use an expression for the property setting. For example, if you want a function named

CalcIt to run when the user clicks a command button, you type =*CalcIt()* as the setting of the On Click property in the Property sheet for that command button. Figure 7-1 depicts the Property sheet with the On Click property set as =CalcIt().

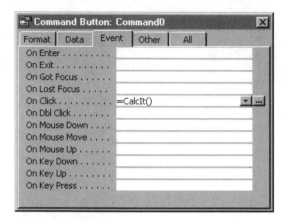

**Figure 7-1.** *Calling a function from an event property.*

You must put an equal sign in front of the function name. This symbol enables Microsoft Access to distinguish the function name from a macro name.

> **NOTE** Because sub procedures cannot return a value, you cannot reference or invoke a sub procedure by assigning a variable to be equal to its result. Therefore, if you try to invoke a sub procedure from a property or even from an event property, Microsoft Access will assume the sub procedure to be a macro name, not a function.

## Using Other Properties to Call Functions

Any property within a form, report, or control can also refer to a function. For this example, create a new form with three text box controls, named txtUnitPrice, txtQuantity, and txtOrderAmount. We want to display the product of the first two text box controls in the third text box. To do this without using a function call, you could place the following expression, which assumes the name of the form is MyForm, in the ControlSource property of the third text box:

```
=Forms!MyForm!txtUnitPrice * Forms!MyForm!txtQuantity
```

This example is a simple calculation that does not really need a function. However, you could place a reference to a function in the ControlSource property of the third text box control, the same way you do in the On Click property of a command button. To change the preceding expression to a function, you could place the following code in a module:

```
Function CalcIt()
    CalcIt = _
        Forms!MyForm!txtUnitPrice * Forms!MyForm!txtQuantity
End Function
```

Using the following syntax in the ControlSource property will have the same effect as the expression we showed you first:

```
=CalcIt()
```

Whenever you place a function in a property of a form, report, or control, the function will return a value. If you do not use the returned value, you should consider calling it from an event property, a topic we discuss in the "Responding to Events" section beginning on page 193.

## Code Behind Forms

When using functions in event properties, if you export the form or report to another database, you must also remember to export the modules you used because Microsoft Access will not do it automatically, unless you use the technique discussed in this section. Also, be sure to test your forms and reports in the new database to make sure you have exported all the necessary modules. To avoid having to worry about whether all the necessary code modules "followed" their forms or reports when exported, you can use *code behind forms,* a process that in effect binds the form and its code together.

Each form and report in a database has a built-in module containing event procedures that respond to events that occur on the form or report. When you write event procedures for a specific event, these procedures are stored in this module. You can create these modules as you are creating your form or report, and they become part of the design of that form or report. For both forms and reports, these modules are referred to as code behind forms. When you export a form or report, the code behind the form or report is exported with it. Code behind forms is the wave of the future, moving Microsoft Access application development a step closer to object-oriented technology. In an object-oriented environment, all objects have code associated with them. This code is encapsulated or hidden from other objects. Wherever an object is used or moved to, the code associated with it goes as well.

You generally use a form or report module to automate tasks specific to that particular form or report. For example, you can use code behind forms to do the following tasks:

- Open another form or report
- Initialize settings in the form or report each time it is opened
- Move to a particular location in the form or report
- Search for a particular record in the record source of the form or report
- Update fields on the form or report
- Perform a calculation and place the result in a control on the form or report
- Verify and control user input

It is simple to open the module for a form or report:

**1.** Select the form or report in the Database window.

**2.** Click the Code button on the toolbar, shown in Figure 7-2.

**Figure 7-2.** *The Code Button on the Form Design view toolbar.*

The module for a form or report looks identical to a module you create from the Database window. However, when using code behind forms you will use the Object and Procedure combo boxes more than you did with standard modules. The Object combo box will list all the form's controls, including the form itself and all its sections. Sections refers to the Detail, Form Header, and Form Footer sections of the form. In the module's General section, you can define variables used by the form's procedures. You cannot define Public constants in code behind forms, only in standard modules. The General section also allows you to define functions that are not event procedures but can be called by more than one event procedure.

Previously, we defined a function called CalcIt that was called by an event property. Let's now convert that function to an event procedure in a form module.

**Standard Modules vs. Code Behind Forms**

Despite the many benefits of using code behind forms, in some situations standard modules are still ideal. In the following cases, you should stick to standard modules rather than use code behind forms:

■ When creating generic code that refers to a form and can be used among other forms and reports

■ When creating utility code, such as that for converting degrees from Fahrenheit to Celsius

■ When using public variables for forms or for other code in standard modules

■ When making calls to the Windows Application Programming Interface (API)

■ When using constants in multiple forms and reports

## Responding to Events

Each form or report module contains predefined event procedures that run in response to events that occur on the form or report. (We cover these events in detail later in the chapter, in the "Form and Report Events" section beginning on page 198.) You can create a custom response to an event by adding Microsoft Visual Basic for Applications code to the event procedure. Rather than placing the name of the function to execute in the On Click property, click the Build button next to the event property (Figure 7-3) to display the Choose Builder dialog box (Figure 7-4).

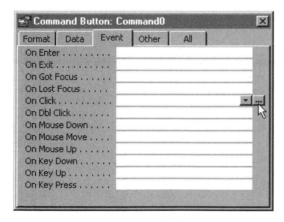

**Figure 7-3.** *The Build button in the Property window.*

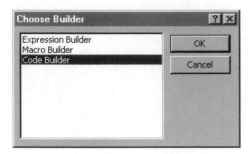

**Figure 7-4.** *The Choose Builder dialog box.*

Select Code Builder, and click OK. The form's Module window opens and displays the appropriate event procedure's Sub and End Sub statements, as shown in Figure 7-5. These statements define the event procedure. Some event procedures, like the KeyPress event, accept arguments in the procedure definition. All arguments that are passed to event procedures are passed by Microsoft Access, not you. However, you can manipulate these arguments' values within an event procedure. You'll see an example of how to do this a little later in the "Form and Report Events" section on page 198.

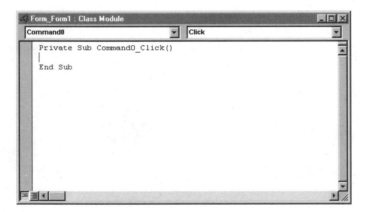

**Figure 7-5.** *The default Click event procedure, which does nothing.*

By default, all event procedures are defined with the Private keyword. A Private procedure can be called only from the form itself or from a procedure in the form module. To call the event procedure from outside the form, change the Private keyword to Public.

In VBA, the name of an event procedure is the name of the control followed by an underscore (_) and the name of the event. This naming convention is typical for VBA programmers, but it does present one major problem: renaming a control after an event procedure has been created. Before you create any event procedures, set the Name property of all your objects. If you change the Name property of an object after you have defined an event procedure, the existing code is moved by Microsoft Access to the General section of the form and a new, empty event procedure with the new name of the control is created. Add a Command button to the form from our previous example, and change its Name property to cmdCalculate and its Caption property to Calculate. Now view the code for the new button.

Since CmdCalculate_Click is an event procedure, which is a sub procedure, no value can be returned. Therefore, you must assign the expression's product equal to the Value property of the txtOrderAmt text box. To do so, place the following code, which is similar to the CalcIt function you previously created, in the Click event procedure:

```
Private Sub CmdCalculate_Click()
    Forms!MyForm!txtOrderAmt = _
        Forms!MyForm!txtUnitPrice * Forms!MyForm!txtQuantity
End Function
```

Now when the form is run, clicking the Calculate button will update the txtOrderAmt text box to reflect the product of txtUnitPrice and txtQuantity. If the form is copied to another database, its module goes with it. If a form or report is deleted, its module is deleted too.

**NOTE** Most of the code presented in this chapter can be found in CHAP07.MDB in the CHAP07 subfolder of the folder in which you installed the companion CD files.

## Class Modules

Code behind forms is also referred to as class modules. Class modules are available by choosing Code from the View menu while viewing a form or report in Design view. Think of a class as a template of an object. A class and an object are closely related, but they do have important differences.

Microsoft Access has three types of class objects that you can create: forms, reports, and user-defined classes. The properties and procedures of forms and reports are considered members of their respective class objects. We will discuss user-defined class modules in the "Creating New Class Modules" section later in this chapter on page 242.

Forms and reports in general are considered to be a base class. A *base class* is a class from which other classes can be created. Any forms or reports that you create are considered subclasses. A *subclass* is a copy of a particular class that has been modified for more specific needs. For example, a new form has certain properties associated with it, but you can modify those properties and add controls or procedures. These changes to the form make that subclass specific to the application's needs.

At this point, you are probably wondering what all this discussion about classes and objects means to you. To help you see how this information relates to your work as a developer, you need to develop an understanding of the scope of class modules.

## Class Module Scope

You have already seen that you can use class modules to create event procedures. You can also use them to design your own properties and methods. All variables that you create in the General Declarations section of a class module with the Public, Private, or Dim keyword become properties of that object. To refer to that property at run time, from outside the class module use the Form keyword followed by an underscore and the name of the form; then add a period and the property name. For example, to refer to the Caption property of a form named Form1, use the following syntax:

```
Form_Form1.Caption = "Hello World!"
```

This syntax is called *predeclared identifiers* and is discussed in detail in the section "Using Predeclared Identifiers" beginning on page 225.

NOTE    Dim has the same scope as Private when used in a class or standard module.

To refer to a user-defined property named intDiscount on a form named Form1, use the following syntax:

```
' In the General Declarations section
Dim intDiscount As Integer

Private Sub cmdDiscount_Click()
    Form_Form1.intDiscount = Form_Form1!txtNewValue
End Sub
```

The example above demonstrates how you might define your own property of the form and set its value at run time to the value of a text box on the form.

If you don't specify the Private keyword, any procedure created in a class module is Public. A Public procedure is available to other class modules as well as to standard modules. A standard module is a module that exists under the

Modules tab of the Database window. Having Public scope allows class module procedures to be accessed from outside a particular form or report. The Public keyword can be used but is not necessary. These Public procedures are considered methods of the object. Using the property we created above, we can make the SetDiscount procedure a Public method of the form that can be called from anywhere. The following code demonstrates how to define a method of the form that accepts an argument:

```
' In the General Declarations section
Dim intDiscount As Integer   ' Private property of form

Public Sub SetDiscount(NewValue As Integer)
    Form_Form1.intDiscount = NewValue
End Sub
```

To call the SetDiscount method, you can use the following syntax:

```
Form_Form1.SetDiscount(10)
```

Here a value of 10 is passed to the SetDiscount method and subsequently assigned to the Private property intDiscount.

**NOTE**  If you declare the above intDiscount variable as Public, you can refer to it outside the form or report with the following syntax:

```
Form_Form1.intDiscount = 10
```

If the Form is not open, it will be opened automatically and hidden. We will discuss opening and hiding forms in the "Multiple Instances of Forms" section beginning on page 232.

Private procedures in class modules can be called only by other procedures attached to that form or class. To declare a procedure as Private, you must use the Private keyword. To declare a procedure as Public, you can use the Public keyword or remove the Private keyword (if one exists) in the first line of the procedure.

The following table lists the default scopes for the different elements you can define in standard and class modules when you do not supply a keyword such as Public, Private, or Dim. Recall that the Dim keyword and Const keyword cause variables and constants to have Private scope when used in a class or standard module.

**PROCEDURE, VARIABLE, AND CONSTANT SCOPE DEFAULTS**

| Coding Element | Default Scope If Scope Is Not Explicitly Declared | Allowed Scope |
|---|---|---|
| Functions and sub procedures in a standard module | Public | Public, Private |
| Functions and sub procedures in a class module | Public | Public, Private |
| Event procedures | Public, but Microsoft Access explicitly adds the Private keyword by default | Private, Public |
| Variables defined in General Declarations section of a standard module | Not applicable—Must use a declaration keyword | Public, Private |
| Variables defined in General Declarations section of a class module | Not applicable—Must use a declaration keyword | Public, Private |
| Constants defined in General Declarations section of a standard module | Private | Private, Public |
| Constants defined in General Declarations section of a class module | Private | Private only |

Even though procedures and constants have default scopes, we suggest that you always use the Public and Private keywords when creating methods. Doing this will make debugging and maintaining your code much easier.

## Form and Report Events

Events in Microsoft Access allow you to create a true Microsoft Windows-style application. Without events, the developer controls the flow of the application. Using events, the user chooses which part of the application will be executed. Both forms and reports can respond to numerous events. In this section we will concentrate on the most commonly used form and report events and their practical uses.

**TIP** The ShowEvents form in the Orders sample database displays the order in which all the different events occur. Use this form, as well as Help, to determine the correct order of events. The Orders sample database can be installed as an option when you set up Microsoft Access.

## Form Events

The order in which form events are discussed in this chapter is the order in which the events occur when a user opens and closes a form.

### Open

The Open event for a form occurs after the underlying query for the form is executed but before the first record is displayed. When creating an event procedure for the Open event, you will notice that only one argument is defined for this procedure: Cancel. The Cancel argument is set to False by default, but you can set it to True within the Open procedure if you want to prevent the form from opening. For example, a form that includes the following code will not open unless the form named Main Form is currently open in Form view:

```
Private Sub Form_Open(Cancel As Integer)
    Const conObjStateClosed = 0
    Const conDesignView = 0
    ' Check if Main Form is open.
    If SysCmd(acSysCmdGetObjectState, acForm, "Main Form") <> _
        conObjStateClosed Then
        ' Check if Main Form is in Design View.
        If Forms("Main Form").CurrentView = conDesignView Then
            ' Close if Main Form is in Design View.
            Cancel = True
        End If
    Else
        Cancel = True  ' Close if Main Form is not open.
    End If
End Sub
```

### Load

The Load event occurs when the form is opened and its records are displayed. Unlike the Open event, the Load event cannot be canceled. You can use your Load event procedure to initialize properties of the form and the controls within it before the user sees the form open.

### Activate

The Activate event occurs when the form receives the focus. If your application has more than one form open simultaneously, the Activate event can be used to display the toolbar appropriate for the form that currently has the focus. The following example uses the constant acToolbarYes to show the toolbar:

```
Private Sub Form_Activate()
    DoCmd.ShowToolbar "Toolbar1", acToolbarYes
End Sub
```

This Sub procedure will make the toolbar named Toolbar1 visible when the form receives the focus. You can hide the toolbar in your Deactivate event procedure.

### Current

The Current event occurs when a record receives the focus or when the underlying record source is requeried. Because this event occurs when the record receives the focus, it is triggered both when you move from record to record and when the form is opened. Placing code in the Current event procedure allows you to synchronize forms or perform calculations on the current record. For example, you could use the following event procedure in the Customers form to synchronize the Orders form and the Customers form in the Northwind Traders database:

```
Private Sub Form_Current()
    ' Current event of the Customers form
    Forms![Orders].FilterOn = True
    ' When setting the Filter property, specify the field
    ' you want to reset on the left side of the equation
    ' and specify the field with which it is to be synchronized on the
    ' right side of the equation.
    Forms![Orders].Filter = _
        "CustomerID = Forms!Customers!CustomerID"
End Sub
```

The above example will work only if the Orders form is open. If the Orders form is not open, an error will occur. You could use the IsLoaded function, which comes with the Northwind database (it is not a built-in function), to verify whether the Orders form is open and running. The IsLoaded function accepts one argument, the form name you are checking. The Current event procedure would look like the following code if the IsLoaded function is used:

```
Private Sub Form_Current()
    ' Current event of the Customers form
    If IsLoaded("Orders") Then
        ' If the form is open, set its Filter Property.
        Forms![Orders].FilterOn = True
        ' When setting the Filter property, specify the field
        ' you want to reset on the left side of the equation
        ' and specify the field with which it is to be synchronized
        ' on the right side of the equation.
        Forms![Orders].Filter = _
            "CustomerID = Forms!Customers!CustomerID"
    End If
End Sub
```

## Unload

The Unload event occurs when the form is being closed but before it is removed from the screen. Use your Unload event procedure to create a prompt that asks the user whether he or she wants to close the form or perform some additional task, such as writing to a table to keep a log. The Unload event occurs before the close event and can be canceled. The following example creates a prompt that asks whether the user wants to exit the application:

```
Private Sub Form_Unload(Cancel As Integer)
    Dim intResponse As Integer

    intResponse = MsgBox("Are you sure you want to exit?", _
        vbYesNo)
    ' If Yes was clicked, exit normally.
    ' If No was clicked, cancel the Unload event.
    If intResponse = vbNo Then
        Cancel = True
    End If
End Sub
```

## Deactivate

The Deactivate event occurs when the form loses the focus. If your application has more than one form open at a time, you can use your Deactivate event procedure to hide a toolbar that is appropriate only for the form losing the focus. The following example will hide the toolbar named Toolbar1 when the form loses the focus:

```
Private Sub Form_Deactivate()
    DoCmd.ShowToolbar "Toolbar1", acToolbarNo
End Sub
```

## Close

The Close event occurs as the last event of a form but before the form is removed from the screen. This event is often used to open other forms in an application. When you are running an application that displays only one form at a time, the Close event should open the next form you want the user to use. For example, when the user closes the Customers form, you could have the Main Switchboard form appear. The Close event procedure for the Customers form might look like the following:

```
Private Sub Form_Close()
    DoCmd.OpenForm "Main Switchboard"
End Sub
```

TIP Rather than opening the Main Switchboard form, you can increase your application's performance simply by toggling its Visible property. By doing so, the Main Switchboard form does not have to be loaded each time you close any other form, and consequently, the user does not have to wait for the Main Switchboard form to load.

## Report Events

Unlike the previous section on Form events, the following Report events are not listed in order of occurrence.

### Close

The Close event of a report occurs when the report's Preview view is being closed or when the report has finished printing. The Close event procedure is useful if you want to redisplay the form that called the report or if you want to return to the main form of the application, as shown here:

```
Private Sub Form_Close()
    ' Assumes the Main Switchboard form is loaded.
    [Form_Main Switchboard].Visible = True
End Sub
```

### NoData

The NoData event occurs only on reports that are bound, that is, reports whose RecordSource property is not blank. If no records are in the report's record source, the NoData event is triggered. You should use your NoData event procedure to cancel printing or previewing of the report if there is no data, as can be done by setting the Cancel argument to True:

```
Private Sub Report_NoData(Cancel As Integer)
    Cancel = True
End Sub
```

### Page

The Page event occurs after a page has been formatted but before it has been printed. This event allows you to add graphics to the report at run time by drawing a border or different color around the report. The following line of code could be added to the Employee Sales By Country report from the Northwind database to produce a blue border:

```
Private Sub Report_Page()
    Me.Line (0, 0) - _
        (Me.LogicalPageWidth, Me.LogicalPageHeight), _
        RGB(0, 0, 255), B
End Sub
```

The Employee Sales By Country report prompts you with two arguments: Beginning Date and Ending Date. Enter *1/1/95* for the Beginning Date and *9/1/95* for the Ending Date to see the blue border.

The preceding example uses the Me keyword, which we will describe in detail later in this chapter. For now, it is important to know that you use the Me keyword in a class module instead of the name of the report when referring to the module's associated form or report. The Me keyword always refers to the form or report that is running the code.

# Working with Forms

As you have surely noticed, the Microsoft Access Forms Designer (Design view of a form) does not provide all the capabilities you will need for all the forms you design. Microsoft Access does, however, allow you to modify your forms and controls at run time, which means that you can add the following functionality:

- Guiding the user's actions (for example, disabling a button until all text boxes contain at least one character)

- Running a calculation on the fly and writing the result to a text box

- Hiding unnecessary controls until needed

- Trapping for errors in user input

Being able to modify these objects at run time gives you the flexibility and control necessary to create a true Windows 95 application. In the next section we will explore how to code these modifications.

## Using the Forms Collection and the Reports Collection

Just what is a collection? A *collection* is a group of objects of the same type. For example, an automobiles collection could contain a Corvette object and a Ferrari object but not a Horse object. The same logic goes for forms and reports. The Forms collection contains only opened forms, the Reports collection only opened reports.

Even though forms and reports are similar, they are not the same kind of object, and you must therefore refer to them in separate collections. Many different collections are available when you are programming in Microsoft Access, and all collections have one property in common: Count. The Count property displays the total number of objects contained within a particular collection. All collections are zero-based, so be careful if you use a For...Next loop to enumerate all the objects in a collection. The following example shows two ways to step through all the forms in the Forms collection and print the name of the form to the Debug window:

```
Sub ListForms()
    Dim intCount As Integer, frmCurrentForm As Form
    For intCount = 0 To Forms.Count - 1
        Debug.Print Forms(intCount).Name
    Next
    ' Do the same thing using a For...Each loop.
    For Each frmCurrentForm In Forms
        Debug.Print frmCurrentForm.Name
    Next
End Sub
```

These collections can be used to enumerate the objects contained in them or to refer to a specific form or report contained within them. Earlier in this chapter we used the sample function IsLoaded, which is included in the Northwind Traders sample database, to determine if a particular form was currently open. This function checks the CurrentView property of a form in the Forms collection. The IsLoaded function follows:

```
Function IsLoaded(ByVal strFormName As String) As Boolean
    ' Returns True if the specified form is open in Form view
    ' or Datasheet view.

    Const conObjStateClosed = 0
    Const conDesignView = 0

    If SysCmd(acSysCmdGetObjectState, acForm, strFormName) <> _
        conObjStateClosed Then
        ' Check current view of the form.
        If Forms(strFormName).CurrentView <> conDesignView Then
            IsLoaded = True
        End If
    End If
End Function
```

You use the SysCmd function to see if the form is open; you could also enumerate the Forms collection. Once you determine that the form is open, you need to find out whether it is in Design view or Form view. Because the name of the form is not known when the function is created, you cannot use a predeclared identifier. Instead, you must use the Forms collection so that the name of the form can be identified at run time.

When using the Forms or Reports collection, you can specify either the name or the ordinal position of the object in the collection. Whenever a form is opened, it is added to the Forms collection. The first form has the ordinal position of zero, the second has the ordinal position of one, the third the ordinal position of two, and so on. The ordinal numbers should be used only when enumerating all the forms in the collection via a For...Next loop because the ordinal numbers of the objects are dynamic. When a form in the collection is closed, it is removed from the Forms collection and the remaining forms are renumbered starting at zero. For example, suppose the database has three forms. The three forms are opened in the following order: FormA, FormB, FormC. The ordinal positions of these forms are FormA—0, FormB—1, FormC—2. If FormA is closed, the ordinal positions of the remaining forms change. Now the forms' ordinal numbers are FormB—0, FormC—1. You can see why you shouldn't refer to the ordinal position unless you are using a loop. For your loop you can use the collection's Count property to determine the number of objects currently opened, as shown in the code snippet ListForms on page 204.

You can also refer to a form or report by name in the collection, as shown here:

```
Debug.Print Forms("Customers").Caption
```

This method was used in the IsLoaded example shown earlier. In that example, the name of the form was passed as an argument to the function rather than hard-coded. Thus, you can refer to any object, by its name, in the collection at run time. In the next section we discuss form and report properties and how you should refer to them.

# Setting Properties on Forms and Reports

You can use properties in Microsoft Access to modify the design and run-time appearance of objects within your application. These properties define the application's appearance and user interface. We won't cover all the many properties available for forms and reports but will instead focus on the most commonly used ones.

## Commonly Used Form Properties

### ActiveControl

The ActiveControl property of the form determines which control currently has the focus.

> **NOTE** The ActiveControl property is available by using a macro or VBA. It is not a property that can be set on a form's property sheet.

### AllowEdits, AllowDeletions, AllowAdditions

These properties determine whether a user is allowed to edit, delete, or add records in a form.

## Cycle

The Cycle property specifies what will happen when the user presses the Tab key in the last control on a bound form. You can set this property to go to the next record, which is the default behavior, or go back to the first control in the tab order for the current record. If the form is subdivided using page-break controls, you can set the Cycle property to force the cursor to go back to the first control in the tab order on the current page.

## Filter

The Filter property allows you to enter criteria that limit (filter) the form's underlying record source to display specific information.

## KeyPreview

Forms have a KeyPreview property that determines whether the form receives the keyboard events before any controls receive the keyboard events. If the KeyPreview property is No, the form does not receive the keyboard events. If KeyPreview is Yes, the form receives each keyboard event before the event is sent to the form's active control. For example, if you want to make your application end when the user presses Shift-Alt-F2 regardless of which control has the focus, you set KeyPreview to Yes and trap for the keys in the KeyDown event. You can also use the KeyPreview property to provide visual cues to the user about which commands are appropriate. For example, if you require the user to fill in all fields before clicking an OK button, you should disable the OK button until the data has been entered in all the fields, as shown in Figure 7-6.

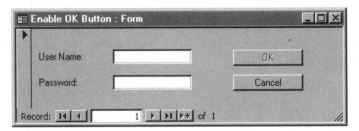

**Figure 7-6.** *Disabling the OK button.*

Assuming this scenario, you could create a form that looks like the dialog box in Figure 7-6 and use the code below to enable the OK button when text has been entered in both text boxes. When there is at least one character in each text box, the OK button is enabled by the code below. Because the KeyPress property of this form is set to True, the form's KeyUp event will be trapped.

```
Private Sub Form_Open(Cancel As Integer)
    ' Disable the OK button when the form is opened.
    Me.cmdOK.Enabled = False
End Sub
```

```
Private Sub Form_KeyUp(KeyCode As Integer, Shift As Integer)
    ' Enable the OK button only if all text boxes
    ' have entries. You must execute different code depending
    ' on which text box is active because the Value property
    ' is not updated until the control loses the focus.
    Select Case Me.ActiveControl.Name
        Case "txtUserName":
            If Me.ActiveControl.Text = "" Or _
                IsNull(Me.ActiveControl.Text) Or _
                Me.txtPassword.Value = "" Or _
                IsNull(Me.txtPassword.Value) Then
                ' at least one text box is empty
                cmdOK.Enabled = False      ' disable OK button.
                Exit Sub
            End If
        Case "txtPassword":
            If Me.ActiveControl.Text = "" Or _
                IsNull(Me.ActiveControl.Text) Or _
                Me.txtUserName.Value = "" Or _
                IsNull(Me.txtUserName.Value) Then
                ' at least one text box is empty
                cmdOK.Enabled = False      ' disable OK button.
                Exit Sub
            End If
        Case Else:      ' on different control than text box.
            Exit Sub
    End Select
    ' Both text boxes have information in them.
    cmdOK.Enabled = True
    Exit Sub
End Sub
```

> **NOTE**   Typically, you do not want anyone to see the password you are entering on the screen, so you can set the InputMask property of the text box to Password. This property will place an asterisk in the text box for each character typed in.

### Picture

The Picture property allows you to specify a picture to display as the background of a form. The picture will take up the whole form. The effect is similar to the watermark on expensive paper. Try setting this picture to any of the bitmap files that come with Microsoft Windows 95 or the Microsoft Windows 95 Plus! Pack to create a cool form.

### ShortcutMenuBar

This property specifies the custom shortcut menu to be displayed when you click the right mouse button on a form or control. Remember, the custom shortcut menu should contain only the most common tasks used, and it should not be the only method the user can use to initiate events or choose menu items in your application.

## Commonly Used Report Properties

### HasData

Use the HasData property to determine whether a report is bound to an empty recordset. The HasData property is available only in macros and VBA, not in the user interface. Three values are possible:

| HasData Property Value | Description |
| --- | --- |
| −1 | Bound report with records |
| 0 | Bound report with no records |
| 1 | Unbound report |

### GrpKeepTogether

Use this property to specify whether the groups that have their KeepTogether property set to Whole Group or With First Detail will be kept together by page or by column. For example, if you printed a list of employees by department in a multicolumn format, you could use this property to keep all members of the same department in the same column. This property has two settings: Per Page and Per Column.

### WillContinue

This property determines when a section will continue on the next page. It is another property that is not on the property sheet; it can be used only in macros and VBA.

### Filter

The Filter property allows you to enter criteria that limit (filter) the report's underlying record source to display specific information, as in this example:

```
Me.Filter = "[Region] = 'WA'"
```

### FilterOn

This property determines whether the report's record source is being filtered. You can set it to either Yes or No.

### RepeatSection

Use this property to specify whether a group header is repeated on the next column or page when a group spans more than one column or page. When printing a report that contains a subreport, the subreport's RepeatSection property will determine if the subreport group headers are repeated across columns or pages.

# Creating Generic Code for Forms and Reports

Your form and report names are often lengthy, and it is tedious to keep typing the names over and over again. When using a form or report module, there is a way of referring to the associated form or report from within the code. You can refer to a form or report generically in several ways:

■ Screen.ActiveForm or Screen.ActiveReport

■ Me

■ CodeContextObject

■ Variables representing form/report names and objects

## Screen.ActiveForm and Screen.ActiveReport

Screen.ActiveForm and Screen.ActiveReport refer to the form or report, respectively, that currently has the focus. These objects can be used only when a form or report is active. If no form or report is active, a run-time error will occur. For example, you can use the following function to change the Caption property of the active form to the current date and time using the Now function:

```
Function ChangeCaption()
    Screen.ActiveForm.Caption = Now
End Function
```

## Me

In a class module in VBA, a variable named Me points to the associated form or report. Me always refers to the object in which the code is running. For example, suppose two forms are currently running: Form1 and Form2. Form1 has a timer control. Form2 currently has the focus, but the Interval property of the timer control in Form1 has just elapsed. If the Timer event procedure in Form1 uses the Me keyword, it will refer to Form1 (even though Form1 does not have the focus) because Form1 is the object in which the code is running. The Me keyword can be used only in class modules.

## CodeContextObject

The CodeContextObject has the same functionality as the Me keyword except that it can be used in a class module or a standard module. Functions using the CodeContextObject can be called only from a form or report object. For example, a form or report can call the following function in a class or standard module:

```
Function ChangeCaption()
    CodeContextObject.Caption = "My Caption"
    CodeContextObject.Visible = True
End Function
```

The form or report that called this procedure will have the Caption and Visible properties set. The advantage the CodeContextObject has over the Me keyword is that it can be used in standard modules.

## Variable Names

One reason to use standard modules is to create reusable code. Using the references listed above, you can refer to form and report objects. You can also create your own object variables to represent forms and reports by declaring variables within your functions to be of type Form or Report, as in the following example:

```
Dim frmMyForm As Form
Dim rptMyReport As Report
```

You can also define a variable to represent a specific form or report by using the following declarations:

```
Dim frmMyForm As Form_Customers
Dim rptMyReport As Report_Report1
```

> **NOTE**  Notice that Form_ or Report_ must be used prior to the name of the form or report when you are defining the object variable. You must do this because forms and reports share the same name space. For example, both a form and a report can be named "Employees." Also note that you must enclose the type specifier in brackets if the form or report name includes any spaces.

Once a variable is declared, it can be initialized. Because a form or report is an object, you must initialize the object variable using the Set statement. The following code demonstrates how to initialize an object variable to represent a form, assuming the form is already opened:

```
Function ChangeCaption()
    Dim frmMyForm As Form
    Set frmMyForm = Forms("Customers")
End Function
```

You can now use the form variable, frmMyForm, to manipulate the Customers form properties or call any methods of the Customers form. For example, to change the Caption property of the form, you could do the following:

```
Function ChangeCaption()
    Dim frmMyForm As Form
    Set frmMyForm = Forms("Customers")
    frmMyForm.Caption = "Hello World!"
End Function
```

This method works great as long as you only want to modify the Caption property of one particular form. But what do you do if you do not know which form you want to manipulate when you are designing the procedure? Use the CodeContextObject or Me. If you use the CodeContextObject or Me, you do not need to declare a form variable because the keywords refer to a specific object at run time. The preceding example can be converted to use the CodeContextObject:

```
Function ChangeCaption()
    CodeContextObject.Caption = "Hello World!"
End Function
```

Regardless of the form or report that calls the function, its Caption property will be changed to "Hello World!"

# Programming with Controls

Up to this point, we have discussed only the properties and events of forms and reports. In this section you will see how to use properties and events of controls.

---

### Bound and Unbound Controls

Before jumping into a discussion of how to manipulate controls, let's discuss the difference between bound and unbound controls. A *bound control* is a control that is associated with a field in a table or query using the ControlSource property. You can use bound controls to enter, display, and update the values stored in your table's fields. These values can be text, dates, numbers, Yes/No values, pictures, graphs, or other OLE objects. Perhaps the most common type of bound control is the text box.

An *unbound control* does not directly affect fields stored in a table. Therefore, the ControlSource property does not directly refer to a field from the record source of the form or report. You can use unbound controls to display information, pictures, lines, or rectangles. The most common type of unbound control is a label.

Microsoft Access comes with several standard controls. Many of them are self-discoverable and easy to understand, so we won't include an exhaustive list of them here. The only control we'll examine in detail is the List Box, one of the more difficult to work with, at least at first. We'll also discuss how you can use and manipulate list boxes at run time.

---

## List Boxes

You might want to display a list of preset choices the user can select from. A list box is ideal for this purpose. It also reduces data entry errors because the user does not type information into a field but just selects it instead. List boxes can have many different properties. Let's look at the properties that must be set to display and retrieve information from a list box.

### ControlSource property

A list box can be either bound or unbound, and because of this it has a ControlSource property. If you want the information the user selects to be written back to a table or query (the form's record source), set the ControlSource property to the name of a field. The information displayed in the list box is determined by two properties: RowSourceType and RowSource.

### RowSourceType and RowSource properties

The RowSourceType property determines the type of information that will be displayed in a list box and works in conjunction with the RowSource property. You can set the RowSourceType property to one of three values:

- Table/Query
- Value List
- Field List

The default, Table/Query, allows you to specify any table, query, or SQL statement in the RowSource property. Setting the RowSourceType property to Value List allows you to put a comma delimited list of items in the RowSource property. A setting of Field List allows you to specify any table, query, or SQL statement in the RowSource property, but only the field names from that item will appear in the list box. Remember that the RowSourceType and RowSource properties allow you to specify both the type of information and the data to display in the list box.

### ColumnCount, ColumnWidths, and BoundColumn properties

When using a list box, you are typically going to present the user only with meaningful information, such as the Company Name but not the Customer ID. To limit the information you show to the user, you will want to use the ColumnCount, ColumnWidths, and BoundColumn properties of the list box. ColumnCount allows you to specify the number of columns to display. The ColumnWidths property allows you to specify the width of each column. For multiple columns, you separate the ColumnWidths values with a semicolon.

You could set the following properties for a list box to display only the Company Name by setting the width for the CustomerID column to 0":

| Property | Setting |
|----------|---------|
| RowSourceType | Table/Query |
| RowSource | Customers |
| ColumnCount | 2 |
| ColumnWidths | 0";1" |
| BoundColumn | 1 |

When the form is executed, the list box looks like Figure 7-7, which shows only the Company Name column.

By setting the width of the first column to zero, we are in effect hiding that column. Although the column is not visible, it can still be referred to. The BoundColumn property specifies the column that will be written back to whatever item was specified in the ControlSource property. In Figure 7-7, CustomerID was specified as the BoundColumn and will be written back to the control source. If the control source is empty, the Value property of the list box can be referenced to find out which CustomerID was selected. This example demonstrates how you might show the user meaningful information when in fact you might be hiding but storing values from an Autonumber column.

**Figure 7-7.** *The Sample Customers list box.*

## Combo Boxes

List boxes and combo boxes have the same data properties that can be set to display data. Therefore, you can apply everything we have just discussed about list boxes to combo boxes.

The advantages of using a combo box over a list box are that the combo box takes up less room on a form or report and the user can enter information not in the preset list.

## Column property

The Column property has two arguments: column and row, respectively. The column and row arguments are zero-based. You can use this property to return the value of a column of any row in a list box or combo box, regardless of whether or not the item is selected. If you do not use the row argument, the Column property will assume the row argument to be the selected row. The ItemData method can also return values whether or not the item is selected, just by supplying a row number.

## MultiSelect property

Microsoft Access allows you to create three different types of list boxes. To specify which type you want, set the MultiSelect property of the list box to one of three values: None, Simple, or Extended. By default, the value will be set to None, thus allowing the user to select only one item. In many situations this restriction is appropriate. However, in some cases the user will need to be able to select more than one item in a list box. Simple multiselection allows the user to move up and down the list box and either press the Spacebar or click an item to toggle its selection state. With an Extended multiselection list box, the user must use the Shift key and click on the first and last items to extend the selection or use the Ctrl key and click for noncontiguous selections. A single mouse click with an Extended multiselection list box will reset the selection to the one item that was clicked.

You can retrieve the data that is selected in a list box using the following property, collection, or method:

- Selected property

- ItemsSelected collection

- ItemData method

**Selected property**    The Selected property allows you to check whether a particular row in the list box is currently selected. If True is returned, the row is selected. When using this property, you must specify the index or row you are referring to in the list box. The index number will always begin with zero. To refer to the fifth row in the list box, you could use the following syntax in the Click event procedure of the list box:

```
Private Sub lstCustomers_Click()
    Debug.Print Me.lstCustomers.Selected(4)
End Sub
```

**ItemsSelected collection**    ItemsSelected is a collection contained in the list box object. This collection contains integer indexes that refer to the selected rows in the list box. This collection supports one property, Count, which specifies the total number of items selected in the list box. You can use a For...Each or For...Next loop to enumerate the items selected. This collection is typically used in conjunction with the ItemData method.

**ItemData method** The ItemData method returns the data in the BoundColumn for the specified row in a list box. Using the same list box we have discussed in this section, set the MultiSelect property to Simple. You'll now be able to select multiple rows in the list box, as shown in Figure 7-8, and print information about the selected items using the ItemsSelected collection.

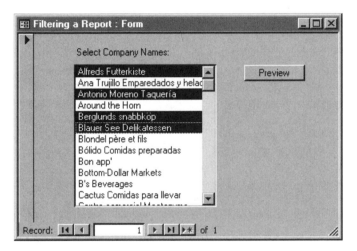

**Figure 7-8.** *The Sample MultiSelect list box.*

The following code could be placed in the Click event of a command button on the form to print the selected items:

```
Private Sub cmdPrintItems_Click()
    Dim intCount As Integer, iCurrentItem As Integer
    For intCount = 0 To Me.lstCustomers.ItemsSelected.Count - 1
        iCurrentItem = Me.lstCustomers.ItemsSelected(intCount)
        ' Print the contents of the first column in the list
        ' box.
        Debug.Print "Company Name: "; _
            Me.lstCustomers.Column(1, iCurrentItem)
        Debug.Print "ItemData: "; _
            Me.lstCustomers.ItemData(iCurrentItem)
    Next
End Sub
```

When the command button is clicked, the companies selected in the list box are printed in the Debug window, as shown here:

```
Company Name: Alfreds Futterkiste
ItemData: ALFKI
Company Name: Antonio Moreno Taquería
ItemData: ANTON
Company Name: Berglunds snabbköp
ItemData: BERGS
Company Name: Blauer See Delikatessen
ItemData: BLAUS
```

The code example above also demonstrates how to use the ItemData method as well as how to retrieve the value from any column in the list box by using the Column property.

> **NOTE**  Column, ItemData, and ListIndex (which returns the total number of rows) apply to combo boxes as well as to list boxes.

## Using a MultiSelect List Box to Filter a Report

Users often don't want to see all the records in a report or form at run time. This preference can cause you headaches when you are designing applications. Microsoft Access heads off these potential migraines by providing a Filter property for forms and reports. You can set the Filter property to an expression, field name, and criteria, thus limiting the total number of records. A MultiSelect list box is a great way to make your application user-friendly when it comes to limiting the data displayed on a form or report.

Suppose you have a report based on a Customers table, which includes all the customers your company does business with. The user might want to see information pertaining only to certain customers. You could create a form that allows the user to select multiple customers from a list box and then print a report with only those customers. To do this, you could create a new (unbound) form and add a list box and a command button to the form. (This example uses the Customers table and the Customer Labels report from the Northwind Traders database.) Set the following properties of the list box:

| Property | Value |
| --- | --- |
| Name | lstCompany |
| RowSource | Customers |
| ColumnCount | 2 |
| ColumnWidths | 0"; 1.5" |
| MultiSelect | Simple |

Setting these properties will display all the customers from the Customers table and allow the user to select multiple entries from the list box. A report based on the Customers table is already included in the Northwind Traders database (Customer Labels), but you do not know what customers your user will want to view at run time. To allow for this unknown factor, add the following code to the Click event procedure of the command button on the new form:

```
Private Sub cmdPreview_Click()
    Dim vntItem As Variant, strFilter As String
    Dim rptMyReport As New [Report_Customers Report]

    For Each vntItem In Me!lstCompany.ItemsSelected
        ' Concatenate single quotes around the customer ID
        ' because the CustomerID field is Text.
        strFilter = strFilter & "[CustomerID] = '" & _
            Me![lstCompany].ItemData(vntItem) & "' OR "
    Next
    ' Remove the OR string from the end of the filter
    ' condition if a filter exists.
    If strFilter <> "" Then
        strFilter = Left(strFilter, Len(strFilter) - 4)
        ' Preview the report using the filter string.
        DoCmd.OpenReport rptMyReport.Name, acPreview, , strFilter
    Else
        MsgBox "No data has been selected!", vbOKOnly
    End If
End Sub
```

When the form is opened and a few customers are selected from the list box, you can click the command button. This automatically opens the Customer Labels report in Print Preview mode and sets its Filter property to limit the number of records. Voila! You've created a great way for the user to view only the records he or she selects.

### Filling a List Box or Combo Box

It is possible to fill a list box or a combo box using a VBA function that you create in Microsoft Access. You might choose to fill a list box if the values you are looking for are not stored in a database, if you are making a calculation, or if your values are constantly changing.

You create the list box or combo box in the same way as before, with one exception. In the RowSourceType property, you would normally select Table/Query, Value List, or Field List; but in this case you type in the name of the function. You do not put an equal sign before the function name or parentheses after it. The RowSource property of the list box should be left empty. Leaving it blank informs Microsoft Access that you want to fill the list box or combo box using a VBA function.

**Creating a function to fill a list box**  When creating a function to fill a list box, you must follow specific guidelines. The first rule is to make sure you are creating a function and not a sub procedure, since values must be returned. The second rule is that the function must accept five arguments: a control variable and four variants. These arguments can be named according to what they represent. The arguments must appear in this order:

```
Function FillList (ctlCurControl As Control, vntID, vntRow, _
    vntCol, vntCode)
```

The first parameter, ctlCurControl, represents the list box to be filled. The second parameter, vntID, is a unique value that identifies the control being filled. The third and fourth parameters represent the row and column being filled, respectively. Remember that the rows and columns in a list box and combo box are always zero-based. The last argument, vntCode, specifies what type of information is being requested. We will talk more about this argument in just a moment.

When you are using a function to fill a list box, the function will be called several times. As a result, you must have some way to save the information or data each time the function is called. There are two ways to do this: with global or with static variables. We will use static variables in our example because the contents of the variables will not be referenced outside the function filling the list box. When Microsoft Access calls this function, each call that is made can request different information from the function. The way to distinguish what information is being requested is to check the value of the vntCode argument. This argument might have a value of 0 through 9, of which two values are for Microsoft Access internal use only. Rather than using multiple If...Then...Else statements in the function, it is easier to use a Select...Case statement in which the value of the vntCode argument is compared to Microsoft Access constants. The constants in the following table can be used when filling a list box.

### CONSTANTS FOR FILLING A LIST BOX

| Code Value | Constant |
| --- | --- |
| 0 | acLBInitialize |
| 1 | acLBOpen |
| 3 | acLBGetRowCount |
| 4 | acLBGetColumnCount |
| 5 | acLBGetColumnWidth |
| 6 | acLBGetValue |
| 7 | acLBGetFormat |
| 9 | acLBEnd |

No constants were created for the values of 2 and 8 because these values are used by Microsoft Access only. The number of times your function is called for each code varies. For codes 0, 1, 3, and 4, Microsoft Access calls the function once. A vntCode value of 5 is called twice, once to set the total width of the list box and once to set the column width. The number of times values of 6 and 7 are called depends on the number of entries in the list box and if the user is scrolling in the list. Microsoft Access passes a value of 9 for the vntCode argument when the form is closed or each time the list box is requeried.

Now that you know what the different vntCode values represent, let's look at a function that will display all the files from the root folder of the hard drive in a list box:

```
Public Function FillListbox(ctlCurControl As Control, vntID, _
    vntRow, vntCol, vntCode)
    ' This function is used in the RowSourceType property
    ' for the unbound list box. It will display the names of
    ' all files in the root folder of the hard drive.
    Static aMyArray() As String, intArrayItems As Integer
    Dim vntReturnVal As Variant
    vntReturnVal = Null

    Select Case vntCode
        Case acLBInitialize
            ' Case 0: initializes the function. Lets the
            ' function know how many elements will be in the
            ' list box. It also initializes the array that
            ' holds the elements.
            intArrayItems = 0
            ChDrive "C" ' Set current drive to C.
            ChDir "C:\" ' Set current folder to root.
            ' Lower bound is 0, so the following means 1 item.
            ReDim aMyArray(0)
            aMyArray(intArrayItems) = Dir("*.*")
            Do Until aMyArray(intArrayItems) = ""
                intArrayItems = intArrayItems + 1
                ReDim Preserve aMyArray(intArrayItems)
                aMyArray(intArrayItems) = Dir
            Loop
            vntReturnVal = intArrayItems

        Case acLBOpen
            ' Case 1: Open. Provides a unique number for the
            ' function. In most cases just use the following
            ' code.
            vntReturnVal = Timer
```

*(continued)*

```
        Case acLBGetRowCount
            ' Case 3: Number of Rows. Lets the function know
            ' how many rows are going to be in the list (can
            ' be zero). Use -1 if number is unknown.
            ' Use intArrayItems here because it is defined as
            ' Static and contains the number of files in the
            ' folder.
            vntReturnVal = intArrayItems

        Case acLBGetColumnCount
            ' Case 4: Number of Columns. (CANNOT be zero.)
            ' Should match value in property sheet. Can use -1
            ' to tell function to use the ColumnCount property
            ' from the control.
            vntReturnVal = -1

        Case acLBGetColumnWidth
            ' Case 5: Column Width. Width of the column is
            ' expressed in twips specified by the vntCol
            ' argument. Use -1 for default widths.
            vntReturnVal = -1

        Case acLBGetValue
            ' Case 6: List Entry. Gives element to be displayed
            ' in the row and column specified by the vntRow
            ' and vntCol arguments.
            vntReturnVal = aMyArray(vntRow)

        Case acLBEnd
            ' Case 9: This is the last call to the function.
            ' Always include this case. This is a good place
            ' for any cleanup code.
            Erase aMyArray
    End Select

    ' Have the function return a value.
    FillListbox = vntReturnVal

End Function
```

The only thing left for you to do to the list box on the form is to set its RowSourceType property to the name of the function FillListbox. When the form is opened in Form view, it will look similar to Figure 7-9 on the following page.

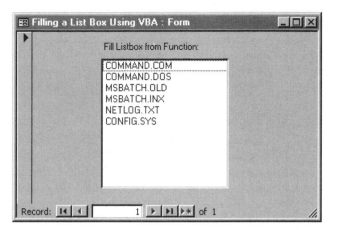

**Figure 7-9.** *Filling a list box with file names using a VBA function.*

# Tab Controls

Like a list box control, a tab control in Microsoft Access 97 can also be manipulated using VBA code. You can use a tab control to increase the amount of information contained on one form without increasing the form's size. A tab control is a container that has a Pages collection containing Page objects in which controls reside. Using the Style property, you can change the appearance of the tabs on a tab control; you can have them displayed either as tabs or buttons—or as neither if you don't want the tabs to appear. Setting the Style property to either Tabs or Buttons changes the tab's appearance but provides the same functionality. If you set the Style property to None, no tabs or buttons are displayed so the user cannot change the page displayed by the tab control. If you set the Style property to None, you must write code that changes the page based on some other user input. Typically, if no tabs or buttons are displayed on a tab control, the form developer is creating some sort of wizard or standard form in which he or she needs to control what is being displayed. For example, a single form could be used to implement a survey, with questions on multiple pages of a tab control.

If you want to change a property of a control on a page in the tab control, you must refer to all the objects that contain that control. For example, the following code changes the Caption property of a label control on page two of a tab control:

```
Forms("MyForm").TabCtl.Pages(1).lblDisplay.Caption = _
    "Hello World!"
```

NOTE Like most collections in Microsoft Access, the Pages collection is zero-based, so Pages(1) refers to the second page in the collection.

To change which page is displayed in the tab control, use the SetFocus method on the page you want to display. The following code demonstrates how to move to the next page in a tab control:

```
Private Sub cmdNext_Click()
    TabCtl.Pages(TabCtl.Value + 1).SetFocus
    If TabCtl.Value + 1 = TabCtl.Pages.Count Then
        cmdNext.Enabled = False
    End If
End Sub
```

The above example uses the Value property of the tab control to get the index of the current page being displayed and adds 1 to it; the command button is then disabled if the last page is displayed. If you have limited space to work with on your form, the tab control is a useful tool to maximize your form's efficiency.

Several other controls ship with Microsoft Access, but typically, manipulating and using them involves only one property setting. You will see examples of manipulating different controls—such as labels and text boxes—in the following section.

## Controls Collection

You can use the Controls collection to refer to controls on forms and reports. Each form and report object has its own separate Controls collection. Just as the Forms collection and Reports collection allow you to refer to form and report properties, the Controls collection allows you to refer to control properties. Many different collections are available when you are programming in Microsoft Access, and all of them have a property named Count. The Count property returns the total number of objects contained within that collection. Remember that all collections are zero-based; so be careful if you use a For...Next loop to enumerate all the objects in a collection. When you refer to an object in the Controls collection, you can use its ordinal position or the name of the control. This flexibility allows you to create generic code that you can reuse in other database applications.

The following example shows two ways to refer to a control in the Controls collection of the current form from the Click event of a command button:

```
Private Sub cmdControlNames_Click()
    Debug.Print Me.Controls(0).Name
    Debug.Print Me.Controls("txtCustomerID").Name
End Sub
```

If the form has one control and its name is txtCustomerID, both lines will print "txtCustomerID" to the Debug window because they are both referring to the same control. Every control on a form will have a Name property. The Name property must be unique for each control on any given form or report because it is used to refer to and distinguish the individual controls at run time.

## Passing in Variable Names

You can declare variables within your functions to be of type Control or of a specific type of control, as shown here:

```
Sub PropertyReference()
    Dim ctlMyControl As Control
    Dim txtMyTextBox As TextBox
End Sub
```

The second variable definition will give faster performance because you are specifying its data type at compile time (called *early binding*), whereas with the first definition Access will not know what type of control the variable represents until run time (called *late binding*). Whenever possible, use early binding for best application performance.

Once a variable is declared, you can initialize it. Because a control is an object, you must initialize the object variable using the Set statement. The following example demonstrates how to initialize an object variable to represent a control on a form:

```
Sub PropertyReference()
    Dim ctlMyControl As Control
    Dim txtMyTextBox As TextBox

    Set ctlMyControl = Forms("Form1")!cmdClose
    Set txtMyTextBox = Forms("Form1")!txtCustomerID
End Sub
```

Now that the variables are initialized, you can refer to them to change and manipulate the controls they represent. Here is an example that changes the Caption property of the command button and the BackColor property of a text box:

```
ctlMyControl.Caption = "Hello World!"
txtMyTextBox.BackColor = RGB(255, 0, 0) ' Red
```

Even though you can declare a variable to be of type Control so that it can represent any type of control, you should use caution when manipulating variables of type Control because different types of controls support different properties. If you want to determine the type of control you are working with at run time, use the ControlType property. The table on the following page lists the control type, associated constant, and constant values of various controls.

### CONTROL TYPES AND ASSOCIATED CONSTANTS

| Control Type | Constant | Value |
|---|---|---|
| Bound Object Frame | acBoundObjectFrame | 108 |
| CheckBox | acCheckBox | 106 |
| ComboBox | acComboBox | 111 |
| Command Button | acCommandButton | 104 |
| Custom Control | acCustomControl | 119 |
| Image | acImage | 103 |
| Label | acLabel | 100 |
| Line | acLine | 102 |
| List Box | acListBox | 110 |
| Option Button | acOptionButton | 105 |
| Option Group | acOptionGroup | 107 |
| Page | acPage | 124 |
| Page Break | acPageBreak | 118 |
| Rectangle | acRectangle | 101 |
| Subform | acSubForm | 112 |
| Tab | acTabCtl | 123 |
| Text Box | acTextBox | 109 |
| Toggle Button | acToggleButton | 122 |
| Unbound Object Frame | acObjectFrame | 114 |

**NOTE** The table above lists the values of the constants. You can use the actual values when using the ControlType property, but we recommend that you always use the constant. The reason for using the constant is that the value might change in future versions of Microsoft Access, but chances are the constant name will remain the same from version to version.

By looking at the ControlType property, you can manipulate a group of controls while looping through the Controls collection. For example, you can disable all text boxes on a form by using the following syntax:

```
Private Sub cmdDisableControls_Click()
    Dim ctlMyControl As Control
```

```
    For Each ctlMyControl In Me.Controls
        If ctlMyControl.ControlType = acTextBox Then
            ctlMyControl.Enabled = False
        End If
    Next
End Sub
```

The example above defined the ctlMyControl variable as type Control because it is looping through the entire Controls collection. Therefore, you need to be able to assign different types of controls to this variable.

## Morphing Controls

Sometimes when you are designing your form you might start out defining the layout of a text box. After testing the application, however, you might realize that this object should really be a combo box. In Microsoft Access for Windows 95, you can change the ControlType property to the type you want, and the relevant properties you defined previously will carry over. The ability to change a control to a different type during execution is called *morphing*.

Unfortunately, you cannot morph at will—there are limits to what controls you can morph into. For example, you cannot morph an Image control into a text box. See Chapter 6 for a complete list of how you can morph controls.

You can set the ControlType property only when the form is open in Design view. The following example demonstrates the code necessary to change a label on a form to a text box, assuming the form is opened in Design view:

```
Forms("Form1").lblCustomerID.ControlType = acTextBox
```

# Extending Your Forms

Up to this point, you have learned how to manipulate the properties of forms, reports, and controls. These objects offer a great deal to the developer, but they do not meet the needs of every developer in every situation. Fortunately, Microsoft Access provides you with the capabilities that will allow you to extend your form's functionality by using predeclared identifiers and creating your own methods and properties.

## Using Predeclared Identifiers

Predeclared identifiers allow you to refer directly to the form or report object under the following conditions:

- Form object is opened in Form view.

- Report object is opened in Print Preview.

- Form and Report objects are closed.

If you try to run code with predeclared identifiers when a form is open in Design view, Microsoft Access generates a run-time error.

When referring to form or report objects using predeclared identifiers, Microsoft Access looks for an open instance of that object. If the object is not already open (for example, a member of the Forms or Reports collection), Microsoft Access opens the hidden form or report. To use a predeclared identifier when referencing an object, you must first specify the class followed by an underscore; then the rest of the syntax is the same as what you have been using. For example, to change the BackColor property of a text box named txtCustomerID to red on the form Form1, you can use the following syntax:

```
Form_Form1.txtCustomerID.BackColor = RGB(255, 0, 0)
```

The class name for all forms is Form, and the class name for all reports is Report. Having predeclared identifiers allows you to refer to an object before it is opened. You need to be aware of some cautions, however.

If the form or report has spaces in its name and you want to refer to them with their predeclared identifier, the class name must be surrounded by brackets. For example, the following code displays the RecordSource property of the form Customer Orders in the Northwind Traders database in a message box:

```
Sub DisplayRecordSource()
    MsgBox [Form_Customer Orders].RecordSource
End Sub
```

If the form or report object is closed to begin with, referring to the object using predeclared identifiers automatically opens the form or report but does not display it. To close the form or report, you must use the Close method of the DoCmd object. So to close the Customer Orders form in the example above, you could use the following syntax:

```
Sub CloseForm()
    DoCmd.Close acForm, "Customer Orders"
End Sub
```

You cannot pass in variable names to refer to a form using predeclared identifiers. For example, the following code works with the Forms collection, but there is no similar method of referring to an object using predeclared identifiers:

```
Sub Referencing()
    Dim strFName As String
    strFName = "Customer Orders"
    MsgBox Forms(strFName).Caption
End Sub
```

## Creating Form and Report Methods

Earlier in the chapter we discussed event procedures and explained how they exist in class modules. You can also create user-defined functions and sub procedures in a class module. In other words, you can create your own custom form and report methods. Whenever you create a Public function in a class module, that function becomes a method of the form or report. To execute that procedure, you must refer to it as a method of the form or report. For example, if you create a Public procedure in a form named MyMethod, you can call it from outside the form, as shown here:

```
Forms("Form1").MyMethod
```

Creating methods for a form or report is beneficial because you can call them from anywhere in the application and they will always be associated with that form or report. Remember from our earlier discussion that if the form or report is exported, so is the class module that contains the form's or report's methods.

When using a method of a form or report object, Microsoft Access will be performing an action on the associated form or report, such as setting its Filter property or manipulating its controls. Using methods is a very powerful use of Microsoft Access objects and is another move toward an object-oriented approach to programming.

## Creating Property Procedures

In Microsoft Access objects you can create special procedures that work similarly to setting and returning predefined property values for forms or reports. These procedures are called *property procedures*. When you create a property procedure, the new property procedure acts as a property of the Microsoft Access form or report that contains the property procedure. You might be wondering why property procedures exist at all. Here are some reasons:

- Microsoft Access is becoming an object-oriented application. Using property procedures is consistent with object-oriented technology. The syntax for calling a property procedure is the same as that for calling or setting a built-in property, such as the Caption property of a form.

- With property procedures, users can create their own properties—ones that perform tasks instead of just storing values.

- Users need to refer to only one property procedure name to both set and return a value, whereas two standard procedures with different names need to be created to set and return a value.

Microsoft Access includes three kinds of property procedures:

- Property Get
- Property Let
- Property Set

You will want to use these property procedures in one of two pairs: Property Get and Property Let or Property Get and Property Set. The reason they are typically used in pairs is that when you create a property you will probably want to both assign and retrieve its value.

## Property Get

With the Property Get statement, you can create a property procedure that returns a property value. Property Get procedures are very similar to Function procedures in that they both return a value. They differ only in that you can define a Property Let or Property Set procedure with the same name and you use the Property and End Property keywords instead of the Function and End Function keywords. Otherwise, procedures created with Property Get are identical to Function procedures.

In this example the Property Get procedure returns the value of a variable local to the class module:

```
' Defined in the General Declarations section of the form
Private intDiscount As Integer

Public Property Get Discount()
    ' Return the value of our private local variable.
    Discount = intDiscount
End Property
```

You can call this procedure with code similar to the following statement, which returns the Discount property value and shows how you might display the value of a user-defined form property:

```
MsgBox Forms("Form1").Discount
```

Notice that like a function the code inside the Property Get procedure must assign the value you want to return to the name of the procedure. Property procedures created with the Property Get statement can take arguments, but they don't have to, and in practice they almost never take arguments. A Property Get procedure declaration takes one less argument than the related Property Let or Property Set declaration. If your Property Get procedure is used in conjunction with one of the other two property procedures, the arguments in the Property Get procedure must have the same name and data type as their counterparts. The following property procedure declarations demonstrate this requirement:

```
Public Property Get MyNameProperty(vntIndex)
Public Property Let MyNameProperty(vntIndex, _
    strName As String)
```

## Property Let

The Property Let statement allows you to create a procedure that sets the value of a property. If you want to validate data before you assign that data to a property value, you can create a property procedure to do so.

Suppose you want to make sure the discount amount is never more than 35 percent. Instead of assuming the discount amount is correct, you can use the Property Let statement to create a property procedure that checks the discount amount before updating the discount property.

The name of this property procedure is Discount. The code inside the procedure checks the amount of the discount and then either stores the discount amount or displays an error message for discount amounts that are greater than 35 percent:

```
' Declared in the General Declarations section of the form
Private intDiscount As Integer

Public Property Let Discount(vntNewValue)
    If vntNewValue <= 35 Then
        intDiscount = vntNewValue
    Else
        MsgBox Prompt:= "Discount too high.", Title:= "Error"
    End If
End Property
```

Notice that the property procedure takes an argument. Property procedures created with the Property Let or Property Set statement must define at least one argument by which they receive the new value of the property. The Property Let procedure is called by setting the property procedure's name to some value, as shown here:

```
Forms("Form1").Discount = 15
```

In this example the Discount property procedure is a property of the form named Form1. The value of the property becomes the value of the vntNewValue argument in the property procedure, which is specified using the value on the right side of the equal sign.

In practice, Property Let procedures nearly always take exactly one argument even though they can take more. When calling a property procedure created with Property Let, the last argument in the argument list contains the value that appears on the right side of the equal sign. The other arguments appear in parentheses following the name of the property. For example, assume the Discount procedure takes two arguments: the retail price of the item and the percentage of the discount. The first line of the property procedure would look like this:

```
Public Property Let Discount (Price, NewValue)
```

Calling the procedure now, you pass the Price argument inside the parentheses, in this case using a variable named Retail, and the value on the right side of the equal sign, in this case 15, is assigned to the NewValue argument:

```
Forms("Form1").Discount(Retail) = 15
```

## Property Set

The Property Set statement allows you to create a property procedure that sets a reference to an object. Because you work only with objects in a Property Set procedure, you must use the Set statements in most places in which the object values are used with the Property Set procedure:

1.  Within the Property Set procedure when you assign the object's value to your private object variable

2.  Within the Property Get procedure that is paired to your Property Set procedure

3.  When calling the Property Set procedure or when assigning the result of its paired Property Get procedure to an object variable

The following example creates a property named LastForm, which contains a reference to the last form that was opened:

```
' In the General Declarations section of the form
Private frmLastForm As Form

Public Property Get LastForm() As Variant
    Set LastForm = frmLastForm
End Property

Public Property Set LastForm(vntNewValue)
    Set frmLastForm = vntNewValue
End Property
```

To assign and retrieve a value of the property procedures, use the following syntax:

```
' Calls the Property Set procedure and makes the form visible.
Set Forms("Form1").LastForm = Form_Customers
Forms("Form1").LastForm.Visible = True

' Calls the Property Get procedure and closes the form.
DoCmd.Close acForm, Forms("Form1").LastForm.Name
```

**Using Property Procedures to Create Read/Write Properties**

By using a Property Get procedure with a Property Let property procedure, you are creating your own read/write properties. You can create your own read only property using just a Property Get procedure since such a procedure will only return a value. You can create a write only property (such as a Password property) using just a Property Let or Property Set procedure since such a procedure will only set a value.

## Why use property procedures?

You might have noticed in all of the preceding examples that we created a Private form level variable. In the Property Get procedure, we simply return the value of that variable; and in the Property Let or Property Set procedure, we simply assign that variable a value. This process brings up three valid questions:

1. Why do we need a form level variable at all?

2. Why not make the form level variable Public and refer to it directly?

3. Why not use two methods rather than property procedures?

Let's answer these questions in order.

1. The form level variable is necessary because a property procedure is nothing more than a function. Therefore, in the Property Let and Property Set statements, the arguments being accepted go out of scope as soon as the procedure ends. Without storing the value to a form-level variable, the Property Get procedure would not be able to return the previously set value.

2. As we have said, using property procedures moves Microsoft Access another step closer to being object oriented. In an object-oriented environment, you never directly expose (make Public) anything that your application relies on. If you do, you open up the possibility that a user could set that variable to an invalid value. For example, if your application expects the variable to contain a number and the user tries to set it to a string instead, the application will have a run-time error. Property procedures provide you with the ability to create two procedures (one to assign a value and one to return a value) that can validate user input and perform an action if necessary. You won't have to worry about whether a user-input value in the property is valid—it will always be valid because the property procedure you create ensures its validity.

**3.** Methods do not offer the same flexibility as property procedures do. The great advantage of property procedures is that you reference/call them the same way you call a built-in property. The way the property is referenced—either retrieving or assigning a value—determines which property procedure will be called. If two methods were used, you would have to know the names of both methods and how to call each one, including which one accepts an argument and which one does not.

## Multiple Instances of Forms

Forms are extremely flexible objects in Microsoft Access. You can create multiple instances of your forms. For example, you can create an application in which the user can simultaneously view multiple instances of the Customers form, each showing different customers.

Each form you design is considered a class. You can use the New keyword to create new instances of that class. (The words "instance" and "object" are interchangeable. For example, saying Rover is a dog object is just like saying Rover is an instance of the class dog.) Each new instance of a form you create is not visible until you set the Visible property to True. Any properties you set will affect that instance of the form only and will not be saved with the form. The following example creates two instances of the Customers form from the Northwind Traders database:

```
Public frmMyForm1 As Form
Public frmMyForm2 As Form

Sub MultipleInstance()
    Set frmMyForm1 = New Form_Customers
    frmMyForm1.Visible = True
    Set frmMyForm2 = New Form_Customers
    frmMyForm2.Visible = True
End Sub
```

If the form variables were defined within the sub procedure, the forms would close automatically when the procedure was finished. The form would close because the variables go out of scope when the procedure is finished executing. Because the form variables are Public, the forms remain open after the procedure has ended. You might have to move the forms around to see them both at once because they will appear on top of each other.

You can also use the New keyword with the Dim statement. Here is the preceding example using the New keyword when the variables are defined:

```
Public frmMyForm1 As New Form_Customers
Public frmMyForm2 As New Form_Customers
```

```
Sub MultipleInstance()
    frmMyForm1.Visible = True
    frmMyForm2.Visible = True
End Sub
```

Notice that the Set statements are not required when using the New keyword to declare a variable to be a specific object. Using this method, a new instance of the Form_Customers object is created as soon as one of its properties is referred to.

## Referencing Multiple Instances of Forms

The form itself is considered to be the default class. When you create an instance of that form with the New keyword, that instance is considered a nondefault instance of that form. You cannot refer to a nondefault instance of a form by name in the Forms collection. You can refer to those instances only by their index numbers. You can create multiple nondefault instances of a form, and each instance will have the same name. Therefore, you can have more than one form with the same name in the Forms collection, without any means of distinguishing them other than by index number. For example, creating multiple instances of the Customers form as shown above creates two instances of the same form name in the Forms collection. To demonstrate, add the statements shown in boldface below to the previous example:

```
Public frmMyForm1 As New Form_Customers
Public frmMyForm2 As New Form_Customers

Sub MultipleInstance()
    Dim frmAllForms As Form
    frmMyForm1.Visible = True
    frmMyForm2.Visible = True
    For Each frmAllForms In Forms
        Debug.Print frmAllForms.Name
    Next
End Sub
```

This displays the following in the Debug window:

```
Customers
Customers
```

To close a single instance of a set of multiple instances of a form class, use the Close method of the DoCmd object by referring to the instance's index in the Forms collection. The following example will close the second form in the Forms collection:

```
DoCmd.Close acForm, Forms(1).Name
```

If the name of the form, Customers, were specified in the preceding line of code, the first form named Customers in the Forms collection would have been closed.

## Understanding the usage of the New keyword

The following table provides examples of the possible combinations of and what you can accomplish with the declared variables both with and without the New keyword.

**USING THE NEW KEYWORD**

| Statement | Result |
|---|---|
| `Dim frmMyForm As _`<br>`    New Form_Employees` | VBA ensures that an instance of the form exists (sometimes called auto-instantiation). VBA automatically creates an instance of the form. The form becomes part of the Forms collection or is created when it is referred to, as in this example:<br><br>`frmMyForm.Visible = True`<br><br>The variable frmMyForm cannot be released by setting it to Nothing. |
| `Dim frmMyForm As _`<br>`    New Form_Employees`<br>`Set frmMyForm = Form_Employees` | VBA ensures that an instance of the form exists (sometimes called auto-instantiation). VBA automatically creates an instance of the form.<br><br>The variable frmMyForm cannot be released by setting it to Nothing. |
| `Dim frmMyForm As Form`<br>`Set frmMyForm = _`<br>`    Forms("Employees")` | VBA will generate an error if the form is not already loaded. |
| `Dim frmMyForm As Form`<br>`Set frmMyForm = Form_Employees` | VBA opens an instance of the form because the predeclared identifier is used. The form is opened with its Visible property set to False.<br><br>To release the variable frmMyForm, set it to Nothing, as here:<br><br>`Set frmMyForm = Nothing`<br><br>The form, however, will still be loaded. |

*(continued)*

| Statement | Result |
|---|---|
| | You can also set the variable frmMyForm to another object by using the following syntax:<br><br>`Set frmMyForm = _`<br>`    Form_Customers`<br><br>In this case, the Employees form and the Customers form will remain loaded. |
| `Dim frmMyForm As New Form`<br>`Set frmMyForm = _`<br>`    Forms("Employees")` | VBA will not open an instance of the form because the New keyword does not refer to an actual form object. It just refers to the form class. VBA will generate an error if the form is not already loaded. |
| `Dim frmMyForm As New Form`<br>`Set frmMyForm = Form_Employees` | VBA creates an instance of the form with its Visible property set to False.<br><br>To release the frmMyForm variable, set it to Nothing. The form will, however, still be loaded because it is referenced in the Forms collection.<br><br>Because the New keyword just refers to the form class and does not refer to an actual object, you can set the frmMyForm variable to another object, as shown in this example:<br><br>`Set frmMyForm = _`<br>`    Form_Customers`<br><br>In this case, the Employees form and the Customers form will remain loaded. |

**NOTE**   When you set an object variable to Nothing, you are disassociating the object variable from the object. When all variables that refer to a particular object are disassociated, memory and system resources associated with that object are released.

## Creating Multiple Instances of a Form Using an Array

You can declare an array of forms with the Private, Dim, ReDim, Static, or Public keywords in the same manner as you would declare an array of any other type. When you declare an array with the New keyword, VBA creates a new instance of the form for each element in the array as you use it. Using an array is a great way to keep track of and control the instances of forms you open.

The following example creates five instances of a form and sets each caption to the form name and an instance number:

```
Public aMyFormArray() As New Form_Customers

Sub CreateFiveForms()
    Dim intFormIndex As Integer
    ReDim aMyFormArray(5)
    For intFormIndex = 0 To 4
        With aMyFormArray(intFormIndex)
            .Caption = "Form1: " & intFormIndex
            .Visible = True
        End With
    Next intFormIndex
End Sub
```

> **NOTE**  You can also declare an array of controls the same way you de-clare an array of any other type. Unlike form arrays, control ar-rays cannot be declared with the New keyword. They can, however, be declared as a specific control type, as in
>
> ```
> Dim txtMyText (5) As TextBox
> ```

## Collection Objects

So far we have discussed three collections: forms, reports, and controls. You also have the ability to create your own Collection object. You can use a collection to group together related objects. The Collection object itself is a useful alter-native to an array because it can hold object references and many other VBA data types. You might prefer to use the Collection object rather than arrays for the following reasons:

- Collection objects use less memory than arrays.

- Collection objects do not require you to ReDim them when objects are added and removed from the collection.

- Collection objects have a more flexible indexing scheme.

- Collection objects have built-in methods to add and delete members.

> **NOTE**  Each collection we have discussed so far is zero-based. All user-defined Collection objects are one-based.

The Collection object has three default methods and one default property, which enable you to insert, delete, and retrieve the members stored in a collection. The following table lists the default methods and properties of the Collection object.

### COLLECTION OBJECT DEFAULT METHODS AND PROPERTIES

| Method or Property | Description |
| --- | --- |
| Add method | Adds an item to the collection. |
| Item method | Returns an item. You can use the item's index or key value to retrieve its data. |
| Delete method | Removes an item from the collection. |
| Count property | Returns the number of items in the collection. |

User-defined Collection objects can contain objects of different types. The properties and methods do not enforce the types of objects being added to a collection. You'll find it easiest to debug and maintain an application that uses Collection objects if each collection contains only one type of object. All Microsoft application collections contain only one type of object. Also, try to name your collection as the plural of the types of objects it contains. This style is not mandatory, but it helps when you're debugging and maintaining your application. For example, if you're keeping track of Car objects, don't create a collection named Transportation, which implies other modes of transport in addition to cars.

To use any of the Collection object methods, you first have to know what indexes and keys are. An *index* is simply a Long Integer between 1 and the number of items in the collection. You use the index to enumerate the items in a collection, using either a For...Next or a For...Each loop, as discussed earlier in the chapter. When you add or remove items from the collection, the value of each item's index may change. A *key* is a variant that evaluates to a string. The key allows you to associate a more meaningful description with an item in the collection.

**WARNING** Be sure to add a unique key to identify each item within the collection; and use the key when you are referring to or deleting items from the collection.

To create a Collection object, declare a variable to be of type Collection. Use the New keyword to indicate that you are creating a new collection:

```
' In the General Declarations section
Dim Employees As New Collection
```

## Adding Items to a Collection

Once you have defined a Collection object, you will probably want to add items to it. You can do this by calling the Add method of the new collection. The Add method allows you to specify the item being added as well as its key. For example, to add an employee object to the collection Employees using the name of the employee and a nickname, use the following:

```
Employees.Add Item:="Bob", Key:="Bobster"
```

This example uses named arguments, which makes it easier to see the values being assigned to the arguments of the Add method. Remember, the Key argument must be a string. If the key is to be a number, use the CStr function to convert it to the string value required by the Key argument, as shown here:

```
Employees.Add Item:="Bob", Key:=CStr(123456789)
```

Using the CStr function, you can use the employee's social security number as the key for the new item.

## Inserting Items Anywhere in a Collection

The Add method has two additional arguments: Before and After. These arguments allow you to specify the order for the objects in the collection. To specify the order of the objects in a collection as they are added, you can use these arguments in the following manner:

■ To specify the order by index position, use a numeric expression that is from 1 to the value of the collection's Count property.

■ To specify the order by key name, use a string expression that corresponds to the key specified when the object being referred to was added to the collection.

The following example uses the Before and After arguments to assign positions to people as they are added to the Employees collection:

```
' In the General Declarations section of the form
Dim Employees As New Collection
```

```
Sub AddEmployees()
    Employees.Add Item:="Bob", Key:=CStr(123456789)
    ' Add Ann to the collection as the first employee in
    ' the collection.
    Employees.Add Item:="Ann", Key:=CStr(234567890), _
        Before:="123456789"
    ' Add Amber to the collection as the first employee
    ' in the collection.
    Employees.Add Item:="Amber", Key:=CStr(345678901), _
        Before:="234567890"
End Sub
```

Now the Employees collection has the following objects in the following order: Amber, Ann, Bob.

## Retrieving or Setting Values for Collection Members

You can retrieve or set values to the objects in their collections just as you can in any other default collection in Microsoft Access. You can use the Item method to retrieve specific members of a custom collection. When referring to an object in the collection, you can refer to the object by its index number in the collection or by its Key value. Remember that the Key value is a string and consequently needs to be specified as such when referring to the item, even if the key contains only numeric data. The following two examples show two ways to retrieve values for objects in a user-defined collection. The first example will enumerate all the objects within the Employees collection.

```
Sub EnumCollection()
    Dim intCount
    For intCount = 1 To Employees.Count
        Debug.Print Employees(intCount)
    Next intCount
End Sub
```

> **NOTE** The Item method is the default method for a Collection object, so you can omit it when you are accessing a member of a collection. For example, to print the first item in the Employees collection, the following two lines of code will produce the same results:
>
> ```
> Debug.Print Employees(1)
> Debug.Print Employees.Item(1)
> ```

The second example uses a collection named MyFormsCollection that stores some of the forms opened in the database. Although this example demonstrates how to retrieve the Name property for each form, you will see in the section "Practical Uses of Collections" on page 240 how you can use a Collection object to handle multiple instances of a form.

```
Sub EnumCollection()
    Dim Frm As Form
    For Each Frm In MyFormsCollection
        Debug.Print Frm.Name
    Next Frm
End Sub
```

## Deleting Collection Members

You can use the Remove method to delete a member of a collection. Like the Item method, Remove allows you to refer to an item in the collection by its index or by its Key value. To remove the first item in a collection, you could use the following syntax:

```
Employees.Remove 1
```

To remove all the items in a collection at one time, set the collection object variable equal to Nothing, as shown here:

```
Set Employees = Nothing
```

## Practical Uses of Collections

A Collection object has many uses. Let's take a look at how collections and forms can work together. Up to this point, we have described collections that can hold values such as strings. Collections can also hold a reference to a form object. This usage is particularly handy when you're working with multiple instances of forms, because it allows you to keep track of each form in your collection—all the instances have the same name in the Forms collection. The following example shows how you might add a form to a collection:

```
' General Declarations section of a standard module
Public MultiForms As New Collection
Sub NewForm()
    Dim frmMyForm As New Form_Customers, strNewKey As String
    strNewKey = "Inst" & Trim(MultiForms.Count)
    MultiForms.Add Item:=frmMyForm, Key:=strNewKey
    With MultiForms(strNewKey)
        .Caption = strNewKey
        .Visible = True
    End With
    ' Clear the form variable because it is referenced
    ' in a collection now.
    Set frmMyForm = Nothing
End Sub
```

Once the form has been added to the collection, the Caption property of the form indicates what instance it is, and then the form is made visible. Rather than setting the Caption property of the Form object, you might consider setting the form's Tag property (or a property that you create using either a Property procedure or a variable declared in the Declarations section of a form module), which would store the Key for that object in the collection. This way, when the form is closed, it can be removed from the collection as well. The Close event procedure of the form might look like the following:

```
Private Sub Form_Close()
    MultiForms.Remove Me.Tag
End Sub
```

No matter how a form that includes the above event procedure is closed, it is always removed from the collection.

## Bookmarks

You can also use collections in conjunction with property procedures. One property that a form provides is called a bookmark. A *bookmark* in Microsoft Access is just what it sounds like: a placeholder. Sometimes you might want to mark your place in the data (say, the record you are currently viewing) and return to it later. You can mark the current record by using a bookmark.

The Bookmark property will return a unique string that you can store in a variable or collection. When you want to return to that record, you set the Bookmark property of the form to the unique string or to the Collection object that was assigned the unique string. This property can be useful when you want to check information in another record and return immediately to the current record. To use the Bookmark property in a form, first create a form-level variable of type String:

```
' In the General Declarations section of the form
Dim bkmrk As String
```

Then add two command buttons to the form that will be used to store and retrieve the bookmark setting. The following code can be used to do this:

```
Private Sub cmdSetBookmark_Click()
    ' Set variable equal to current record on the form.
    bkmrk = Me.Bookmark
End Sub

Private Sub cmdRetrieveBookmark_Click()
    ' Set form's bookmark equal to variable.
    Me.Bookmark = bkmrk
End Sub
```

This code allows you to mark a record on your form and return to it from any other record in that form. In Chapter 8 we will study another example that uses bookmarks, collections, and property procedures together.

### Notes about collection objects

When working with collection objects, keep in mind the following guidelines:

■ The size of the collection is adjusted automatically as each new item is added.

■ The New keyword in the declaration for the Collection object variable causes the Collection object to be created the first time the variable is referred to in code.

■ The collection is an object, not a data type. For this reason, you must create it and keep a reference to it in a variable.

■ Like any other object, the Collection object will be destroyed when the last variable that contains a reference to it is set to Nothing or goes out of scope. All the object references it contains will be released.

■ If you use a collection to keep track of forms, use the collection's Remove method to delete the object reference from the collection when closing the form, and set its object variable to Nothing.

## Creating New Class Modules

As discussed earlier in this chapter, a class module is a container that holds the properties and methods that make up a particular class. A class module can be associated with a form or report and is automatically created when you add code to any object on the form or report. For example, if a command button exists on the form and you click the Build button and select Code Builder, the form now has a class module associated with it. A form that does not have a class module associated with it is called a lightweight form. The reason for this is that when an instance of the form is created at run time, additional start-up time and memory are not needed to load any code in addition to the form.

You can also add a class module to your database from the Database window by choosing Class Module from the Insert menu. Once the class module is saved, it will appear in the Modules tab of the Database window. You can then add properties to the class module by using property procedures or by creating Public variables. Methods are added to the class by creating Public functions or sub procedures.

Using class modules gives you the ability to group similar functionality within a single object. As a result, you cannot use any of the properties or methods defined for the class until an instance of the class is created. The following example will demonstrate this. Using a class module named FileClass, the following class definition can be used as a starting point to group common file I/O operations. This example will define a property named FileName and a method named Import.

**NOTE** The Import method in this example assumes that data in the file is delimited by a comma and that only two fields will be added to the table. If the number of fields were unknown, you could add a loop inside the Do...Loop that would search for the delimited character and add a string to the field.

```
Option Compare Database
Option Explicit

Private strFileName As String

Public Property Get FileName() As Variant
    ' Return the name of the file.
    FileName = strFileName
End Property

Public Property Let FileName(ByVal vNewValue As Variant)
    ' Set the name of the file.
    strFileName = vNewValue
End Property

Public Sub Import(ByVal strTableName As String)
    Dim db As Database, rs As Recordset
    Dim strNewRow As String, iComma As Integer

    Set db = CurrentDb()
    Set rs = db.OpenRecordset(strTableName)
    ' Open the file for input.
    Open FileName For Input As #1
    ' Retrieve each line from the file
    ' and add it as a record to the table.
    Do While Not EOF(1)
        Line Input #1, strNewRow
        ' Each field is delimited by a comma.
        iComma = InStr(1, strNewRow, ",")
        rs.AddNew
        ' Subtract 1 from iComma so that the comma is not included.
        rs(0) = Left(strNewRow, iComma - 1)
        ' Add 1 to iComma so that the comma is not included.
        rs(1) = Mid(strNewRow, iComma + 1)
        rs.Update
    Loop
    Close #1  ' Close the file.
End Sub
```

To create an instance of the FileClass, use the New keyword specifying the name of the class module, as shown in the following sub procedure, which would be defined in a standard module:

```
Sub AddCustomers()
    Dim oAFile As New FileClass
    oAFile.FileName = "NewCust.TXT"
    oAFile.Import "Customers"
End Sub
```

The above code example shows how to create a new instance of the FileClass and then use its properties and methods to add records to the Customers table.

As you can see, class modules that exist outside of a form or report provide you with the ability to create reusable objects. To use the properties or methods of the object, all you need to do is create an instance of the class.

# Microsoft Access Object Model

The Microsoft Access model is structured to include all its objects under one hierarchy: the Application object. This structure allows Automation client applications to take advantage of the features of Microsoft Access.

## Application

The Application object is at the top of the object hierarchy, and all other Microsoft Access objects and collections are members of it. In Microsoft Access the application itself has its own exposed object hierarchy. The Application object is used to apply methods or property settings to the entire Microsoft Access application. The Application object, as well as each object in the hierarchy, can support methods and properties. For a complete list of methods and properties supported by the objects discussed below, search in Help under the object name. The object hierarchy is discussed in detail in Chapter 9.

One method the Application object supports is BuildCriteria. This method allows you to easily create a parsed criteria string that can be used in an object's Filter property. For example, you could add a command button to the Employees form in the Northwind Traders database to filter the form. Use the following code in the Click event procedure of the command button:

```
Private Sub cmdFilter_Click()
    Dim strMsg As String
    Dim strInput As String, strFilter As String

    strMsg = "Enter one or more letters of the Employee's "
    strMsg = strMsg & "last name followed by an asterisk."
    ' Prompt the user for input.
```

```
    strInput = InputBox$(strMsg)
    ' Build the criteria string (dbText is a constant that
    ' indicates the field type).
    strFilter = BuildCriteria("LastName", dbText, strInput)
    ' Set the Filter property of the form to apply the filter.
    Me.Filter = strFilter
    ' Set the FilterOn property to show the filtered records.
    Me.FilterOn = True
End Sub
```

When the form is opened in Form view and the command button is clicked, you are prompted with an input box to enter a criteria. If you enter a criteria like D*, you will see that the form shows only those records whose LastName field starts with "D."

The Application object supports the objects and collections shown in Figure 7-10.

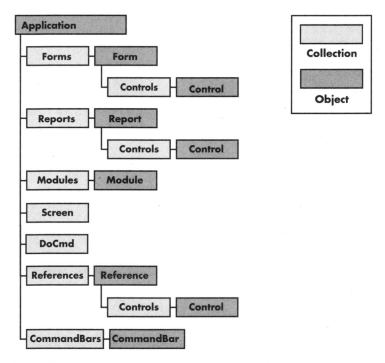

**Figure 7-10.** *Microsoft Access object hierarchy.*

## Forms

The Forms collection contains references to all open Form objects in the current database.

## Reports

The Reports collection contains references to all open Report objects in the current database.

## Controls

The Controls collection refers to all controls on an open form or report in the current database. Each form and report has a separate Controls collection.

## Screen

The Screen object is used to refer to the particular form, report, or control that currently has the focus. The following examples use the Screen object:

```
Screen.ActiveForm.Caption = "Hello World!"
MsgBox Screen.ActiveReport.RecordSource
Screen.ActiveControl.Visible = True
```

## DoCmd

The DoCmd object allows the user to run Microsoft Access macro actions using VBA. For example, to open a form you could use the following syntax:

```
DoCmd.OpenForm "Customers"
```

When you convert any macro to VBA code, you use the DoCmd object with the associated method. There are several actions that DoCmd cannot perform. The following table lists these actions and indicates how the conversion wizard implements the necessary changes.

**MACRO ACTIONS NOT SUPPORTED BY THE DOCMD OBJECT**

| Actions not Supported by DoCmd | Macro Conversion Wizard Solution |
| --- | --- |
| AddMenu | The conversion wizard comments out these lines and notifies the user that it has done so. |
| MsgBox | Uses the MsgBox function. |
| RunApp | Uses the Shell function to run another application. |
| RunCode | Uses the Call statement to execute the function directly in VBA. Remember that a function's return value is discarded when using the Call statement. |
| SendKeys | Uses the SendKeys statement. |
| SetValue | Sets the value directly in VBA. |
| StopAllMacros | Uses the End statement. |
| StopMacro | Uses the Exit function. |

To call the Conversion Wizard, open a macro in Design view. Choose Save As/ Export from the File menu. In the dialog box that appears, select Save As Visual Basic Module. All the macro actions, except those listed in the preceding table, are changed to methods of the DoCmd object. The macro actions not supported are commented out in code using the apostrophe (').

## Modules Collection

The Modules collection contains a list of all open standard and class modules defined in the database. Each Module object can be manipulated by using its properties and methods. The methods exposed by the Module object allow you to insert procedures and lines of code. Typically, you will use this collection only if you are writing a wizard for Microsoft Access.

## References Collection

In Microsoft Access 97, you can add a References collection to your database by selecting References from the Tools menu when a module is open in Design view. This allows you to include object libraries from ActiveX servers or other Microsoft Access databases. The References collection allows you to see which references exist in a particular database. It contains references only to the items selected in the References dialog box for the current database. You can use the References collection to add and remove references through code.

# Creating Command Bars with Code

Creating command bars manually through the user interface is by far the easiest and most efficient method and usually provides you with what you need to make your application robust. In some instances, however, you will need to use code to take full advantage of the flexibility of command bars. For example, with code you can add command buttons, drop-down (combo box style) controls, and gauges, or you can dynamically display and change command bars. To work with command bars using code, you must understand the CommandBar object model, which is shown in Figure 7-11.

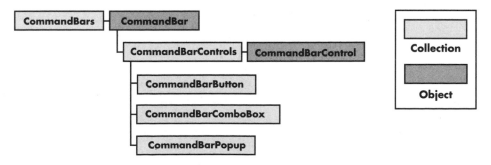

**Figure 7-11.** *CommandBar object hierarchy.*

The Application object contains the CommandBars collection, which contains all the CommandBar objects, both built in and custom. Within each CommandBar object is a CommandBarControls collection, which contains all the CommandBarControl objects—both built in and custom. In the Command-BarControls collection, you can work directly with CommandBarButton, CommandBarComboBox, and CommandBarPopup controls. All other command bar controls are considered CommandBarControl objects.

To refer to a CommandBarControls collection that contains any type of Control object, you use the Controls collection for the syntactic reference. With cascading menu command bar controls created with the CommandBarPopup control, you can have additional Controls collections with their own Control objects, and even those objects can have Controls collections as long as those control objects are CommandBarPopup controls.

## Using the Command Bar Object Model

When working with the CommandBar object model, the indexes in the collections are one-based instead of zero-based. So when you want to refer to the first command bar in the CommandBars collection, you must use Command-Bars(1). All the collections in this hierarchy are one-based.

You can declare a CommandBar object either by index or by name, as shown here:

```
Dim CB As CommandBar
Set CB = CommandBars(1)
' or
Set CB = CommandBars("MyToolbar")
```

To refer to the top-level command bar controls on your command bar, you must use an index since a name cannot be given to the control. The index values are from left to right on the command bar and begin with 1. Therefore, to refer to the first control on the first command bar, use the following syntax using the Controls collection of the CommandBar object:

```
Dim CB As CommandBar
Dim CBControl As CommandBarControls

Set CB = CommandBars(1)
Set CBControl = CB.Controls(1)
```

If the control is a cascading menu control that has other controls on it, you can use the following syntax to refer to the first control on the cascading menu:

```
Set CBControl = CB.Controls(1).Controls(1)
```

To use the CommandBars collection and all of its objects, you must create a reference to the Microsoft Office 8.0 Object Library. To add this reference via the user interface, open the Debug window by pressing Ctrl+G. From the Tools menu, choose References. In the References dialog box, select Microsoft Office 8.0 Object Library, and click OK.

> **TIP** To add this reference with code, open the Debug window, type the following code in the Immediate pane, and press Enter:
>
> ```
> References.CreateFromFile("C:\windows\system\mso97.dll")
> ```
>
> Make sure you have the correct path to MSO97.DLL. You can verify that the reference was added by viewing the References dialog box.

To determine what is available via the Microsoft Office 8.0 object model, open the Object Browser and select Office in the Project/Library drop-down list, as shown in Figure 7-12.

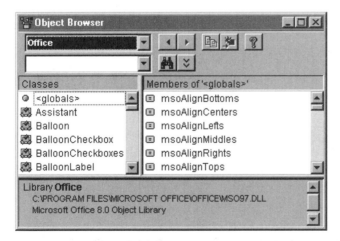

**Figure 7-12.** *Microsoft Office 8.0 Object Library in the Object Browser.*

In the following sections, we will focus on some common tasks you might want to perform using code and some you can perform only with code.

### Creating and modifying command bars

To create a command bar, call the Add method of the CommandBars collection using the following syntax:

```
CommandBars.Add(Name, Position, MenuBar, Temporary)
```

The following table lists the arguments for the Add method of the CommandBars collection.

| Argument | Description |
| --- | --- |
| Name | Optional argument that gives the CommandBar object a unique, friendly name that will show up as the command bar name in the user interface. If omitted, a default name is assigned. |
| Position | Optional argument that determines the location of the newly created command bar. The following constants are used to determine the position: msoBarLeft, msoBarTop, msoBarRight, msoBarBottom, msoBarFloating (the default), msoBarPopup (creates a pop-up command bar), msoBarMenuBar (creates a menu bar command bar). |
| MenuBar | Optional argument that replaces the position of the active menu bar with the new command bar when set to True. The default value is False. |
| Temporary | Optional argument that makes the command bar temporary when set to True. Once you close the database application, the command bar is deleted. The default value is False. |

The following code adds a simple command bar called Test Toolbar to the CommandBars collection:

```
Sub CreateCommandBar()
    CommandBars.Add Name:="Test Toolbar"
End Sub
```

Notice that after you create the command bar it is not visible. You can make it visible manually by choosing View from the Toolbars menu in the Database window and then selecting the toolbar name. If you want to make the command bar visible using code, add this line of code:

```
CommandBars("Test Toolbar").Visible = True
```

**TIP** When you practice creating toolbars with code, set the Temporary argument to True to avoid having to delete your command bars manually later. Remember that you can simply close the database to remove temporary command bars.

Now that you can create a command bar using code, perhaps you would like to have it replace the position of the currently active menu bar. To do so, you must set the MenuBar argument to True and select the proper Position argument. Typically, your active menu bar is in the top position of your application. Therefore, you would set the Position argument of your command bar to be on top also, as shown here:

```
Sub CreateCommandBar()
    CommandBars.Add Name:="Test Toolbar", _
        Position:=msoBarTop, MenuBar:=True, temporary:=True
    CommandBars("Test Toolbar").Visible = True
End Sub
```

**NOTE**    If you had left the MenuBar argument False, the command bar that you just created would have appeared on top of the application window but underneath all the command bars that were already docked on top.

Creating a command bar to replace the active menu bar is not a problem. But what if the active menu bar is docked to the left or right or at the bottom of your application? Unless you prevent users from moving command bars, how will you know what position the active menu bar is in? The answer to these questions is to use a property of the CommandBars collection named ActiveMenuBar property. This property identifies the active menu bar in the application. To ensure that you always find the correct position of the currently active menu bar, change the Position argument to the following:

```
CommandBars.Add Name:="Test Toolbar", _
    Position:=CommandBars.ActiveMenuBar.Position, _
    MenuBar:=True, Temporary:=True
```

## Adding and deleting command bar controls

The next step after you have created a command bar is to put some controls on it. To do so, you call the Add method of the Controls collection of the CommandBar object using this syntax:

```
CommandBars("My Toolbar").Controls.Add _
    (Type, Id, Parameter, Before, Temporary)
```

The table on the following page lists the arguments for the Add method of the Controls collection.

| Argument | Description |
|----------|-------------|
| Type | Optional Variant argument that determines the type of control to be added to the specified command bar. You can use the following constants: msoControlButton (create command button control), msoControlEdit (create a text box control), msoControlDropdown (create a drop-down list box control), msoControlComboBox (create a combo box control), or msoControlPopup (create a menu control). The default is msoControlButton. |
| Id | Optional Integer argument that specifies a built-in control. If this argument is set to 1 or omitted, a blank custom control of the specified type will be added to the command bar. |
| Parameter | Optional Variant argument that associates any custom information to a particular command bar control. This argument could be useful for determining whether the command bar control should be available for a particular form. |
| Before | Optional argument that places the new command bar control just before the control that is identified by this argument. If left blank, the control's position will be last on the command bar. |
| Temporary | Optional argument that makes the command bar control temporary when set to True. Once you close the database application, the command bar control is deleted from the command bar. The default value is False. |

**TIP**

If you want to create a command bar control on your custom command bar that duplicates the functionality of one of the built-in command bars, use the ID argument of the Add method. To do this, you must determine the correct ID. You can obtain the correct ID by typing the following code into the Immediate pane of the Debug window:

```
?CommandBars _
    (<Name of Command Bar>).Controls(<Position of Control>).Id
```

To determine the ID of the New Object drop-down control on the Database toolbar so that you can duplicate its appearance and functionality on your custom command bar, type the following code into the Immediate pane of the Debug window:

```
?CommandBars("Database").Controls(21).Id
```

To add the control, enter the following code in the Immediate pane:

```
CommandBars("Test Toolbar1").Controls.Add Id:=2599
```

Next, to add the AutoForm and AutoReport command to this control, use the Controls collections of the New Object drop-down command bar control where the New Object drop-down control is the first control on the command bar. To add an item to the New Object drop-down control, you must first set an object variable representing that control as is done in the following code. (When doing this in a procedure, declare the ctlMyList variable to be of type CommandBarControl.)

```
Set ctlMyList = CommandBars("Test Toolbar1").Controls(1)
ctlMyList.Controls.Add Id:=581
ctlMyList.Controls.Add Id:=582
```

To delete a control from a command bar, simply use the Delete method of the Control object, as shown here:

```
CommandBars("Test Toolbar1").Controls(2).Delete
```

To delete an entire command bar from the database application, simply refer to the command bar and use the Delete method of the CommandBars collection, like this:

```
CommandBars("Test Toolbar1").Delete
```

## Extending and manipulating command bars

Most toolbar types have buttons, drop-downs, or other controls that simplify user tasks. Through VBA you can extend and manipulate your command bars at run time, making your application much more flexible.

## Adding functionality to your command bar controls

Now it's time to make your command bars functional by using the OnAction property of your command bar Control objects. The OnAction property tells Microsoft Access which procedure to execute when the user clicks a particular control. The OnAction property can be set to a macro name or a function name. For example, the following code creates a command bar and a command bar button control. Then the built-in message box function is assigned to the OnAction property of that control. Keep in mind that this can also be a user-defined function.

```
Sub AddOnAction()
    Dim CB As CommandBar
    Dim CBControl As CommandBarButton

    ' Create a new command bar that is temporary.
    Set CB = CommandBars.Add _
```

*(continued)*

```
            (Name:="New Toolbar", Temporary:=True)
        CB.Visible = True
        ' Add a command button to the command bar.
        Set CBControl = CB.Controls.Add(msoControlButton)
        CBControl.OnAction = "=MsgBox('Hello')"
End Sub
```

When you execute the preceding code, a floating toolbar with a single, blank button will appear. Click the button to see the message box.

**TIP** Like an event procedure, the OnAction property can have the name of a function preceded by an equal sign or just the name of a macro.

To give the user another method to execute the same function that is used on the command bar control, you could just call the function in the OnClick event of a form's command button. If you change the OnAction property during run time to use a different function, however, you'll also have to use decision logic in the OnClick event to make sure that you are calling the appropriate function. To eliminate confusion and the extra coding required for the command button on the form, simply call the Execute method of that particular command bar control. Using the command bar we just created, you can trigger the OnAction function from another procedure or from the Immediate pane of the Debug window, as shown here:

```
CommandBars("New Toolbar").Controls(1).Execute
```

## Improving the appearance of your command bar controls

The user should be able to quickly identify the purpose of the command bar and its controls. To ensure that the appearance of your command bar controls enhances their usability, you can change their text, use images, and create screen tips for them. Add text to the command button control you created above by adding the following code at the end of the AddOnAction procedure:

```
CBControl.Caption = "Hello MsgBox"
CBControl.Style = msoButtonCaption
```

Use the Immediate pane of the Debug window to delete the toolbar before rerunning the AddOnAction procedure.

To use an image rather than text, replace the code above with the following, which uses the FaceId property of the CommandBarControl object:

```
CBControl.Style = msoButtonIcon
CBControl.FaceId = CommandBars("Database").Controls(2).FaceId
```

**TIP** You cannot use an image from a file. You can select an image of a built-in command bar or custom command bar by referring to its FaceId property.

You can also display both text and an image on a control. To do so, replace the preceding code with the following:

```
CBControl.Caption = "Hello MsgBox"
CBControl.Style = msoButtonIconAndCaption
CBControl.FaceId = CommandBars("Database").Controls(2).FaceId
```

When you pass the cursor over the command bar, you will notice that the ScreenTip text is the same as the caption. If you want to display more descriptive information in the ScreenTip text, just set the ScreenTip property by adding the following line of code:

```
CBControl.TooltipText = _
    "This Toolbar Button Will Display A Message Box"
```

If you want to separate (group) your controls by a vertical bar, you can use the BeginGroup property of the CommandBarControl object. When set to True, this property will place a vertical bar just before the control.

Unfortunately, there is no EndGroup property, so you must use another BeginGroup property for the control that you first create outside that group:

```
CBControl.BeginGroup = False
```

## Managing the availability of your command bars

Occasionally, it might not be appropriate for your command bar to be available. You also might not want to rely on the user to decide when the toolbar should be displayed. To display the custom command bar or any built-in command bar, use the Visible property of the particular CommandBar object. (This property does not apply to pop-up menus.)

```
CommandBars("New Toolbar").Visible = True
CommandBars("Database").Visible = True
```

If you set the Visible property to False, the command bar will disappear. However, the user can still make the command bar visible by selecting it from the list of command bars after choosing View from the Toolbars menu. To prevent the user from having any access to the command bar, use the Enabled property of the CommandBar object. By setting Enabled to False, the command bar will disappear and will not be available by choosing View from the Toolbars menu option:

```
CommandBars("New Toolbar").Enabled = False
CommandBars("Database").Enabled = False
```

To display the command bar again, set the Enabled property to True.

Remember that you can also control the location of the command bar by using the Position property of the CommandBar object or of the CommandBars collection's ActiveMenuBar property. You can use the CommandBar object's Top and Left properties to position a floating command bar from the top and left boundaries of the application window using pixels as the measurement unit. You can also use the Height and Width properties to determine the command bar's shape. In addition, you can use the RowIndex property of the CommandBar object to change the order in which currently visible command bars are stacked on top of each other.

To retain even more control over command bars, you can use the Protection property of the CommandBar object. You can use the constants described in the following table as values for the Protection property.

### PROTECTION PROPERTY CONSTANTS

| Protection Constants | Value | Description |
| --- | --- | --- |
| msoBarNoProtection | 0 | By default, user can customize and relocate the command bar. |
| msoBarNoCustomize | 1 | User cannot customize the command bar. |
| msoBarNoResize | 2 | User cannot resize the command bar. |
| msoBarNoMove | 4 | User cannot move the command bar. |
| msoBarNoChangeVisible | 8 | User cannot make the command bar either visible or invisible. |
| msoBarNoChangeDock | 16 | User cannot change the current docking of the command bar. |
| msoBarNoVerticalDock | 32 | User cannot dock the command bar vertically. |
| msoBarNoHorizontalDock | 64 | User cannot dock the command bar horizontally. |

Notice the values of each constant. You can combine any of these constants to achieve the appropriate level of protection for a particular command bar. For example, to prevent a user from docking your command bar either vertically or horizontally, you can use the following code:

```
CommandBars("New Toolbar").Protection = _
    (msoBarNoVerticalDock + msoBarNoHorizontalDock)
```

This code works great if the command bar is already floating. If the command bar is already docked, however, you will receive an error. You can use the Position property of the CommandBar object to determine whether the command bar is floating (or docked), as shown in the following code:

```
Sub FloatToDock()
    Dim CB As CommandBar
    Set CB = CommandBars("New Toolbar")

    ' Determine if the command bar is docked.
    If CB.Position <> msoBarFloating Then
        ' If the command bar is docked, make it floating.
        CB.Position = msoBarFloating
    End If
    CB.Protection = _
        (msoBarNoVerticalDock + msoBarNoHorizontalDock)
End Sub
```

**TIP** If you do allow your user to customize your command bars, you can use the Reset method of the CommandBar object to restore them to their original state.

### Further managing your command bar controls

Sometimes most of the controls on your command bar apply to certain contexts but individual command bar controls do not. For example, if you create a command bar control that is used to save the current record, you could disable that control until the user has filled in all of the appropriate information. To disable a specific control, set its Enabled property to False, as shown here:

```
CommandBars("New Toolbar").Controls(2).Enabled = False
```

To make a command bar control disappear from the command bar, set its Visible property to False:

```
CommandBars("New Toolbar").Controls(2).Visible = False
```

When the control is disabled or made invisible, you can still execute its OnAction property via code as well by using other methods and properties. The user, however, cannot click the command bar control.

You can also set the focus to a specific command bar control by using the SetFocus method:

```
CommandBars("New Toolbar").Controls(2).SetFocus
```

This method would be ideal in the scenario mentioned previously, where the Save Record control is disabled until all of the information is supplied. Once the information is supplied and the control is enabled, you could also set the focus to that control. Then, the user just has to press Enter to execute the Save Record control. This eliminates any extra mouse movements required to select the command bar control.

> **TIP** You can use the Move method of a command bar control to re-position it within the command bar. You can also use the Priority property to determine the importance of a particular control when there are more controls on a command bar than can be displayed on the screen.

You can designate the appearance of a command bar button by using the State property of the particular button control using the constants in the following table.

### STATE PROPERTY CONSTANTS

| State Constants | Value | Description |
|---|---|---|
| msoButtonUp | 0 | By default, the button control is in the up position. After the user clicks the button, it returns to the up position. |
| msoButtonDown | −1 | By default, the button control is in the down position. After the user clicks the button, it returns to the down position. |
| msoButtonMixed | 2 | The button can remain either in the up or down position. (For example, the buttons designating boldface or italic type remain down when you are using them and up when you are not.) |

Here is the code you would use to place a button in its down position:

```
CommandBars("New Toolbar").Controls(2).State = msoButtonDown
```

Most of your command bar controls will be the buttons. However, at times you will need the flexibility that is found only in controls you create with code. These controls include Edit controls, DropDown (ComboBox) controls, and Gauge controls.

## Using the Edit command bar control

To create an Edit control, you must specify msoControlEdit as the Type argument of the Add method of the Controls collection, as shown here:

```
Function CreateEditControl()
    Dim CB As CommandBar
    Dim CBControl As CommandBarControl

    ' Create a new command bar that is temporary.
    Set CB = CommandBars.Add _
        (Name:="New Toolbar", Temporary:=True)
    CB.Visible = True
    ' Add a command bar Edit control.
    Set CBControl = CB.Controls.Add(msoControlEdit)
End Function
```

Now that you have an Edit control, you need to do something with it. To add or retrieve text with code, you can use the Text property of the Edit control. The following example adds some default text to the Edit control when it is first created:

```
Function CreateEditControl()
    Dim CB As CommandBar
    Dim CBControl As CommandBarControl

    ' Create a new command bar that is temporary.
    Set CB = CommandBars.Add _
        (Name:="New Toolbar", Temporary:=True)
    CB.Visible = True
    ' Add a command bar Edit control.
    Set CBControl = CB.Controls.Add(msoControlEdit)
    ' Place text into the Edit control.
    CBControl.Text = "Initial text in my edit control"
End Function
```

You'll notice that when you create the control not all of the text fits nicely. To adjust the width of the Edit control, you can use the Width property of the control, which is set in pixels:

```
CBControl.Width = 150
```

Using the Text property, you are able to add, change, and retrieve information from the Edit control.

To make the Edit control perform a task whenever a user types a value into it, use the OnAction property of the control, as shown here:

```
Function CreateEditControl()
    Dim CB As CommandBar
    Dim CBControl As CommandBarControl
```

*(continued)*

```
' Create a new command bar that is temporary.
Set CB = CommandBars.Add _
    (Name:="New Toolbar", Temporary:=True)
CB.Visible = True
' Add a command bar Edit control.
Set CBControl = CB.Controls.Add(msoControlEdit)
' Place text into the Edit control.
CBControl.Text = "Initial text in my Edit Control"
' Automatically adjust the width of the Edit control.
CBControl.Width = Len(CBControl.Text) * 7
' After the user types in text,
' execute the following code.
CBControl.OnAction = "=Open_MsgBox()"
CBControl.Tag = "MyEdit"
End Function
```

Notice that we set the Tag property to MyEdit. This can be a good way to create a name for your controls. Keep in mind that the ID can be only of type Long, and it can be difficult to remember which ID belongs to which control when you have a highly populated command bar. The Tag property gives you a more descriptive way to identify the control.

The following function, Open_MsgBox( ), will open a message box containing the text in the Edit control as its Prompt argument when the user presses Enter in the Edit control. In addition, this function will resize the Edit control to fit the newly typed text.

```
Function Open_MsgBox()
    Dim CBControl As CommandBarControl

    ' Locate the appropriate Edit control.
    Set CBControl = _
        CommandBars("New Toolbar").FindControl _
        (Type:=msoControlEdit, Tag:="MyEdit")
    ' Adjust the width of the Edit control.
    CBControl.Width = Len(CBControl.Text) * 7
    ' Open a message box with the text as the prompt.
    MsgBox CBControl.Text
End Function
```

The code above introduced a new method of the CommandBar object named FindControl. This method allows you to locate any control on any command bar in your application. The FindControl method has the following arguments:

FindControl(Type, Id, Tag, Visible, Recursive)

| Argument | Description |
|----------|-------------|
| Type | If you are looking for a specific type of control on the command bar, type in any of the msoControlType constants, such as msoControlEdit, msoControlButton, and so on. This argument is optional. |
| Id | This optional integer argument specifies a built-in control. |
| Tag | A tag is a property of the command bar control that can be assigned a string. If you use tags, you do not have to remember the ID number of that particular control. This argument is optional. |
| Visible | If set to True, the FindControl method will look at only those controls that are currently visible on the command bar. By default, this value is set to False. This argument is optional. |
| Recursive | If set to True, the FindControl method will search the entire command bar and all of its sub pop-up command bars. By default, this value is set to False. This argument is optional. |

**NOTE** The FindControl method will stop at the first control that meets the specified criteria. If a control is not found, the method will return Nothing. For more information on the FindControl method, see online Help.

You can use the FindControl method to search a specific command bar, as shown in the Open_MsgBox function on the previous page. You can also search for a control on all of the command bars in the database. The following code does this and also checks to see whether the FindControl method returns a valid control. If it finds the control, the function will display a message box saying that it finds the control; otherwise, it displays a message box indicating that it has not. If it has not found a control, the CommandBarControl variable will store Nothing. You must use the Is operator when checking the value of an object variable.

```
Function FindCBControl(PassTag As String)
    Dim CBControl As CommandBarControl

    Set CBControl = CommandBars.FindControl(Tag:=PassTag)
    If CBControl Is Nothing Then
        MsgBox "Did Not Find It"
    Else
        MsgBox "Found It"
    End If
End Function
```

This function uses the Tag property to locate the command bar control. You could also modify the function to search for a control using any criteria that you can specify using the arguments of the FindControl method.

### Using the ComboBox command bar control

To create a ComboBox control, you must specify msoControlComboBox as the Type argument of the Add method of the Controls collection, as shown here:

```
Function CreateComboBoxControl()
    Dim CB As CommandBar
    Dim CBControl As CommandBarComboBox

    ' Create a new command bar that is temporary.
    Set CB = CommandBars.Add _
        (Name:="New Toolbar", Temporary:=True)
    CB.Visible = True
    ' Add a command bar Edit control.
    Set CBControl = CB.Controls.Add(msoControlComboBox)
End Function
```

You can use the constant msoControlDropdown if you want a control that works like a list box, in which you can only select values and not type them in. You would also have to declare the CBControl variable as type CommandBarControl since no specific object type is available for a list box. You can also adjust the width of the ComboBox control, as you did with the Edit control.

When you click the combo box, you will notice that no values are stored there. Therefore, you will need to modify the code above to add values using the AddItem method, as shown here:

```
Function CreateComboBoxControl()
    Dim CB As CommandBar
    Dim CBControl As CommandBarComboBox

    ' Create a new command bar that is temporary.
    Set CB = CommandBars.Add _
        (Name:="New Toolbar", Temporary:=True)
    CB.Visible = True
    ' Add a command bar Combo Box control.
    Set CBControl = CB.Controls.Add(msoControlComboBox)
    CBControl.Tag = "MyComboBox"
    ' Add items to the combo box.
    CBControl.AddItem "Employees"
    CBControl.AddItem "Customers"
End Function
```

The AddItem method has the arguments listed in the following table.

| Argument | Description |
|---|---|
| Text | Indicates the displayed value to be added to the combo box. This argument is required. |
| Index | Determines the position of the item in the list. This argument is optional; if it is not used, the item will be added to the end of the list. |

**TIP**  You could also add items to a combo box control with the values in a table or query or a list of database objects by using Data Access Objects (DAO), which is discussed in Chapter 9.

Some additional properties of the ComboBox control are described in the following table.

| Property | Description |
|---|---|
| DropDownWidth | Controls the width of the list of items in the combo box control. |
| DropDownLines | Controls the number of lines displayed in the list. If the number of items is greater than the number of lines specified in the DropDownLines property, the user will see a scroll bar displayed. |
| List | Returns the text associated with an item in the list based on its index number. |
| ListCount | Determines the total number of items in the list. |
| ListIndex | Returns the index number of the item that is selected. If no item is selected, the ListIndex property returns zero. |
| ListHeaderCount | Creates a line separator in your list and indicates the number of items to be placed above it. A ListHeaderCount property value of −1 indicates that there is no separator line in the combo box control. |

Once your combo box is filled, you might want to assign a function to the control's OnAction property so that when a value is selected in the combo box a particular action occurs. The following example will open the form selected from the combo box list created in the code on the previous page:

```
Function OpenComboBoxForm(FName As String)
    DoCmd.OpenForm FName
End Function
```

For this function to be executed when a form name is selected from the combo box, you will need to add the following line of code to the end of the CreateComboBoxControl( ) function:

```
' Add OnAction function
CBControl.OnAction = _
    "=OpenComboBoxForm(CommandBars.ActionControl.Text)"
```

You use the ActionControl property to determine which command bar control has executed the function in the OnAction property.

Sometimes a default list is not enough. You might want the user to be able to add items to your combo box control. To allow this, you could use the following code in the OnAction property of a command button control:

```
Function AddToComboBox()
    Dim CBControl As CommandBarComboBox
    Dim AddText As String

    Set CBControl = CommandBars.FindControl(Tag:="MyComboBox")
    ' Open an input box to allow the user to add an item.
    AddText = InputBox("Add Your Item")
    If Len(AddText) = 0 Then
        ' If the Cancel button was clicked,
        ' the InputBox function returns a zero
        ' length string.
        MsgBox "Did not add the item"
    Else
        ' Add the value typed in the input box.
        CBControl.AddItem AddText
        MsgBox "Item Added"
    End If
End Function
```

If you want to remove all of the items from the combo box control, you can use the Clear method. You could create a command button control that allows the user to clear the items. To do so, you could use the following code in the OnAction property of the command button control:

```
Function ClearItems()
    Dim CBControl As CommandBarComboBox

    Set CBControl = CommandBars.FindControl(Tag:="MyComboBox")
    ' Remove all items from the combo box control.
    CBControl.Clear
    MsgBox "All Items Removed"
End Function
```

If you want to remove only one item at a time, you can use the RemoveItem method. You could create a command button control that allows the user to remove the selected item. To do so, you could use the following code in the OnAction property of the command button control:

```
Function ClearOneItem()
    Dim CBControl As CommandBarComboBox

    ' Locate the correct combo box control.
    Set CBControl = CommandBars.FindControl(Tag:="MyComboBox")

    ' Remove just the item selected in the combo box control.
    CBControl.RemoveItem CBControl.ListIndex
    MsgBox "The Item Has Been Removed"
End Function
```

## Manipulating menu bars

The easiest way to create menu bars is through the graphical user interface. However, at times you'll want to manipulate your menu bar items through code, for example, to arrange the following actions:

- Add and remove check marks for menu items

- Enable and disable menu items

- Hide or unhide menu items

- Add and remove menu items

To add a check mark to a menu item, set the State property of the menu bar control to True. The following code will check the first menu item under the first menu control on a command bar named Custom Menu Bar:

```
CommandBars("Custom Menu Bar").Controls(1).Controls(1).State = True
```

To remove a check mark from a menu item, set the State property of the menu bar control to False. You can check and uncheck menu items if an image is associated with the menu item.

To disable a menu item, set the Enabled property of the menu bar control to False. The following code will disable the first menu item under the first menu control on the built-in menu bar:

```
CommandBars("Menu Bar").Controls(1).Controls(1).Enabled = True
```

To enable a menu item, set the Enabled property of the menu bar control to True. To hide a menu item, set the Visible property of the menu bar control to False. The following code will hide the first menu item under the first menu control on the built-in menu bar:

```
CommandBars("Menu Bar").Controls(1).Controls(1).Visible = True
```

To unhide a menu item, set the Visible property of the menu bar control to False.

> **NOTE**
> Remember that you can use the Visible property of a menu bar type command bar to show or hide a specific menu. You can use the ShowPopup method of the CommandBar object to display a pop-up menu command bar:
>
> ```
> CommandBars("My Popup Menu Bar").ShowPopup
> ```
>
> The Position property of the command bar must be equal to msoBarPopup, and the Enabled property must be set to TRUE.

To add a menu item to a menu bar control, you can use the Add method of the control. The following code adds a cascading menu under the first menu control and then adds a control button underneath that one:

```
CommandBars("Custom Menu Bar 1").Controls(1).Controls.Add _
    Type:=msoControlPopup
CommandBars("Custom Menu Bar 1").Controls(1).Controls.Add _
    Type:=msoControlButton
```

To create a cascading menu, you must set the Type argument of the Add method to the msoControlPopup constant. To add additional cascading menus or command bar controls to a cascading menu, simply use the Add method for the Controls collection of that control. The following code adds an additional cascading menu to the one added above:

```
CommandBars("Menu Bar").Controls(1).Controls(1).Controls.Add _
    Type:=msoControlPopup
```

To remove a menu item, use the Delete method of the Controls collection of the particular menu item control. The following code removes the second menu item from the first menu control:

```
CommandBars("Menu Bar").Controls(1).Controls(2).Delete
```

> **NOTE**
> If you delete a cascading menu, all cascading menus within the deleted menu are also deleted.

## PREVIEW of the next chapter

Forms and reports in Microsoft Access 97 are very flexible objects. They are the fundamental objects that a user will see when running your database application, so be sure that you design and use these objects appropriately. The next chapter will take the concepts you've learned about forms and class modules and apply them in mini-applications.

# 8

# Solutions with Forms

In Chapter 7 we discussed how you could use functions with the properties, events, and controls of forms and reports to tailor your applications. In this chapter we will go a step further and demonstrate three solutions that rely on added code to accomplish powerful tasks. We will use collections and property procedures to modify the Customers form in the Northwind Traders database; create a multipage form, or wizard, that you can use to welcome users to your application; and show you how to let your users customize the forms in your application.

Obviously, forms have many uses within an application. The solutions we present in this chapter are tasks that are not fully documented or uses of forms that you might not have thought of. These solutions are also provided on the companion CD.

## Using Collections and Property Procedures

In Chapter 7 we introduced collection objects and property procedures, but we didn't discuss how to use these features together. As you'll recall, collections can contain any type of object or data type. You can add, retrieve, and remove items from a collection by calling the appropriate methods of the collection object. To simplify this process, you can call these methods from a property procedure. In this section we will use a collection of bookmark properties to show how the collection object and property procedures can work together.

### Using Bookmarks

Suppose you need to design an application that allows the user to view data from a Microsoft Access table. This task is rather simple. You create a form and set its Record Source property to the table name. Each control on the form could then represent a field within the table. But what if the user also wants to be able to mark any number of records while in the form so that he or she can quickly return to them when needed? Although arranging for this capability is a bit more involved than making table data accessible, you can do it using bookmarks.

In Microsoft Access, bookmarks allow the user to keep track of his or her location within a recordset. Similar to a bookmark in a book, they allow the user to mark a position that he or she wants to go back to. When a form's Record Source property is not empty, the form is considered to be bound. All bound forms create an internal recordset object that allows you to view the data from the underlying table or query. In Chapter 7 we demonstrated how to use a single bookmark to save your position within a recordset so that you could return to it later.

You can create as many bookmarks as you need within a recordset object as long as you use a different variable to represent each bookmark. Because the user wants to be able to mark any number of records, a collection object would be a good way to keep track of the bookmarks. The user would simply add an item to the collection whenever he or she wanted a new bookmark. Because a collection can contain an unlimited number of items, you are not limiting the number of bookmarks you can define. If you used variables to represent the bookmarks, when you were first creating your application you would have to define the total number of variables you would need. Having to decide this so early on would consequently limit the number of bookmarks the user could set. To show you how to use multiple bookmarks, we will use property procedures to add and retrieve items from a collection. We will demonstrate on the Customers form from the Northwind Traders sample database. (If you have previously modified the sample database that comes with Microsoft Access, you can use the NWIND.MDB database from Chapter 6, located in the CHAP06 subfolder of the folder in which you installed the companion CD files. A finished version of the application described in this chapter is included in the CHAP08 subfolder.)

## Modifying the Customers Form

Let's first consider how to set and retrieve the various bookmarks the user will create through your code. The easiest way might be to use two command buttons: one to set the bookmark and one to go to it. With this in mind, add two command buttons to the Customers form, and set the following properties:

| Property | Value |
| --- | --- |
| **First button** | |
| Name | SetBookmark |
| Caption | Set Bookmark |
| **Second button** | |
| Name | GetBookmark |
| Caption | Get Bookmark |

Now that you have added the command buttons to the form, open the code module for the form by choosing Code from the View menu. In the General Declarations section of the form, you need to define a Private collection variable. This collection will hold the bookmarks. You can define this variable by using the following syntax:

```
Private MyBookmarks As New Collection
```

Now let's add code to the command buttons. Open the Click event procedure for the SetBookmark button. In this event procedure, you want to add an item to the collection MyBookmarks. The item in this case will be a bookmark that represents the current record you are on in a form. To do this, call the Add method of the collection object and pass in the bookmark as the Item:

```
Private Sub SetBookmark_Click()
    ' Create a new item in the collection.
    MyBookmarks.Add Item:=Me.Bookmark
End Sub
```

The line of code above will add a bookmark object to the collection called My Bookmarks. Because this bookmark is the first one added to the collection, you can retrieve it by using the following syntax:

```
' Retrieve the item from the collection.
Me.Bookmark = MyBookmarks(1)
```

Add the line of code above to the click event procedure of the GetBookmark command button. Now let's test the code and see what it does. If you run the form, you can see all the records from the Customers table. Go to any record in the form. Click the button labeled Set Bookmark. Now move to another record in the form. Click the Get Bookmark button. You should be on the same record as when you set the bookmark.

## Adding Multiple Items to a Collection

Now that you have the essential code to set and retrieve a bookmark on the form, the next step is to add multiple items to the collection. Let's first think of the best way to save multiple bookmarks. Because we are not using variables in this example, we cannot create a new variable to represent each bookmark. Rather, we must add a new item to the collection to represent the new bookmark. You can retrieve items in a collection by their Index or Key value. The Index value may change when items are added or removed from the collection, so it is best to create a Key for each bookmark. The Key value of an item is a unique string that will identify the item in the collection. Using the Key value, you name each bookmark in the collection. To name each bookmark, use the InputBox function, which will prompt the user for a string value and use the result as the Key value for the new item. Now modify the Click event procedure for the SetBookmark command button to look like the following:

```
Private Sub SetBookmark_Click()
    Dim strResponse As String
        strResponse = InputBox$ _
            ("What would you like to call this bookmark?")
    ' If the Cancel Button is pressed, exit the procedure.
    If Len(strResponse) = 0 Then Exit Sub
    ' Create a new item in the collection.
    MyBookmarks.Add Item:=Me.Bookmark, Key:=strResponse
End Sub
```

The other half of the problem is to retrieve these items from the collection using the Key value. You could use an InputBox text box to ask the user for the name of the bookmark. But what if the user forgets or misspells the name? From the user's standpoint, the best design would involve using the Microsoft Access combo box control to provide a list of available bookmarks.

## Adding a Combo Box to a Form

By adding a combo box to the Customers form, you let the user choose which bookmark to use. Set the following properties of the combo box:

| Property | Value |
| --- | --- |
| Name | BMCombo |
| Row Source Type | Value List |
| Limit To List | Yes |

The Row Source Type property is set to Value List because items—for example, the names of the bookmarks—will be added to the list at run time. So if you plan to have the user select the bookmark name from the combo box, you should add the bookmark to the combo box when the bookmark is initially set. You can add the bookmark names to the Row Source property of the combo box. The Row Source property must be a semicolon delimited list whenever you have more than one bookmark. Therefore, you must know if anything is already in the Row Source property before you add something. You could use an If...Then...Else statement to test the value of the Row Source property so that you can add a comma if necessary. Modify the Click event procedure of the SetBookmark button to look like the following:

```
Private Sub SetBookmark_Click()
    Dim strResponse As String
        strResponse = InputBox$ _
            ("What would you like to call this bookmark?")
```

```
    ' If the Cancel Button is pressed, exit the procedure.
    If Len(strResponse) = 0 Then Exit Sub
    With Me.BMCombo
        ' Check the RowSource property of the combo box
        ' so that the new bookmark name may be added.
        If Len(.RowSource) = 0 Or IsNull(.RowSource) Then
            .RowSource = strResponse
        Else
            ' If the RowSource has an item, add a comma
            ' followed by the name of the new bookmark.
            .RowSource = .RowSource & ";" & strResponse
        End If
    End With
    ' Create a new item in the collection.
    MyBookmarks.Add Item:=Me.Bookmark, Key:=strResponse
End Sub
```

Now the SetBookmark command button will add a bookmark to the collection with any name the user gives it and will add the name to the combo box.

## Retrieving Bookmarks via the Combo Box

To retrieve the bookmark, the user must select the name of the bookmark in the combo box and then click the Get Bookmark command button. In the Click event procedure of the GetBookmark command button, a message box that tells the user to select an item in the combo box if one is not currently selected needs to be displayed. To display such a message box, place the following code in the Click event for the GetBookmark command button:

```
Private Sub GetBookmark_Click()
    If IsNull(Me.BMCombo.Value) Or _
        Len(Me.BMCombo.Value) = 0 Then
        MsgBox "Please select bookmark to go to."
        Me.BMCombo.SetFocus
    Else
        ' Return the form back to the bookmark.
        Me.Bookmark = MyBookmarks(Me.BMCombo.Value)
    End If
End Sub
```

Test the application to see how it works. Go to any record on the form, and click the Set Bookmark command button. Enter any name for the bookmark in the InputBox text box. Move to another record. Select the name from the BM-Combo combo box, and click the Get Bookmark command button. Try this with several bookmarks.

## Clearing Bookmarks

The user may want to remove all the bookmarks stored in the collection and start over with new ones. To clear bookmarks, add a command button to the Customers form and set the following properties:

| Property | Value |
|----------|-------|
| Name | ClearBookmarks |
| Caption | Clear Bookmarks |

In the Click event of the ClearBookmarks command button, add the following code to remove the bookmarks from the collection and reset the BMCombo combo box so that its list is empty:

```
Private Sub ClearBookmarks_Click()
    Dim intBM As Integer

    ' Remove all bookmarks in the collection.
    For intBM = MyBookmarks.Count To 1 Step -1
        MyBookmarks.Remove intBM
    Next

    ' Clear the RowSource of the combo box.
    Me.BMCombo.RowSource = ""
    Me.BMCombo.Value = ""
End Sub
```

## Adding Property Procedures

As an alternative to placing all the code to manipulate the collection in the command buttons, you could create property procedures that could be a common feature for all your forms. You could then use the property procedures to manipulate the collection. The command buttons would not call the methods of the collection but rather would simply refer to the property procedures.

Remember that you are not only adding items to a collection but also retrieving them. Therefore, if you are going to use property procedures to do this, the Property Get procedure needs to accept at least one argument. This argument will be used to find a particular item within the collection. You can use the Property Let procedure to add an item to the collection because a bookmark is only a string. The Property Let procedure should accept two arguments: the bookmark and the Key value. The code on the facing page shows what the property procedures look like and how to call them from the command buttons on the form.

```
Private MyBookmarks As New Collection

Public Property Get CurrentBookmark(KeyValue As String) _
    As String
    ' Return an item from the collection.
    CurrentBookmark = MyBookmarks(KeyValue)
End Property

Public Property Let CurrentBookmark(KeyValue As String, _
    strBookmark As String)
    ' Create a new item in the collection.
    MyBookmarks.Add Item:=strBookmark, Key:=CStr(KeyValue)
End Property

Private Sub SetBookmark_Click()
    Dim strResponse As String

    strResponse = InputBox$ _
        ("What would you like to call this bookmark?")
    ' If the Cancel Button is pressed, exit the procedure.
    If Len(strResponse) = 0 Then Exit Sub
    With Me.BMCombo
        ' Check the RowSource property of the combo box
        ' so that the new bookmark name may be added.
        If Len(.RowSource) = 0 Or IsNull(.RowSource) Then
            .RowSource = strResponse
        Else
            .RowSource = .RowSource & "," & strResponse
        End If
    End With
    ' Pass the key value and the bookmark to the Property Let
    ' procedure.
    Me.CurrentBookmark(strResponse) = Me.Bookmark
End Sub

Private Sub GetBookmark_Click()
    If IsNull(Me.BMCombo.Value) Or _
        Len(Me.BMCombo.Value) = 0 Then
        MsgBox "Please select a bookmark to go to."
        Me.BMCombo.SetFocus
    Else
        ' Return the form back to the bookmark.
        Me.Bookmark = Me.CurrentBookmark(Me.BMCombo.Value)
    End If
End Sub
```

NOTE Remember that the argument name you use in the Property Get procedure must be the same as the first argument in the Property Let procedure.

Notice that the only change to the Click event procedures of the command buttons is that instead of referring to the collection they refer to the property of the form. Test the application again, and you should be able to add bookmarks and go to them.

## Creating Multipage Forms

Occasionally, you may need a form to include more information than can be displayed on one screen; or you may want the user to follow a particular sequence of steps. Multipage forms are a good solution for these situations. The best examples of multipage forms in Microsoft Access are wizards. Any wizard in Microsoft Access presents questions and then creates an object based on the answers given. In all wizards, you can go forward or backward to the various pages.

The trick to creating a multipage form is to keep the pages the same size. So your first decision is how big to make each page. Once you decide on the page size, you can copy the format of the first page to the remaining pages. In this solution, the form will have a total of three pages and each page will be 3 inches in height. The form will allow the user to select which customers they wish to view in a report by means of a multiselect list box. The data for this solution comes from the Customers table in the Northwind sample database.

### Creating the Pages

To begin, create a new form, and set the following properties for it:

| Property | Value |
| --- | --- |
| Scroll Bars | Neither |
| Record Selectors | No |
| Navigation Buttons | No |
| Auto Center | Yes |
| Border Style | Thin |
| Control Box | No |
| Min Max Buttons | None |
| Close Button | No |

Because a multipage form depends on exact measurements for the placement of items, you should use the properties sheet to set properties such as Top, Left,

Width, and Height. Click on the Detail section of the form, and set the Height property to 9.0". This will allow for three 3" pages to be created on the form.

To separate each page of the form, you must use the page-break control. Place two page-break controls on the form. Set the Top property of one page-break control to 3.00" and the other to 6.00". The form now has three pages defined. When working with multiple-page forms, it's a good idea to define the area on each page where controls should be placed. You could do this by adding a rectangle object to each page. Set the Top property of each rectangle to 0.05" below the top of the page.

## Page 1

In most wizards the first page includes information that describes the wizard and a picture that shows what the finished object will look like. With this idea in mind, make sure the control wizard is on and add an Unbound Object Frame control to page 1. Select Create From File, and choose any bitmap. (You can use the T-WIZ.BMP from the CHAP08 subfolder of the companion CD.) Move the object to the desired location on page 1, and note the value of the Top property. Once this object exists on the page, copy it and paste it. Set the Top property of the object to 3 inches more than the first object. Now the object will be placed at the same location as the first object except on page 2. Do the same for page 3.

The first page of the form should inform the user what this wizard will do. Think of it as a welcome screen. Add a label to the form that has this information: "Welcome to the Customers Report Wizard. Click the Next button to select the customers you wish to view."

Since the user will ultimately print the report, add a text box to page 1 that allows the user to change the report's page header. Set the Name property of the text box to txtTitle. When completed, page 1 should look like Figure 8-1.

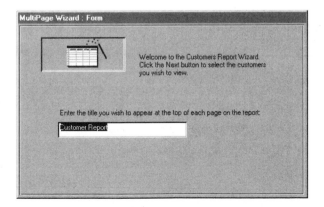

**Figure 8-1.** *Page 1 of the multipage form solution.*

## Page 2

On page 2 you will present the user with a list of Company Names from which to base his or her report. The best way to present this information is via a list box. A list box can show all the customers' companies and allow the user to select any number of them.

Add a list box to page 2, and set the following properties:

| Property | Value |
|---|---|
| Name | lstCompany |
| Row Source | Customers |
| Column Count | 2 |
| Column Widths | 0"; 1" |
| Multi Select | Simple |

Notice that the Column Count property is set to 2 and that the first column will be hidden because its ColumnWidth is set to 0. The first column in the Customers table, CustomerID, is hidden because it is a primary key of the table and will be used to filter the table so that the user can view only the selected records. The list box will show only the CompanyName field. When completed, page 2 will look like Figure 8-2.

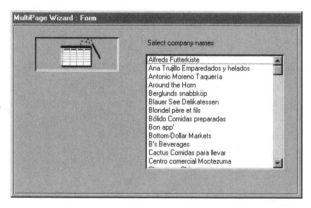

**Figure 8-2.** *Page 2 of the multipage form solution.*

## Page 3

Page 3 of the multipage form will indicate that the user can preview the customer report. In a real wizard you might allow the user to open the report in different views; to keep things simple here, however, we are showing only a preview of the report. Place a label on the third page of the form with the following text for its Caption property: "Customers Report Wizard. Click the Preview button to preview the report with your selected customers." Page 3 should now look like Figure 8-3.

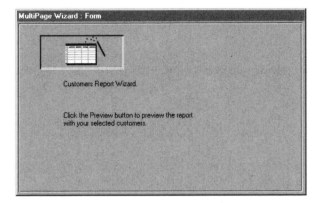

**Figure 8-3.** *Page 3 of the multipage form solution.*

## Adding Navigation Buttons

Now that you have designed the form's interface, you need to provide command buttons to allow the user to go from page to page. You'll want to add the Next, Previous, Preview, and Close navigation buttons. These command buttons need to appear on each page. Rather than adding copies of these buttons to each page, however, add them to the form's footer. To open the form footer, select Form Header/Footer from the View menu (when the form is opened in Design view). Set the Height property of the form header to 0, and add four command buttons to the form footer. Two of the command buttons will allow the user to move from page to page (Next and Previous). One button will preview the report, and the last will close the form.

Set the following properties for the Next navigation command button:

| Property | Value |
| --- | --- |
| Name | cmdNext |
| Caption | Next |

Set the following properties for the Previous navigation command button:

| Property | Value |
| --- | --- |
| Name | cmdPrevious |
| Caption | Previous |

Set the following properties for the Preview navigation command button:

| Property | Value |
| --- | --- |
| Name | cmdPreview |
| Caption | Preview |
| Visible | No |

Set the Visible property for the cmdPreview button to No because you don't want the user to try to preview the report without selecting which customers will be in it. This button should be enabled only when the user reaches the last page of the form.

Set the following properties for the Close form navigation command button:

| Property | Value |
| --- | --- |
| Name | cmdClose |
| Caption | Close |

## Adding VBA Code

To close the form, place the following code in the Click event of the cmdClose button:

```
Private Sub cmdClose_Click()
    DoCmd.Close acForm, Me.Name
End Sub
```

Before you can add any code to the navigation buttons, the form has to have some way to determine which page the user is currently on. The form needs to be able to track the user's current location so that the cmdPreview button can be made visible when the last page is reached and so that the cmdPrevious and cmdNext buttons can be enabled and disabled appropriately. The best way to notify the form of the user's location is to create a set of property procedures.

### Property procedures

You'll need two properties: one to store the maximum number of pages on the form and one to store the current page. Let's name these properties MaxPages and CurrentPage, respectively. Adding property procedures for the MaxPages property is easy because you need only to set and retrieve a value. Add the following code to the form to do this:

```
' General Declarations section of form
Private iMaxPages As Integer    ' Stores maximum pages of form

Public Property Get MaxPages() As Variant
    MaxPages = iMaxPages
End Property
```

```
Public Property Let MaxPages(ByVal vNewValue As Variant)
    iMaxPages = vNewValue
End Property
```

The CurrentPage property should allow you to set and retrieve a value. When this property is set, the form needs to be updated to show the new page and enable the appropriate command buttons so that they are visible and enabled. It is also important to notify the form from which the Property Let procedure was called. For example, if it is called from the cmdNext button, the user wants to go to the next page (increase the value of CurrentPage). You can add the following code to the form to keep track of the CurrentPage:

```
' General Declarations section of form
Private iCurrentPage As Integer       ' Stores current page

Public Property Get CurrentPage() As Variant
    CurrentPage = iCurrentPage
End Property

Public Property Let CurrentPage(ByVal vNewValue As Variant)
    On Error GoTo CurrentPageErr
    ' Generic way to determine which control
    ' called the procedure
    Select Case Me.ActiveControl
        Case "cmdNext":
            If vNewValue < MaxPages Then
                vNewValue = vNewValue + 1
            End If
        Case "cmdPrevious":
            If vNewValue > 1 Then
                vNewValue = vNewValue - 1
            End If
        Case Else
            ' CurrentPage was set to correct page from
            ' a procedure.
    End Select
ChangePage:
    Me.GoToPage vNewValue      ' Go to new page

    ' If last page, then disable the Next button
    ' and show the Preview button.
    If vNewValue = MaxPages Then
        Me!cmdPreview.Visible = True
        ' Put the focus to the Preview button.
        Me!cmdPreview.SetFocus
        Me!cmdNext.Enabled = False
```

*(continued)*

**281**

```
        Else
            Me!cmdNext.Enabled = True
            Me!cmdPreview.Visible = False
        End If

        ' If page 1, then disable the Previous button.
        If vNewValue = 1 Then
            Me!cmdPrevious.Enabled = False
        Else
            Me!cmdPrevious.Enabled = True
        End If

        iCurrentPage = vNewValue

Exit Property
CurrentPageErr:
    If Err.Number = 2474 Or Err.Number = 2427 Then
    ' Form is opening, and no control is active.
        Resume ChangePage
    Else
        Resume Next
    End If
End Property
```

Now that we have defined the property procedures, it is time to create the VBA code for the cmdNext and cmdPrevious buttons.

### Open event

The form should first open to page 1. To make sure this happens, you must set the MaxPages and CurrentPage properties in the Open event of the form. The following VBA syntax will do this:

```
Private Sub Form_Open(Cancel As Integer)
    Me.MaxPages = 3     ' Set the maximum number of pages.
    Me.CurrentPage = 1  ' Set the current page to 1.
End Sub
```

### Changing the current page

The cmdNext and cmdPrevious Click events are equally easy to set. Just add 1 to or subtract 1 from the CurrentPage property. Here is the VBA syntax to do this:

```
Private Sub cmdNext_Click()
    Me.CurrentPage = Me.CurrentPage + 1
End Sub
```

```
Private Sub cmdPrevious_Click()
    Me.CurrentPage = Me.CurrentPage - 1
End Sub
```

Save the form as MultiPage Wizard. Now that most of the code is complete, you can test the form. Open the form and advance through the different pages. Notice how the Next and Previous buttons are enabled and disabled appropriately and the Preview button is visible only on the last page.

> **NOTE**　You can also simulate a multipage form by using the Tab control and setting its Style property to None. To move from page to page, use the SetFocus method of the Page object (described in Chapter 7) in the Click event procedures of the Previous and Next command buttons.

## Creating the Customers Report

Before you add code to the cmdPreview button, you need to create a report. This solution does not require a fancy report. Use the AutoReport feature of Microsoft Access to create the report. Save it as Customers Report.

Open the report in Design view, and select the label control in the Page Header section. Change the Name property of the label to lblHeader. This label will be used to display the text from page 1 of the form MultiPage Wizard. To change this label at run time, place the following code in the Open event procedure of the report:

```
Private Sub Report_Open(Cancel As Integer)
    Me.lblHeader.Caption = Forms![MultiPage Wizard]!txtTitle
End Sub
```

Notice that the Caption property of the label is set to the text box on page 1 of the form MultiPage Wizard.

Close and save the report. You're done! The essentials are completed. Feel free to tinker with the report interface if you're feeling creative!

### Filtering the Customers report

Previously, we added a multiselect list box to page 2 of the form MultiPage Wizard. Open this form in Design view.

The form's cmdPreview button should display the Customers Report in Print Preview with only the records selected in the list box. To use only selected records, you must use the ItemsSelected property of the list box, because each selected item is enumerated and concatenated to a string variable. Once the filter condition is completed, the string variable can be passed as the fourth argument to the OpenReport method, as shown here:

```
Private Sub cmdPreview_Click()
    Dim vntItem As Variant, strFilter As String
    Dim rptMyReport As New [Report_Customers Report]

    For Each vntItem In Me!lstCompany.ItemsSelected
        ' Concatenate single quotes around the customer ID
        ' because the CustomerID field is Text.
        strFilter = strFilter & "[CustomerID] = '" & _
            Me![lstCompany].ItemData(vntItem) & "' OR "
    Next
    'Determine if a filter has been generated.
    If Len(strFilter) > 0 Then
        ' Remove the extra OR condition at the end of the string.
        strFilter = Left(strFilter, Len(strFilter) - 4)
    End If
    ' Preview the report, and pass the filter string.
    DoCmd.OpenReport rptMyReport.Name, acPreview, , strFilter
End Sub
```

The variable, strFilter, will come out with the following format:

```
[CustomerID] = 'ALFKI' OR [CustomerID] = 'ANTON'
```

In this example, ALFKI and ANTON represent Customer IDs that were selected in the list box. The MultiPage Wizard form is now complete. Try it out!

# Allowing Users to Customize Forms

Most Microsoft Windows–based applications give users the ability to customize the user interface. Microsoft Access provides an easy way for you to include this capability in your applications. In this section you will learn how to create a form that allows the user to change the Back Color property of the form's Detail section and save that color so that when the user opens the form again, the colors will be the same. Although this example uses only the Back Color property of the Detail section, you could easily modify the example to include font and control changes the user could customize.

## Creating a Color Picker Form

Since the ultimate goal is to allow the user to change the background color of a form, the first form you'll need to create will be a color picker. This form should show the user the available colors. Figure 8-4 shows what this form will look like when it's completed.

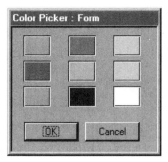

**Figure 8-4.** *Color Picker form.*

This form will act simply as a dialog box, so you must change many of the form's properties to reflect this. Set the following properties of the form:

| Property | Value |
| --- | --- |
| Scroll Bars | Neither |
| Record Selectors | No |
| Navigation Buttons | No |
| Auto Center | Yes |
| Modal | Yes |
| Control Box | No |
| Min Max Buttons | None |
| Close Button | No |

## Adding controls and properties

Add nine rectangle objects and two command buttons to the form. Set the Back Style property of the rectangles to Normal, and change the Back Color property of each to reflect a different color. Now the user can click the rectangle that has the desired color. The trick is to save the color the user selected so that the form calling the Color Picker form can refer to it. The easiest way to do this is to create a property of the form to store the color selected. Remember, when creating any property, you need a Private variable that can store the value passed in after the procedures have finished executing. Add the following code to your form to create a property called NewColor:

```
Private strSelectedColor

Public Property Get NewColor() As Variant
    NewColor = strSelectedColor
End Property

Public Property Let NewColor(ByVal vNewValue As Variant)
    strSelectedColor = vNewValue
End Property
```

Now that a property of the form exists to store the selected color, you must add code to the Click event of each rectangle object. In this event procedure, you need to set the form's property (NewColor) equal to the Back Color property for that rectangle. The following code shows what the Click event of Box0 will look like:

```
Private Sub Box0_Click()
    Me.NewColor = Me!Box0.BackColor
End Sub
```

Add the same code to the Click event of the other rectangles, but change the reference from Box0 to the appropriate name of the rectangle you are working with.

Change the captions of the command buttons to OK and Cancel and change their names to cmdOK and cmdCancel. In the Click event of the cmdCancel button, add the code necessary to close the form, as shown here:

```
Private Sub cmdCancel_Click()
    DoCmd.Close
End Sub
```

In the Click event of the cmdOK button, hide the form but do not close it. The calling form still needs to refer to the NewColor property. Add the following code to its Click event procedure:

```
Private Sub cmdOK_Click()
    Me.Visible = False
End Sub
```

The form is now complete. Save it as Color Picker.

Next you want to create the form that the user may customize.

## Customizable Forms

It may sound difficult to create a form that saves user settings, but it's not with Microsoft Access. In fact, it's easy.

First you need to consider where to save user settings information. Microsoft Access saves all its settings in the Registry. The Registry is used by many Windows-based applications to store information about the application and its environment. The Registry is the best place to save the settings for your application, too.

Microsoft Access has two main functions that allow you to write information to and retrieve information from the Windows Registry: GetSetting and SaveSetting. The best times to use these functions are when the form is opened and closed, respectively. The events that correspond with these actions are, as you might guess, the Open and Close events of the form.

The next step in completing our application is to create a new form in Microsoft Access. To this form, add two command buttons. Although you can have as many controls as necessary on the form, in this example we are adding only the basics. Change the Caption properties of the command buttons to Choose Back Color and Close and change the names to cmdColor and cmdClose. Figure 8-5 shows what this form will look like when it's completed. Save the form as Customize Form Color. Now open the new form's Close event procedure. In this event you will want to use the SaveSetting procedure to save the Back Color of the form's Detail section. This procedure has a few arguments that you must specify. Two arguments describe the sections in the Registry where the information will be written, one describes the key, and the fourth specifies the value. The two arguments that deal with the Registry sections are AppName and Section. You should pass as values to these two arguments the name of your application (AppName) and the name of the form or object that you're saving information about (Section). The key allows you to describe exactly what it is that you are saving. For example, you could use "Detail Color" because you'll be saving the Back Color of the form's Detail section. The setting is the value that you're storing, for example, the color. You can use the following syntax to store this information in the Registry:

```
Private Sub Form_Close()
    SaveSetting AppName:="MyApp", Section:=Me.Name, _
        Key:="Detail_Color", Setting:=Me.Detail.BackColor
End Sub
```

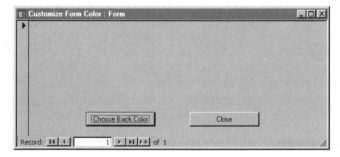

**Figure 8-5.** *Sample customizable form solution.*

Because the information has been saved in the form's Close event, it should be retrieved in the form's Open event.

The GetSetting function has nearly the same arguments as the SaveSetting statement. It does not, however, have the Setting argument. Instead, it has an argument called Default that allows you to specify a value to be used if there is no information in the Registry for the sections you specified. The following example uses the Default argument to specify the Back Color of the Detail section that the form definition was originally saved with if no other information can be found:

```
Private Sub Form_Open(Cancel As Integer)
    Me.Detail.BackColor = GetSetting(AppName:="MyApp", _
        Section:=Me.Name, Key:="Detail_Color", _
        Default:=Me.Detail.BackColor)
End Sub
```

## Calling the Color Picker Form

The essentials for saving and retrieving the customized options are now complete. All that remains is to open the form that has the options the user can choose.

In the Click event procedure of the cmdClose button on the Customize Form Color form, add the following code to close the form:

```
Private Sub cmdClose_Click()
    DoCmd.Close
End Sub
```

This code automatically invokes the Close event procedure.

In the Click event procedure of the cmdColor button, add the following code to display the Color Picker form:

```
Private Sub cmdColor_Click()
    DoCmd.OpenForm ("Color Picker")
End Sub
```

When the Color Picker form is displayed, it is modal. This means that you cannot give focus to any form within Microsoft Access until the Color Picker form is closed. This fact is important, because the Activate event of the form will be triggered when the Color Picker form is closed. This allows you to change the Back Color of the form to what was selected in the Color Picker form. In this event procedure you should also close the Color Picker form, so the Back Color of your form is not changed every time the Activate event occurs. The following code shows what the Activate event of your form might look like:

```
Private Sub Form_Activate()
    ' Ignore any errors that may occur if the Color
    ' Picker form is not open.
    On Error Resume Next
    Me.Detail.BackColor = Forms![Color Picker].NewColor
    DoCmd.Close acForm, "Color Picker"
End Sub
```

Close the form and run it. You should now be able to click the Color Picker button and choose any color. The form's Back Color should change to the correct color, and that color should remain the same if you close the form and reopen it.

## PREVIEW of the next chapter

This chapter showed some techniques that you will find useful when creating your own custom solutions. The next chapter focuses on Data Access Objects. These are objects that can be used to manipulate your database, primarily your tables and data, through VBA.

# PART

# THREE

## Working with Data

# 9

# Data Access Objects (DAO)

In this chapter we'll explain why and how to use Microsoft Data Access Objects, commonly referred to as DAO. We'll begin the chapter by discussing some terminology used with DAO. Then we'll introduce the DAO hierarchy, which is a hierarchy of programmable objects you can use to access and manipulate data. From a general overview of the hierarchy, we'll move to a detailed examination of each object in the hierarchy. We'll describe the collections and objects and their methods and properties and give practical code examples for each object. Because you'll probably be working mostly with the objects that fall below the database object in the DAO hierarchy, we'll cover these in more detail than we do the upper-level objects.

Before we get into specifics, however, let's briefly consider why you would want to use DAO. You could create an entire database using DAO and some of the Microsoft Access built-in procedures. Can you guess why this would not be wise? Obviously, some tasks are easier to accomplish through the user interface, such as creating a query or setting up relationships among tables. Some methods and properties of DAO objects, however, can be useful because they automate and improve routines that are tedious or redundant via the user interface. Remember that one of the key purposes for creating your application is to reduce the amount of time and effort it takes for the user to complete tasks. The most common uses of DAO are manipulating data, processing transactions on data, and setting up security for the data.

Through DAO you can work only with data; you cannot build or manipulate parts of the user interface. For example, you cannot create a form using DAO even though it is part of the database, because a form is not data. You can create a table, however. In general, anything that you can do with tables, with queries, or with data itself can be done through DAO. The only thing you can do through DAO with the user interface is retrieve the names of objects. For example, through the Containers object you can retrieve the names of forms or the names of reports.

# DAO Terminology

Because of DAO's consistency with object-oriented technology, you should find it relatively easy to understand Microsoft DAO objects and program with them. The DAO hierarchy, like many other object-oriented applications, has objects and collections that allow for easy manipulation, in this case by using the Microsoft Jet Database Engine. These objects and collections have properties and methods that allow you to identify and manipulate any item within the DAO hierarchy. The following sections give an overview of objects and collections and their properties and methods as they relate to DAO.

## Objects

An object in the DAO hierarchy is a specific entity that exists inside the database engine or in your database. These objects include the database engine itself; the workspace that you log on to before you open your database; your database; and your tables, queries, relationships, and security permissions. Each DAO object logically builds on the others, as is the case in any good object hierarchy. Many DAO objects contain collections of other objects that they support. For example, you cannot have a Microsoft Access table without it first being contained within a Microsoft Access database. Each DAO object serves a purpose and has methods and properties that allow you to develop and manage the object and any object that it contains. Without access to these methods and properties, the user would have to manage your database entirely through the user interface. As a solution provider, you want to bypass the user interface and automate certain tasks to ensure that they are completed successfully.

## Collections

A collection is a set of objects of the same type. Each object in a collection can also contain collections of other objects. So, a collection can contain zero or more objects of the same type, and an object can contain zero or more different collections. For example, a Rooms collection could contain Kitchen, Bedroom, and Office objects. (The Rooms collection would never, however, contain an Automobile object.) Each room object could have various collections of objects. For instance, the Office object could have a Persons collection (you, your housemate) and a Personal Computers collection.

In DAO, the Databases collection contains Database objects, each of which in turn contains a Containers, a QueryDefs, a Recordsets, a Relations, and a TableDefs collection.

## Properties

A property describes one aspect of an object's state or characteristics. A House object, for example, might have a Color property, which is set to green. A DAO object's Properties collection describes all of the object's state and characteristics. (DAO collections have only a single property, the Count property.)

You can set or retrieve properties for a DAO object. You might see that a house is green and decide to paint it yellow. Likewise, you might retrieve a control object's enabled property and then set it to False. You can also use properties to distinguish objects in a collection, and you can use a collection's Count property to determine the number of objects in that collection, as shown in the following code:

```
Dim intPropCount As Integer
intPropCount = DBEngine.Properties.Count
```

## Methods

The DAO objects provide services to you; that is, they perform actions. In an object-oriented application, these services or actions are called methods. Each object has its own specific methods, depending on the object's purpose. For example, a Guitar object would have a Play method, whereas a Person object would have a Sleep method. It would not make sense for a Guitar object to have a Sleep method.

Collections also have methods, but collections have a limited number of methods. A Guitar collection, for example, contains Guitar objects. If you are an active guitar collector, your collection of Guitar objects is subject to change. In the DAO hierarchy, collections can have the following methods to facilitate such change:

- An Append method, which adds an object to the collection. When using the Append method, you append an object that has whatever properties you specify.

- A Delete method, which removes an object from the collection. When you delete an object using the Delete method, you need to refer only to the object name; specifying the object's properties is unnecessary because the name alone will accurately identify it as the object to be deleted.

- A Refresh method, which verifies the number and/or characteristics of objects in a collection after they have been added or removed.

# The DAO Hierarchy

Figure 9-1 shows the Microsoft Access DAO hierarchy. In the following sections, we'll introduce most of these objects and explain where they fit into the hierarchy.

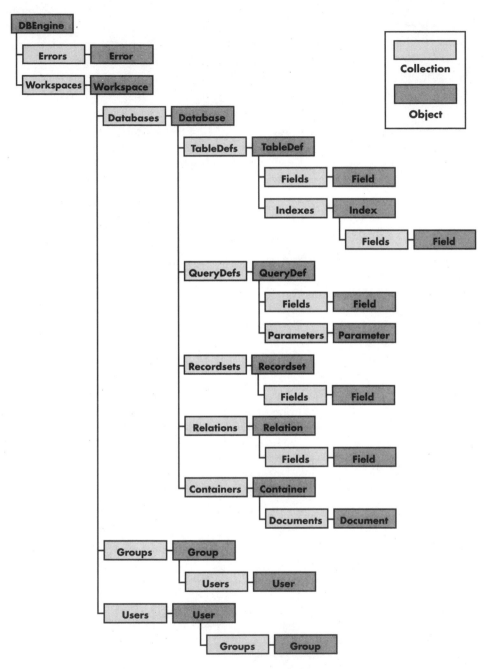

**Figure 9-1.** *Microsoft Access DAO hierarchy.*

## DBEngine

At the top of the DAO hierarchy is the DBEngine object, the object through which you manipulate the Microsoft Jet Database Engine. (Jet is an acronym for Joint Engine Technology.) All the objects within the DAO hierarchy are dependent on or based on this object. The DBEngine object is the only DAO object that isn't contained in a collection.

Because there is no collection of DBEngine objects, you can have only a single instance of the Jet Database Engine in any Microsoft Access session. You could simultaneously run as many sessions of Access as your PC's memory allows, thereby creating multiple instances of the DBEngine object. But there's really no reason to do so, and doing so isn't recommended.

## Workspace

The DBEngine object contains a collection of Workspace objects. The purpose of the Workspace object is to maintain a separate transaction log. Whenever you work with workspaces and the transactions within them, be aware that a transaction cannot span multiple workspaces. This feature allows you to isolate one group of transactions so that they can be rolled back (undone) if necessary, without affecting other transactions. Using workspaces to separate transactions also allows you to run simultaneous transactions.

Whenever Microsoft Access is started, a default Workspace object is automatically created. To refer to the default Workspace object, use the following code:

```
Set wsMyWorkspace = DBEngine.Workspaces(0)
```

The zero in the collection is the default and represents the first object added to the collection. You can create as many Workspace objects as you need.

## User and Group

Each Workspace object has a collection of User and Group objects. One of the primary uses of User and Group objects is to provide security, a topic we'll cover in depth in Chapter 12. Here we'll just mention some of the aspects of the security model in DAO. By default, when Microsoft Access is first started, the user is automatically logged on as the Admin user. Your application can create a new workspace and force the user to log on with a more specific ID. You can use the CurrentUser function to see which user is logged on to Microsoft Access. This capability plays an important role in Microsoft Access security, as you'll see in Chapter 12.

### Referencing Objects Within Their Collections (Containers)

Objects can be referenced in several ways.

- **By index** In indexed references, you refer to an object by its index in the collection. All DAO collections are indexed beginning with zero:

```
Collection(0)
```

- **By object data type** To represent an object, declare a variable of that object's data type and use that variable to manipulate that object:

```
Dim xyz As SpecificObjectType
```

- **Implicitly** In implicit references, objects are referred to directly:

```
Object
```

- **Explicitly** In explicit references, you refer to an individual object by referring explicitly to the collection that contains it:

```
Collection("Object Name")
Collection![Object Name]
```

Using an exclamation point to reference an object performs what is known as early binding. *Early binding* tells Microsoft Access at compile time which object is to be referenced at run time. Using parentheses to refer to an object is known as late binding. *Late binding* waits until run time to tell Microsoft Access which object to use. Within Microsoft Access, early binding can sometimes be faster than late binding. With late binding you have the advantage of creating more flexible and generic code because you can use a variable to reference the object name. The following pseudocode, for example, uses a string variable called strObjName to allow you to specify any object name of a given collection, thus creating reusable generic code:

```
Collection(strObjName)
```

The Group object allows you to set up permissions for multiple users so that you don't have to set up the permissions individually. You can place a user in a group, or you can add the group to the user's Groups collection. Either method establishes the user as the member of a group.

**Making Use of Workspaces, Users, and Groups in Your Application**

The Microsoft Access user interface provides for only a single workspace, a single database, and a single user at any one time. But an application running under Access can create a second workspace, log on as a different user, and open a second database. Once multiple workspaces are open, your application can move data between multiple databases, can manipulate data in multiple databases, or can even display a form that draws its contents from tables that several different users have permission to use.

## Database

The Database object has five collections: TableDefs, QueryDefs, Relations, Recordsets, and Containers. These collections allow your application to access the different parts of a database.

## TableDef

A TableDef object represents a table within your database. Each TableDef object has a collection of Field objects. In Microsoft Access you can define up to 255 fields for a table, but the size limitation for the set of fields in a record for Microsoft Access is 2 KB.

To demonstrate this size limitation, let's start Microsoft Access and create a new table. For a field name, type *F1*. For the data type, choose text with a field size of 255. Repeat this process nine more times (rename your fields sequentially as F2, F3, and so on). You will have created 10 fields within the table. Save the table and open it to enter data. Add sample data to each field, from F1 to F10, filling up all 255 characters in each field. As soon as you exceed 2 KB of data, Access will tell you that the record is too large.

Memo fields are an exception to this size limit. Memo fields store a pointer to the data, so they can hold up to 64 KB of text while taking up only a very small portion of the record. You should also be aware that Text fields, although defined as a maximum size, are actually variable in length. A text field takes up only as much space as what is typed into it. A numeric field, however, takes up the predefined size of that field regardless of what number is typed into it. With numeric data types, you should use the smallest size required to store the largest number that will be entered in the field.

## QueryDef

QueryDef objects are used primarily to create new queries or modify existing ones. When you create a QueryDef object, you are simply creating a query via a program. You can then use the QueryDef object's methods to execute the query.

A query can have up to 255 fields, and an SQL statement can have approximately 64,000 characters. If you are going to output several fields, keep your field and table names short. When Access builds the SQL statement, it specifies both the table name and the field name for each field, so if you have long table names and long field names, you might reach this 64,000 character limit. QueryDef objects can have Field objects and Parameter objects.

## Relation

You can use Relation objects to create relationships among tables. Relationships are much easier to create through the user interface, but there are reasons you might need to create relationships from within an application. For example, to make design updates easier, you might split your database into a front end (queries, forms, reports, macros, and modules) and a back end (tables and data) so that you have two files. The front-end database can link to all the tables in the back-end database. Then you can modify the front end at any time without overwriting any data. But suppose your user wants you to add a new table and relate it to an existing table. You can place this new table and the new relationship into the back-end database using a module that tests for the new table and checks to see whether the desired relationship exists. If it does not, then the module creates it using a Relation object.

## Recordset

Recordset objects are used for retrieving the data from the TableDef or QueryDef object. A Recordset object can be opened as a table, a dynaset, or a snapshot. (A dynaset is a set of records that can contain fields from multiple tables or queries.) Tables and dynasets are normally read-write. A snapshot is a read-only recordset. You open a Recordset object as a table only for Microsoft Access tables that exist within the database file itself, not for linked tables. All linked tables must use the dynaset-type recordset. (Recordsets, tables, dynasets, and snapshots are discussed in much more depth in Chapter 10.)

## Container

Container objects, as their name suggests, refer to the objects contained in the database, such as Tables (including Queries), Forms, Reports, Scripts (Macros), Modules, and Relationships. Container objects simply hold a Documents collection. Document objects hold the name and summary information for specific items that exist within the database and are used primarily for security within a database application.

# DAO in Detail

Now that you have a general idea of what the higher level objects in the DAO hierarchy are and what they do, we will shift our focus and examine each object in detail. We will include practical code examples for each object.

## Using the DBEngine Object

The DBEngine is the highest-level object in the DAO object model. No other collections or objects contain it. It, however, contains and controls all the other collections and objects in the DAO hierarchy. The DBEngine allows you to use and manipulate your database, just as your car's engine provides the power so you can operate your car. Without the engine, a car is just a pile of metal and plastic. And without the DBEngine, your database would be just another file on your hard drive.

### Using the properties of the DBEngine object

The following list includes the most commonly used properties of the DBEngine object. (You can find a complete list of DBEngine properties in online Help.)

**IniPath**  This property returns the path to the Registry key that specifies the location of the Workgroup Information File (SYSTEM.MDW), which Microsoft Access uses for storing user and group information for security purposes. This property cannot be changed within the Microsoft Access programming environment. You can read this property as follows:

```
Dim prMyProp As String
prMyProp = DBEngine.IniPath
```

After running this code, the prMyProp variable stores the following default Registry path:

> SOFTWARE\Microsoft\Office\8.0\Access\Jet\3.5

This property cannot be set from within Microsoft Access, however. You would use this property from other VBA applications, such as Microsoft Visual Basic and Microsoft Excel, when opening an Access database that has security set on it. This allows you to specify which Registry entry will be used to point to the SYSTEM.MDW file.

**SystemDB**  This property returns the file path (the location on your hard disk) of the SYSTEM.MDW file as stored in the Registry key returned by the IniPath property. This property cannot be changed within the Microsoft Access programming environment. As with the IniPath property, you would rarely use this property from Microsoft Access because it is more useful in other VBA applications. You can read it, however, with the following code:

```
Dim prMyProp As String
prMyProp = DBEngine.SystemDB
```

After running this code, the prMyProp variable stores the following default SYSTEM.MDW file path:

```
C:\Windows\System\system.mdw
```

**LoginTimeout**   This property is used to specify the number of seconds that the database engine will wait before returning a logon time-out error for Open Database Connectivity (ODBC) data sources.

Microsoft Access is a great front-end application for ODBC databases such as Microsoft SQL Server. However, you can receive an error when trying to connect and log on to the ODBC data source. The error could be caused because the network is down, because the network traffic is too heavy, or maybe even because the SQL Server is offline. By default, the Jet Database Engine will wait 20 seconds before producing a connection error. If your network is slow, you can increase the number of seconds to wait, as shown here:

```
' Set the LoginTimeout to 2 minutes.
DBEngine.LoginTimeout = 120
```

If you want the Engine to keep trying to connect until it succeeds, you can set the value to 0, but you will most likely want to set this property to some large number, because at some point you will want the Engine to stop trying to log on.

**Version**   This property returns the version of the Database Engine being used. You can determine the version as follows:

```
Dim prMyProp As String
prMyProp = DBEngine.Version
```

For Microsoft Access, the prMyProp variable stores version 3.5 after running this code.

### Using the methods of the DBEngine object
To maintain the integrity of your database, you can use the following methods of the DBEngine object.

**RepairDatabase**   Use this method to repair a database that has become corrupted. The following code will repair MYDATABASE.MDB:

```
Dim strDBName As String
strDBName = "C:\Files\MyDatabase.MDB"
DBEngine.RepairDatabase strDBName
```

This method cannot be used to repair the database it is being called from. It also cannot be used to repair a database that is open.

**CompactDatabase**    Use this method to compact a database. The following code will compact MYDATABASE.MDB into MYCOMPACTDB.MDB:

```
Dim strDBName As String, strNewDBName As String
strDBName = "C:\Files\MyDatabase.MDB"
strNewDBName = "C:\Files\MyCompactDB.MDB"
DBEngine.CompactDatabase olddb:=strDBName, newdb:=strNewDBName
```

This method cannot be used to compact the database it is being called from. It also cannot be used to compact a database that is open.

The CompactDatabase method has the following optional arguments:

- **Locale** Specifies a collating order other than that of the original database.

- **Options** Compacts the database into an encrypted or decrypted state and specifies the version of the Microsoft Jet Database Engine with which to compact it. You can combine the encrypt/decrypt and version options by summing their constants together.

- **Password** Compacts the database if it is password protected *if* the database file itself is given a password. The string ";pwd=" must be placed before the actual password string. This argument is not the same as the user-level security model password.

**RegisterDatabase**    If your application uses an ODBC data source, you can use this method to make entries in the ODBC.INI file and in the Registry to ensure that your application will always have this data source available. The following code, for example, registers the "SQL Backend" ODBC data source, which allows the user to access the data in the Pubs database on the Coyote SQL Server:

```
Dim vntAttribs
vntAttribs = "Description=SQL Backend" & vbCr
vntAttribs = vntAttribs & "OemToAnsi=No" & vbCr
vntAttribs = vntAttribs & "Server=Coyote" & vbCr
vntAttribs = vntAttribs & "Database=pubs"
DBEngine.RegisterDatabase "My SQL Server", _
    "SQL Server", True, vntAttribs
```

NOTE Do not put any spaces after the equal signs in your call to Register Database. Each attribute must be separated by a carriage return character denoted by the internal constant vbCr.

This data source can also be viewed by the 32-bit ODBC Administrator application located in the Microsoft Windows 95 Control Panel.

**Idle**   This method allows the database engine to complete any background processing by suspending data processing. As a result, the DBEngine can complete any optimization tasks. This method is necessary only in a multiuser environment in which each user needs to see the most up-to-date data.

**CreateWorkspace**   This method can be used to log on to another workspace as a different user in order to access a database using different security permissions. (This process is examined in Chapter 12.) It can also be used with ODBCDirect functionality, as discussed in the "DAO and ODBCDirect" section beginning on page 348. This method can also be used for transaction processing, as we will see in Chapter 10.

## Performing common tasks with the DBEngine object
As a solution provider, some of the common tasks you might want to perform using the database engine are repairing and compacting a database application through a utility database and registering ODBC data sources used by a database application.

**Repairing and compacting your database**   As users of your database add and delete records, your database will grow and the information in it will become stored discontiguously. To avoid corruption and unnecessary database size, you can create a utility database that allows the user to repair and compact your database application. You can call the procedures below from the AutoExec macro or the StartUp form of a utility database to repair and compact your databases. (These procedures also test to see whether the methods complete successfully.)

Pass the name and complete path of a database file into the vntRepDB function to repair that database.

```
'************************************
' vntRepDB accepts a database name and path, for example:
' "C:\Path\DB.MDB"
' vntRepDB repairs the specified database if it is not open.
'************************************
Function vntRepDB(strDBPathName As String)
    ' Initiate error handling routine.
    On Error GoTo err_vntRepDB
    ' Repair the database using the RepairDatabase method.
```

```
    DBEngine.RepairDatabase strDBPathName
    ' If the database is repaired successfully, vntRepDB will
    ' return a successful response of "Pass".
    vntRepDB = "Pass"
    Exit Function
err_vntRepDB:
    ' Error routine handles any attempt to repair an open
    ' database and additional unexpected errors.
    Select Case Err.Number
        Case 3356
            MsgBox Err.Description & vbLf & _
                "Please close all instances of this " & _
                "database and try again."
        Case Else
            MsgBox Err.Description
    End Select
    ' If an error occurs, the vntRepDB function returns
    ' user-defined run-time error 65535.
    vntRepDB = CVErr(65535)
End Function
```

**TIP** You can also create an icon that uses the /Repair switch to repair a closed database.

Pass the name and complete path of a database file into the vntComDB function to compact that database, as shown here:

```
'**********************************
' vntComDB accepts a database name and path.
' vntComDB compacts the specified database if it is not opened.
'**********************************
Function vntComDB(strDBPathName As String)
    ' Initiate error handling routine.
    On Error GoTo err_vntComDB
    Dim strTempName As String
    ' Create a temporary database using a random number in the
    ' Windows Temp directory. The input database will be
    ' compacted into this temporary database.
    ' The Environ Function returns the setting for the specified
    ' operating system variable.
    Randomize
    strTempName = Environ("Temp") & "\TempDB" & _
        Int((99 * Rnd) + 1) & ".MDB"
    ' Compact the database into a temporary database.
    DBEngine.CompactDatabase strDBPathName, strTempName
    ' If the database is compacted successfully, delete the
```

*(continued)*

```
    ' original database and rename the temporary database to
    ' the original database's name.
    Kill strDBPathName
    Name strTempName As strDBPathName
    ' If the database is compacted successfully, vntComDB will
    ' return a successful response of "Pass".
    vntComDB = "Pass"
    Exit Function
err_vntComDB:
    ' Error routine handles any attempt to compact an open
    ' database and additional unexpected errors.
    Select Case Err.Number
        Case 3356
            MsgBox Err.Description & vbLf & _
                "Please close all instances of this " & _
                "database and try again."
        Case Else
            MsgBox Err.Description
    End Select
    ' If an error occurs, the vntComDB function returns
    ' user-defined run-time error 65534.
    vntComDB = CVErr(65534)
End Function
```

> **TIP**
> You can also create an icon that uses the /Compact switch to repair a closed database. To repair and compact the database from the same icon, use the /Repair and /Compact switches together.

The procedures vntRepDB and vntComDB are separate procedures that perform specific tasks. You might decide to use them individually in your database, or you can use the procedure below to both repair and compact your database.

> **TIP**
> Repairing a database validates system tables, indexes, and data pages. Compacting a database removes any empty spaces or unused data pages, so it's always a good idea to repair a database before compacting it.
>
> To repair and compact a database, you must have Open Exclusive permissions for the database. By default, all users are members of the Users group; also by default, the Users group has Open Exclusive permissions.

```
'**********************************
' CompactRepair accepts a database name and path.
' CompactRepair calls the repair and compact
' procedures vntRepDB and vntComDB.
'**********************************
```

```
Sub CompactRepair(strDBPathName As String)
    ' vntRepReturn and vntComReturn store the
    ' results of the vntRepDB and vntComDB procedures.
    Dim vntRepReturn, vntComReturn
    ' Execute the vntRepDB procedure.
    vntRepReturn = vntRepDB(strDBPathName)
    ' Test for "Pass" or user-defined error.
    If IsError(vntRepReturn) Then
        MsgBox "Repair Failed" & vbLf & _
            "Please Notify Your Database Administrator"
    Else
        MsgBox "Repair Successful"
    End If
    ' Execute the vntComDB procedure.
    vntComReturn = vntComDB(strDBPathName)
    ' Test for "Pass" or user-defined error.
    If IsError(vntComReturn) Then
        MsgBox "Compact Failed" & vbLf & _
            "Please Notify Your Database Administrator"
    Else
        MsgBox "Compact Successful"
    End If
End Sub
```

**Registering your ODBC database**   If you are distributing your database to different machines and using an ODBC data source for linking tables or running SQL pass-through queries, you need to register the data source on those different machines. The RegisterDatabase method of the DBEngine object gives you this capability. The RegisterDatabase method has the following arguments:

- **DSN**  This is the name of the ODBC data source you want to reference.

- **driver**  This argument represents the name of the ODBC driver being used. For example, "SQL Server" is the name that represents the ODBC driver SQLSRV32.DLL.

- **silent**  When registering a database through code, set this numeric value to True. You do this because you do not want your users to be prompted with driver-specific information. As a result, you must include all the ODBC driver setup information in the attributes argument of this method.

- **attributes**  This argument is a string expression that includes all the ODBC driver setup information. Because some of the setup information already has default values, you don't need to include these values unless the default is not acceptable. These values will be added to the machine's Registry. The setup information must be separated by a carriage-return–delimited string.

You can also register your database through the user interface. The following steps show you how to register an SQL Server ODBC database manually. They are followed by code to accomplish the same result.

1. Click the 32bit ODBC icon in the Control Panel to open the ODBC Administrator. You will see the ODBC Data Source Administrator dialog box shown here:

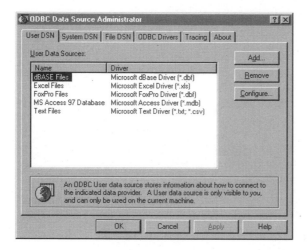

2. Click the Add button on the User DSN tab to open the following Create New Data Source dialog box. Select the SQL Server driver. You specify this value using the driver argument in the RegisterDatabase method.

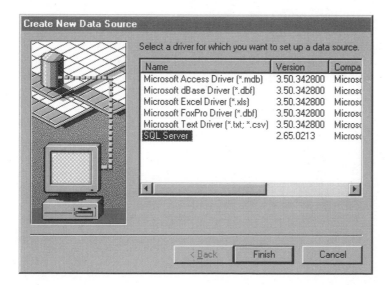

**3.** Click Finish to open the ODBC SQL Server Setup dialog box shown below. Click the Options button to expand the dialog box. You specify the Data Source Name using the DSN argument in the RegisterDatabase method. You specify the rest of the information in this dialog box using the attributes argument in the RegisterDatabase method.

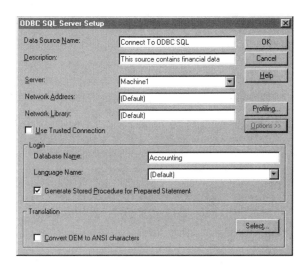

**4.** Click OK, and you will be returned to the ODBC Data Source Administrator dialog box in which your new SQL Server database DSN is displayed in the User DSN tab, as shown here:

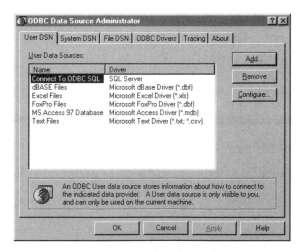

The procedure on the following page accomplishes the same result using the RegisterDatabase method.

```
Sub RegisterODBCDatabase()
    On Error GoTo err_RegisterODBCDatabase
    Dim vntAttribs
    vntAttribs = "Description=This source contains " & _
        "financial data." & vbCr
    vntAttribs = vntAttribs & "Server=Machine1" & vbCr
    vntAttribs = vntAttribs & "Database=Accounting"
    ' All other data source options are left at their
    ' default settings.

    DBEngine.RegisterDatabase DSN:="Connect To ODBC SQL", _
        driver:="SQL Server", silent:=True, _
        attributes:=vntAttribs
    Exit Sub
err_RegisterODBCDatabase:
    MsgBox "Registration of ODBC Data Source Failed."
    Exit Sub
End Sub
```

> **NOTE**    If the database source information is already in the Registry, the existing information will be updated by your code. If the RegisterDatabase method fails to execute successfully, no changes will be made to the Registry.

## Referring to the collections of the DBEngine object

Because the DBEngine object is at the top of the hierarchy, it must support or contain collections of all the other objects that rely on the Database Engine. The following collections are supported by the DBEngine object.

**Workspaces (default)**    When you start Microsoft Access, you are automatically logged on to a session of the Microsoft Jet Database Engine. You can log on as another user through code by creating a Workspace object. This object is useful for programming security or for executing simultaneous transactions on a database object.

Because the Workspaces collection is the default collection of the DBEngine object, you can reference the collection implicitly:

```
' Explicit Reference to the Workspaces collection
Debug.Print DBEngine.Workspaces(0).Name
' Implicit Reference to the Workspaces collection
Debug.Print DBEngine(0).Name
```

**Errors**    This collection allows you to trap for errors generated when programming with DAO.

**Properties**  By default, every DAO object has a Properties collection. To return a list of properties in the Properties collection supported by DBEngine, use the following code:

```
Dim prDBEProp As Property
For Each prDBEProp In DBEngine.Properties
    Debug.Print prDBEProp.Name
Next
```

## Using the CreateProperty Method

DAO objects have a predefined set of properties for each object and collection. In some instances, however, you might find this limiting because you or a host application that uses the Microsoft Jet Database Engine (such as Microsoft Access) would benefit from additional properties for those objects. To work around this limitation, you or the host application can use the CreateProperty method that several of the DAO objects have. The Jet Database Engine does not understand or use properties created by the CreateProperty method.

For example, although a Field object in a table can have a Caption property, you cannot reference the Caption property unless the value has been set through code or through the user interface. When you first type the Caption property of a field in a table in the Microsoft Access user interface, Access executes a CreateProperty method (as you would have to do through code if you did not use the user interface). Once the CreateProperty method has been called (by Access or by your code), you can reference the new property explicitly without creating a run-time error. The following code shows how to reference a created property:

```
Dim strMyCaption As String
strMyCaption = _
    DBEngine(0)(0).TableDefs("Customers"). _
    Fields("CustomerID").Properties("Caption")
```

You cannot reference a created property the same way you would a built-in property. For example, the following code does not work:

```
strMyCaption = _
    DBEngine(0)(0).TableDefs("Customers"). _
    Fields("CustomerID").Caption ' Wrong!!!
```

To determine which properties are supported by the Microsoft Jet Database Engine, see online Help about the object or use the Object Browser. If you do not find the property in either location, the property is specific to Microsoft Access and must be referenced explicitly through the object's Properties collection.

## Using the Workspaces Collection and the Workspace Object

The most common task of the Workspace object is to open a database through code in order to manipulate recordsets. The next most common task is to use the Workspace object to perform security operations on a database or system database known as the Workgroup Information file (SYSTEM.MDW).

The Workspaces collection has only one property: Count.

**Count**   Count returns the number of Workspace objects in the collection. When you start Microsoft Access, the Workspaces collection has one Workspace object, which is known as the default workspace. At this point, the Workspaces collection will have a count of one object. You can verify this with the following code:

```
Dim intWrkSpcCount As Integer
intWrkSpcCount = DBEngine.Workspaces.Count
```

The Workspaces collection also has just one method: Append.

**Append**   When you create a Workspace object, you must add it to the Workspaces collection in order to be able to reference it outside of the procedure in which you created it.

```
Dim wsMyWrkSpc As Workspace
' Create a new Workspace while logged on as the Admin user.
Set wsMyWrkSpc = DBEngine.CreateWorkspace _
    (Name:="NewWorkSpace", UserName:="Admin", Password:="")
' Display the count of the Workspaces collection, which
' will be equal to 1.
MsgBox DBEngine.Workspaces.Count
' Append the Workspace object to the Workspaces collection.
DBEngine.Workspaces.Append wsMyWrkSpc
' Display the count of the Workspaces collection, which
' will now be equal to 2.
MsgBox DBEngine.Workspaces.Count
```

**NOTE**   The scope or availability of the Workspace object depends on the scope of the variable used to create the object. When the object variable is no longer in scope, the Workspace object created is no longer available unless it has been appended to the Workspaces collection.

Remember that whenever you start Microsoft Access you are automatically logged on to a workspace. By default, you are logged on to the Database Engine as the user "Admin" but with no password. This situation is the same as leaving your car door unlocked with the keys in the ignition. Anyone could enter your car. We will discuss the security implications of the Workspace object in more detail in Chapter 12. Creating multiple workspaces allows you to execute multiple transactions on the same or different databases. We will look at this important aspect of the Workspace object in Chapter 10.

## Using the properties of the Workspace object

The following list contains the commonly used properties of Workspace objects. (For a complete list, see online Help.)

**Name**   This property refers to the name of the Workspace object. When you first start Microsoft Access, you log on to the default workspace. The name of the default workspace is #Default Workspace#. All three of the following lines of code display the same thing (#Default Workspace#):

```
Debug.Print DBEngine.Workspaces(0).Name
Debug.Print DBEngine.Workspaces("#Default Workspace#").Name
Debug.Print DBEngine(0).Name
```

> **NOTE**   References to objects in the Workspaces collection are zero based, as they are in the Forms and Reports collections. Therefore, 0 represents the first object in the Workspaces collection, which is always the default workspace.

**UserName**   This property refers to the name of the user who is logged on to that Workspace object. You can find this value using the following code:

```
Dim strLoginName As String
strLoginName = DBEngine.Workspaces(0).UserName
```

## Using the methods of the Workspace object

The Workspace object has the following methods.

**OpenDatabase**   This method allows you to open any data source that you can open in the user interface. Opening a database through code allows you to manipulate that database's objects quickly and efficiently when intervention through the user interface is not necessary. For example, if you want to append records from one table to another without user interaction, you can create code that does the appending behind the scenes. This code can also trap for possible errors that may occur and resolve those conflicts. The OpenDatabase method is one way to ensure that the integrity of your database is controlled by you, rather than by a user who may be uncertain about how to deal with problems. The following code shows how to open a database:

```
Dim dbMyDB As Database, strDBName As String
strDBName = "C:\Files\MyDatabase.MDB"
Set dbMyDB = DBEngine.Workspaces(0).OpenDatabase(strDBName)
```

**Close**   Use this method to close a Workspace object. Closing the Workspace object removes it from the Workspaces collection. The following code shows how to close a workspace:

```
Dim wsMyWrkSpc As Workspace
' Enter the CreateWorkspace method on one line.
Set wsMyWrkSpc = DBEngine.CreateWorkspace _
    (Name:="NewWorkSpace", UserName:="Admin", Password:="")
' Do other processing here, then close the workspace
' when finished using it.
wsMyWrkSpc.Close
```

> **NOTE**   You cannot close the default Workspace object because you are still operating within the Microsoft Access user interface.

**CreateDatabase**   This method allows you to create a new, empty database that is then opened to be accessed by code. When creating a database, you must include a collating order. The constant dbLangGeneral is for collating orders in English, German, French, Portuguese, Italian, and Modern Spanish. For other collating orders, see online Help. This method is not a common one, but you can use it in a custom backup procedure to create a backup database. Here's how to call this method:

```
Dim dbMyDB As Database, strDBName As String
strDBName = "C:\Files\NewDatabase.MDB"
Set dbMyDB = DBEngine.Workspaces(0). _
    CreateDatabase(strDBName, dbLangGeneral)
```

The CreateDatabase method also has the optional argument *options*, which you can use to create a database in an encrypted or decrypted state as well as in a specified version of the Microsoft Jet Database Engine. You can combine the encrypt/decrypt and version options by summing their constants together.

**BeginTrans, CommitTrans, and Rollback**   These three methods allow you to treat multiple transactions as a unit. You can either commit (save) a group of transactions all at once or decline to commit those transactions if certain conditions occur. For example, imagine that you are writing a real-time application that requires the most up-to-date information possible. The only problem is that you must continually update large groups of data that depend on certain conditions to become true. So, to save time while waiting for your condition to become true, you can begin your transaction and process your information. Once the condition becomes true, all of your processed information can be written to the table immediately. If the condition proves to be false, however, you can roll back, or cancel, the transaction without losing any of your vital data.

You can also use these methods to eliminate unnecessary hard drive access. For example, if you are adding 10,000 new records to a table through code, each time a record is saved Access writes the record to the hard drive. If these additions were saved in groups, the need to access the hard drive would be greatly reduced.

**CreateUser and CreateGroup**   You use these methods to create new users and groups and to add users to groups. These methods allow an authorized user to add other users to a secured database without giving the authorized user the ability to make any other changes that involve security.

### Referring to the collections of the Workspace object
The following collections are contained within the Workspace object.

**Databases (default)**   This collection contains all the Database objects opened in a particular workspace. When you start Microsoft Access and log on to the default workspace, the database you open in the user interface is the first object in the Databases collection. It cannot be removed unless the database is closed through the user interface or through code. Even though more than one database can be open at a time, only one database can appear in the user interface per session of Microsoft Access. Because the Databases collection is the default collection of a Workspace object, you can reference the collection implicitly, as shown here:

```
' Explicit Reference to the Databases collection
Debug.Print DBEngine.Workspaces(0).Databases(0).Name
' Implicit Reference to the Databases collection
Debug.Print DBEngine(0)(0).Name
```

**Users and Groups**   These collections contain all the different users and groups available in the Workgroup Information file (SYSTEM.MDW). You can manage those individual User and Group objects with these collections. These collections and their objects are discussed in detail in Chapter 12.

**Properties**   This collection is the same for all DAO objects.

## Using the Errors Collection and the Error Object
The Errors collection has only one property and has no methods.

**Count**   Count returns the number of Error objects in the collection. The Errors collection will contain an Error object only for errors generated using DAO programming. For example, if a data type mismatch error occurs because a string value is assigned to an integer variable, it will not appear in the Errors collection. If you try to open a table through DAO that does not exist, however, an

Error object will be added to the Errors collection. Here's how to reference the Count property:

```
Dim intErrorCount As Integer
intErrorCount = DBEngine.Errors.Count
```

The set of Error objects in the Errors collection describes a single error. Any operation involving DAO can generate one error that adds one or more Error objects, which detail that error, to the Errors collection. The Errors collection is cleared only when another DAO operation generates a different error. There is no method available to clear an Error object or to remove it from the Errors collection.

> **NOTE** Do not confuse the Error object and the Errors collection with the Err object. The Error object and Errors collection apply only to DAO. The Err object is not part of the Errors collection.

## Using the properties of the Error object

The Error object has the following properties. (It has no methods.)

**Number**   This property returns the error number.

**Description**   This property describes the error message that corresponds to the Number property. This is the default property of the Error object.

**Source**   This property is a string expression that names the object or application that originally generated the error.

**HelpFile**   This property gives the name of the Help file that contains information about the error.

**HelpContext**   This property provides the Help file context ID for the error corresponding to the Number property.

The following code shows how to reference these properties:

```
Dim lngErrNum As Long, strErrDes As String
Dim strErrSource As String, strErrHelpFile As String
Dim lngErrHelpContext As Long
lngErrNum = DBEngine.Errors(0).Number
strErrDes = DBEngine.Errors(0).Description
strErrSource = DBEngine.Errors(0).Source
strErrHelpFile = DBEngine.Errors(0).HelpFile
lngErrHelpContext = DBEngine.Errors(0).HelpContext
```

## Performing common tasks with the Error object

The Errors collection is useful when you are using ODBC data sources. One ODBC action can cause multiple errors. If multiple errors are returned by the ODBC data source, they will be appended in order of importance: the most general errors are placed at the end of the collection, and the most detailed errors (or those errors closest to the source of the error) are placed at the beginning. For example, if an error is generated using ODBC with SQL Server, the SQL Server error will become the first Error object in the Errors collection even though the initial error, such as "ODBC—call failed," was generated by the client (Microsoft Access).

The following sample function returns multiple errors when it is executed:

```
Sub CollectErrors()
    On Error GoTo err_CollectErrors
    Dim dbMyDB As DATABASE, rsMyRS As Recordset
    Dim errMyErr As Error

    Set dbMyDB = DBEngine(0)(0)
    ' dbo_authors is from the SQL Server sample Pubs database.
    Set rsMyRS = dbMyDB.OpenRecordset("dbo_authors")
    ' Adding only a value to au_id will cause an error
    ' because the other fields cannot store null values.
    rsMyRS.AddNew
        rsMyRS![au_id] = "555-KL-1212"
    rsMyRS.UPDATE
    Exit Sub
err_CollectErrors:
    For Each errMyErr In Errors
        Debug.Print "(" & errMyErr.Source & ")" & _
            errMyErr.Description
    Next
End Sub
```

The Debug window returns the following information about the four Error objects in the Errors collection when the CollectErrors procedure is executed:

```
(ODBC.Recordset)[Microsoft][ODBC SQL Server Driver][SQL Server]
The column au_lname in table dbo.authors may not be null.
(ODBC.Recordset)[Microsoft][ODBC SQL Server Driver][SQL Server]
The column au_fname in table dbo.authors may not be null.
(ODBC.Recordset)[Microsoft][ODBC SQL Server Driver][SQL Server]
The column contract in table dbo.authors may not be null.
(DAO.Recordset)ODBC--call failed.
```

NOTE Even though the *ODBC—call failed* error occurs first, the Errors collection places it at the end because it is the least descriptive. The more descriptive errors are placed at the beginning of the Errors collection so that you can quickly ascertain the cause of the problem without searching through all the Error objects.

## Using the Databases Collection and the Database Object

The Database object can be very useful when manipulating the database itself and the objects contained in its hierarchy. For example, you can determine the exact location of the database using the Name property as discussed on page 319 or create additional objects that can be contained within the database. The Databases collection has only one property and no methods.

**Count**   The Count property returns the number of Database objects in the collection. When you start Microsoft Access and open a database, the Databases collection has one Database object by default, the database opened in the user interface. At this point, the Databases collection will have a count of one object. Here's how you might reference the Count property:

```
Dim intDBCount As Integer
intDBCount = DBEngine.Workspaces(0).Databases.Count
```

The Databases collection is just what you'd imagine—a collection of Database objects in code. The Databases collection is the default collection of the Workspace object. Even though the Workspace object supports the Users and Groups collections (and, of course, a Properties collection), most of its usage is with the Databases collection. (Now you see why it is the default collection!) When you start Microsoft Access and open a database, that database is always the first object in the Databases collection. With the Databases collection you can open many instances of the current database or of other databases, including your Indexed Sequential Access Method (ISAM) and ODBC databases. You cannot open a database without first being in a workspace, because the security features that are always present in Access require a Workspace object.

You can use Database objects to manage the objects they contain. For the most part, Database objects are created to manage and manipulate data in databases. Some of the methods and properties of the Database object will be mentioned here, but you will use them more extensively later in this book.

### Using the properties of the Database object

The following list contains the commonly used Database object properties. (See online Help for a complete listing.)

**Connect**   This property can be used to create linked tables from an ISAM, ODBC database, or Microsoft Access.

**Name**    This property returns the name and full path location of the Database object. Here's how to access this property:

```
Dim strDBName As String
strDBName = DBEngine.Workspaces(0).Databases(0).Name
```

**QueryTimeout**    This property is used to determine the number of seconds the database will wait before returning a query time-out error for ODBC data sources. A query time-out error might occur when you are trying to query (access data) from an ODBC data source. This error could be caused for various reasons: the network is down; the network has too much traffic; or the SQL server is offline. By default, the QueryTimeout is 60 seconds. If your network is slow, you might want to increase the number of seconds to wait. Here's how to reference this property:

```
Dim intQTO As Integer
intQTO = DBEngine.Workspaces(0).Databases(0).QueryTimeOut
```

**RecordsAffected**    You can run or execute an action query through code by using either an SQL statement or a QueryDef object. When an action query is executed in the user interface, the user is prompted with the number of records that will be deleted, updated, or inserted. The RecordsAffected property returns the number of affected records for action queries executed through code.

**Updatable**    This property can be used to determine whether you can make changes to a Database object. The Updatable property will return either True (–1) or False (0). For example, if you open a Database object as read-only, the Updatable property will return False. Here's how to check this property:

```
Dim blnUpdateOK As Boolean
blnUpdateOK = DBEngine.Workspaces(0).Databases(0).Updatable
```

**Version**    This property returns the version of the Microsoft Jet Database Engine that created the database. This property does not refer to the version of Microsoft Access, because other applications, such as Microsoft Visual Basic 3.0 and 4.0, can create databases with the Microsoft Jet Database Engine. For example, if a database were created using Microsoft Jet Database Engine version 3.0, the version property would return 3.0. A converted database has the version number of the Microsoft Jet Database Engine that converted it. Here's how to retrieve this setting:

```
Dim MyProp As String
MyProp = DBEngine.Workspaces(0).Databases(0).Version
```

## Using the methods of the Database object

The Database object has the following methods:

**Close**   This method is used to close any Database object you open in code. Any other objects opened using the Database object will also be closed because the Database object will no longer exist. The following code shows how to close a database:

```
Dim dbMyDB As Database, strDBName As String
strDBName = "C:\Files\MyDatabase.MDB"
Set dbMyDB = DBEngine.Workspaces(0).OpenDatabase(strDBName)
' Close the database, and remove it from the Databases
' collection.
dbMyDB.Close
```

**CreateTableDef, CreateQueryDef, CreateRelation, and CreateProperty**   These methods allow you to create tables, queries, relationships, and custom properties. The CreateTableDef method is especially useful for linking Microsoft Access tables and other data files such as Microsoft FoxPro files. The other methods are not often used because it is easier to achieve the same result through the user interface. However, they could be useful if you are designing a wizard that needs to create tables, queries, relationships, and properties. The following three procedures show how to create queries, relationships, and properties, respectively:

```
'***********************************
' Create a query using the CreateQueryDef method.
'***********************************
Sub CreateAQueryDef()
    Dim qdMyQuery As QueryDef, strQName As String
    Dim strQSQL As String
    strQName = "New Query Object"
    strQSQL = "SELECT * FROM Employees WHERE EmployeeID > 5;"
    Set qdMyQuery = DBEngine(0)(0).CreateQueryDef()
    qdMyQuery.Name = strQName
    qdMyQuery.SQL = strQSQL
    ' Append the QueryDef to the QueryDefs collection.
    DBEngine(0)(0).QueryDefs.Append qdMyQuery
    qdMyQuery.Close
End Sub

'***********************************
' Create a relationship using the CreateRelation
' method.
' OneTable is the table name from the one side, and
' ManyTable is the table name from the many side.
'***********************************
```

```
Sub CreateARelation(OneTable As String, ManyTable As String)
    Dim dbMyDB As Database, rlMyRelation As Relation
    Dim fldMyField As Field

    Set dbMyDB = DBEngine(0)(0)
    Set rlMyRelation = _
        dbMyDB.CreateRelation("OneToManyCascadeUandD")
    rlMyRelation.Table = OneTable
    rlMyRelation.ForeignTable = ManyTable
    ' Create a One To Many relationship with Cascading Updates
    ' and Deletes. To create a nonenforced relationship (no
    ' referential integrity), such as that between a table and
    ' a query, add the (dbRelationDontEnforce) attribute.
    rlMyRelation.Attributes = _
        dbRelationUpdateCascade + dbRelationDeleteCascade
    ' Determine the fields to be used in the relationship from
    ' both tables. If two fields are going to be used to create
    ' a relationship, repeat the following three lines of code
    ' identifying the different field names.
    Set fldMyField = rlMyRelation.CreateField("CustomerID")
    fldMyField.ForeignName = "CustomerID"
    rlMyRelation.Fields.Append fldMyField
    ' Save the Relationship.
    dbMyDB.Relations.Append rlMyRelation
End Sub


'*************************************
' Create a custom database property using the CreateProperty
' method.
'*************************************
Sub CreateAProperty()
    Dim prNewProp As Property, strPropName As String
    strPropName = "DesignVersion"
    Set prNewProp = DBEngine(0)(0).CreateProperty(strPropName)
    ' Set the data type and value of the new property.
    ' See the Type property in online Help for a list of
    ' Type constants.
    prNewProp.Type = dbText
    prNewProp.Value = "3.27.67"
    ' Add the new property to the Database object's Properties
    ' collection.
    DBEngine(0)(0).Properties.Append prNewProp
End Sub
```

Examples using the CreateTableDef and CreateRelation methods are discussed in the TableDefs and Relations collections sections later in this chapter.

**Execute** This method allows you to run an action query through code. This query can be a QueryDef object or an SQL statement. This method is used in conjunction with the RecordsAffected property, which determines how many records an action query will involve. Here's an example:

```
Sub ExecuteActionQuery()
    Dim dbMyDB As Database, strQSQL As String
    Dim lngRecAff As Long
    On Error GoTo err_ExecuteActionQuery

    Set dbMyDB = DBEngine(0)(0)
    ' SQL statement used in a Delete action query
    strQSQL = _
        "DELETE FROM Employees WHERE Title = 'Sales Representative';"
    ' Execute the action query SQL statement.
    dbMyDB.Execute strQSQL, dbFailOnError
    ' Display the number of records to be deleted.
    lngRecAff = dbMyDB.RecordsAffected
    MsgBox lngRecAff & " record(s) deleted."
    Exit Sub
err_ExecuteActionQuery:
    ' Trap for updating failures.
    MsgBox "Update Failed"
    Exit Sub
End Sub
```

> **NOTE** Use the dbFailOnError option with the Execute method so that updates will be rolled back if an error occurs.

**OpenRecordset** This method is one of the most widely used in DAO because it allows you to open recordsets in code based on tables, queries, and SQL statements. The following code shows how to call this method:

```
Dim dbMyDB As Database, rsMyRS As Recordset
Set dbMyDB = DBEngine(0)(0)
Set rsMyRS = dbMyDB.OpenRecordset("Orders Table")
```

**MakeReplica and Synchronize** These methods allow you to create replicated databases and then update them by synchronizing them.

## Performing common tasks with the Database object
Solution providers often use the Database object to open a Recordset object and to create linked tables. We cover the subject of opening a Recordset object in great detail in Chapter 10.

To link Microsoft Access tables to another Access database, use the Create-TableDef method of the Database object. You need the following information:

- The new table name for the linked table (for example, "New Linked Orders Table").

- The database from which the table will be linked (for example, C:\ Files\BackEndDB.MDB). This value is stored in the Connect property of the linked table object.

- The name of the table from the database you are linking to (for example, "Orders Table"). This value is stored in the SourceTableName property of the linked table object.

The following code shows how to link a table:

```
Function blnLinkAccessTable(strLinkTableName As String) _
    As Boolean
    Dim dbMyDB As Database, tblMyTableDef As TableDef
    On Error GoTo err_blnLinkAccessTable
    Set dbMyDB = DBEngine.Workspaces(0)(0)
    ' Create a link to a Microsoft Access table.
    Set tblMyTableDef = dbMyDB.CreateTableDef(strLinkTableName)
    tblMyTableDef.Connect = ";DATABASE=C:\Files\BackEndDB.MDB"
    ' Name of the table in BackEndDB.MDB to be linked
    tblMyTableDef.SourceTableName = "Orders Table"
    ' Link the table by appending it to the TableDefs
    ' collection.
    dbMyDB.TableDefs.Append tblMyTableDef
    ' Return True if link is successful.
    blnLinkAccessTable = True
    Exit Function
err_blnLinkAccessTable:
    ' Return False if an error occurs.
    blnLinkAccessTable = False
    Exit Function
End Function
```

One of the strongest features of Microsoft Access is its ability to link to and update different database types, such as SQL Server and Microsoft FoxPro. To link ISAM database tables to a Microsoft Access database, use the CreateTableDef method of the Database object. You need the following information:

- The new table name for the linked table (for example, "New Linked ShipDBF Table").

- The database type and path where the ISAM database exists. (For example, to link to a dBase IV database, use "dBase IV;DATABASE=C: \Files\".) This value is stored in the Connect property of the linked table object. (The appropriate Connect property values for all other ISAM drivers are available in online Help in the Connect property topic.)

- The name of the table from the ISAM database you are linking to (for example, "ShipDBF"). This value is stored in the SourceTableName property of the linked table object.

```
Function blnLinkISAMTable(strLinkTableName As String) _
    As Boolean
    Dim dbMyDB As DATABASE, tblMyTableDef As TableDef
    On Error GoTo err_blnLinkISAMTable

    Set dbMyDB = DBEngine.Workspaces(0)(0)
    ' Create a link to a dBase IV table.
    Set tblMyTableDef = dbMyDB.CreateTableDef(strLinkTableName)
    ' Link dBase IV table ShipDBF in database directory C:\Files.
    tblMyTableDef.Connect = "dBase IV;DATABASE=C:\Files\"
    ' Name of the table in the ISAM database to be linked
    tblMyTableDef.SourceTableName = "ShipDBF"
    ' Link the table by appending it to the
    ' TableDefs collection.
    dbMyDB.TableDefs.Append tblMyTableDef
    ' Return True if link is successful.
    blnLinkISAMTable = True
    Exit Function
err_blnLinkISAMTable:
    ' Return False if an error occurs.
    blnLinkISAMTable = False
    Exit Function
End Function
```

> **NOTE** Linking to ODBC data source tables is the same as linking to ISAM databases except that the Connect property value is a little more complicated. For example, the Connect property value for linking to a table in the "My SQL Server" ODBC SQL Server data source would be ODBC; DATABASE=pubs; UID=UserNameBob; PWD=Bob'sPassword; DSN=My SQL Server.

Maintaining the links to these tables is discussed in the section titled "Performing common tasks with the TableDef object" on page 328.

## The collections of the Database object

The Database object supports the following collections:

**TableDefs (default)**  This collection contains all the tables stored in the database, including hidden and system tables. Because the TableDefs collection is the default collection of the Database object, you can reference the collection implicitly, as shown here:

```
' Explicit Reference to the TableDefs collection
Debug.Print DBEngine(0)(0).TableDefs(0).Name
' Implicit Reference to the TableDefs collection
Debug.Print DBEngine(0)(0)(0).Name
```

**QueryDefs**   This collection contains all the query objects stored in the database.

**Recordsets**   This collection contains all the recordsets that are opened in code based on tables, queries, and SQL statements.

**Containers**   The Microsoft Jet Database Engine keeps track of the database and the objects stored in it according to type. For example, the forms you create belong to the Forms container, and your relationships belong to the Relationships container. The Containers collection is used primarily for security purposes. Some of the objects in this collection are created by the Microsoft Jet Database Engine, and some are created by Microsoft Access.

**Relations**   This collection contains all the relationships stored in the database.

**Properties**   This collection is the same for all DAO objects.

## Using the TableDefs Collection and the TableDef Object

The TableDefs collection contains all the TableDef (table) objects in the database, including those that are linked. The TableDefs collection is the default collection of the Database object. The TableDefs collection has one property: Count.

**Count**   The Count property returns the number of TableDef objects in the TableDefs collection for a particular Database object. Here's how to reference this property:

```
Dim intTblCount As Integer
intTblCount = DBEngine(0)(0).TableDefs.Count
```

The TableDefs collection has the following methods:

**Append**   When creating TableDef objects, local or linked, you need to append them to the TableDefs collection so that you can refer to those new TableDef objects in code outside of the procedure that created them.

**Delete**   This method will remove a TableDef object, local or linked, from the TableDefs collection. If the TableDef object is a linked table, only the link will be removed. The original data will not be affected.

**Refresh**   Use this method to make sure that the TableDefs collection accurately represents its objects. Whenever appending, deleting, or modifying a TableDef object, it is good programming practice to refresh the TableDefs collection, especially if you are in a multiuser environment.

The following code shows how to use these methods:

```
Function blnLinkFoxTable(strLinkTableName As String) As Boolean
    Dim dbMyDB As DATABASE, tblMyTableDef As TableDef
    On Error GoTo err_blnLinkFoxTable
    Set dbMyDB = DBEngine(0)(0)
    Set tblMyTableDef = dbMyDB.CreateTableDef(strLinkTableName)
    ' Link FoxPro table FoxTBL in database directory
    ' C:\Files\.
    tblMyTableDef.Connect = "FoxPro 2.6;DATABASE=C:\Files\"
    ' Name of table to be linked
    tblMyTableDef.SourceTableName = "FoxTBL"
    ' Use the Append method to add FoxTable to the TableDefs
    ' collection.
    dbMyDB.TableDefs.Append tblMyTableDef
    ' Use the Refresh method to ensure the accuracy of the TableDefs
    ' collection.
    dbMyDB.TableDefs.Refresh
    ' Use the Delete method to remove FoxTable.
    dbMyDB.TableDefs.Delete strLinkTableName
    ' Use the Refresh method to ensure the accuracy of the TableDefs
    ' collection.
    dbMyDB.TableDefs.Refresh
    blnLinkFoxTable = True
    Exit Function
err_blnLinkFoxTable:
    ' Return False if an error occurs.
    blnLinkFoxTable = False
    Exit Function
End Function
```

In addition to containing all the tables that you create in your database, the TableDefs collection contains the System tables that the Microsoft Jet Database Engine creates by default. Through the TableDefs collection and its individual TableDef objects, you can return and modify most aspects of the table design for any of these tables, including a table's fields and indexes. You have to use the object hierarchy as a means of getting to those levels of a table's structure.

## Using the properties of the TableDef object

The most commonly used properties of TableDef objects are listed below. (For a complete list of the TableDef object's properties, consult online Help.)

**Attributes**  With this property, you can determine whether a table in the Table-Defs collection is a system table, a hidden table, a linked ISAM table, or a linked

ODBC table. This information can be useful if you want to display a list of tables available to the user that does not include system and hidden tables. You can also determine which linked tables are ISAM or ODBC tables in order to refresh their links.

**Name** This property returns the name of the TableDef as it appears in the Database container and in the user interface.

**Connect and SourceTableName** The Connect property is used to determine the type and location of a linked table. The SourceTableName property is the true name of the table that is linked. (You can rename the linked tables in the client database.)

**ConflictTable** This property returns the name of the table that contains record-level replication errors for a particular table.

## Using the methods of the TableDef object

The TableDef object has the following methods.

**CreateField** This method allows you to create a field for an existing table or for a new table. When creating a field, provide a field name, data type, and size, as shown here:

```
Sub CreateAField()
    Dim dbMyDB As Database, tblMyTableDef As TableDef
    Dim fldMyField As Field
    Set dbMyDB = DBEngine(0)(0)
    ' Create a new table.
    Set tblMyTableDef = dbMyDB.CreateTableDef("NewTable")
    ' Create a new field for the table.
    Set fldMyField = tblMyTableDef.CreateField("FirstName")
    ' Specify the data type of the field.
    fldMyField.Type = dbText
    ' Specify the size of the field.
    fldMyField.Size = 35
    ' Add the field to the TableDef's Fields collection.
    tblMyTableDef.Fields.Append fldMyField
    ' Save the TableDef by adding the object to the
    ' TableDefs collection.
    dbMyDB.TableDefs.Append tblMyTableDef
    ' Refresh the TableDefs collection.
    dbMyDB.TableDefs.Refresh
End Sub
```

**CreateIndex** This method allows you to create an index for an existing table or for a new table. The example on the following page creates an index using the First Name and Last Name fields.

```
Sub CreateAnIndex()
    Dim dbMyDB As Database, tblMyTableDef As TableDef
    Dim fldMyField As Field, ixMyIndex As Index

    Set dbMyDB = DBEngine(0)(0)
    Set tblMyTableDef = dbMyDB.TableDefs("Employees")
    ' Create the Full Name Index.
    Set ixMyIndex = tblMyTableDef.CreateIndex("Full Name")
    ' Establish the fields to be used in the index.
    Set fldMyField = ixMyIndex.CreateField("LastName")
    ' LastName is in descending order (the default
    ' is ascending order).
    fldMyField.Attributes = dbDescending
    ixMyIndex.Fields.Append fldMyField
    Set fldMyField = ixMyIndex.CreateField("FirstName")
    ixMyIndex.Fields.Append fldMyField
    ' Save the Index.
    tblMyTableDef.Indexes.Append ixMyIndex
    tblMyTableDef.Indexes.Refresh
End Sub
```

**CreateProperty**   This method allows you to create custom properties for a table just as you can for individual Database objects. This method includes the Filter and OrderBy properties, which Microsoft Access uses and maintains because the Microsoft Jet Database Engine does not recognize these properties. Once again, creating a property is much easier to do in the user interface, so you won't often use this method unless you are developing a wizard that creates tables.

**OpenRecordset**   You use this method to directly create a Recordset object on your TableDef object in order to manipulate the data stored in that table. We will discuss this method in more detail in Chapter 10.

**RefreshLink**   If the location of a linked table changes, the Connect property might no longer be valid. You use the RefreshLink method to update the connection and establish a new link if the location of the back-end data source has changed.

## Performing common tasks with the TableDef object

The most common task of the TableDef object is to refresh the connections of linked tables to ensure that the tables are available to the Database object. You use the Attributes property of the TableDef object to determine which tables are linked. Then use the RefreshLink method to update those connections. If the back-end data source cannot be located, you must be able to prompt the user for the new source location.

You can use the following sample code in the AutoExec macro of a Program database that links to a back-end Microsoft Access database. The procedure refreshes the links of the Microsoft Access tables. If the database cannot be located, the user is prompted for the new location and the link is then re-established.

```
Function blnRefreshAndRelink(strAccDBName As String) As Boolean
    Dim dbMyDB As Database, tblMyTableDef As TableDef
    Dim strNewPath As String, strNewConnect As String

    On Error GoTo err_blnRefreshAndRelink
    strNewPath = ""
    Set dbMyDB = DBEngine(0)(0)
    ' Loop through the TableDefs collection, and refresh the links
    ' to non-ODBC linked tables.
    For Each tblMyTableDef In dbMyDB.TableDefs
        If tblMyTableDef.Attributes = dbAttachedTable Then
            tblMyTableDef.RefreshLink
            Debug.Print tblMyTableDef.Name
        End If
    Next
    blnRefreshAndRelink = True
    Exit Function
err_blnRefreshAndRelink:
    Select Case Err.Number
        ' Cannot find non-ODBC linked table file
        Case 3024
            ' Check if a new path location has already been set.
            If strNewPath = "" Then
                strNewPath = InputBox _
                    (prompt:="Please Enter New Path", _
                    title:=tblMyTableDef.Name & _
                    " Table Location", _
                    Default:=strAccDBName)
            End If
            ' Check for a valid path.
            Do Until Dir(strNewPath, vbNormal) <> ""
                strNewPath = InputBox _
                    (prompt:="Please Enter New Path", _
                    title:=tblMyTableDef.Name & _
                    " Table Location", _
                    Default:=strAccDBName)
                ' If the Cancel command button is clicked, exit
                ' error trapping.
                ' Return to the next RefreshLink method for the
                ' next non-ODBC linked table.
                If strNewPath = "" Then
                    MsgBox tblMyTableDef.Name & _
                        " will not be available."
```

*(continued)*

```
                    Resume Next
                End If
            Loop
            ' Establish the new link.
            strNewConnect = ";DATABASE=" & strNewPath
            tblMyTableDef.Connect = strNewConnect
            tblMyTableDef.RefreshLink
            Resume Next
        ' Trap for unexpected errors.
        Case Else
            MsgBox Err.Description
            blnRefreshAndRelink = False
    End Select
End Function
```

### The collections of the TableDef object

The following collections are supported by the TableDef object.

**Fields (default)**   This collection contains all the fields (and their properties) that are part of the definition (design) of your tables. Because the Fields collection is the default collection of the TableDef object, you can reference the collection implicitly.

```
' Explicit Reference to the FieldDefs collection
Debug.Print DBEngine(0)(0)(0).Fields(0).Name
' Implicit Reference to the FieldDefs collection
Debug.Print DBEngine(0)(0)(0)(0).Name
```

**Indexes**   This collection contains all the indexes that are part of the definition (design) of a given table.

**Properties**   This collection is the same for all DAO objects.

## Using the QueryDefs Collection and the QueryDef Object

The QueryDefs collection contains all the QueryDef (query) objects in the database. You use the QueryDefs collection to refer to and manipulate the QueryDef objects. The QueryDefs collection, as do all DAO collections, has a Count property to determine the number of objects in the collection.

**Count**   Count returns the number of QueryDef objects in the QueryDefs collection for a particular Database object. You can reference it as follows:

```
Dim intQDCount As Integer
QDCount = DBEngine(0)(0).QueryDefs.Count
```

The QueryDefs collection has the following methods:

**Append**  When creating QueryDef objects, you need to append them to the QueryDefs collection so that you can refer to them in code outside of the procedure in which you create them.

**Delete**  Use this method if you want to remove a QueryDef object from the QueryDefs collection.

**Refresh**  Use this method to make sure that the QueryDefs collection accurately represents its objects. Whenever appending, deleting, or modifying a QueryDef object, it is good programming practice to refresh the QueryDefs collection—especially if you are in a multiuser environment.

The following code shows how to use these methods:

```
Sub RefreshQueryDefs()
    Dim dbMyDB As Database, qdMyQuery As QueryDef
    Set dbMyDB = DBEngine(0)(0)
    Set qdMyQuery = dbMyDB.CreateQueryDef()
    qdMyQuery.Name = "NewQuery"
    qdMyQuery.SQL = "DELETE * FROM Employees;"
    ' The above QueryDef creates a Delete action query.
    ' Use the Append method to add NewQuery to the
    ' QueryDefs collection.
    dbMyDB.QueryDefs.Append qdMyQuery
    ' Use the Refresh method to ensure the accuracy of the
    ' QueryDefs collection.
    dbMyDB.QueryDefs.Refresh
    ' Use the Delete method to remove NewQuery.
    dbMyDB.QueryDefs.Delete "NewQuery"
    ' Use the Refresh method to ensure the accuracy of the
    ' QueryDefs collection.
    dbMyDB.QueryDefs.Refresh
End Sub
```

The QueryDef object can represent any type of query that you can create in the Microsoft Access user interface. These queries include the typical Select queries as well as Delete, Update, Append, Make Table, Union, Data Definition, and SQL Pass-Through queries. Tables just contain data; queries are used to filter and organize data into valuable and meaningful information or to perform actions on data, such as deleting, appending, and updating records.

## Using the properties of the QueryDef object

The following list includes the commonly used properties of QueryDef objects. (For a complete listing, see online Help.)

**Name**  The Name property returns the name of the QueryDef object. The TableDef and QueryDef objects cannot share the same name.

**SQL**  This property returns the Structured Query Language statement that matches the query object's graphical design. By changing this property, you change the query.

**Type**  You can use this property to specify or determine what type of query the QueryDef object represents. For a complete list of Type values, see the Type property topic in online Help. The following code shows how to reference this property:

```
Dim qdMyQuery As QueryDef
For Each qdMyQuery In DBEngine(0)(0).QueryDefs
    ' Determine whether the Query is a Select Query.
    If qdMyQuery.Type = dbQSelect Then
        Debug.Print qdMyQuery.Name
    End If
Next
```

**RecordsAffected**  You can run or execute an action query through code by using either an SQL statement or a query object. When an action query is executed in the user interface, the user is prompted with the number of records that will be deleted, updated, or inserted. The RecordsAffected property returns the number of those affected records for action queries executed through code.

**ReturnsRecords and Connect**  The ReturnsRecords property can be used to either set or return a True/False (Boolean) value indicating whether an SQL pass-through query returns records from an ODBC SQL Server data source. SQL pass-through queries can be used to execute Store Procedures or Updates, which do not return any records. The Connect property for QueryDef objects is used only when creating an ODBC SQL pass-through query. The syntax for the Connect property is the same as that for creating links to ODBC SQL Server tables. The Connect property must be set before the ReturnsRecords property is set. Here's an example of how to use this property:

```
Sub CreatePassThroughQuery()
    Dim dbMyDB As Database, qdMyQuery As QueryDef
    Set dbMyDB = DBEngine.Workspaces(0)(0)
    ' Create an SQL pass-through query.
    Set qdMyQuery = dbMyDB.CreateQueryDef()
    With qdMyQuery
        .Name = "My SQL PT"
        ' Use SQL Server Syntax.
        .SQL = "SELECT * FROM authors WHERE au_id = " & _
            "'172-32-1176'"
        ' Set the Connect property for the ODBC SQL Server
        ' data source.
        .Connect = "ODBC; DATABASE=pubs; " & _
```

```
                "UID=UserNameBob; PWD=BobsPassword; " & _
                "DSN=Road Runner"
        ' This query returns a recordset.
        .ReturnsRecords = True
    End With
    ' Append the SQL pass-through query to the
    ' QueryDefs collection.
    dbMyDB.QueryDefs.Append qdMyQuery
End Sub
```

**ODBCTimeout**   This property is the same as the QueryTimeout property for the Database object. However, you can apply a different amount of time to an individual query object if the default set by the Database object is not sufficient. The ODBCTimeout property applies only to the query object that you change the property for.

**LogMessages**   If set to Yes, Microsoft Access will create a user-defined message table in your database that will store messages returned from the SQL database that you access. By default, this property is set to No.

**FailOnError**   You can use this property to force an update or delete query to terminate and roll back the transaction on an ODBC data source if an error occurs.

**UseTransaction**   You can use this property on an action query for an ODBC data source to specify whether the action query runs as a single transaction. In other words, if set to No and the action query fails partially, the information changed up to that point will be committed and not rolled back. Therefore, you must have some means of completing any changes that should have been made or rolling back changes that shouldn't have been made. Set this property to No only if performance considerations are more important than data accuracy.

**MaxRecords**   You can use this property to set the maximum number of records that an ODBC data source will return.

### Using the methods of the QueryDef object
The QueryDef object has the following methods:

**Execute**   With this method, you can run an action query.

**CreateProperty**   This method allows you to create custom properties for a query just as you can for individual database and table objects. This property includes the Description and Filter properties, which Microsoft Access uses and maintains because the Microsoft Jet Database Engine does not recognize them. Once again, creating properties is much easier to do in the user interface, so you won't use this method often unless you are developing a wizard that creates QueryDefs.

**OpenRecordset**   You use this method to directly create a Recordset object on your QueryDef (query) object in order to manipulate the data returned by a SELECT query.

## Performing common tasks with the QueryDef object

Solution providers often use the QueryDef object to open a Recordset object and to execute an action query. Opening a recordset based on a query object that returns records is discussed in great detail in Chapter 10.

To execute an action query using a QueryDef object, you call the Execute method for that object. This method is used in conjunction with the Records-Affected property, which returns the number of records the action query will affect.

```
Sub ExecuteActionQuery2()
    Dim dbMyDB As Database, qd As QueryDef, lngRecAff As Long

    On Error GoTo err_ExecuteActionQuery
    Set dbMyDB = DBEngine(0)(0)
    ' This QueryDef is a delete query that will
    ' delete employees from the Employees table where
    ' their title is equal to Sales Representative.
    Set qd = dbMyDB.QueryDefs("DeleteEmployees")
    ' Execute the action query SQL statement.
    qd.Execute dbFailOnError
    ' Return the number of records to be deleted.
    lngRecAff = qd.RecordsAffected
    MsgBox lngRecAff & "record(s) deleted."
    Exit Sub
    ' Trap for updating failures.
err_ExecuteActionQuery:
    MsgBox "Update Failed"
    Exit Sub
End Sub
```

> **TIP** Use the dbFailOnError option with the Execute method so that updates will be rolled back if an error occurs.

## The collections of the QueryDef object

The following collections are supported by the QueryDef object:

**Parameters (default)**   This collection contains all parameters used by a query to dynamically customize the results of its recordset. Because the Parameters collection is the default collection of the QueryDef object, you can reference the collection implicitly.

```
' Explicit Reference to the Parameters collection
Debug.Print DBEngine(0)(0).QueryDefs(0).Parameters(0).Name
' Implicit Reference to the Parameters collection
Debug.Print DBEngine(0)(0).QueryDefs(0)(0).Name
```

**Fields**   This collection contains all the fields (and their properties) that are part of the definition (design) of your queries.

**Properties**   This collection is the same for all DAO objects.

## Using the Recordsets Collection and the Recordset Object

The Recordsets collection and Recordset object are the most widely used of all DAO objects. Recordsets allow you to add, delete, update, and manipulate your data. With Recordset objects you can create custom searches and data manipulation routines. Because you will be doing a majority of your DAO programming using Recordset objects, we have dedicated most of Chapter 10 to this subject.

## Using the Relations Collection and the Relation Object

The Relations collection contains all the Relation (relationship) objects in the database. You use the Relations collection to refer to, create, and manipulate the Relation objects. You typically need to do this only if you are creating a relationship or database wizard. Like all DAO collections, the Relations collection has a Count property that determines the number of objects in the collection.

**Count**   Count returns the number of Relation objects in the Relations collection for a particular Database object. Here's how to reference this property:

```
Dim intRLCount As Integer
intRLCount = DBEngine(0)(0).Relations.Count
```

The Relations collection has the following methods:

**Append**   When creating Relation objects, you need to append them to the Relations collection so that you can refer to them in your code.

**Delete**   This method will remove a Relation object from the Relations collection.

**Refresh**   Use this method to make sure that the Relations collection accurately represents its objects.

The Relation objects are the relationships that you create. Relationships can enforce referential integrity between tables, or they can simply join tables or queries. Relationships allow you to normalize your database to save space and reduce the likelihood of data entry errors, which can be a problem in flat file database systems.

---

**Referential Integrity and Normalization**

You can set up a table so that any fields that are linked to other tables cannot contain values that don't exist in those other tables. This is called *referential integrity*. As an example, imagine you have a table that contains addresses and includes a State field. If you link the State field to a table of valid state abbreviations using referential integrity, a user will not be able to enter invalid state abbreviations into an address.

The term *normalization* refers to a phase of database design during which you try to eliminate duplication of data among tables and to ensure that all data is appropriately linked among your tables.

---

## Using the properties of the Relation object

Relation objects have the following properties. (For a complete list, see online Help.)

**Name**    The Name property returns the name of the Relation object. When you create a relationship in the Microsoft Access user interface, a name is automatically assigned.

**Attributes**    With this property, you can specify or determine the type of relationship that exists. For example, you can check whether a relationship uses cascading updates or cascading deletes, you can enforce referential integrity, and so on.

**Table and ForeignTable**    The Table property returns the name of the primary table, such as the "one" table in a one-to-one or one-to-many relationship. The ForeignTable property returns the name of the table used as the other part of the relationship, such as the "many" table in a one-to-many relationship. If referential integrity is not enforced, the Foreign Table property can also be used to refer to joins between tables or queries.

## Using the method of the Relation object

The Relation object has only one method: CreateField.

**CreateField**    This method is used to specify which fields will be used in the Relation object and whether the relationship has enforced referential integrity or is just a join.

### The collections of the Relation object
The following collections are supported by the Relation object:

**Fields (default)**  This collection contains all the fields (and their properties) that are part of the definition (design) of your relationships. The Fields collection is the default collection of the Relation object.

**Properties**  This collection is the same for all DAO objects.

## Using the Parameters Collection and the Parameter Object
The Parameters collection contains all the Parameter objects in a specific Query-Def object. You use the Parameters collection to refer to and pass values to those parameters defined in the query. The Parameters collection, as do all DAO collections, has a Count property to determine the number of objects in the collection.

**Count**  The Count property returns the number of Parameter objects in the Parameters collection for a particular QueryDef object. You can reference this property as follows:

```
Dim intParamCount As Integer
intParamCount = _
    DBEngine(0)(0).QueryDefs("Query1").Parameters.Count
```

The Parameters collection has only one method: Refresh.

**Refresh**  Use this method to make sure that the Parameters collection accurately represents its objects. (This method is rarely used for the Parameters collection.)

Parameters allow you to pass different criteria to a query in order to dynamically change the resulting recordset. Parameter objects can be created only through the Structured Query Language statement (SQL property) of a Query-Def object.

### Using the properties of the Parameter object
Parameter objects have the following properties:

**Name**  The Name property returns the name of the Parameter used in a Query-Def object. This property is read-only because the parameters are established with the QueryDef object's SQL statement.

**Type**  This property returns the data type of the parameter that is being used within a QueryDef. For example, you can have a parameter that needs to pass in data or integers. For a complete list of Type values, see the Type property topic in online Help.

**Value**    Use this property to return or set the value of the parameter to be used to affect the QueryDef object's resulting recordset.

The Parameter object has no methods and supports only the Properties collection (which is the same for all DAO objects).

## Using the Indexes Collection and the Index Object

The Indexes collection contains all the Index objects in an individual TableDef object. You use the Indexes collection to refer to and manipulate Index objects. Typically, you would need to do so only if you were creating a table wizard. The Indexes collection, as do all DAO collections, has a Count property to determine the number of objects in the collection.

**Count**    Count returns the number of Index objects in the Indexes collection for a particular TableDef object. You can reference this property as follows:

```
Dim intIndexCount As Integer
intIndexCount = _
    DBEngine(0)(0).TableDefs("Employees").Indexes.Count
```

The Indexes collection has the following methods:

**Append**    When creating Index objects in a TableDef, you need to append them to the Indexes collection so that you can refer to them in code outside of the procedure in which you create them.

**Delete**    This method will remove an Index object from the Indexes collection of a TableDef.

**Refresh**    Use this method to make sure that the Indexes collection accurately represents its objects.

The Index object can be an index made up of one or more fields. You can sort the fields in the index as a combination of ascending and descending order. You can also decide whether the index will be the PrimaryKey in the table, a unique index, or just an index that allows duplicate values.

### Using the properties of the Index object

The following list contains the most commonly used properties for QueryDef objects. (See online Help for a complete list.)

**Name**    The Name property returns the name of the Index object. The index name could be the name of the field or fields used to create the index, but you can assign any name to an index. For example, an index created from the First Name and Last Name fields might be called Full Name.

**Primary**    This property returns a True value (–1) if the index is the primary key in the TableDef.

**Unique** This property returns a True value (−1) if the index can contain only unique values.

**DistinctCount** This property returns the number of unique values, or keys, in an index. For example, if a text field in a table with a unique index has the following values, it will return a DistinctCount of 3:

A;A;A;B;C;C

**Foreign** This property will return a True value (−1) if the index is used as a Foreign key in a relationship and a False value (0) if it is not.

**IgnoreNulls** If this property is set to a True value (−1), then null values will not be included. Subsequently, the amount of storage space needed for that index will be reduced, especially if many of the values in the index are null.

### Using the methods of the Index object
The Index object has the following methods:

**CreateField** This method allows you to specify the fields that will be used to create an Index object.

**CreateProperty** This method allows you to create custom properties for an index just as you can for individual Database and Table objects.

### The collections of the Index object
The following collections are supported by the Index object:

**Fields (default)** This collection contains all the fields (and their properties) that are part of the definition (design) of a given query. The Fields collection is the default collection of the Index object.

**Properties** This collection is the same for all DAO objects.

## Using the Fields Collection and the Field Object
The Fields collection contains all the Field objects in an individual TableDef, QueryDef, Recordset, Index, or Relation object. You use the Fields collection to refer to and manipulate Field objects. You might use this collection frequently with the Recordset objects, but with the other objects you will typically use the Fields collection only if you are building a wizard. Like all DAO collections, the Fields collection has a Count property that determines the number of objects in the collection.

**Count** The Count property returns the number of Field objects in the Fields collection for a particular TableDef, QueryDef, Recordset, Index, or Relation object. You can reference this property as shown on the following page.

```
Dim intFCount As Integer
intFCount = <DAOobject>.Fields.Count
```

The Fields collection has the following methods:

**Append**  When creating Field objects, you need to append them to their appropriate Fields collection so that you can refer to them in code outside of the procedure in which you create them.

**Delete**  This method will remove a Field object from a Fields collection.

**Refresh**  Use this method to make sure that the Fields collections are accurate.

The Fields collection applies to five different DAO objects: TableDef, QueryDef, Recordset, Index, and Relation. All five of these objects consist of fields and require a Fields collection and Field objects for their definition.

## Using the properties of the Field object

This section lists the most commonly used properties of Field objects with respect to the various objects that use fields. (For a complete list, see online Help.)

The TableDef object commonly uses the following properties of the Field object in its Fields collection:

**Name**  The Name property returns the name of the Field object.

**Type**  The Type property determines the data type of a field.

**Size**  This property determines the size of the field's data type. For example, a field that is a Text data type can have a size between 1 and 255 characters.

**Attributes**  The most common use of this property is to create an AutoNumber field using the dbAutoIncrField constant. Use the Attributes property in conjunction with the Size property to determine if the AutoNumber is incremental or random.

**DefaultValue, ValidationRule, ValidationText, and Required**  These properties determine the integrity of the data to be stored in that field.

The following code shows how to use some of these properties:

```
Sub CreateAutoNumberField()
    Dim dbMyDB As Database
    Dim tblMyTableDef As TableDef, fldMyField As Field
    Set dbMyDB = DBEngine(0)(0)
    ' Create a new table.
    Set tblMyTableDef = dbMyDB.CreateTableDef _
        ("Table with AutoNumber Field")
    ' Add a field MyAutoNum to the table.
```

```
        Set fldMyField = tblMyTableDef.CreateField()
        fldMyField.Name = "MyAutoNum"
        fldMyField.Type = dbLong
        fldMyField.Attributes = dbAutoIncrField
        fldMyField.Size = 2
        tblMyTableDef.Fields.Append fldMyField
        dbMyDB.TableDefs.Append tblMyTableDef
End Sub
```

The QueryDef and Index objects commonly use the following property of the Field object in their Fields collections:

**Name**    The Name property returns the name of the Field object.

The Recordset object commonly uses the following properties of the Field object in its Fields collection:

**Name**    The Name property returns the name of the Field object.

**ValidateOnSet**    By default, a Field's validation rule will not be executed until you try to save the entire record. However, if you want to validate the field before the record is saved, you can set the field's ValidateOnSet property to True to automatically trigger the validation rule as soon as the field's value is changed.

The Relation object commonly uses the following properties of the Field object in its Fields collection:

**Name**    The Name property returns the name of the Field object.

**Foreign Name**    When creating a relationship, you must create in the Relation object the field or combination of fields that will be used in the relationship. When you create the field in the Relation object's Fields collection, this field applies only to the "one" table in a one-to-one or one-to-many relationship. To establish the relationship with a field from the other table or query, you must specify the linking field in the ForeignName property for the field referencing the "one" table.

## Using the methods of the Field object

The Field object has the following methods. (For a complete list of methods of the Field object, see online Help.)

**FieldSize, AppendChunk, and GetChunk**    These methods are used with Recordset objects to retrieve and append Memo or OLE field data that is greater than 64 KB.

**CreateProperty**    This method allows you to create custom properties for a field just as you can for individual database and table objects. If the field collection is in a TableDef object, you can create a Caption or Format property, which Microsoft Access uses but the Microsoft Jet Database Engine does not.

### The collections of the Field object

The following collections are supported by the Field object:

**Properties**   This collection is the same for all DAO objects.

## Using the Containers Collection and the Container Object with the Documents Collection and the Document Object

The Containers collection stores all the Container objects in the database. The Containers collection and the Documents collection can be used to implement or change security for your database. The only other use of these collections is to return a list of all the objects in the database container (the tables, queries, forms, reports, macros, and modules) and to access some of the custom database properties. The Container objects and their corresponding Document objects cannot be changed or manipulated for any purpose other than for establishing and maintaining a secured database.

The following list shows the names of the Container objects in a database that are defined by the Microsoft Jet Database Engine:

**Databases**   This Container object can be used to refer to the custom and summary information properties of the Database object.

**Tables**   This Container object refers to the saved tables and queries in the database. Remember that "Tables" is just the name of the container; it also refers to queries.

**Relations**   This Container object refers to the saved relationships in the database.

The following list shows the names of the Container objects in a database that are defined by Microsoft Access:

**Forms**   This Container object refers to the saved forms in the database. The group of saved forms is different from the forms in the Forms collection, which refers only to forms that are open in the user interface.

**Reports**   This Container object refers to the saved reports in the database. The group of saved reports is different from the reports in the Reports collection, which refers only to reports that are open in the user interface.

**Scripts**   This Container object refers to the saved macros in the database.

**Modules**   This Container object refers to the saved modules in the database.

NOTE In addition to the containers listed above are two named SysRel and Relationships. They store permissions information about the graphical view of the Relationships window and the permissions on relationships themselves. These containers are used internally by Microsoft Access and are not useful for any type of solution development.

Each of these Container objects has a Documents collection. The Document objects in the collection contain information about the individual objects in your database. Documents are used to determine and change the security permissions assigned to those objects. They can also have a Replicable property, which is used to replicate those objects if the database is replicated. With UserDefined and SummaryInfo documents in the Databases container, you can access a database's SummaryInfo and UserDefined properties (custom database properties). The security aspects of the Containers and Documents collections are discussed in Chapter 12.

### Performing common tasks with Containers and Documents

The following tasks are done with Containers and Documents collections:

- Returning a list of documents in the database container
- Returning the SummaryInfo and Custom properties of the database

The other common tasks performed with these collections involve security and are discussed in Chapter 12.

**Filling a combo box with a list of documents**   Sometimes you may want to give the user access to a list of the objects in the database. Using the Containers collection, you can return a list of all the objects in the database by using a particular Container object's Documents collection. The following code fills a list box with a list of the objects you select. Other than creating the procedure, the only thing you need to do to run this example is to create a list box on a form and set its Row Source Type property to the name of the function, vntFillListBoxAgain.

```
Public Function vntFillListBoxAgain(ctlMyCtrl As Control, _
    vntid, vntrow, vntcol, vntcode) As Variant
'***************************************************************
' This function name is used as the Row Source Type for an
' unbound list box. It will display the names of all of a
' specific Container object's Documents collection.
'***************************************************************
```

*(continued)*

```
Static aMyArray() As String, intArrayItems As Integer
Dim vntReturnVal As Variant
vntReturnVal = Null
Select Case vntcode
  Case acLBInitialize
    '*****************************************************
    ' Case 0: Initializes the function. Lets the function
    ' know how many elements will be in the list box. It
    ' also initializes the array that holds the elements.
    '*****************************************************
    intArrayItems = 0
    Dim dbMyDB As Database, tblMyTableDef As TableDef
    Dim qdMyQuery As QueryDef, cntMyContainer As Container
    Dim docMyDoc As Document, strContainerName As String

    Set dbMyDB = DBEngine(0)(0)
    intArrayItems = 0
    ' Possible values for the strContainerName variable are
    ' Databases, Tables, Relations, Queries, Forms, Reports,
    ' Scripts, or Modules.
    strContainerName = "Forms"
    Select Case strContainerName
        Case "Tables"
          ' Loop through the TableDefs collection
          For Each tblMyTableDef In dbMyDB.TableDefs
            If (tblMyTableDef.Attributes And _
                dbSystemObject) Or _
                (tblMyTableDef.Attributes And _
                dbHiddenObject) Then
                ' Skip the System and Hidden Tables.
            Else
                ' Show only tables that are not
                ' System or Hidden tables.
                ReDim Preserve aMyArray(intArrayItems)
                aMyArray(intArrayItems) = _
                    tblMyTableDef.Name
                intArrayItems = intArrayItems + 1
            End If
          Next
        Case "Queries"
          ' Loop through the QueryDefs collection.
          For Each qdMyQuery In dbMyDB.QueryDefs
            ReDim Preserve aMyArray(intArrayItems)
            aMyArray(intArrayItems) = qdMyQuery.Name
            intArrayItems = intArrayItems + 1
          Next
        Case Else
```

```
            ' Loop through the Documents collection
            ' based on the Databases, Relations, Forms, Reports,
            ' Scripts, or Modules Container object.
            Set cntMyContainer = _
                dbMyDB.Containers(strContainerName)
            For Each docMyDoc In cntMyContainer.Documents
                ReDim Preserve aMyArray(intArrayItems)
                aMyArray(intArrayItems) = docMyDoc.Name
                intArrayItems = intArrayItems + 1
            Next
    End Select
    vntReturnVal = intArrayItems

Case acLBOpen
    '*********************************************************
    ' Case 1: Open. Provides a unique number for the
    ' function. In most cases, just use the following code.
    '*********************************************************
    vntReturnVal = Timer

Case acLBGetRowCount
    '*********************************************************
    ' Case 3: Number of Rows. Lets the function know how
    ' many rows are going to be in the list (can be zero).
    ' Use -1 if number is unknown.
    ' Used iArrayItems here because it is defined as Static
    ' and it indicates the number of rows in the list box.
    '*********************************************************
    vntReturnVal = intArrayItems

Case acLBGetColumnCount
    '*********************************************************
    ' Case 4: Number of Columns. (CANNOT be zero.) Should
    ' match value in property sheet. Can use -1 to tell
    ' function to use the Column count property from the
    ' control.
    '*********************************************************
    vntReturnVal = -1

Case acLBGetColumnWidth
    '*********************************************************
    ' Case 5: Column Width. Width of the column is
    ' expressed in twips specified by the Col argument.
    ' Use -1 to use default widths.
    '*********************************************************
    vntReturnVal = -1
```

*(continued)*

```
    Case acLBGetValue
        '*****************************************************
        ' Case 6: List Entry. Gives element to be displayed in
        ' the rows and column specified by the Row and Col
        ' arguments.
        '*****************************************************
        vntReturnVal = aMyArray(vntrow)

    Case acLBEnd
        '*****************************************************
        ' Case 9: This is the last call to the function. Always
        ' include this case. This is a good place for any
        ' cleanup code.
        '*****************************************************
        Erase aMyArray


    End Select
    ' Return the value.
    vntFillListBoxAgain = vntReturnVal
End Function
```

**SummaryInfo and custom database properties**   The SummaryInfo and custom database properties are shown in Figure 9-2. This dialog box is from the Northwind Traders sample database.

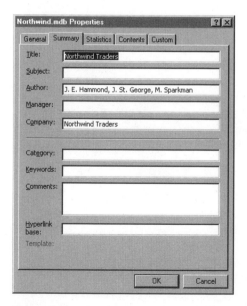

**Figure 9-2.** *SummaryInfo and custom database properties.*

You can change or create the SummaryInfo and custom database properties using the following syntax, respectively:

```
Function vntGetSummaryInfo()
    ' This function returns the value of the
    ' Title property of the SummaryInfo (Summary Information)
    ' document. These properties are Microsoft Access database
    ' properties.
    Dim dbMyDB As Database, cntMyContainer As Container
    Dim docMyDoc As Document

    Set dbMyDB = DBEngine(0)(0)
    Set cntMyContainer = dbMyDB.Containers("Databases")
    Set docMyDoc = cntMyContainer.Documents("SummaryInfo")
    ' Since Title is a Microsoft Access property,
    ' you must refer to it through the Properties
    ' collection of the Document object SummaryInfo.
    vntGetSummaryInfo = docMyDoc.Properties("Title")
End Function

Function vntGetDBVersion()
    ' This function returns the value of the
    ' CustomDatabase property MyDBVersion of the
    ' UserDefined Document object's Microsoft Access Properties
    ' collection.
    Dim dbMyDB As Database, cntMyContainer As Container
    Dim docMyDoc As Document

    Set dbMyDB = DBEngine(0)(0)
    Set cntMyContainer = dbMyDB.Containers("Databases")
    Set docMyDoc = cntMyContainer.Documents("UserDefined")
    ' Since MyDBVersion is a user-defined property,
    ' you must refer to it through the Properties
    ' collection of the Document object UserDefined.
    vntGetDBVersion = docMyDoc.Properties("MyDBVersion")
End Function
```

**NOTE** If the properties referenced in the above procedures do not already exist, you will first have to use the CreateProperty method to create those properties since they are used only by Microsoft Access and not by the Microsoft Jet Database Engine. For more information, see online Help for the SummaryInfo and custom database properties topics.

# DAO and ODBCDirect

So far, we have examined how you can use the DAO hierarchy to manipulate objects that exist within a Microsoft Access database. Now we'll turn to a section of the DAO hierarchy that allows you to manipulate external databases such as Microsoft SQL Server and Oracle databases without using the Microsoft Jet Database Engine.

As discussed earlier in the chapter, the Microsoft Jet Database Engine is a very powerful part of Microsoft Access that allows you to access your data and manipulate objects using both the user interface and VBA code. In previous versions of Microsoft Access, the Jet Database Engine is used also to manipulate databases that do not inherently use Jet, such as SQL Server. Consequently, the Jet components are still loaded into memory, and data retrieval is slower than with other methods. You can still use Jet in Microsoft Access 97 to manipulate non-Jet databases, or you can use ODBCDirect. In Microsoft Access 97, ODBCDirect is built into the DAO hierarchy and allows you to choose whether to use either the Jet Database Engine or ODBC to manipulate the data you are retrieving. In this section we will focus on the data retrieval capabilities, using ODBC to access and manipulate data from a back-end database such as an SQL Server database.

## Creating an ODBCDirect Workspace

Using the DBEngine object, you can set the DefaultType property to either dbUseJet or dbUseODBC. The default, dbUseJet, will create Workspace objects that connect to the Microsoft Access Jet Database Engine. Setting the DefaultType property to dbUseODBC allows you to create Workspace objects that connect to an ODBC data source. The DAO hierarchy for the DBEngine and Workspace objects is the same whether using ODBCDirect or Jet, except that there is also a Connections collection you can access if you use ODBCDirect workspaces. Figure 9-3 shows the ODBCDirect hierarchy.

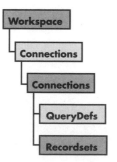

**Figure 9-3.** *DAO hierarchy with ODBCDirect objects and collections.*

To create a new ODBCDirect workspace, you must use the CreateWorkspace method from the DBEngine object. (The default workspace is always a Microsoft Access Jet workspace.) The following code shows how to create an ODBCDirect workspace:

```
Dim ws As Workspace
Dim conPubs As Connection

DBEngine.DefaultType = dbUseODBC
Set ws = DBEngine.CreateWorkspace("wrkODBC", "admin", "")
```

Once you have an ODBCDirect Workspace object, you can create a connection to the back-end data source.

### Connections collection

The Connections collection contains a list of all Connection objects that you can create using ODBC Data Sources. This collection is very similar to the Databases collection in that when you create a Connection object you specify which ODBC database you want that object to represent.

**TIP** To find out how to create an ODBC Data Source, see the "Registering your ODBC database" section beginning on page 307.

The OpenConnection method, which exists for Workspace objects, allows you to specify the name of the connection, options for the connection, and whether it is read-only. You specify the Data Source you have defined in the Connect Options argument. The following code uses the OpenConnection method to connect to a database that exists on the data source named "MyServer."

```
Dim ws As Workspace
Dim conPubs As Connection

DBEngine.DefaultType = dbUseODBC
Set ws = DBEngine.CreateWorkspace("wrkODBC", "admin", "")

Set conPubs = ws.OpenConnection("Pubs", dbDriverNoPrompt, _
    False, "ODBC;DATABASE=pubs;UID=sa;PWD=;DSN=MyServer")
```

Once a connection is established, you can access the data that exists in the tables of the database and create Recordset and QueryDef objects to manipulate the data. Certain back-end databases, such as SQL Server, allow only a specific number of connections to the server at one time. The Connections collection allows you to control the number of connections your application makes to the server.

TIP

If you don't want to create a data source name via the ODBC Data Source Administrator or the RegisterDatabase method, you can create a File DSN. A File DSN is simply a text file that provides information about which ODBC driver to use and its configuration information, as shown below:

```
[ODBC]
DRIVER=SQL Server
UID=sa
DATABASE=pubs
SERVER=MyServer
```

To use this File DSN with the OpenConnection property, save it in a file named MyServer.DSN, then use the following code:

```
Set conn = wrk.OpenConnection("MyConnect", _
    dbDriverNoPrompt, False, _
    "ODBC;FILEDSN=c:\MyServer.dsn;UID=sa;PWD=;")
```

## Connection object properties

The following list includes the commonly used properties of the Connection object. For a complete list, consult online Help.

- **QueryTimeOut** sets or returns the number of seconds to wait for a query to finish executing.

- **RecordsAffected** returns the number of records affected during an update or a delete operation.

- **StillExecuting** indicates whether the query is still running.

- **Transactions** indicates whether the connection supports transactions.

- **Updatable** indicates whether objects in this connection are updatable.

## Connection object methods

The following list contains the commonly used methods of the Connection object. See online Help for more information.

- **Cancel** terminates a query if it is in the middle of executing. This method is useful if the query is taking too long in returning records.

- **CreateQueryDef** creates a temporary QueryDef object that can be used to manipulate data.

- **Execute** executes an SQL string to update, delete, or insert data into a table.

- **OpenRecordset** creates a Recordset object that can be used to manipulate data.

## ODBCDirect QueryDefs

When using an ODBCDirect workspace, you do not have access to the definitions or objects in the database. This is because the database typically resides on a server, and network performance would be seriously degraded if DAO provided a means to access the tables and all of their data and definitions directly. The QueryDefs collection for ODBCDirect workspaces contains a temporary list of QueryDef objects that are defined for a connection.

You can create a QueryDef object in an ODBCDirect workspace the same way you create one within a Microsoft Access Jet workspace—using the Create-QueryDef method, but executing this method on a Connection object. In addition to the properties shown previously for QueryDef objects, in an ODBCDirect workspace you can set the Prepare and CacheSize properties.

- **Prepare** Allows you to specify whether a temporary stored procedure will be created on the server before you execute the query. Creating a stored procedure on the server yields better performance for the query if the query is referenced repeatedly.

- **CacheSize** Allows you to set the number of records that should be retrieved and stored in the local cache. (A *cache* is a space reserved on the local machine for holding data.) Caching can improve performance, especially if users ask for the same data again later in the session.

Like the QueryDef object in Microsoft Access Jet workspaces, the ODBCDirect QueryDef object supports a Parameters and Fields collection, both of which function alike and serve exactly the same purpose as their Jet counterparts.

The ODBCDirect functionality provided with Jet 3.5 is a very powerful and flexible way of accessing ODBC data without having to load all of the Jet engine into memory. We did not cover this topic in detail in this book only because there are too many nuances to the topic, depending on your individual installation. Once you understand the particular back end you are working with in your installation, using the ODBCDirect functionality in Jet 3.5 to manipulate the data is less of a challenge because the same syntax is used to manipulate the objects as is used in the DAO hierarchy for Microsoft Access databases.

## PREVIEW of the next chapter

In Chapter 10 we will continue our discussion of DAO. The chapter will focus primarily on working with data, which is what we use DAO for in the first place. You will learn how to create transactions, move data from one table to another, search for records, edit records, and much more.

# 10

## Accessing Data Using DAO

In Chapter 9 we discussed the objects in the DAO hierarchy in detail. In this chapter we will apply what we learned about DAO to working with data. We will examine how to access data in multiple databases, how to process transactions, and how to use Microsoft Access SQL (Structured Query Language) to create queries. We will spend the bulk of the chapter, however, in studying Recordset objects and their many uses, because you will probably be working with these DAO objects more than with any others.

Before we discuss the Recordset object, however, let's cover the Database object in more detail than we did in Chapter 9.

### The Database Object

In Chapter 9 you learned how to reference the currently open database using either variation of the same syntax shown in the following code:

```
Dim dbMyDB As Database
Set dbMyDB = DBEngine.Workspaces(0).Databases(0)
Set dbMyDB = DBEngine(0)(0)
```

When referring to the current database through the code above, the database variable (dbMyDB) refers to the open instance of that database. The limitation of this is that if you use more than one database variable, any changes you make to one variable will apply to any other variables that were also set using the DBEngine(0)(0) syntax, as shown in the example on the following page.

```
Sub ChangeDBProperty()
    Dim dbMyDB1 As Database, dbMyDB2 As Database
    Set dbMyDB1 = DBEngine(0)(0)
    Set dbMyDB2 = DBEngine(0)(0)
    Debug.Print dbMyDB1.QueryTimeout; dbMyDB2.QueryTimeout
    dbMyDB1.QueryTimeout = 250
    Debug.Print dbMyDB1.QueryTimeout; dbMyDB2.QueryTimeout
End Sub
```

In this code example, both database variables will return the new QueryTimeout value for the database.

If you want to create truly different database variables—in which a change to one will not affect the others—use the CurrentDB function. This function creates a copy of the Database object that can be manipulated independently of other variables referring to the same current database, as shown here:

```
Sub ChangeDBProperty()
    Dim dbMyDB1 As Database, dbMyDB2 As Database
    Set dbMyDB1 = CurrentDB()
    Set dbMyDB2 = CurrentDB()
    Debug.Print dbMyDB1.QueryTimeout; dbMyDB2.QueryTimeout
    dbMyDB1.QueryTimeout = 250
    Debug.Print dbMyDB1.QueryTimeout; dbMyDB2.QueryTimeout
End Sub
```

In this code, using CurrentDB, dbMyDB1.QueryTimeout will return 250, whereas dbMyDB2.QueryTimeout will return the default QueryTimeout value. The returned values for QueryTimeout can be different because they are in different copies of the database rather than in the same instance of the database pointed to by two variables.

We used the DBEngine(0)(0) syntax to demonstrate the logic of the DAO hierarchy. At this point, we will use the CurrentDB function to work with Database objects. In fact, you could also use the CurrentDB object in the code examples in Chapter 9.

## Opening Another Database

You might sometimes want to open another database through code instead of using the current database. Databases you might prefer to open through code could include native Microsoft Access databases and ISAM and ODBC data sources. And sometimes you do not want to create linked tables; instead, you need their information only when you are using certain procedures. To access other data sources without creating linked tables, use the OpenDatabase method discussed in Chapter 9. The OpenDatabase method, which is a method of the Workspace object, has the following arguments:

**dbname**   This required argument is the name of the database (data source) to be opened.

**exclusive**   By default, a Microsoft Access database is opened as shared. However, you can use this optional argument to open a database as exclusive. This argument has a True/False Boolean value.

**read-only**   By default, a Microsoft Access database is opened as read/write. However, you can use this optional argument to open a database as read-only. This is a True/False Boolean value.

**source**   This is a string value you use to open a data source. In Microsoft Access, you can use it to pass in a share-level password. In ISAM and ODBC data sources, this source argument is the same information as is used in the Connect property.

> **NOTE**   When opening a Microsoft Access database that has a share-level password, you must specify the source argument as ";PWD=" followed by the password. You must also supply the exclusive and read-only arguments.

The following code demonstrates how code is used to open different types of databases:

```
Sub OpenMultiDatabases()
    ' To run this example, you will need to change
    ' \\Server\Share to point to a valid network location
    ' to which you have the appropriate level of access.

    ' Open a Microsoft Access database with share-level
    ' password and Read/Write access.
    Dim dbMyDB As Database
    Set dbMyDB = DBEngine(0).OpenDatabase _
        ("\\server\share\a.mdb", False, False, ";pwd=password")

    ' Open a Microsoft FoxPro 2.6 table.
    Dim dbMyFoxDB As DATABASE
    Dim rsMyRS As Recordset
    Set dbMyFoxDB = DBEngine(0).OpenDatabase _
        ("\\server\share", False, False, "FoxPro 2.6;")
    ' Open a Recordset object based on the FoxPro table
    ' named FoxTable.DBF.
    Set rsMyRS = dbMyDB.OpenRecordset("FoxTable")
```

*(continued)*

```
' Open an ODBC data source.
Dim dbMyODBCDB As DATABASE
Set dbMyODBCDB = DBEngine(0).OpenDatabase _
    ("", False, False, _
    "ODBC;DSN=Publishers;DATABASE=pubs;UID=sa;PWD=")
End Sub
```

Keep in mind that if you close the Database object variable, any other objects opened or referenced through this variable will be closed as well.

## The Recordset Object

Opening a recordset is like opening a Table object or a Query object in Datasheet view, but in memory rather than on the screen. A Recordset object does not appear in the user interface. So why use a Recordset object if it is only a representation of a table or query when you already have that table or query stored in the database container? If you use the Table or Query object through the user interface, you are allowing the user to control how information is processed. With the Recordset object, you can control how the information is processed through code. You can create custom edit routines for bulk data processing. You can also create custom searches that allow your users to find the information they need quickly.

### Defining Recordsets

You can create three different types of Recordset objects: tables, snapshots, and dynasets. Each type of object has advantages and disadvantages, as you will see in the following sections.

#### Table

A table-type Recordset object can be created only with local Microsoft Access tables. It cannot be created with linked Microsoft Access, ISAM, or ODBC tables. When you create a table-type recordset, it is the same as opening a table in Datasheet view in the user interface. When opened in code, all the records are loaded into memory. The main advantage of opening a table-type recordset is that you can quickly search for values based on an index of the table.

#### Snapshot

A snapshot is a read-only set of records that can be based on a table, a query, or an SQL statement. It can be used for nonlocal Microsoft Access tables and for ISAM and ODBC data sources. A snapshot is not just a read-only set of records but is also a static set that represents the status of the records at the time the Recordset object was created. So if those records are changed, the snapshot will not reflect the changes. A good example of a snapshot is a Report object. When you execute a report, that report takes a picture, or snapshot, of that data at the time the report is run. If the report did not use a snapshot to provide a static set of data, the report would continually rerun calculations and arrange data, attempting to stay current with an ever-changing data source. As with tables, all records are opened into memory. Because no record locking is required, a snapshot is an extremely fast method for using a recordset if viewing the data is the only requirement of the recordset or if there aren't many records.

### Dynaset

A dynaset is an updatable set of records that can be based on a table, a query, or an SQL statement. A dynaset can be used for nonlocal Microsoft Access tables and for ISAM and ODBC data sources. It is the most commonly used type of Recordset object because its strengths make up for the weaknesses of table and snapshot recordsets. For example, a dynaset-type Recordset object does not open all of the records into memory. Instead, it uses bookmarks or pointers to the records to retrieve records. The Microsoft Jet Database Engine will retrieve only the actual data (the fields themselves) when you need to refer to that data. So for large amounts of data, dynasets are very efficient because they load only pointers into memory rather than entire records. Dynasets, unlike snapshots, can be updated and manipulated, and they reflect the changes made to their underlying data sources. When you create this kind of recordset, use only those columns (fields) that you really need. Keeping the recordset as small as possible will give you the best performance.

## Creating Recordsets

To open a recordset, use the OpenRecordset method for the Database object. You must also declare an object variable as a Recordset object. When used with the Database object, the OpenRecordset method has three parameters:

**source**  This parameter is the name of the table (either local or linked), query, or SQL statement the recordset will be based on.

**type**  This parameter specifies the type of recordset you want to create: table (dbOpenTable constant), snapshot (dbOpenSnapshot constant), or dynaset (dbOpenDynaset constant).

**options**  These options optimize the Recordset object being opened for performance reasons. You can use some options in combination with each other. For a list of options, see the Help file "OpenRecordset Method" topic.

### Table-type recordsets

Remember that a table-type recordset can be created only with local Microsoft Access tables, not with linked tables. You can create a table-type recordset using either of the methods shown in the code on the following page.

```
Dim dbMyDB As Database, rsMyRS As Recordset
Set dbMyDB = CurrentDB

Set rsMyRS = dbMyDB.OpenRecordset("LocalTable")
' Or you can use the following with the default table object
' type specifier.
Set rsMyRS = dbMyDB.OpenRecordset("LocalTable", dbOpenTable)
```

To open a local table as a table-type object, it is not necessary to use the dbOpenTable type constant, because this constant is the default recordset type of local tables. For table-type objects, you can use the following optional arguments to optimize your use of the recordset:

**dbDenyWrite**   This option will prevent other users from editing or adding records to a particular table through the user interface or through another Recordset object using that table as a source. The Recordset object must be closed before other users can edit and add records. The following code demonstrates how to use this option:

```
Dim dbMyDB As Database, rsMyRS As Recordset
Set dbMyDB = CurrentDB
Set rsMyRS = dbMyDB.OpenRecordset _
    ("LocalTable", dbOpenTable, dbDenyWrite)
```

**dbDenyRead**   This option will prevent other users from editing, adding, and even viewing records of a table. The table becomes exclusively locked by this recordset variable, and the table cannot be viewed or used until the recordset variable is closed. The following code shows how to use this option:

```
Dim dbMyDB As Database, rsMyRS As Recordset
Set dbMyDB = CurrentDB
Set rsMyRS = dbMyDB.OpenRecordset _
    ("LocalTable", dbOpenTable, dbDenyRead)
```

**dbReadOnly**   This option will allow other users to view the data, but only in a read-only state until the Recordset object is closed. Here is how you set this option:

```
Dim dbMyDB As Database, rsMyRS As Recordset
Set dbMyDB = CurrentDB
Set rsMyRS = dbMyDB.OpenRecordset _
    ("LocalTable", dbOpenTable, dbReadOnly)
```

Once you are finished using the Recordset object, use the Close method of the object to remove it from memory. It is also good programming practice to close the database variable if it is no longer needed after the recordset variable is closed. The following code shows how to close these objects:

```
Dim dbMyDB As Database, rsMyRS As Recordset
Set dbMyDB = CurrentDB
Set rsMyRS = dbMyDB.OpenRecordset _
    ("LocalTable", dbOpenTable, dbDenyWrite)
' Close the Recordset object if it is no longer used.
rsMyRS.Close
' Close the Database object if it is no longer used.
dbMyDB.Close
```

## Snapshot-type recordsets

When creating a snapshot, you can use local and linked tables as well as queries and SQL statements. The following code shows how a snapshot-type recordset can be created from various sources:

```
Dim dbMyDB As Database, rsMyRS As Recordset
Set dbMyDB = CurrentDB

' From a local table
Set rsMyRS = dbMyDB.OpenRecordset _
    ("LocalTable", dbOpenSnapshot)

' From a linked table
Set rsMyRS = dbMyDB.OpenRecordset _
    ("LinkedTable", dbOpenSnapshot)

' From a Query object
Set rsMyRS = dbMyDB.OpenRecordset _
    ("Query1", dbOpenSnapshot)

' From an SQL statement
Set rsMyRS = dbMyDB.OpenRecordset _
    ("SELECT * FROM Employees;",dbOpenSnapshot)
```

To open a snapshot-type object, you must use the dbOpenSnapshot type constant because a snapshot is not the default recordset type for any of its possible sources. For snapshot-type objects, you can use the following options:

**dbForwardOnly** This option creates a forward-scrolling snapshot. You can move *only* forward through the recordset. This option can be useful if you need to evaluate a recordset only once. A snapshot that scrolls only forward is faster than a regular snapshot because it does not allow you to refer to the previous records once you move past them. Here is how you use this option:

```
Dim dbMyDB As Database, rsMyRS As Recordset
Set dbMyDB = CurrentDB
Set rsMyRS = dbMyDB.OpenRecordset _
    ("LocalTable", dbOpenSnapshot, dbForwardOnly)
```

**dbDenyWrite and dbReadOnly**  These options work in the same manner as they do for table-type recordsets, but they are not really useful because when you create a snapshot you have a recordset that is already frozen in time—that is, other edits and additions have no effect on the recordset.

## Dynaset-type recordsets

When creating a dynaset, you can use local and linked tables as well as queries and SQL statements. The following code shows how a dynaset-type recordset can be created from various sources:

```
Dim dbMyDB As Database, rsMyRS As Recordset
Set dbMyDB = CurrentDB


' From a local table
Set rsMyRS = dbMyDB.OpenRecordset("LocalTable", dbOpenDynaset)


' From a linked table
Set rsMyRS = dbMyDB.OpenRecordset("LinkedTable")
' Or you can use
Set rsMyRS = dbMyDB.OpenRecordset("LinkedTable", dbOpenDynaset)


' From a Query object
Set rsMyRS = dbMyDB.OpenRecordset("Query1")
' Or you can use
Set rsMyRS = dbMyDB.OpenRecordset("Query1", dbOpenDynaset)


' From an SQL statement
Set rsMyRS = dbMyDB.OpenRecordset("SELECT * FROM Employees;")
' Or you can use
Set rsMyRS = dbMyDB.OpenRecordset _
    ("SELECT * FROM Employees;", dbOpenDynaset)
```

To open a dynaset-type object, you need to use the dbOpenDynaset type constant only when opening a local table, because a dynaset is the default recordset type of all other data sources. For dynaset-type objects, you can use the following options to optimize your use of the recordset:

**dbAppendOnly**  This option will allow you only to add new records to your dynaset. This option does not allow you to edit existing records. Use the following code to implement this option:

```
Dim dbMyDB As Database, rsMyRS As Recordset
Set dbMyDB = CurrentDB
Set rsMyRS = dbMyDB.OpenRecordset _
    ("Query1", dbOpenDynaset,dbAppendOnly)
```

**dbDenyWrite and dbReadOnly**   These options work in the same manner as they do for table-type recordsets.

**dbInconsistent and dbConsistent**   Because the values of these constants are mutually exclusive, you cannot use both of them together. Inconsistent updates are allowed when using the dbInconsistent constant. With inconsistent updates, you can update any column in a table, even if that would break the relationship between the two tables. Consistent updates using the dbConsistent constant preserve the integrity of your relationships because the key field of a many-side table cannot be changed to a value that is not already in the one-side table. This is the default for relationships with referential integrity in Microsoft Access.

## Recordsets from other recordsets

In the previous section you created a recordset from the Database object. You can also call the OpenRecordset method directly on TableDef, QueryDef, and Recordset objects.

- Using the OpenRecordset method with a local TableDef object will create a table-type recordset by default.

- Using it with a QueryDef object will create a dynaset-type recordset by default.

- By default, when using the OpenRecordset method with a Recordset object, the new recordset will inherit the type, such as dynaset or snapshot, unless the Recordset object is a table-type object, in which case the new recordset will be a dynaset-type object. The OpenRecordset method cannot be used with a Recordset object that is a forward-scrolling-only snapshot.

**Using the OpenRecordset method with a TableDef object**   There is really no advantage to creating a recordset from the TableDef object directly rather than from the Database object. However, if you want to use the OpenRecordset method with a TableDef object, you can do so by using the following code:

```
Dim dbMyDB As Database, rsMyRS As Recordset
Set dbMyDB = CurrentDB
' Create a table-type recordset.
Set rsMyRS = dbMyDB.TableDefs("Employees").OpenRecordset()
' Create a dynaset-type recordset.
Set rsMyRS = dbMyDB.TableDefs("Employees"). _
    OpenRecordset(dbOpenDynaset)
```

**Using the OpenRecordset method with a QueryDef object** The OpenRecordset method is extremely useful with a QueryDef object when you are creating recordsets from parameter queries, as you will see in the "Working with parameter queries" section beginning on page 380. A QueryDef object generally provides an easy way for you to view records in multiple tables or to filter the records from a table. Where possible, use a QueryDef object rather than an SQL statement when opening a recordset. Doing so will provide the best performance because a QueryDef object is compiled by Microsoft Access when it is saved rather than at run time. The following code shows how to use the OpenRecordset method with a QueryDef object:

```
Dim dbMyDB As Database, rsMyRS As Recordset
Dim qdMyQuery As QueryDef
Set dbMyDB = CurrentDB
' Create a QueryDef object.
Set qdMyQuery = dbMyDB.CreateQueryDef _
    ("Query1",SELECT * FROM Employees;")
' Open a recordset based on the new query.
Set rsMyRS = qdMyQuery.OpenRecordset()
```

**Using the OpenRecordset method with a Recordset object** The OpenRecordset method is also extremely useful with a Recordset object when you want to create a separate recordset after you make changes to an existing one. For example, you can use the Filter property of a recordset to further limit the number of records in a recordset and thereby manipulate fewer records. To make changes to a dynaset- or snapshot-type Recordset object (but not a table-type one), you can use the following properties:

- **Filter** This property can be used to further limit the records of a dynaset- or snapshot-type Recordset object.

- **Sort** This property can be used to further sort records of a dynaset- or snapshot-type Recordset object.

The following code demonstrates how you can use the Filter and Sort properties:

```
Dim dbMyDB As Database, rsMyRS1 As Recordset
Dim rsMyRS2 As Recordset
Set dbMyDB = CurrentDB
' Create an initial recordset based on a table's dynaset.
Set rsMyRS1 = dbMyDB.OpenRecordset("Employees", dbOpenDynaset)
' Open a recordset based on a filtered and sorted
' set of records.
rsMyRS1.Filter = "Title = 'Sales Representative'"
' Sort LastName ascending and FirstName descending.
rsMyRS1.Sort = "LastName Asc, FirstName Desc"
Set rsMyRS2 = rsMyRS1.OpenRecordset()
```

---

For small recordsets, the Filter and Sort properties are sufficient. Occasionally, however, especially with larger recordsets, it is faster to open a recordset with an SQL statement that uses the appropriate sorting (ORDER BY) statement and filtering (WHERE) statement.

## Using Recordsets

Now that you can create Recordset objects, the next step is to find out how best to navigate through those objects to locate information. You will also want to manipulate the data, editing, adding, or deleting values and records based on your own predetermined conditions. Recordset objects are valuable because with them you can create custom search routines, process bulk transactions in a completely controlled environment, and give your application flexibility that extends beyond that provided by the user interface.

### Using the Fields collection and the Field object of a recordset

Once you create a recordset, you will want to be able to refer to the values of the fields in each record. To do that, you must use the Fields collection and its objects. You can refer to a field in a recordset in the following manner:

```
Sub PrintLastName()
    Dim dbMyDB As Database, rsMyRS As Recordset
    Set dbMyDB = CurrentDb
    Set rsMyRS = dbMyDB.OpenRecordset _
        ("Employees", dbOpenDynaset)

    rsMyRS.MoveFirst
    ' Reference a field by index in the Fields collection
    ' (print the contents of the field).
    Debug.Print rsMyRS.Fields(0)
    ' Reference a field by name in the Fields collection.
    Debug.Print rsMyRS.Fields("LastName")
    ' Reference a field by just the name, because the
    ' Fields collection is the default collection of the
    ' Recordset object.
    Debug.Print rsMyRS("FirstName")
    ' Reference a field using object syntax.
    Debug.Print rsMyRS![FirstName]
    rsMyRS.Close
End Sub
```

The RS("FirstName") and RS![FirstName] syntaxes are the most common and readable methods for referring to a field. Also notice that you did not need to explicitly reference the Value property because it is the default property of the Fields collection of a Recordset object.

## Navigating through recordsets

To scroll backward and forward through a recordset, use the following methods of the Recordset object:

- **MoveFirst** allows the user to move to the first record in a recordset.

- **MoveLast** allows the user to move to the last record in a recordset.

In both of these methods, if the recordset is empty, the user will receive a trappable error stating that there is no current record. The user can also use both of these methods to establish a current record position when opening a recordset that contains records.

- **MoveNext** allows the user to move to the next record in a recordset.

- **MovePrevious** allows the user to move to the previous record in a recordset.

- **Move** allows the user to move forward or backward within a recordset by a user-specified number of moves.

With all of these three methods, if the user steps outside (or past) the first or last record of the recordset, he or she will receive a trappable error stating that there is no current record.

The following code demonstrates how you might encounter and trap for the No Current Record error.

```
Sub RSMoveError()
    Dim dbMyDB As Database, rsMyRS As Recordset
    ' Trap for No Current Record when moving outside
    ' (going beyond) the recordset.
    On Error GoTo err_RSMoveError
    Set dbMyDB = CurrentDb
    Set rsMyRS = dbMyDB.OpenRecordset _
        ("Employees", dbOpenDynaset)
    ' Move to the first record.
    rsMyRS.MoveFirst
    ' Move to the third record.
    rsMyRS.Move 3
    ' Move to the last record.
    rsMyRS.MoveLast
    ' Move to the EOF record.
    rsMyRS.MoveNext
    ' Move to the next record so an error will occur.
    rsMyRS.MoveNext
    ' Display the contents of the first
    ' field in the current record.
```

```
        Debug.Print rsMyRS(0)
        rsMyRS.Close
        dbMyDB.Close
        Exit Sub

err_RSMoveError:
    ' Error 3021 = "No Current Record"
    If Err.Number = 3021 Then
        MsgBox "You have moved outside the recordset."
        Resume Next
    End If
End Sub
```

You can prevent your users from moving outside a recordset when scrolling through it in a variety of ways through code. One method is to write code that checks whether the user is at the beginning of a file or at the end, by using the following properties:

**BOF**   The beginning-of-file property indicates whether the current record position is before (precedes) the first record. BOF will return True if the record position precedes the first record.

**EOF**   The end-of-file property indicates whether the current record position is after (follows) the last record. EOF will return True if the record position follows the last record.

> **NOTE**   BOF and EOF will both return True if the Recordset object contains no records.

The following code shows how to use the BOF and EOF properties:

```
Sub BOFandEOF()
    Dim dbMyDB As Database
    Dim rsMyRS As Recordset
    ' Trap for No Current Record when moving outside
    ' (going beyond) the recordset.
    On Error GoTo err_BOFandEOF
    Set dbMyDB = CurrentDb
    Set rsMyRS = dbMyDB.OpenRecordset _
        ("Employees", dbOpenDynaset)

    ' Establish current record.
    rsMyRS.MoveFirst
```

*(continued)*

```
    Do While Not rsMyRS.EOF
        Debug.Print rsMyRS("EmployeeID")
        rsMyRS.MoveNext
    Loop
    ' The Final MoveNext will move the record position
    ' past the last record. EOF will return True.
    Debug.Print "EOF = " & rsMyRS.EOF

    ' Establish current record.
    rsMyRS.MoveLast

    Do While Not rsMyRS.BOF
        Debug.Print rsMyRS("EmployeeID")
        rsMyRS.MovePrevious
    Loop
    ' The Final MovePrevious will move the record position
    ' before the first record. BOF will return True.
    Debug.Print "BOF = " & rsMyRS.BOF
    rsMyRS.Close
    dbMyDB.Close
    Exit Sub

err_BOFandEOF:
    ' Error 3021 = "No Current Record"
    If Err.Number = 3021 Then
        MsgBox "You have moved outside the recordset."
        Exit Sub
    End If
End Sub
```

> **NOTE** Be careful when using the Move method, because you can still go outside (or beyond) the recordset and generate the No Current Record error.

Another way to move forward and backward through a recordset is by using a For...Next loop in conjunction with the RecordCount property.

**RecordCount**   This property returns the number of records in a Recordset object. If the recordset is empty, the RecordCount property returns 0. When code execution first opens a recordset, all of the records or bookmarks (pointers) might not be in memory. To get an accurate record count, do a MoveLast method, forcing all records to be accessed. When records are added or deleted, the record count needs to be refreshed to be accurate. To refresh a recordset, use the Requery method of the Recordset object.

NOTE When working with linked TableDef objects, the RecordCount property setting is always −1. To get an accurate record count, you can open a dynaset-type recordset on the linked table, move to the last record, and retrieve the count.

The following code illustrates how the RecordCount property and For loop are used:

```
Sub PercentPosExample()
    Dim dbMyDB As Database, rsMyRS As Recordset
    Dim fldMyField As Field, lngRecCount As Long
    Dim lngInitial As Long

    Set dbMyDB = CurrentDb
    Set rsMyRS = dbMyDB.OpenRecordset("Customers")
    ' Exit function if the recordset is empty.
    If rsMyRS.RecordCount <= 0 Then Exit Sub
    ' If RecordCount > 0, move to the last record
    ' to retrieve an accurate count.
    rsMyRS.MoveLast
    lngRecCount = rsMyRS.RecordCount
    ' Move back to the first record.
    rsMyRS.MoveFirst
    ' Forward scroll through the recordset.
    For lngInitial = 1 To lngRecCount
        ' Print the value of each field in the record.
        For Each fldMyField In rsMyRS.Fields
            Debug.Print fldMyField.Value
        Next
        rsMyRS.MoveNext
    Next lngInitial
    ' Move to the last record.
    rsMyRS.MoveLast
    ' Backward scroll through the recordset.
    For lngInitial = lngRecCount To 1 Step -1
        ' Print the value of each field in the record.
        For Each fldMyField In rsMyRS.Fields
            ' The Value property is not necessary
            ' because it is the default
            ' property of the Field object.
            Debug.Print fldMyField
        Next
        rsMyRS.MovePrevious
    Next lngInitial
    ' Close the Recordset object.
    rsMyRS.Close
    ' Close the Database object.
    dbMyDB.Close
End Sub
```

**The PercentPosition property, the AbsolutePosition property, and the GetRows method**   Use the PercentPosition property to return the approximate percentile that the current record is in or to move to a current record in a certain percentile of all three recordset types (range 0–100 percent).

Use the AbsolutePosition property (zero based) to return the exact ordinal position of the current record or to move to a current record based on its ordinal position in a dynaset or snapshot recordset. AbsolutePosition will return –1 if there are no records in the recordset. Neither the AbsolutePosition nor the PercentPosition property applies to forward-scrolling-only snapshots or to a Recordset object opened from an SQL pass-through query.

You can also use the GetRows method to move through a recordset and store the record values in an array. For more information on this method, see online Help.

## Locating records

Knowing how to move through a recordset is important, but for most developers it is just the beginning. For example, you might want to create a custom search routine to find specific records in a recordset. You could use the following methods to devise a custom search through dynaset- and snapshot-type recordsets. Each method uses criteria that you specify (similar to the syntax used by the Filter property).

**FindFirst**   This method will start at the beginning of a recordset and search to the end of the recordset until it finds the desired record.

**FindLast**   This method will start at the end of a recordset and search to the beginning of the recordset until it finds the desired record. This method tends to be slower than the FindFirst method because it must access all the records in the recordset before it can commence.

**FindNext**   This method will find the next record that satisfies the search criteria.

**FindPrevious**   This method will find the closest previous record that satisfies the search criteria.

> **NOTE**   You cannot use the Find methods with table-type Recordset objects or with forward-scrolling snapshots.

The criteria used by the Find methods is similar to the Filter property and to the WHERE condition of an SQL statement without the WHERE keyword:

- "[EmployeeID] > 5"
- "[LastName] = 'Smith'"
- "[HireDate] = #1/1/96#"

- "[EmployeeID] > 5 And [LastName] <> 'Smith' And [HireDate] < #1/1/96#"

- "[HireDate] < Date()"

The following code shows how to sort data and specify search criteria for the Find methods:

```
Sub FindFirstEx()
    Dim dbMyDB As Database, rsMyRS As Recordset
    Dim strCriteria As String

    Set dbMyDB = CurrentDb
    ' Sort on EmployeeID since the following code
    ' will search on this field.
    Set rsMyRS = dbMyDB.OpenRecordset _
        ("SELECT * FROM Orders ORDER BY EmployeeID;")
    If rsMyRS.RecordCount <= 0 Then Exit Sub
    ' Specify criteria for the Find methods.
    strCriteria = "[EmployeeID] = 1"

    ' Find the first match.
    rsMyRS.FindFirst strCriteria
    Debug.Print rsMyRS("OrderID")

    ' Find the second match.
    rsMyRS.FindNext strCriteria
    Debug.Print rsMyRS("OrderID")

    ' Find the last match.
    rsMyRS.FindLast strCriteria
    Debug.Print rsMyRS("OrderID")

    ' Find the match before the last one.
    rsMyRS.FindPrevious strCriteria
    Debug.Print rsMyRS("OrderID")
    rsMyRS.Close
    dbMyDB.Close
End Sub
```

## Using variables and form references for criteria

In the previous example, you hard-coded the values for the criteria used by the Find methods to locate records within a Recordset object. To create flexible and custom search procedures, you should use variables or references to controls on a form as part of your criteria string. The following sections demonstrate how to concatenate different data types that are stored in variables or control references by using the ampersand (&) character as well as quotation marks and the pound sign (#).

**Concatenating numeric values**   When concatenating a numeric value stored in a variable, use the ampersand and double quotation marks in the following manner:

```
Dim intMyNumber As Integer, strCriteria As String
intMyNumber = 25
strCriteria = "[EmployeeID] = " & intMyNumber & " "
```

When concatenating a numeric value stored in a control on a form, use the ampersand and the double quotation marks as shown here:

```
Dim strCriteria As String
strCriteria = "[EmployeeID] = " & Forms![Employees]![EmpID] & " "
```

**Concatenating string (text) values**   When concatenating a string value stored in a variable, use the ampersand, single quotation marks, and double quotation marks in the following way:

```
Dim strMyString As Integer, strCriteria As String
strMyString = "Smith"
strCriteria = "[Last Name] = '" & strMyString & "' "
```

When concatenating a string value stored in a control on a form, use the ampersand, single quotation marks, and double quotation marks like this:

```
Dim strCriteria As String
strCriteria = "[Last Name] = '" & Forms![Employees]![LName] & "' "
```

**Concatenating string (text) values that contain apostrophes**   You will often need to work with string values that contain an apostrophe, such as names like "O'Donnell" or contractions like "can't." In the preceding example, the SELECT statement would fail if you passed a last name of "O'Donnell" because of the additional apostrophe in the SELECT statement.

The following code shows the preferred method for working with string values. This method works regardless of whether the string value contains an apostrophe.

```
Dim db As Database
Dim rs As Recordset
Set db = CurrentDb
Dim strName As String
Dim sql As String

strName = "O'Brien"
sql = "SELECT * FROM employees WHERE [LastName] = " & Chr(34) & _
    strName & Chr(34) & ";"
```

```
Set rs = db.OpenRecordset(sql)
rs.MoveLast
MsgBox rs.RecordCount
```

**Concatenating date/time values**   When concatenating a date or time value stored in a variable, use the ampersand, pound sign (#), and double quotation marks in the following manner:

```
Dim datMyDate As Date, strCriteria As String
datMyDate = #01/01/1995#
strCriteria = "[Birth Date] = #" & datMyDate & "# "
```

When concatenating a date value stored in a control on a form, use the ampersand, pound sign, and double quotation marks as shown here:

```
Dim strCriteria As String
strCriteria = "[Birth Date] = #" & Forms![Employees]![BDate] & "# "
```

**Building a simple criteria using the BuildCriteria method**   Using the BuildCriteria method, you can easily create a simple parsed criteria string that can be used with the Find methods. The method requires the following arguments:

- **field** This argument is the name of the field to be searched on. Only one field name can be used at a time.

- **fieldtype** This is the data type of the field. You can use the constants listed in the Type property topic in online Help.

- **expression** This is the value that you will use to search on the field. The expression can contain multiple values.

The following code shows how to implement these arguments of the Build-Criteria method:

```
Sub BuildExpression()
    ' Use an InputBox to retrieve user input
    ' for a custom search using the FindFirst
    ' and BuildCriteria methods.
    Dim dbMyDB As Database, rsMyRS As Recordset
    Dim strInput As String, strCriteria As String
    Dim strMsg As String

    Set dbMyDB = CurrentDb
    Set rsMyRS = dbMyDB.OpenRecordset _
        ("Employees", dbOpenDynaset)
```

*(continued)*

```
        strMsg = "Enter one or more letters of the Employee's " & _
            "last name, followed by an asterisk."

        ' Prompt user for input.
        strInput = InputBox(strMsg)
        ' Build a criteria string.
        strCriteria = BuildCriteria("LastName", dbText, strInput)
        ' Apply the criteria to the FindFirst method.
        rsMyRS.FindFirst strCriteria
        Debug.Print rsMyRS("FirstName") & " " & _
            rsMyRS("LastName")
        rsMyRS.Close
        dbMyDB.Close
End Sub
```

## Determining whether a record is located

If a Find method cannot locate a record, it will *not* generate an error. To determine whether one of the Find methods has located a record, use the NoMatch property:

**NoMatch**  This property returns True if the Find method did not locate the record specified by the criteria. It returns False if the Find method did locate the record specified by the criteria. If a record is located, that record will be in the current position in the recordset; if the record was not located, the record position will not change.

The following code shows how to use the NoMatch property:

```
Sub BuildExpression()
        ' Use an InputBox to retrieve user input
        ' for a custom search using the FindFirst
        ' and BuildCriteria methods.
        Dim dbMyDB As Database, rsMyRS As Recordset
        Dim strInput As String, strCriteria As String
        Dim strMsg As String

        Set dbMyDB = CurrentDb
        Set rsMyRS = dbMyDB.OpenRecordset _
            ("Employees", dbOpenDynaset)
        strMsg = "Enter one or more letters of the Employee's " & _
            "last name, followed by an asterisk."

        ' Prompt user for input.
        strInput = InputBox(strMsg)
        ' Build a criteria string.
        strCriteria = BuildCriteria("LastName", dbText, strInput)
        ' Apply the criteria to the FindFirst method.
        rsMyRS.FindFirst strCriteria
```

```
    ' Make sure a record was found.
    If Not (rsMyRS.NoMatch) Then
        Debug.Print rsMyRS("FirstName") & " " & _
            rsMyRS("LastName")
    Else
        Debug.Print "No matching records were found."
    End If
    rsMyRS.Close
    dbMyDB.Close
End Sub
```

In some applications, just finding the first or last record is not enough. You may want to search an entire recordset until every record that meets the criteria is found. To do this, you can use the BOF and EOF properties or the For...Next loop in conjunction with the RecordCount property. The NoMatch property is critical for exiting the loops once no more records are found. The following code shows how you can do this:

```
Sub FindAllRecords()
    Dim dbMyDB As Database, rsMyRS As Recordset
    Dim lngRecCount As Long, lngInitial As Long
    Dim strCriteria As String

    Set dbMyDB = CurrentDb
    Set rsMyRS = dbMyDB.OpenRecordset _
        ("SELECT * FROM Orders ORDER BY EmployeeID;")
    If rsMyRS.RecordCount <= 0 Then Exit Sub
    ' Specify criteria for the Find methods.
    strCriteria = "[EmployeeID]  > 5"

    ' Return an accurate record count.
    rsMyRS.MoveLast
    lngRecCount = rsMyRS.RecordCount
    ' Position the current record at the first record.
    rsMyRS.MoveFirst
    rsMyRS.FindFirst strCriteria
    Debug.Print rsMyRS("OrderID")
    ' Search from the beginning of the recordset.
    Do Until rsMyRS.EOF
        rsMyRS.FindNext strCriteria
        ' If a match cannot be found, exit the loop.
        If rsMyRS.NoMatch = True Then Exit Do
        Debug.Print rsMyRS("OrderID")
    Loop
    ' Position the current record at last record.
```

*(continued)*

```
    rsMyRS.MoveLast
    rsMyRS.FindLast strCriteria
    Debug.Print rsMyRS("OrderID")
    ' Search from the end of the recordset.
    For lngInitial = lngRecCount To 1 Step -1
        rsMyRS.FindPrevious strCriteria
        ' If a match cannot be found, exit the loop.
        If rsMyRS.NoMatch = True Then Exit For
        Debug.Print rsMyRS("OrderID")
    Next lngInitial
    ' Close the Recordset object.
    rsMyRS.Close
    ' Close the Database object.
    dbMyDB.Close
End Sub
```

## Finding records in a table-type recordset

You cannot use the Find methods to locate records for table-type Recordset objects. Instead, you use the Seek method in conjunction with the Index property. A big limitation of the Seek method is that even though there might be more than one record that satisfies search values, the Seek method will not cycle through those records. Once the Seek method finds a match, it stops its search. The Seek method is useful only for quickly finding an instance of a record based on an index. For complete search routines, create a dynaset- or snapshot-type recordset and use the Find methods.

As just mentioned, the Seek method and Index property can be used only with table-type Recordset objects. If an index is not present in the table, you cannot use the Seek method. The Seek method searches for a value based on the index named by the Index property. The Seek method has these arguments:

**comparison** When searching through the fields in the index, you can use one of the following comparison operators: equal to (=), greater than (>), greater than or equal to (>=), less than (<), or less than or equal to (=<).

> **NOTE** For the comparison operators =, >=, and >, Seek begins its search at the beginning of the index. If you use < or <=, Seek begins its search at the end of the index and works backward. (If the index allows duplicates, the Seek could start at any point among the duplicate index entries.)

**key1, key2, key3, ...** These are the actual values you want to search for, dependent on the number of fields in the index. If three fields make up an index, you must supply three values of the appropriate data type to search on those fields in the index. You must supply the key arguments in the order that the fields appear in the index. For example, if you have an index named "Full Name," with FirstName followed by LastName, you must pass in "Bob" as the first key and "Smith" as the second key, and not the other way around. If a primary key is defined for the table, the name of the index is "PrimaryKey." The following code illustrates how to use the Seek method and Comparison argument to find a record:

```
Sub SeekingRecords()
    Dim dbMyDB As DATABASE, rsMyRS As Recordset

    Set dbMyDB = CurrentDb
    Set rsMyRS = dbMyDB.OpenRecordset("Employees")
    ' Specify the Index Name to use for the search.
    rsMyRS.INDEX = "LastName"
    ' Specify the values to be used to search on the Full Name
    ' index that is composed of FirstName and LastName
    ' fields, in that order.
    rsMyRS.Seek "=", "Buchanan"
    If rsMyRS.NoMatch = False Then
        MsgBox "Record Found"
        Debug.Print rsMyRS(1)
    Else
        MsgBox "Record Not Found"
    End If
    rsMyRS.Close
    dbMyDB.Close
End Sub
```

**NOTE** The Seek method can be used only on local Microsoft Access tables. To use this method for linked Microsoft Access tables, use the OpenDatabase method and base a table-type Recordset object on that database variable. Then use the Seek method on the recordset.

## Adding, Editing, and Deleting Records

You store data in tables so that you can retrieve that data as information. Being able to move through a recordset and search for values based on specified criteria is a powerful functionality of the Recordset object. Data is not static, however; users continually need to add new data, delete unnecessary records, and update invalid data. To accomplish these tasks, use the following methods with dynaset- or table-type Recordset objects:

**AddNew**   This method allows the user to add a new record to an updatable recordset. It requires the Update method to save the addition.

**Edit**    This method allows the user to change an existing record in an updatable recordset. It requires the Update method to save the change to the record.

**Update and CancelUpdate**    The Update method saves the additions or changes to the recordset initiated by the AddNew and Edit methods. If the AddNew and Edit methods are not followed by the Update method, their additions or changes are not saved. The CancelUpdate method will undo any additions or changes initiated by the AddNew and Edit methods as long as the Update method has not been executed.

**Delete**    This method allows the user to delete an existing record in an updatable recordset. The Delete method does not require the Update method to remove records from the recordset. Once the Delete method is executed, the record cannot be recovered.

**NOTE**    You might be wondering why the Delete method does not require the Update method, whereas the AddNew and Edit methods do. Well, here's the reason: when you delete a record from a table or query in the user interface, it is automatically removed; but when you add or edit a record, your changes are not stored until you save (update) that record.

The following code shows how you can set up a recordset so your users can add to it, edit it, and delete from it. (The form Employees must be open to run this code.)

```
Sub AddingRecords()
    Dim dbMyDB As Database, rsMyRS As Recordset
    Dim intResponse As Integer

    Set dbMyDB = CurrentDb
    Set rsMyRS = dbMyDB.OpenRecordset("Table1", dbOpenDynaset)
    rsMyRS.MoveFirst
    ' Edit the first record.
    rsMyRS.Edit
        rsMyRS("FirstName") = "Mark"
        rsMyRS("Address") = "1003 Burnett Street"
    rsMyRS.UPDATE

    rsMyRS.MoveLast
    ' Delete the last record.
    rsMyRS.Delete

    ' Add a new record based on values from
    ' controls on an unbound form.
    rsMyRS.AddNew
```

```
        rsMyRS("FirstName") = Forms!Employees!FirstName
        rsMyRS("LastName") = Forms!Employees!LastName
        rsMyRS("Address") = Forms!Employees!Address
        rsMyRS("City") = Forms!Employees!City
    ' Prompt the user to save the record.
    intResponse = MsgBox("Save the record", vbYesNo)
    If intResponse = vbYes Then
        ' If the response is Yes, save the record.
        rsMyRS.UPDATE
    Else
        ' If the response is No, do not add the record.
        rsMyRS.CancelUpdate
    End If
    ' Close the Recordset object.
    rsMyRS.Close
    ' Close the Database object.
    dbMyDB.Close
End Sub
```

When adding, editing, or deleting records from a recordset, keep in mind the following considerations:

■  The recordset must be updatable. You can use the Updatable property of the Recordset object to determine whether changes can be made. If the Updatable property returns True, the recordset can be changed.

■  Validation rules are the limits or conditions on data entered into a field, and they must be considered when you are making changes to the fields in a recordset. Validation rules will be evaluated when you update the record. However, you can evaluate the validation rule of each field before you update the record by using the ValidateOnSet property, which forces that particular field's validation rule to be applied.

■  Relationships must also be considered when you are making changes to the fields in a recordset. For example, if you delete information from a primary table in a one-to-many relationship, an error will occur if the relationship does not have cascading deletions. (If the relationship does not have cascading deletions, you must delete the data from the many-side tables first.)

■  Multiuser considerations, which will be discussed later in this chapter, have special needs.

## More About Recordsets

The Recordset object is the most flexible and functional object in the DAO hierarchy. Without it, DAO programming would consist only of creating databases and implementing security. The versatile Recordset object also allows you to use bookmarks to retrieve and to display records, to create a recordset based on a parameter query, and to work with ActiveX object and Memo fields.

## Using bookmarks to retrieve records

In recordsets, bookmarks work in the same way as they do in forms: they are placeholders that allow you to explore your recordset and then return to specific records. As in forms, a recordset bookmark is a String variable, and you can have as many bookmarks as you want. Without a bookmark, you would have to store certain unique values of a recordset, such as a primary key, into variables and then use a Find method to return to that record. This method is not acceptable and can entail quite a complex routine.

The following properties apply to using bookmarks in a recordset:

**Bookmark**   A bookmark uniquely identifies the current record in the recordset. Setting a recordset's Bookmark property to a bookmark stored in a variable will return you to the record that the bookmark identifies.

**LastModified**   This bookmark is automatically generated when you update a record after invoking the AddNew or Edit method. It allows you to move to that particular record in the recordset. For example, when a record is added to a recordset, the current position of the cursor is not on the new record. Instead, it is on whichever record was current when the AddNew method was invoked. You can use the LastModified property to move to the new record.

| NOTE | When declaring variables for bookmarks, use the String data type. By default, bookmarks are stored as a Variant array of Byte data, and the Option Compare Database statement could result in incorrect evaluation of the bookmark. When you assign the bookmark to a String variable, you avoid this problem. |
|------|------|

The following code shows how to set bookmarks within a recordset:

```
Sub GotoBookMark()
    Dim dbMyDB As Database, rsMyRS As Recordset
    Dim strBM As String

    Set dbMyDB = CurrentDb
    Set rsMyRS = dbMyDB.OpenRecordset _
        ("Employees", dbOpenDynaset)

    ' Move the current record to the fifth record.
    rsMyRS.Move 5
    ' Display the FirstName field.
    MsgBox rsMyRS("FirstName")
    ' Set a bookmark for the fifth record.
```

```
    strBM = rsMyRS.Bookmark
    ' Add a new record.
    rsMyRS.AddNew
        rsMyRS("FirstName") = "Mary"
        rsMyRS("LastName") = "Kay"
    rsMyRS.UPDATE
    ' Move the current record to the new record.
    rsMyRS.Bookmark = rsMyRS.LastModified
    ' Display the FirstName field.
    MsgBox rsMyRS("FirstName")
    ' Return to the fifth record.
    rsMyRS.Bookmark = strBM
    ' Display the FirstName field.
    MsgBox rsMyRS("FirstName")
    ' Close the Recordset object.
    rsMyRS.Close
    ' Close the Database object.
    dbMyDB.Close
End Sub
```

Keep in mind the following notes about using bookmarks with your recordsets:

- Use a Recordset object's Bookmarkable property to determine if a recordset can use bookmarks. For example, a forward-scrolling snapshot does not support bookmarks and would therefore return a False value for the Bookmarkable property.

- If you set a bookmark and the record is deleted, you will receive the trappable error 3167—"Record is deleted"—if you try to set the recordset's Bookmark property to that bookmark variable.

- Bookmarks from one Recordset object cannot be used with another Recordset object unless the second Recordset object is created using the Clone method. The Clone method creates an identical but not independent recordset that refers to the recordset from which it was created.

### Using a recordset bookmark to display a record in a form

When you create a bound form, it has its own recordset and therefore its own bookmarks. As you saw in Chapter 8, you can use a form's Bookmark property to return to specified records in that form. By creating a recordset clone of that form's recordset, you can do custom search routines in the clone. If the search routine finds a match, you can then display the record found in the recordset clone in the form itself.

The code on the following page demonstrates how to clone a recordset and use a recordset bookmark to display a record in a form.

```
Private Sub Command01_Click()
    ' Place this code in the event procedure of a
    ' command button's Click event.
    Dim rsMyRS As Recordset

    ' Create a recordset clone of the form's recordset.
    Set rsMyRS = Me.RecordsetClone
    ' Perform a search on the Title field based on
    ' what the user types in the EnterLastName text box.
    rsMyRS.FindFirst "[LastName] = '" & Me!EnterLastName & "'"
    If rsMyRS.NoMatch = False Then
        MsgBox "Record Found"
        ' A match is found. To display the found record
        ' in the form, set the form's bookmark equal to
        ' the bookmark of the recordset clone.
        Me.Bookmark = rsMyRS.Bookmark
    Else
        MsgBox "Record Not Found"
    End If
End Sub
```

You can also use this routine with the other Find methods to enhance the user's search capabilities.

## Working with parameter queries

Opening a recordset based on a query is quite easy unless it is a parameter query. A parameter query is used to either prompt the user or pull values from a form control (typically an unbound text box) to dynamically apply criteria to a query. However, if you try to create a recordset based on a parameter query, you will receive error message 3061: "Too few parameters. Expected 1". To pass in the appropriate parameters to the query, you must reference the Parameter object in a QueryDefs Parameters collection and use the OpenRecordset method of the QueryDef object, as shown below. (The form MyParamForm must be open to run this code.)

```
Sub RSfromParamQuery()
    Dim dbMyDB As Database, qdMyQuery As QueryDef
    Dim rsMyRS As Recordset, strMySQL As String
    Dim lngParam1 As Long

    ' Create an SQL statement using a parameter
    ' "EnterEmployeeID".
    strMySQL = "PARAMETERS EnterEmployeeID Long;" & _
        "SELECT EmployeeID, LastName, FirstName" & _
        " FROM Employees" & _
        " WHERE EmployeeID=[EnterEmployeeID];"
```

```
      Set dbMyDB = CurrentDb
      Set qdMyQuery = dbMyDB.CreateQueryDef _
          ("My New Query", strMySQL)

      ' Set the parameter value to a field on a form using
      ' the parameter's name; or use the Parameters collection.
      qdMyQuery.Parameters("EnterEmployeeID") = _
          Forms!MyParamForm!txtEmployeeID
      Set rsMyRS = qdMyQuery.OpenRecordset()
      ' Process the recordset.
      ' ...
      ' ...
      ' ...
      ' Close the Recordset object.
      rsMyRS.Close
      ' Close the Database object.
      dbMyDB.Close
End Sub
```

You can also use the syntax below to set the parameter value to a variable using the parameter's index in the Parameters collection.

```
lngParam1 = 5
qdMyQuery.Parameters(0) = lngParam1
Set rsMyRS = qdMyQuery.OpenRecordset()
```

Or you could use the following syntax:

```
lngParam1 = 5
qdMyQuery.Parameters![EnterEmployeeID] = lngParam1
Set rsMyRS = qdMyQuery.OpenRecordset()"
```

> **NOTE** If a query has more than one parameter, you need to set all of the Parameter object's values before you can create a recordset.

## Working with ActiveX objects and Memo fields

Because an ActiveX object or a Memo field can store large amounts of data, you might want to refer to the data in separate pieces rather than as a whole. (ActiveX objects are stored in the OLE object field type in Design view of a table.) Storing a large ActiveX object or Memo field to a variable can use up a lot of memory. To break down those fields into small, efficient storage blocks, you can use the following methods of the Recordset object:

**FieldSize**  This method returns the number of bytes used to store an object in an ActiveX object field or text in a Memo field. You can use this method to determine the size and the number of pieces you want to break the field into.

**GetChunk**    This method returns all or a part of an ActiveX object or Memo field.

**AppendChunk**    This method appends all or part of an ActiveX object or Memo field's data to the appropriate field type in a recordset.

You can use these three methods in several combinations. The following example uses a variable to retrieve values from a text field in one table. The example then uses the AppendChunk method to append each of those values to one Memo field of a record in another table.

```
Sub AppendAChunk()
    Dim dbMyDB As Database, lngRecCount As Long
    Dim lngInitial As Long, strStoreLastName As String
    Dim rsMyRS1 As Recordset, rsMyRS2 As Recordset

    Set dbMyDB = CurrentDb
    Set rsMyRS1 = dbMyDB.OpenRecordset _
        ("Accumulation", dbOpenDynaset)
    Set rsMyRS2 = dbMyDB.OpenRecordset _
        ("Employees", dbOpenDynaset)

    rsMyRS2.MoveLast
    ' Return the record count of the Employees table.
    lngRecCount = rsMyRS2.RecordCount
    ' Move to the first record of the Employees table.
    rsMyRS2.MoveFirst

    ' Add a new record to the Accumulation table.
    rsMyRS1.AddNew
        ' Loop through the Employees table to retrieve the
        ' LastName values of all records in the table.
        For lngInitial = 1 To lngRecCount
            ' Store the last-name information from the
            ' Employees table.
            strStoreLastName = rsMyRS2("LastName")
            ' Append the last-name data into one Memo field
            ' in the Accumulation table.
            rsMyRS1("LastNameMemo"). _
                AppendChunk (strStoreLastName)
            rsMyRS2.MoveNext
        Next lngInitial
    ' Save the record once all last-name values
    ' have been appended.
```

```
        rsMyRS1.Update
        rsMyRS2.Close
        rsMyRS1.Close
        dbMyDB.Close
End Sub
```

# Multiuser Functionality and Transaction Processing

As you have seen in this chapter, working with recordsets is a straightforward process. At times, however, you must be aware of and trap for errors that can occur in a multiuser environment. In this section we will focus on issues that come up in multiuser environments. We'll also define transaction processing and explain how to use it.

## Multiuser Environments

Microsoft Access has built-in multiuser functionality. When creating a multiuser application, you can either use one database that contains all of your objects or split the database, placing just the tables in one database and the rest of the objects in another. You could call the two databases the Program database and the Data database. When several users open a single database over the network, they are pulling the entire database over the network because Microsoft Access is a file server application, not a client/server application like Microsoft SQL Server.

A file server application is an application that must process the data on a local client machine. A client/server application does all of the processing on the server machine and sends the results only to the local client machine. For example, let's say you have a server that is a dual Pentium with 128 MB of RAM, and your local client machine is a 486 with 16 MB of RAM. Because Microsoft Access is a file server application, when you run a query over the network, Microsoft Access must open the entire database over the network, and the processing will be done only on the local client machine. However, if you use Microsoft Access as a front end (Program database) to Microsoft SQL Server, all of the querying will be done on the much faster server machine, and only the results of the query will be sent over the network, instead of the entire database were the processing to be done locally on the client. Even if your application does not require the use of Microsoft SQL Server, you can still greatly improve performance with the two-database system. With the Program database locally on the client, when you query the Data database on the server, only the table information is pulled over the network, thus increasing your performance.

---

**The Add-In Database Splitter in Microsoft Access**

Microsoft Access has an Add-In database splitter that will split your database into a Program database and a Data database. The Add-In database splitter lets you place your database on the server of your choice and will automatically link your tables to the Program database. To use this great tool, in Database view choose Add-Ins from the Tools menu and then select Database Splitter and follow the instructions. Remember that by splitting your database, your tables are linked and cannot be opened as table-type Recordset objects unless you use the OpenDatabase method on the Data database as discussed earlier in this chapter.

---

As with any multiuser applications, you must consider locking issues. Microsoft Access handles all your multiuser locking problems. In fact, Microsoft Access comes with three levels of locking that help protect the integrity of your data: database-level, recordset-level, and page-level locking.

### Database-level locking

By default, Microsoft Access opens a database as *shared,* meaning that multiple users can open the database at the same time. When a database is opened as *exclusive,* however, only a single user can access the data; no other users can make changes. In a single-user application, this is not an issue or a problem. If you are developing a multiuser application, however, a database should be opened as exclusive only when performing bulk updates on data, to avoid locking out users.

You can open a database as exclusive through the user interface by using the Exclusive check box in the Open Database dialog box. You can also open a database as exclusive through code executed from another database. This second approach becomes important when using a two-database application and you want to open the Data database as exclusive for the reason mentioned above. The following code demonstrates how to open one database as exclusive from another database:

```
Dim dbMyDB As Database
Set dbMyDB = DBEngine.Workspaces(0).OpenDatabase _
    ("c:\data.mdb",exclusive:=True)
```

**NOTE**   When you use the OpenDatabase method, your database will be opened as shared unless you set the exclusive argument to True. If the database is already opened, Microsoft Access will return an error that you can trap and handle in an error routine.

### Recordset-level locking

When the user opens a database as shared, he or she might still want to prevent others from opening or editing a recordset while he or she is making changes. For example, say that a user is transferring money from accounts and does not want anyone making changes to that same set of data. You can lock an entire recordset through a form or through a recordset opened in code to guarantee that only a single user can work on the recordset at one time. To lock an entire recordset on a form, set the RecordLocks property of the Form to All Records. To lock a recordset through code, you can use the following options with the OpenRecordset method:

```
Dim dbMyDB As Database, rsMyRS As Recordset
Set dbMyDB = CurrentDB
Set rsMyRS = dbMyDB.OpenRecordset _
    ("Query1", dbOpenDynaset, dbDenyWrite)
```

If the recordset is already opened with recordset-level locking, Microsoft Access will return an error that you can trap and handle in an error routine.

### Page-level locking

Page-level locking is the most commonly used level of locking. In Microsoft Access, you cannot explicitly do record-level locking. Microsoft Jet stores your records in 2-KB page frames in memory. Depending on the size of the records, one 2-KB page frame could have one or several records. You cannot do record-level locking because records are stored as variable length. An application such as Microsoft Visual FoxPro can have record-level locking because its data is stored as fixed length. For example, in Microsoft Visual FoxPro you can create a Text field that can store 255 characters. If you type the word "Hello," 255 characters will still be stored in that field. In Microsoft Access, only 5 characters will be stored in the field even though you can add 250 more characters. Because the storage size can fluctuate, it is not possible to do record-level locking unless you were to stuff enough data into a record so that every record fills a 2-KB page frame. However, doing this is not efficient.

NOTE    If you want true record-level locking, you can store your data in FoxPro tables and link them to your Program database. That way, you will be working with data that is not stored as variable length.

When it comes to page-level locking in a multiuser environment, you can run into locking problems. For example, say that User A is editing a record. User B then edits the same record and saves his changes before User A. User A then attempts to save her version of the record. Which user's changes will be saved? Microsoft Access provides you with two different ways to handle page-level locking issues: optimistic locking and pessimistic locking. (You will find out much more about optimistic and pessimistic locking in Chapter 11.)

**Optimistic locking**   With optimistic locking, users can edit the same records within the same 2-KB page frame. If User A edits a record and User B edits the same record, the first person to save his or her changes wins. However, the last person to save changes to the record will be prompted by the Microsoft Access user interface with the dialog box shown in Figure 10-1.

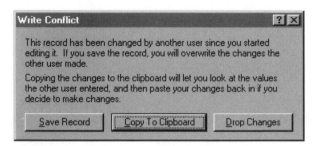

**Figure 10-1.**  *Optimistic-locking conflict dialog box.*

A user can choose to drop or accept the changes made by the other user or copy the changes to the clipboard to compare them to those the other user saved.

**Pessimistic locking**   With pessimistic locking, users cannot edit the same records within the same 2-KB page frame. If User A edits a record and User B tries to edit the same or even a different record in the same 2-KB page frame, only User A will be able to make changes. User B is locked out of the 2-KB page frame until User A saves her changes and therefore relinquishes her hold on the data. If User A never finishes saving the record, that is, remains in Edit mode, User B will never be able to edit that particular 2-KB page frame.

**Working with optimistic and pessimistic locking**   You can utilize optimistic and pessimistic locking through a form or through a recordset opened in code. To set optimistic locking for an entire recordset on a form, set the RecordLocks property of the form to No Locks, which is the default. To set pessimistic locking for an entire recordset on a form, set the RecordLocks property of the form to Edited Record.

To help control optimistic and pessimistic locking through the user interface, you can set the following options that will apply to your entire application:

■ **Number of Update Retries**  Microsoft Access will try more than once to save a user's changes to a recordset that is locked by another user.

The default is 2 retries, but between 0 and 10 are possible. You can set this option by choosing Options from the Tools menu and then selecting the Advanced tab. You can also set it through code:

```
Application.SetOption "Number of Update Retries", 7
```

■ **Update Retry Interval (milliseconds)** This property works in conjunction with the Number of Update Retries. This property specifies the amount of time between update retries. The default is 250 milliseconds but between 0 and 1000 can be selected. You can set this option by choosing Options from the Tools menu and then selecting the Advanced tab or through this code:

```
Application.SetOption "Update Retry Interval (msec)", 500
```

The frequency of updates to the same 2-KB page frames will determine how high you need to set the above properties. Try different settings until you find the combination that works best for your situation.

With optimistic locking, when you modify a record through code the 2-KB page frame is not locked until the Update method is used. With pessimistic locking, when you modify a record through code the 2-KB page frame is locked as soon as the Edit method is used. To utilize optimistic and pessimistic locking for a recordset through code, you can use the LockEdits property with your Recordset objects:

■ **LockEdits** This property allows you to determine whether your recordset will support optimistic or pessimistic locking. The default value is True, which is pessimistic locking. To set the recordset to use optimistic locking, set the value equal to False.

The following code shows how you can use the LockEdits method:

```
Dim dbMyDB As Database, rsMyRS As Recordset
Set dbMyDB = CurrentDb
Set rsMyRS = DB.OpenRecordset("Query1", dbOpenDynaset)
' Optimistic Locking
rsMyRS.LockEdits = False
rsMyRS.MoveFirst
rsMyRS.Edit
    rsMyRS("LastName") = "Smith"
rsMyRS.UPDATE
```

NOTE With ODBC data sources, all recordsets have a LockEdits property set to False because it is the server's responsibility to control the locking.

## Trapping Multiuser Errors

Common page-locking errors that can occur in a multiuser environment include errors 3167, 3186, 3197, and 3260.

### Locking error 3167

This error message reads "Record is deleted." This error occurs when a user is trying to update a record that has just been deleted by another user. You can write an error handling routine that could either requery the recordset using the Requery method or do an AddNew method (if you feel it is necessary to keep that data stored in the database). The following code is a generic sample of an error handling routine:

```
If Err.Number = 3167 Then
    ' The record has been deleted
    ' by another user.
    intMsgResponse = MsgBox _
        ("Record has been deleted by another user " _
        & "refresh records?", vbYesNo)
    ' If the user selects No, the recordset will
    ' not requery.
    If intMsgResponse = vbYes Then
        rsMyRS.Requery
        Exit Function
    Else
        ' Use the AddNew method to reestablish
        ' the record that was deleted by the
        ' other user.
    End If
End If
```

### Locking error 3186

This error message says "Couldn't save; currently locked by user 'Item2' on machine 'Item1'." If a 2-KB page is locked by another user, the user will have to wait and try again to update that record in the 2-KB page. The following error handling routine traps for error 3186:

```
' Trap for the number of times you want to
' try to update the record before giving up.
Select Case Err.Number
    Case 3186
        ' Wait some time before trying the
        ' update again.
```

```
        DoEvents
        For intCounter = 0 To 10
        Next intCounter
        DoEvents
        intNumberOfTries = intNumberOfTries + 1
        If intNumberOfTries > 3 Then
            ' At this point you can write code
            ' to exit the function or prompt the
            ' user to try again later.
        End If
        Resume
    Case Else
        ' Generic error handling
        MsgBox Err.Description
        ' Close the Recordset and the Database
        ' objects if no longer needed.
        rsMyRS.Close
        dbMyDB.Close
        Exit Function
End Select
```

## Locking error 3197

This error message reads "Data has changed; operation stopped." This error occurs with optimistic locking when a user has made a change to a record after another user began editing it but before that second user was able to execute the Update method. The user could still save his or her changes and overwrite the previous user's changes by executing the Update method again. The following error handling routine traps for this error:

```
Select Case Err.Number
    Case 3197
        DoEvents
        For intCounter = 0 To 10
        Next intCounter
        DoEvents
        ' The Resume statement will execute the
        ' Update method again to overwrite the
        ' other user's changes with yours.
        Resume
        ' If you do not want to overwrite the
        ' other user's changes, use the
        ' recordset.CancelUpdate method
        ' instead of the Resume statement
        ' and then do a Resume Next to bypass
        ' executing the Update method.
```

*(continued)*

```
        Case Else
            ' Generic error handling
            MsgBox Err.Description
            ' Close the Recordset and the Database
            ' objects if no longer needed.
            rsMyRS.Close
            dbMyDB.Close
            Exit Function
End Select
```

### Locking error 3260

This error message reads "Couldn't update; currently locked by user 'Item2' on machine 'Item1'." A user might receive this error when trying to update an optimistically locked recordset or to edit a pessimistically locked recordset when another user has that data page open or locked. You can modify one of the sample error handling routines above to handle this error.

### Page-level locking errors on bound forms

Page-level locking errors occur most often when you are using bound forms. The user accesses bound forms probably 90 percent of the time when using your application. You could create unbound forms and use code to manipulate the values and trap for locking issues, but that would defeat the purpose of using the quite efficient bound forms, which greatly reduce your development time. To trap for errors on a bound form, you will need to use the OnError form event. You'll learn how to create bound forms that handle pessimistic and optimistic locking in Chapter 11.

How you handle locking depends on many factors, such as business rules, the technical level of the user, and the degree to which you want to control how data is updated. The information you have learned so far in this section and in the preceding "Multiuser Environments" section will start you well on your way to creating a practical and successful multiuser database system.

## Transaction Processing

Transaction processing is used to quickly and efficiently make changes to data when bulk updates are required for a recordset. These changes can include any combination of the following:

- A series of updates, additions, or deletions made to a Recordset object using the Edit, AddNew, and Delete methods

- Several action queries performed at one time using the Execute method of either the Database object or the QueryDef object

- A series of changes made to Microsoft SQL Server using several SQL pass-through queries

Transactions are necessary when users need to make bulk changes in which all records have to be saved or no records are to be saved. If some updates fail, you might not want to commit any of the updates. For example, imagine that in a transfer of funds from one bank account to another your funds are deducted from but not deposited to the appropriate account. In this case, you would want to roll back the entire transaction.

Even if a complete set of updates is not required, transactions can increase the performance of your application. For example, if you use a For...Next loop to update a recordset, you are going to be writing to the hard drive just about every time the Update method is executed. With a large number of individual updates, this will cause a lot of disk access, which will slow down your application. With transactions, the updates will be processed as groups. For example, if you group updates by 50 records, all 50 records will be written to disk as 1 process, not as 50 separate processes.

All transactions are done in a workspace because a transaction can involve several Database objects and subsequent recordsets. To utilize transactions, use the following methods of the Workspace object:

**BeginTrans**   This method initiates a new transaction in a workspace.

**CommitTrans**   Once the bulk changes of the current transaction have been processed, this method saves all the changes at one time.

**Rollback**   This method ends the current transaction and restores the databases in the Workspace object to the state they were in when the current transaction began.

The following code illustrates how you can use these methods:

```
Sub Transactions()
    Dim dbMyDB As Database, wsMyWrkSpc As Workspace

    On Error GoTo err_Transactions
    Set wsMyWrkSpc = DBEngine.Workspaces(0)
    Set dbMyDB = CurrentDb
    ' Start the transaction.
    wsMyWrkSpc.BeginTrans
        ' Execute bulk action queries.
        With dbMyDB
            .Execute "DELETE * FROM TempTable;", dbFailOnError
            .Execute "INSERT INTO BackupTable SELECT * FROM " & _
                "Orders", dbFailOnError
```

*(continued)*

```
        End With
        ' If all updates execute successfully,
        ' commit the transaction.
    wsMyWrkSpc.CommitTrans
    Exit Sub
err_Transactions:
    ' If any errors occur while making the updates,
    ' all of the changes will be rolled back (not saved).
    Debug.Print Err.Number, Err.Description
    MsgBox "Start the transaction again, updating problems"
    wsMyWrkSpc.Rollback
    Exit Sub
End Sub
```

When working with transactions, keep in mind these important considerations:

- Transactions can be nested up to five levels within Microsoft Access for local and ISAM data sources. For Microsoft SQL Server, Microsoft Access will translate (send) only the outermost transaction to the server.

- You can undo a committed transaction only if it is a nested transaction for which an outer level can be rolled back.

- If you are performing one transaction and are going to do different transactions with different record sources, make sure to begin the new transaction in another Workspace object. If you do not create a new Workspace object for multiple transactions, the final outermost Rollback method invoked will affect the other transactions started in that Workspace. The following code will give you an idea of how to structure your code to do different transactions with different record sources:

```
Dim wsMyWrkSpc1 As Workspace, wsMyWrkSpc2 As Workspace

Set wsMyWrkSpc1 = DBEngine.Workspaces(0)
' Create a separate workspace for
' multiple transactions.
Set wsMyWrkSpc2 = DBEngine.CreateWorkspace _
    ("SecondWS", "Admin", "")
wsMyWrkSpc1.BeginTrans
    ' ...
    ' ...
    ' ...
    wsMyWrkSpc2.BeginTrans
        ' ...
        ' ...
        ' ...
```

```
    If ... Then wsMyWrkSpc2.Rollback
  wsMyWrkSpc2.CommitTrans
wsMyWrkSpc1.CommitTrans
```

■ With pessimistic locking, the page is locked for all recordsets in the transaction once the BeginTrans method is executed. The page is not released until a CommitTrans or Rollback method is executed. With optimistic locking, the page is both locked and then released for a recordset (recordset.LockEdits = False) when the CommitTrans method is executed.

# Structured Query Language

The queries that you create in Microsoft Access are graphical. This allows you to create both simple and complex queries easily. However, the design grid is really just a graphical interpreter and translator of SQL statements. In essence, Microsoft Access is a mini–SQL Server. It uses a Structured Query Language that is very similar—in most parts, identical—to that of Microsoft SQL Server.

Instead of going into the Design view of a query, you could type your own SQL statements in the SQL view that will automatically be translated into a graphical representation. However, doing so would defeat the purpose of having the graphical interface, which is a much more efficient method of generating the SQL statements needed for Microsoft Access to get to your data. The best part about programming with SQL statements is that you can generate them in the graphical Design view of a query and then switch to SQL view to copy and paste the statements into code.

## Anatomy of an SQL Statement

Even though the graphical Design view of your Query object easily and efficiently generates the SQL statements you need, it is important for you to understand how an SQL statement is constructed. In this section you will see what makes up an SQL statement for the typical SELECT statement, which can return a dynamic updatable recordset, as well as action queries and SQL-specific queries.

NOTE    Although the SQL statements discussed in this section might appear on multiple lines, they should be placed on one line or assigned to the same variable when used in code. No line continuation character can be used in the SQL language.

An SQL statement is constructed much like a sentence in the English language. In Microsoft Access, you type an SQL statement the way you would logically think to ask a question of your data. For example, say you want to select the

Last Name and First Name fields from your Employees table. This request in SQL is almost identical to the way in which you would verbalize the request:

```
SELECT [Last Name], [First Name] FROM Employees;
```

In this line, the SELECT keyword identifies the fields or expressions that you want to display in your resultant recordset when you execute the query in the user interface as well as in code. The FROM keyword identifies which table or tables the fields or expressions are coming from. If you have more than one field from more than one table or query identified in the FROM portion of the SQL statement, you must precede each field name with the name of the data source, as shown here:

```
SELECT Employees.[Last Name], Employees.[First Name],
     Orders.[Order Num]
   FROM Employees INNER JOIN Orders
       ON Employees.[EmployeeID] = Orders.[EmployeeID];
```

You use a semicolon (;) to let Microsoft Access know that an SQL statement is completed.

If you want to select all the fields from a table but you do not want to type all the names, you can use an asterisk (*) in the SELECT portion of your SQL statement:

```
SELECT * FROM Employees;
```

**NOTE**    Although SQL keywords, such as SELECT and FROM, are not case-sensitive in Microsoft Access, the readability of the statements will be improved if you leave the keywords uppercase. This is especially true as you develop larger and more complex SQL statements.

## Sorting records using the ORDER BY keyword

Sometimes you might want to view the recordset of a query in a certain order. For example, you might want to view the Employees table recordset in alphabetical order based on the employees' last names. For Microsoft Access, use the ORDER BY keyword for sorting, as shown here:

```
SELECT * FROM Employees ORDER BY LastName;
```

By default, the sort order is ascending; but you can specify the sort order to be descending:

```
SELECT * FROM Employees ORDER BY LastName DESC;
```

## Limiting your recordset using criteria

One of the main uses of queries is to return a specific set of records from an entire data source. To do this, you must restrict the recordset by applying criteria to certain fields in the query. In Microsoft Access, the WHERE clause will restrict the rows that a query returns. In the following example, the query will return only those records from the Employees table in which the employee ID is less than 5:

```
SELECT * FROM Employees WHERE EmployeeID < 5;
```

**NOTE**    You can use a combination of WHERE and HAVING keywords in your SQL statement. The WHERE keyword will limit the recordset before the grouping can occur, which can result in a faster return because a smaller set of the records is then grouped.

The following code shows how to use the WHERE and HAVING keywords:

```
SELECT CustomerID, Count(Orders.OrderID)
    FROM Orders
    WHERE CustomerID Like "c*"
    GROUP BY CustomerID
    HAVING Count(Orders.OrderID)>10;
```

## Evaluating groups of data

You will often want to group information and evaluate another field or fields based on that group. For example, you might want to count the number of orders each customer has made. Use the GROUP BY statement to break up the Orders table into groups of customers, and then use the aggregate function COUNT to count all the orders, as shown here:

```
SELECT CustomerID, Count(OrderID)
    FROM Orders
    GROUP BY CustomerID;
```

Microsoft Access supports the following aggregate functions:

- SUM (sum a field's values per group)
- AVG (average a field's values per group)
- COUNT (count a field per group)
- MAX, MIN (return the maximum and minimum values within a group)
- FIRST, LAST (return the first and last values within a group)
- STDDEV, VAR (return the standard deviation or variance within a group)

### Setting criteria for groupings

Sometimes you might want to limit the values that can be grouped upon and/ or limit the values returned by an SQL aggregate function. For example, you might want to count the number of orders for a group of companies that begin with the letter *C*. You might also want to see only those companies beginning with the letter *C* having a count of orders greater than 10. To set criteria for groups and their aggregates, use the HAVING keyword as follows:

```
SELECT CustomerID, Count(OrderID) AS [OrderCount]
    FROM Orders
    GROUP BY CustomerID
    HAVING CustomerID Like "c*" AND Count(Orders.OrderID)>10;
```

### Using an alias for a field

An alias allows you to assign a more meaningful name to a query output column. In the code above, the name OrderCount is assigned to the column that does the calculations (counting). Let's look at another example:

```
SELECT LastName AS [Employees Last Name] FROM Employees;
```

### Using joins to relate records

In Microsoft Access you can create equi-joins, which return values only between recordsets that contain a match or outer joins to returned matched records as well as unmatched records from one of the recordsets involved. The following example creates an equal join between the two tables using the INNER JOIN keyword:

```
SELECT DISTINCTROW Employees.[LastName], Orders.[ORDER ID]
    FROM Employees INNER JOIN Orders
        ON Employees.[EMPLOYEE ID] = Orders.[EMPLOYEE ID];
```

Outer joins can be created using the LEFT OUTER JOIN or RIGHT OUTER JOIN keyword.

As your queries become more complex, use the graphical interface to generate and test your SQL statements. Remember, you can just copy and paste an SQL statement from the SQL view of a query and use that statement in your code.

### Using action queries

Action queries are also just SQL statements that are generated and translated through the graphical interface of query Design view. The following are examples of SQL statements generated for action queries.

■ Delete action query

```
DELETE * FROM Employees;
```

- Update action query

```
UPDATE Employees SET City = "Oviedo"
    WHERE PostalCode="32765";
```

- Append action query

```
INSERT INTO Customers ( PostalCode, Country )
    SELECT EmpPostalCode, EmpCountry
    FROM Employees;
```

- Make-table action query

```
SELECT Employees.* INTO [New Employees Table]
    FROM Employees;
```

## Using SQL-specific queries

In Microsoft Access, not all SQL statements can be displayed graphically. The only way to use the queries that cannot be displayed graphically is to explicitly write the SQL statements. Microsoft Access has three types of SQL-specific queries: Data Definition Language (DDL), union, and SQL pass-through.

**Data Definition Language (DDL)**   This kind of query allows you to create only native Microsoft Access tables and indexes. You can create fields and assign them data types and sizes only when creating a table, which means that you cannot assign validation rules, formats, captions, and so on. It is better to create your tables using the user interface or DAO, which gives you the ability to create tables with their complete functionality.

One use for DDL queries is to create a unique index for a linked ODBC table that does not have one. If you link to an ODBC Microsoft SQL Server table that does not have a unique index, the table is read-only. Through DDL, you can create a unique index that is stored in Microsoft Access that allows you to edit that table. This unique index does not affect the ODBC table in which it is stored.

Here is an example of a DDL query:

```
CREATE UNIQUE INDEX MYUniqueIndex
    ON dbo_customers (CustomerID);
```

**Union query**   With a union query, you can create a query that combines fields from two or more tables. Sometimes you might want to view records from two tables that store the same information but some of the records are different and some of the records are the same. For example, say you import a Microsoft Excel worksheet as a table that has employee information. You also import a FoxPro table that has employee information. The problem is that each table contains duplicate records as well as different records. A union query will allow you to view those tables as one recordset in which you will see the values that are different in the two tables as well as only one instance of duplicate values. The following SQL statement creates a union query based on TableA and TableB in Microsoft Access:

```
SELECT [Employee ID], [Last Name] FROM TableA
    UNION
    SELECT [Employee ID],[Name] FROM TableB;
```

The union query uses two or more SELECT statements separated by the keyword UNION. When creating a union query, you can just copy and paste the SQL statements from the individual queries and separate them by a union keyword. Notice that a semicolon (;) is at the end of only the last SQL statement, to notify Microsoft Access that the union query is complete.

Keep in mind the following facts about SELECT statements in a union query:

■ The columns (fields) in SELECT statements must be in sequential order.

■ The SELECT statements must all have the same number of columns (fields). If you need to create an extra column, use "Null As Expr1" as a substitute column.

■ Any aliasing must be done in the first SELECT statement.

■ The ORDER BY statement must appear in the last SELECT statement.

**SQL pass-through**   An SQL pass-through query allows you to write SQL statements in Microsoft SQL Server's native SQL language and pass them back to the server to be executed on that server. For example, you cannot grant user permissions on an ODBC SQL Server table using Microsoft Access code, but you can type in the SQL statement that Microsoft SQL Server uses to grant permissions and then execute that statement by running the SQL pass-through query. Like a linked ODBC SQL Server table, your SQL pass-through tables must have a Connect string that can be established by using the builder in the "ODBC Connect Str" property of the SQL pass-through query.

## Nested queries

You can use one query's result as the criteria for a field in another query. The advantage of this is that without this method, if the initial query's result changes over time, you would have to change the other query's criteria (WHERE condition) to ensure that it uses accurate data. This kind of SQL statement is known as a subselect statement. For example, you can have one query return the average age of all persons within a certain demographic region. You could then use that SQL statement as the criteria for a sales table in which you show the sales for people whose age is greater than or equal to the demographic region's value. To accomplish this, you can create the query that returns the average age value and then copy and paste the SQL statement into the criteria section of the other query.

The following SQL statement returns the average age:

```
SELECT Avg(Age) AS AvgAge
    FROM DemoGraphicsTable;
```

The following is the SQL statement of the sales table with the average age value hard-coded into the WHERE condition:

```
SELECT Age, UnitSales
    FROM Sales
    WHERE Age>=25;
```

Now we will use the first SQL statement as a subselect statement to be used in the WHERE condition of this query to allow for dynamic and accurate results whenever this query is executed:

```
SELECT Age, UnitSales
    FROM Sales
    WHERE Age>= (SELECT Avg(Age) AS AvgAge
    FROM DemoGraphicsTable);
```

**NOTE**   The subselect statement does not require a semicolon at the end of it because the overall SQL statement provides this closure.

The above scenario will work only as long as the subselect statement returns only one value. However, you might want to use a subselect statement that will return more than one value to be applied as criteria. To do this, you must use the IN keyword:

```
SELECT Age, UnitSales
    FROM Sales
    WHERE Age IN
    (SELECT Age FROM DemoGraphicsTable
            GROUP BY Age
            HAVING Age = Between 15 And 30);
```

If you want to return values other than what the subselect statement returns, use the NOT operator in front of the IN statement:

```
SELECT Age, UnitSales
    FROM Sales
    WHERE Age NOT IN
    (SELECT Age FROM DemoGraphicsTable
            GROUP BY Age
            HAVING Age = Between 15 And 30);
```

NOTE The subselect statement is executed only once in the criteria section of the query before the regular SELECT statement is executed, which makes for an efficient use of subselect statements because they are executed only once, not for every record.

# DAO and ODBCDirect Recordsets

ODBCDirect recordsets have many similarities to their Jet counterparts. Recordsets are the actual view of the data. They can be created from either a Connection object or a QueryDef object using the OpenRecordset method. You can create four types of Recordset objects for ODBCDirect workspaces: dynaset, snapshot, forward-only, and dynamic.

## Dynaset Recordsets

A dynaset-type recordset can have updatable records. These recordsets are dynamic in that they reflect modifications other users have made to existing records but do not reflect additions or deletions. If a record that has been deleted by another user is accessed, a trappable error occurs. Dynaset recordsets can consist of one or more tables and are updatable. This kind of recordset is most similar to an ODBC keyset cursor.

## Snapshot Recordsets

A snapshot-type recordset is a static copy of a set of records from which you can search or display information. A snapshot recordset cannot be updated nor does it reflect changes to data made by other users. This type of recordset corresponds to an ODBC static cursor and is useful if your users will be searching for data or if they require read-only functionality.

## Forward-Only Recordsets

In a forward-only-type recordset, individual rows in the recordset can be accessed and updated, but the current record pointer can be moved only toward the end of the recordset. If you need to look at the data only once, this type of recordset will provide the best performance. This type of recordset corresponds to an ODBC forward-only cursor.

## Dynamic Recordsets

A dynamic-type recordset reflects modifications to existing records that other users have made. You can use a dynamic recordset to add, change, or delete rows from an underlying table or tables. Membership in a dynamic recordset is not fixed, meaning that the Recordset object will be updated appropriately when other users add and delete records. Because the membership is not fixed, this type of recordset carries the most overhead; it constantly retrieves the latest information from the database. This type of recordset corresponds to an ODBC dynamic cursor.

## Creating ODBCDirect Recordsets

You can create a recordset by using the OpenRecordset method of a Connection object or a QueryDef object. When defining your recordset, remember to include only the records you will need and define the recordset to use only the functionality you require. For example, if the user wants only names that start with *W,* include only the records in which the name begins with *W.* If the user is simply looking up the information, provide a snapshot or forward-only recordset. If the SELECT statement might be used more than once in the application, consider creating a QueryDef object—a recordset created from a QueryDef object will be faster than a SELECT statement by itself because QueryDefs can be compiled on the server, giving you the best performance possible. The following code shows how to create a recordset that retrieves only authors whose last name starts with *W:*

```
Sub ODBCtoSQL()
    Dim ws As Workspace, rs As Recordset
    Dim conPubs As Connection

    DBEngine.DefaultType = dbUseODBC
    Set ws = DBEngine.CreateWorkspace("wrkODBC", "admin", "")
    Set conPubs = ws.OpenConnection("Pubs", _
        dbDriverNoPrompt, False, _
        "ODBC;DATABASE=pubs;UID=sa;PWD=;DSN=MyServer")
    Set rs = conPubs.OpenRecordset _
        ("SELECT * FROM authors WHERE au_lname LIKE 'W*'")
    Debug.Print rs(0), rs(1), rs(2)
    rs.Close
    conPubs.Close
    ws.Close
End Sub
```

The contents of the first three fields in the above recordset are displayed in the Debug window. Remember that the syntax you use for your QueryDef and Recordset objects is specific to the back-end database you are using, so be sure to consult the appropriate documentation if you are unsure about the syntax.

ODBCDirect workspaces provide an easy means of retrieving and manipulating data using ODBC, while still allowing you to use the DAO hierarchy and virtually the same syntax as if the objects were native Jet databases. Be aware that the functionality you have in ODBCDirect workspaces is based on the ODBC driver that you are using; so something that works for an SQL Server back end might not work exactly the same way for another type of server.

## PREVIEW of the next chapter

Now that you are familiar with accessing and manipulating your data using DAO, in the next chapter you will create a sample application that uses DAO in a multiuser environment. The application in Chapter 11 will take you deeper into pessimistic and optimistic page-level record locking.

# 11

# Creating Multiuser Solutions

In previous chapters you learned how to create and use Recordset objects to manipulate your data. You also discovered that multiuser functionality is built into Microsoft Access and therefore into your application. When developing in a multiuser environment, you must consider and anticipate locking conflicts when several users update the same data at the same time. In this chapter you'll get to do just that. Because working with bound forms is the most common and efficient means of adding, editing, and deleting data, you will create two multiuser solutions in this chapter. One solution will implement pessimistic page-level record locking, and the other will implement optimistic page-level record locking.

## Page-Level Record Locking

In this chapter you will use one table and two forms based on that table. The only difference between the two forms will be that one implements pessimistic locking and the other implements optimistic locking. To implement pessimistic locking, you must force the user to save his or her record and thus the changes so that other users may make their necessary changes to the same set of records in that particular 2-KB page frame. To implement optimistic locking, you must give the user the ability to accept or discard his or her changes made to the same record that a second user has changed while the first user is editing it.

Here is a simple analogy to help you understand how Microsoft Access uses 2-KB page frames. Think of all the records in your database as sentences in a book. With both books and databases, you need some method of separating the information into manageable pieces. Books group sentences into pages, and Microsoft Access groups records into 2-KB pieces of memory, which are called page frames.

## Pessimistic Locking

As we just mentioned, the user may want to prevent anyone from editing a record until he or she has finished updating it. You can easily arrange this for the user by setting the RecordLocks property of the form to Edited Records. However, one problem can occur that can stop *anyone* from editing the records in that 2-KB page frame. If a user edits a record in the form but does not save it, no one can make changes to the records in that 2-KB page frame. Imagine how the other users would feel if that user then went on a two-week vacation, forgetting to save the record! Even if the user base is small, no one wants to prowl from office to office trying to figure out who is responsible for locking up a set of records by not having saved an edited record.

You can prevent users from accidentally locking other users out of a form's underlying recordset by not saving their changes for extended periods of time. Using the Timer event of the form, you can force the form to save the current record automatically after a specified time interval. The form will automatically save whatever edits the user has made and free that 2-KB page for other users. To set up such an arrangement, take the following steps:

NOTE The completed application is saved as CHAP11.MDB in the CHAP11 subfolder of the folder in which you installed the companion CD files. You can open the completed application or build it with the following instructions.

1. Create a new database called LOCKING.MDB.

2. Import the Employees table from NORTHWIND.MDB. (This sample database is installed with Microsoft Access in the C:\Program Files\ Microsoft Office\Office\Samples subfolder.)

3. Create a new blank form that is bound to the Employees table in the new database.

4. Set the following form properties:

| Property Name | Value |
|---|---|
| Record Source | Employees |
| Caption | Pessimistic Locking |
| Record Locks | Edited Record<br>This sets the form to pessimistic locking. |
| Dividing Lines | No |
| Auto Center | Yes |
| Timer Interval | 900000<br>The Timer Interval represents the interval in which the Timer event gets executed. When set to 0, the Timer event will *not* execute. The property is in milliseconds, with possible values between 0 and 2,147,483,647. 900,000 milliseconds equals 15 minutes. |

**5.** In Design view of the form, add the fields EmployeeID, LastName, First-Name, and Title from the form's record source (Employees table), as shown in Figure 11-1.

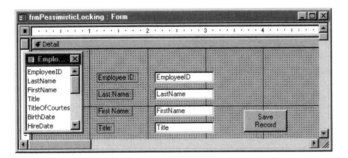

**Figure 11-1.** *Design view of the pessimistic locking form.*

**6.** Add a Command button as shown in Figure 11-1.

**7.** Set the following Command button properties:

| Property Name | Value |
|---|---|
| Name | cmdSave |
| Caption | Save Record<br>You can change the appearance of the caption by placing the cursor on the space between Save and Record and entering Ctrl-Enter. You may need to adjust the height of the button to display both words. |

**8.** Save the form as "frmPessimisticLocking".

In the Declarations section of the form, type in the following code:

```
Dim blnFlag As Boolean
```

In the OnLoad event of the form, type in the following code:

```
Private Sub Form_Load()
    ' Initialize the blnFlag variable to False.
    ' Use this to indicate whether the Record has
    ' been in edit mode for more than 15 minutes.

    blnFlag = False

End Sub
```

In the cmdSave event of the form, add the following code:

```
Private Sub cmdSave_Click()
    On Error GoTo Err_cmdSave_Click
    DoCmd.DoMenuItem acFormBar, acRecordsMenu, _
        acSaveRecord, , acMenuVer70
    Exit Sub

Err_cmdSave_Click:
    MsgBox Err.Description
    Exit Sub
End Sub
```

In the On Timer event of the form, add the following code:

```
Private Sub Form_Timer()
    ' When the Timer Interval reaches
    ' 900000 milliseconds (15 minutes),
    ' use the Dirty property to check
    ' whether the record is being edited.
    ' If the record is dirty, save it by
    ' setting the Dirty property to False.

    ' Check whether the record is being edited by
    ' checking the value of the form's Dirty property.
    If Me.Dirty = True Then
        ' If blnFlag = False, then the record has been
        ' in edit mode for less than 15 minutes.
        If blnFlag = False Then
            blnFlag = True
        Else
```

```
        ' If blnFlag = True, then the record has been in
        ' edit mode for at least 15 minutes; therefore,
        ' force the record to be saved and reset the
        ' blnFlag variable.
        blnFlag = False
        Me.Dirty = False
      End If
    End If
End Sub
```

By using just the Timer Interval property and the Timer Event, you can resolve the problem with pessimistic locking by saving the record for the user through code after a predetermined time. In the code above, you will force the record to be saved within 15 to 30 minutes after being edited. You can increase or decrease this time frame by changing the Timer Interval property of the form. To test this form, follow these steps:

1. Open two instances of Microsoft Access on your machine to simulate a multiuser environment.

2. Open your database (LOCKING.MDB or CHAP11.MDB) in both instances.

3. Open the frmPessimisticLocking form in both instances.

4. Begin editing the first record of the form in instance 1, but do not save the record.

5. Now try editing the first record of the form in instance 2. Your Record Selector will display a locking symbol, indicating that you cannot edit this record. (See Figure 11-2.)

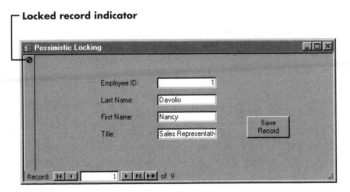

**Figure 11-2.** *Pessimistically locked record indicator.*

You will not be able to edit the first record in instance 2 because that particular 2-KB page frame is already locked by instance 1. But the Timer Event will save the record in instance 1 within 15 to 30 minutes. Once the record has been saved, you will be able to add, edit, and delete records in the 2-KB page frame in instance 2.

## Optimistic Locking

In most cases, you will want to use optimistic locking with bound forms. With optimistic locking, in a multiuser environment you are able to edit other records in the same 2-KB page frame that one user may be in the middle of changing. With pessimistic locking, the 2-KB page frame is locked as soon as one of the users starts to edit one of the records. With optimistic locking, the 2-KB page frame is locked only when the user saves the record. Optimistic locking is ideal in a multiuser situation in which your users are making many updates to common records. Optimistic locking has one drawback, however: more than one user may be editing the same record; the first person to save the record wins. The other user or users by default get prompted from Microsoft Access to either save their changes, copy them to the clipboard, or drop them, as shown in Figure 11-3.

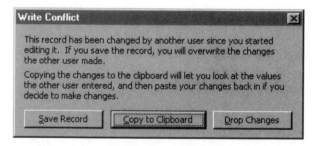

**Figure 11-3.** *Microsoft Access default Write Conflict dialog box.*

As a solution developer, you might not want the users to see the Microsoft Access solution to the problem. You might instead decide to create your own custom routine that automatically saves or drops a user's changes, or maybe even prompts the user to compare the differences and save a combination of both users' changes.

The generic code on pages 409–412 can be used with any form. If two users edit the same record, the last user to update will be prompted either to discard the changes or evaluate the differences. The code will automatically change to red the font color of those fields in which changes have taken place. The user will then be prompted one field at a time either to save her version of the field's data or to keep the data that the other user saved. Either open CHAP11.MDB or do the following:

1. While in the LOCKING.MDB Database window, select frmPessimistic-Locking. Next, select Copy from the Edit menu, select Paste from the Edit menu, and name the new form frmOptimisticLocking.

2. Open frmOptimisticLocking in Design view, and set the following form properties:

| Property Name | Value |
|---|---|
| Record Source | Employees |
| Caption | Optimistic Locking |
| Record Locks | No Locks<br>This sets the form to optimistic locking. |
| Dividing Lines | No |
| Auto Center | Yes |
| Timer Interval | 0 |

3. View the form module, and delete the sub procedures Form_Load and Form_Timer.

4. Save the form.

When a user tries to save her record after another user has already saved his changes to the same record, a locking error will result for the first user. In the form's On Error event, add the following code to trap for any multiuser locking errors:

```
Private Sub Form_Error(DataErr As Integer, Response As Integer)
    Dim MsgResponse As Integer

    ' Trap for Locking errors on the form.
    If (DataErr >= 3187 And DataErr <= 3262) _
        Or DataErr = 3167 Or DataErr = 7787 Then
        ' Suppress the Microsoft Access user interface
        ' message box by letting Response = 0.
        Response = 0
        If DataErr = 3167 Then
            ' The record has been deleted
            ' by another user.
            ' Undo the Save Record action.
            DoCmd.DoMenuItem 0, 1, 0, 0, acMenuVer70
            MsgResponse = MsgBox("Record has been deleted" & _
                " by another user, refresh records?", vbYesNo)
            ' If the user selects No, the form will not
            ' requery and the user will see #Deleted in the
            ' controls of the deleted record.
```

*(continued)*

```
                    If MsgResponse = vbYes Then
                        Me.Requery
                    End If
                    Exit Sub
                End If
                ' Call Locking Routine to drop your changes
                ' and accept the other user's, or compare the other
                ' user's changes and select the values to keep.
                Call HandleLocks(255, 0)
            End If
        End Sub
```

Once the On Error event of the form traps the multiuser locking error, you need to provide a way for the user to compare her values to the other user's changes that were saved. The following code, typed into the Declarations section of the form, will give the user the ability to discard her changes and accept the other user's changes or to compare them and keep only the desired field entries.

```
        ' This routine will be called if there is
        ' a multiuser locking problem on a record.
        ' ChangeColor is the font color to be used to
        ' show the changed fields, and OriginalColor is
        ' the font color before the change.

Sub HandleLocks(ChangeColor As Long, OriginalColor As Long)
    Dim ctl As Control
    Dim MsgResponse As Integer, Msg As String
    Dim ChangedFields As New Collection, CF As Control, _
        CollectCount As Integer
    Dim RS As Recordset
    Dim RSC As Recordset

    ' Open the form's RecordsetClone.
    Set RSC = Me.RecordsetClone

    ' Move the form's RecordsetClone to the current record.
    ' This also refreshes the underlying data to show
    ' stored changes made by another user.
    RSC.Bookmark = Me.Bookmark

    ' Loop through the form controls to compare changes
    ' to bound fields.
    For Each ctl In Me.Controls
        ' Look only at text fields; but you can include
        ' other control types that are bound in your routine.
        If ctl.ControlType = acTextBox Then
            ' If the form values and the RecordsetClone values
            ' do not match, change the font of the text box
```

```
            ' to the ChangeColor variable.
            ' Also set the control's Tag property to the value
            ' in the RecordsetClone.
            If ctl <> RSC((ctl.ControlSource)) Then
                ctl.ForeColor = ChangeColor
                ctl.Tag = RSC((ctl.ControlSource))
                ' Add changed controls to the ChangedFields
                ' collection to loop through later in the code.
                ChangedFields.Add ctl
            End If
        End If
Next

MsgResponse = MsgBox("Someone has just changed this record." & _
    " You can choose YES to drop the changes you just made." & _
    " If you choose NO, you can compare values." & Chr(13) & _
    Chr(13) & "Drop your changes?", vbYesNo)

If MsgResponse = vbYes Then
    ' Your changes will be dropped.
    ' Loop through the ChangedFields collection.
    For Each CF In ChangedFields
        ' Make the control's value equal to its
        ' Tag property.
        CF = CF.Tag
        ' Change font color back to original.
        CF.ForeColor = OriginalColor
        ' Clear the control's Tag property.
        CF.Tag = ""
    Next

    ' Clear the ChangedFields collection.
    For CollectCount = ChangedFields.Count To 1 Step -1
        ChangedFields.Remove CollectCount
    Next CollectCount
    ' Exit this procedure; the other user's values
    ' have been saved.
    Exit Sub
End If

' You decided to compare your changes with those of
' the other user.
For Each CF In ChangedFields
    Msg = "Change value of the " & CF.Name & " field to" & _
        Chr(13) & CF.Tag
    MsgResponse = MsgBox(Msg, vbYesNo)
```

*(continued)*

```
            If MsgResponse = vbYes Then
                ' You chose to discard your data for that field.
                ' Make the control's value equal to its
                ' Tag property.
                CF = CF.Tag
                ' Change font color back to original.
                CF.ForeColor = OriginalColor
                ' Clear the control's Tag property.
                CF.Tag = ""
            Else
                ' You chose to keep your data for that field.
                ' Open another recordset based on the form and
                ' move to that record.

                ' Because the underlying record source has already
                ' been changed by another user, you must open
                ' a new recordset and apply the values that
                ' you stored in the ChangedFields collection.

                ' This allows you to write back your values
                ' without causing locking errors on the form.

                ' In fact you are reediting the record and
                ' masking that fact through this code.
                Set RS = CurrentDb.OpenRecordset((Me.RecordSource), _
                    dbOpenDynaset)
                RS.MoveLast
                RS.MoveFirst
                ' Set the new recordset position equal to the
                ' record on the form. If the form has a filter
                ' applied, you must also filter the new recordset.
                RS.AbsolutePosition = Me.CurrentRecord -1
                RS.Edit
                RS((CF.ControlSource)) = CF.Value
                RS.Update
                ' Change font color back to original.
                CF.ForeColor = OriginalColor
                ' Clear the control's Tag property.
                CF.Tag = ""
            End If
        Next

        ' Clear the ChangedFields collection.
        For CollectCount = ChangedFields.Count To 1 Step -1
            ChangedFields.Remove CollectCount
        Next CollectCount

    End Sub
```

By using just the On Error event to trap multiuser locking errors and a custom routine to give the user the ability to compare differences in those records, you create a solution using optimistic locking. To test this form, follow these steps:

1. Open two instances of Microsoft Access on your machine to simulate a multiuser environment.

2. Open your database (LOCKING.MDB or CHAP11.MDB) in both instances.

3. Open the frmOptimisticLocking form in both instances.

4. Begin editing the first record of the form in instance 1, but do not save the record.

5. Edit the same record of the same form in instance 2.

6. Save the edited record in the form in instance 2 by clicking the Save Record Command button.

7. Save the edited record in the form in instance 1. You will see the message box shown here:

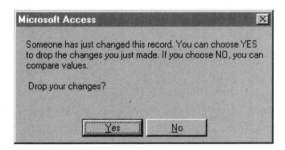

8. If you select Yes, you will lose your changes and the procedure will end. Select No to compare your changes to the changes in other instances. Once you select No, the font color of those fields that are different than your version of the record will become red. You will then be given the opportunity to keep your individual changes or drop them, as shown here:

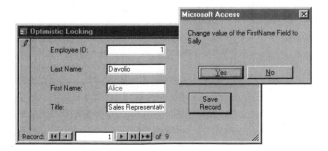

When you are to the point at which you can make a comparison, the record has already been saved to the table by the other user. However, since your changes have not yet been committed and therefore the record has not yet been saved, your form will still display your edits. If you choose your edits over those saved by the other user, the HandleLocks sub procedure writes back to the table via the Recordset object that you create.

In the HandleLocks sub procedure, you can modify the code to handle the locks differently based on your needs and on the amount of trust you have in the user's ability to make decisions.

> **NOTE**    Variations of the optimistic locking solution can also be applied to unbound forms and to recordsets that you create in code. By using unbound forms and subsequently handling the recordsets entirely through code, you give yourself more control over your application's execution. Of course, this results in a lot more coding on your part.

## PREVIEW of the next chapter

In Chapter 12 you will learn how to protect your Microsoft Access database applications using the built-in security features of Access. These features include password security, which is simple password protection; user-level security, which is based on user and group permissions; and MDE files, which you can create if you want to protect your code from being viewed or edited. In addition, you will learn how to apply and manipulate your application's security with VBA code through DAO.

# 12

# Implementing Security

Creating a robust application takes time and hard work, so when you distribute your application, you might not want others to look at and copy your code or modify objects in your database. You can prevent such actions by implementing security on the database. In this chapter, we will examine the two types of security schemes available in Microsoft Access 97: password security and user-level security. Then we will see how to implement and maintain security by using Microsoft Visual Basic for Applications (VBA). We will also discuss converting your application to an .MDE file, which prevents anyone from editing or viewing module code.

> **TIP** Before implementing password or user-level security, always make a backup copy of your database and of your default workgroup information file (SYSTEM.MDW) and put them in a physically secure location.

## Password Security

A user who doesn't need to implement security based on Microsoft Jet's in-depth security model still might want to keep others out of a database. Jet 3.5 introduces the ability to set a password on a database so that only those who know the password can open the database. Setting a password on a database leaves user-level security intact—that is, even if someone knows the password of a database, he or she still must have user-level permissions to perform actions on the database and its objects. (See the "User-Level Security" section beginning on page 417.) If the user forgets the password, there is no way of changing it or of opening the database.

To set or remove a password on a database, you must have the database opened exclusively and you must either be the owner of the database, be a member of the Admins group, or have Administer permission on the database.

## Creating and Working with a Database Password

To add a password to a database, choose Security from the Tools menu and select Set Database Password. Set the password using the dialog box, as shown in Figure 12-1.

**Figure 12-1.** *Setting a database password.*

### Removing the password from a database

To remove the password from a database, choose Security from the Tools menu and then select UnSet Database Password. Once you have done this, password security is removed.

### Adding, removing, or changing a database password programmatically

To add, remove, or change a database password programmatically, call the NewPassword method on the Database object. Here is the syntax:

```
Object.NewPassword OldPassword, NewPassword
```

Object represents a variable of an Object data type that is the User or Microsoft Jet 3.5 Database object whose Password property you want to change. OldPassword represents a string expression that is the current setting of the Password property of the User or Jet 3.5 Database object. NewPassword is a string expression that is the new setting of the Password property of the User or Jet 3.5 Database object.

To add a database password, use the following code:

```
Dim MyDB As Database
Set MyDB = CurrentDb()
MyDB.NewPassword "", "password"
```

To change a database password, use the following code:

```
Dim MyDB As Database
Set MyDB = CurrentDb()
MyDB.NewPassword "password", "ChangedPassWord"
```

To remove a database password, use the following code:

```
Dim MyDB As Database
Set MyDB = CurrentDb()
MyDB.NewPassword "ChangedPassWord", ""
```

# User-Level Security

In Microsoft Access, user-level security is always on. Every database you create or use contains information specifying which users have permissions to each of the objects within the database. Many users are not concerned with security, so by default Microsoft Access logs you on as a user who has full permissions to all objects, an administrator known as the user Admin. If a database is secured using user-level security, however, users must supply a valid user name and password in order to gain access to the database. The user can then access objects to which they have been granted specific permissions by a database administrator.

## The Workgroup Information File

Each time you start Microsoft Access, user and group information is accessed from a Workgroup information file called SYSTEM.MDW, which is created automatically when Microsoft Access is installed. You may also choose to create a new Workgroup information file by running the Workgroup Administrator application (WRKGADM.EXE) by clicking on the MS Access Workgroup Administrator shortcut that is installed in your Microsoft Office folder.

Within a Workgroup information file, you can create user accounts and groups. Different Workgroup information files can store entirely different users and groups. To log in as a particular user, you must first "join" the Workgroup information file in which that user account was created. To join a Workgroup information file, run the Workgroup Administrator and click the Join button. Click the Browse button, and select the Workgroup information file you want to join. Click OK in the Select Workgroup Information File dialog box, click OK in the Workgroup Information File dialog box, and click OK when the Workgroup Administrator tells you the Workgroup information file has been successfully joined. Finally, click the Exit button in the Workgroup Administrator dialog box.

### Users

One default user account is part of every new Workgroup information file. The default user is named "Admin" and has no password, so Microsoft Access automatically attempts to log you on as user Admin, with no password. If the

Admin user's password has changed, a logon dialog box will appear when you start Microsoft Access. In that case, you must log on as a particular user and specify the appropriate password. (See Figure 12-2.)

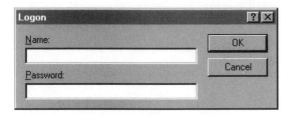

**Figure 12-2.** *Logon dialog box.*

Two other special accounts always exist and are established and maintained internally by Jet: Creator and Engine. These accounts do not appear in the User And Group Accounts dialog box. The permissions assigned to these accounts cannot be changed.

## Groups

In Microsoft Access, you can create groups to which users may belong. This makes it much easier to assign identical permissions to multiple users. Groups do not have passwords, and you cannot log on to a Jet system using a group alias. By default, two groups are created in all Workgroup information files: Admins and Users. The user Admin is a member by default of both the Admins and Users groups.

Because there must always be one user who is a member of the Admins group, you cannot remove the user Admin from this group unless another user also belongs to the Admins group. This ensures that at least one user has the ability to add other users, reset passwords, and perform other database administration tasks. Members of the Admins group can assign permissions, delete objects, and clear the password of any other user.

When users are added via the Microsoft Access security interface, the new users are automatically made members of the Users group. You cannot delete users from this group through the interface, but you can assign users to any number of additional groups. By default, all users can perform the following tasks:

- Create new databases
- Create new database objects
- Change system preferences
- Repair databases
- Compact databases

## Creating users and groups

Now that we have discussed the default users and groups in Microsoft Access, let's see how you can create your own users and groups. To create a new user or group, you must be logged on as a user who is a member of the Admins group. If you are not prompted to supply a user name and password when you start Microsoft Access, you are logged on as user Admin, with no password. (Remember, the Admin user is a member of the Admins group by default.)

When you add a new user or group to a Workgroup information file, you must supply the user or group name and a personal ID (PID). The name is what will be used to identify the user or group in the user interface. Together the name and the PID will be used by Jet to automatically create a system ID (SID). The PID can be any combination of characters and numbers and can be from 4 to 20 characters in length. Jet uses the PID in combination with the name to distinguish users with the same name in different Workgroup information files.

For example, suppose you create a user named Gary. You give Gary a password and full permissions to your tables, and you take permissions away from all other users and groups. Then you copy your database to a network. I come along and install Microsoft Access on my machine, and I also create a user named Gary in my Workgroup information file. Is your database secured? Yes—unless I happen to know the PID you entered for *your* user named Gary. As you can see from this example, if PIDs did not exist, anyone who created a user name identical to someone else's would have access to that user's system.

| TIP | Write down the user name and PID that you choose when you create each user or group and physically secure this list. If you do not know the user name and PID used to create your users and groups, you will not be able to re-create them. Both are case-sensitive, so be accurate when you save this information. |

## Adding new users and groups

To add a new user or group to a Workgroup information file, first make sure you are joined to the appropriate Workgroup information file and then take the following steps:

1. Choose Security from the Tools menu, and then select User And Group Accounts. The User And Group Accounts dialog box will be displayed. (See Figure 12-3 on the next page.)

2. Click the Users tab.

3. Click the New button, and enter the user name and PID in the New User/Group dialog box. (Be sure to keep a record by writing the user name and PID exactly as you entered them; remember, Microsoft Access user names and PIDs are case-sensitive when creating users and groups.)

**4.** Click the OK button.

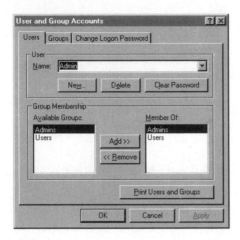

**Figure 12-3.** *User And Group Accounts dialog box.*

The SID, not the user name, is the identifier that is stored in the system table of each database and associated with object permissions. The permissions themselves are stored only in the databases to which those objects belong. To verify the password for each user and map that user name to a SID, Jet uses a table in the Workgroup information file called MSysAccounts. Once you have clicked the OK button in the New User/Group dialog box, Microsoft Access creates a SID in the MSysAccounts table of the current Workgroup information file for the new user or group. Note that an MSysAccounts table exists in the database as well as in the Workgroup information file. Therefore, the SID is stored in both the database and the Workgroup information file. It has to be stored in both places so that as the user opens a database, Access can find a match between the SID in the Workgroup information file and the SID that the database has stored for the user. Once there is a match, Access can validate this user as being able to access the database based on this user's permissions.

The following table shows that if there are matching SIDs, the user can access the database with the permissions assigned to him or her. (The SIDs shown in the following table are not actual SIDs. SIDs are stored in binary format.) If a database is completely secured and if a user tries to open that database while joined to another Workgroup information file, he or she will not be able to open that database, unless the Users and Groups are the same in both Workgroup information files. If the original Workgroup information file is lost or corrupted, to make the database accessible you will have to re-create the same users and groups in a new Workgroup information file, using exactly the same names and PIDs.

**Database: MSysAccounts**

| Account | SID |
|---------|-----|
| Admin | Default |
| Admins | Based off Workgroup SID |
| Users | Default |
| Michele | SYS1234 |
| Jason | SYS4567 |

match
match
match
no match
match

**Workgroup: MSysAccounts**

| Account | SID |
|---------|-----|
| Admin | Default |
| Admins | Unique value |
| Users | Default |
| Michele | RBG6789 |
| Jason | SYS4567 |

To log in as a user other than Admin, you must first change the password for the Admin user by taking the following steps:

1. Choose Security from the Tools menu, and then select User And Group Accounts.

2. Click the Change Logon Password tab.

3. Do not specify an old password. (By default, there isn't a password for new users.) Press the Tab key to move the cursor to the New Password text box.

4. Type in a new password.

5. Type the same password in the Verify textbox, and click the OK button.

6. Exit Microsoft Access, and then restart it.

## Permissions

Before an object can be accessed, the user must have permission to access it. Users and groups each have their own sets of permissions. Microsoft Access 97 uses the least-restrictive-permissions model, which contains two types of permissions: implicit and explicit.

*Implicit permissions* are those granted to a group. When a user is added to a group, that user receives all the permissions of that group. For example, if a user has no permissions to any of the objects in a database but is a member of a group that does have all permissions, that user inherits those permissions.

*Explicit permissions* are those given directly to a user. When explicit permissions are granted, no other users are affected. For example, if a user has permissions to all the database objects and is then added to a group that does not have any permissions to those objects, the user can still access all the database objects; even though this user has acquired the permissions of the group to which he or she was added, the least restrictive permissions still apply.

For example, suppose a database includes Employees, Payroll, and Division tables. The Workgroup information file contains two users, Andy and Christine, and two groups, Managers and AllEmployees. Assume the AllEmployees group has explicit permission to the Employees table, the Managers group has explicit permission to the Payroll table, and the user Christine has explicit permission to the Division table. If Andy and Christine are members of the AllEmployees group but only Andy is a member of the Managers group, Andy will have implicit permission to both the Employees table and the Payroll table, and Christine will have implicit permission to only the Employees table. This is shown in the following table:

| Table | Users and Groups | | | |
|---|---|---|---|---|
| | **Andy** | **Christine** | **Managers Group** | **AllEmployees Group** |
| **Employees** | I | I | | E |
| **Payroll** | I | | E | |
| **Division** | | E | | |

Key: E = Explicit permission
     I = Implicit permission

As a developer, you should assign users to groups for the following reasons:

■ **Organizational concerns** It makes sense to put managers in the Managers group and secretaries in the Secretaries group.

■ **Maintenance** If you need to change the implicit permissions for multiple users and the users are already in a group, you can update all the users in a single step.

■ **Maintenance and time savings** If there are several hundred objects in a database, it is easier to assign permissions to a couple of groups (remember that users inherit group permissions) than to assign permissions to hundreds of users.

The Microsoft Jet database engine stores permission information for an object (such as information about whether a user has full permissions or no permissions) in the database that contains that object. For example, if a user is assigned permissions to a data table in MYDATA.MDB, Jet will store those permissions in a MYDATA.MDB system table. Then when the user attempts to access the data table, Jet takes the user's SID and the SIDs of the groups to which the user belongs and compares these SIDs with the entries in the MYDATA.MDB system table to verify that the user has permissions to that data table.

Permissions are not kept in the Workgroup information file because multiple databases use that file to compare SIDs. Also, because permissions apply only to a specific database, it makes sense to store them only in the database.

For example, Database A has the following users and groups with their associated SIDs:

| Users/Groups | SID |
| --- | --- |
| Andy | Andy1234 |
| Christine | Christine6789 |
| Employees | ABC123 |

Both users are assigned permissions to the Employees Table object, as shown in the following table. Because their SIDs are now associated with that object's permissions, the following permissions are granted to the users and groups based on their SIDs:

| Employees Table Object Permissions | Users/Groups | Users/Groups SID |
| --- | --- | --- |
| Full | Andy | Andy1234 |
| Read data | Christine | Christine6789 |
|  | Employees | ABC123 |
| Delete data | Employees | ABC123 |

The following illustration shows the matchup between the SIDs in the Workgroup information file and those assigned to the object:

**Object Permissions/
SIDs in Database**

| Permissions | SID |
| --- | --- |
| Full | Andy1234 |
| Read Data | ABC123 |
|  | Christine6789 |
|  | Andy1234 |
| Delete Data | ABC123 |
|  | Christine6789 |
|  | Andy1234 |

match
match
match
match
match
match
match

**SIDs in Workgroup Information File**

| Account | SID |
| --- | --- |
| Andy | Andy1234 |
| Employees | ABC123 |
| Christine | Christine6789 |
| Andy | Andy1234 |
| Employees | ABC123 |
| Christine | Christine6789 |
| Andy | Andy1234 |

If this database is taken to another workgroup, the users in the other workgroup will not be able to view the Employees table, since that workgroup has different users and groups with different SIDs.

To assign permissions to users or groups by way of the Microsoft Access security interface, choose Security from the Tools menu and then select User And Group Permissions to open the User And Group Permissions dialog box. (See Figure 12-4.) The User/Group Name list box on the left side of the dialog box shows all the users and groups in the system. The Object Name list box on the right side of the dialog box displays the objects in the database. To select more than one object at a time, hold down the Ctrl key and click the primary mouse button. The lower half of the dialog box displays the types of permissions you can assign to a given object. Not all permissions apply to all objects. For example, Insert Data does not apply to a Form object, but it does apply to Table and Query objects.

**Figure 12-4.** *User And Group Permissions dialog box.*

There are nine types of permissions altogether. Let's discuss what each type means.

- **Open/Run** gives the user permission to run a macro or open a form or database.

- **Open Exclusive** gives the user permission to open a database exclusively.

- **Read Design** allows the user to look at the design of an object (for example, the design of a form or a table).

- **Modify Design** automatically gives the user Read Design permissions so that the object can be modified. If you have Modify Design permissions, you can change the structure of a table or modify a form, for example.

- **Read Data** applies to tables and queries and allows the user to look at the data.

- **Update Data** automatically gives the user Read Data permission and allows the user to update the data in a table or query.

- **Insert Data** automatically gives the user Read Data permission and allows the user to add data to a table or a query.

- **Delete Data** automatically gives the user Read Data permission and allows the user to delete the data in a table or query.

- **Administer** permission gives the user total control over the object. This permission allows a user to assign permissions to others. A user must have Administer permission on the database to perform the following tasks:

  - Set a password for the database

  - Replicate the database

  - Set the StartUp properties of the database

  For Database objects, this permission allows users full access to objects and data and includes the ability to assign permissions. Objects, of course, include the databases and all its tables, queries, forms, reports, macros, and modules. By default, the Users group, the Admins group, and the creator of a database will have Administer permission for the database. If a user has Administer permissions for Database objects only, the user can make changes to that object but not to other objects in the database.

## What Permissions Do You Need?

Now that we know what each of these permissions means, let's see how they apply to our database objects and how they affect our ability to perform tasks and view data within a Microsoft Access application.

### Tables

Permissions to tables are fairly simple to understand. If you have Read Data permission, you may view both the table's data and its structure. (Read Design is implied by Read Data.) You can assign Update Data, Insert Data, and Delete Data permissions to allow users to change, add, or delete records, and Modify

Design permission to allow users to change the table's structure or delete the entire table. With permissions to tables, you cannot assign Read permission only to particular columns or records. To achieve security at that level of granularity, you must use queries, forms, or VBA.

### Queries

By using queries, you can implement column-level security and give users the ability to add or delete records, even if they do not have Read Data permissions to a table. The query property Run Permissions (which you can set by clicking the Properties toolbar button while viewing a query in Design view) makes it possible for the administrator to allow a query to be used for certain tasks that users are not allowed to perform directly on the query's underlying table.

For example, suppose you have a secure database with an Employees table and in the Employees table you store the salary of each employee. If you do not want employees to see other employees' salaries, you can revoke all permissions to the Employees table. Then you can create a query that selects every column from the Employees table except the Salary column, and you can then set the Run Permissions property of the query to Owner's. The query property, Run Permissions, makes it possible for the administrator to allow users to perform certain tasks via a query that they are not allowed to perform on the table directly. Ownership of objects is discussed in the "Owners" section on page 428.

### Forms

You cannot use forms to give users access to data that they otherwise would not be able to see or modify. If you base a form on a table to which the user has no permissions and if you give the user Open/Run permissions to that form, the user will not be able to open the form and view the data. You can give users the ability to modify data to which they have no direct access only by using queries that have the Run Permissions property set to Owner's, as discussed in the previous section, or by using VBA to open a workspace based on another user and creating a Recordset object.

### Reports

Reports are used only for viewing data. Therefore, the user needs only Read Data permissions to the underlying RecordSource of a report. To print or preview the report, the user must have Open/Run permission for the report itself.

### Macros

To run a macro, the user needs Open/Run permission. In macros, it is not possible to check permissions or trap for errors, so you must create different macros for different users to prevent their macros from failing. (You could also create VBA functions that check the permissions of users, as described later in this chapter in the "Using DAO to Set Permissions and to Program Security" section.)

## Modules

Modules have only three types of permissions: Administer, Read Design, and Modify Design. If no permissions are assigned to a user, he or she still has the ability to execute the functions and sub procedures contained within a module. Assign permissions to modules only if you want the user to be able to view the code in them.

# Understanding Default Security in Microsoft Access

When you create a Workgroup information file, the default users and groups are the ones shown in the following tables.

**DEFAULT USERS AND GROUPS**

| Users | SID | Default Permissions | Group Membership |
|-------|-----|---------------------|------------------|
| Admin | Same for all Workgroups | All | Admins Users |

| Groups | SID | Default Permissions | |
|--------|-----|---------------------|--|
| Admins | Different for all Workgroups | All | |
| Users | Same for all Workgroups | All | |

## The Admin user

The Admin user is the default user account. If you are using Microsoft Access without logging on, you are using the Admin account. The Admin user's SID is identical across all installations of Microsoft Access, so any permissions given to the Admin user will be available to the Admin user in all Workgroup information files. It is not recommended that you assign permissions to the Admin user simply because this user is identical on all systems. By default, the Admin user is the only member of the Admins group, has full explicit permissions to all of the objects, and can create and change objects because of these permissions.

## The Admins group

A user who is a member of the Admins group is the true administrator of a Workgroup information file and of a database. An Admins group member can set and remove permissions to database objects and can create new users and groups in the Workgroup information file.

## The Users group

All users belong to the Users group, so any permissions assigned to that group are also given to every individual user in any Workgroup information file. For a secure database, it is not recommended that you give explicit permissions to the Users group. Permissions are given to the Users group by default so that user-level security is transparent until a database is fully secured. Removing all permissions from the Users group is one of the steps required to secure a database.

### Owners

When a user first creates a new database, that user is the owner of the new database. Even if this user is not in the Admins group, he or she can still set permissions to that new database: whoever creates a database owns it and can do anything he or she wants with it.

It is very important that you know the owner of all objects within the database, including the Database object itself, because the owner of an object will always have the ability to assign himself or herself permissions to that object. For example, if user Ginny creates a table called Table1 and if you then revoke all of Ginny's permissions to Table1, Ginny will not be able to open the table. She can go into the User And Group Permissions dialog box, however, and assign herself permissions to Table1 because she is the owner of that object. You cannot permanently revoke all permissions to an object from its owner. You can change owners, however, using the Change Owner tab of the User And Group Permissions dialog box, and then remove all permissions from the previous owner. However, you must be a member of the Admins group, have Administer permissions on the object, or be the owner of the object.

# Securing and Unsecuring a Database

When you secure or unsecure a database, you should follow specific steps. The SID for the Admin user and the Users group is the same across all Workgroup information files. What this means is that if you assign permissions to the Admin user on your system, anyone can log on as the Admin user on his or her system and have those same permissions. By default, the Admin user (if he or she created all the objects) and the Users group have full permissions to all objects in a database.

## Securing a Database Manually

The following steps outline how to manually secure a database with Microsoft Access 97:

1. Create a backup of your database file.

2. When the Admins group account is automatically created, Jet retrieves your user name and company name information and uses it to create a unique SID. Since this information is often easy to determine, it's possible for unauthorized users to create another version of your Workgroup

information file and consequently assume the irrevocable permissions of an administrator account (a member of the Admins group) in the workgroup defined by that Workgroup information file. To prevent this, create a new Workgroup information file to specify a Workgroup ID (WID). Be sure to write down the information and put it in a safe place so you can re-create the Workgroup information file if you need to. (See the online Help topic titled "Create a new Microsoft Access workgroup information file" for details.)

3. After you create the new Workgroup information file, only the default accounts exist, so you must create all necessary users and groups in the new Workgroup information file.

4. Create a new user account called Developer (or whatever name you choose) under which you will administer the database and the Workgroup information file, and add that user to the Admins group so that user can set permissions and create other accounts.

5. In the new Workgroup information file, create a password for the Admin user.

6. Log on as Developer. Remove the Admin user from the Admins group.

7. Revoke all permissions on all objects for the Admin user and the Users group. This ensures that no default accounts have access to any objects in the database. If you want all users to have read-only access, set the appropriate permissions for the Users group. Now you can assign permissions for your application's accounts.

8. Change the Owner property of all objects, including the Database object, to Developer.

If you plan to distribute your database, make sure you test the application while logged on under the different account names. Also test your application with a different Workgroup information file to be sure the default accounts have the appropriate permissions (or lack of permissions) for your database.

## Securing a Database with the User-Level Security Wizard

If the steps just outlined seem tedious, you can implement security with the User-Level Security Wizard. This wizard is built into Microsoft Access 97 and automatically creates user-level security on a database. The wizard secures a database in the following ways:

■ It checks to make sure the user has Read Data permission to MSysObjects. By default, all members of the Admins and Users groups have this permission.

- It asks for the types of objects to be secured (all objects or selected tables, queries, forms, reports, macros, and modules).

- It creates a new, empty, encrypted database. The encrypting of the database ensures file-level security in the operating system.

- It exports all the objects from the original database to the new database.

- It re-creates table relationships and table links in the new database.

- It makes the current user the owner of the database and gives the current user permission to all objects in the database.

- For those objects selected to be secured and for any new objects that will be created (tables, queries, and forms, for example), it revokes all the permissions of the Users group. If other users and groups have been created, those permissions will also be revoked. (It does *not* revoke Open/Run permissions from the Database object itself.)

Before running the User-Level Security Wizard, you need to take the following steps:

1. Create and join a new Workgroup information file. Make sure the Workgroup information file is created with a unique Workgroup ID.

2. Create a password for the Admin user.

3. Create a new user (for example, Developer), and add that user to the Admins group.

4. Exit and restart Microsoft Access.

5. Log on as the new user in the Admins group.

6. Remove the Admin user from the Admins group. If a user other than the new user (Developer) should be the owner of the database and all the objects in it, exit Microsoft Access and log on as that user. At the minimum, that user needs to have Read Data and Read Design permissions to all objects in the database that are to be secured.

7. Open the database that is to be secured.

To run the User-Level Security Wizard, do the following:

1. Choose Security from the Tools menu, and then select User-Level Security Wizard.

2. Select the objects you want to secure, and then click OK.

3. Choose a filename and location for the secured version of the database in the Destination Database dialog box. The original database will not

be modified by Access. Click the Save button. The wizard may take a few minutes to secure a database completely.

**4.** When Access displays a dialog box indicating that the new copy of the database is now secured, click OK.

**5.** Open the new secured database.

**6.** Create any custom users and groups in the new Workgroup information file, and assign them permissions to the appropriate objects.

The original database is not changed in any way and can be accessed as it was before the User-Level Security Wizard was invoked. To avoid breaches of security, therefore, it would be a good idea either to delete the original database or to store it in a safe location.

After the wizard has been used to create the new secured database, only members of the Admins group of the particular Workgroup information file you created will have access to the secured objects in the new database, and the Users group will have no permissions to the secured objects. Therefore, users who are not members of the Admins group will not be able to access those objects. For those other users in the Workgroup information file to have access to the objects in the secured database, permissions can be granted only by a user who is a member of the Admins group or by the user who is the owner of the database.

## Unsecuring a Database

At some point, you may want to unsecure your database. Once a database has been unsecured, the Admin user becomes the owner and the Users group has full permissions to all objects in the database.

The easiest way to unsecure a database, assuming no data has changed in the secured version, is to use your backup copy of the database, which you should have saved before the database was secured. If you do not have a backup copy of the database or if the data in the secured version has changed and must be retained, however, you can unsecure your database by taking the following steps:

**1.** Log on as a member of the Admins group. (For example, this member could be the Developer account you created when you secured the database.)

**2.** Put the Admin user back into the Admins group.

**3.** Assign the Users group full permissions to all objects.

**4.** Exit and restart Microsoft Access.

**5.** Log on as the Admin user.

**6.** Reset the Admin password to be blank.

**7.** Change the Owner property of all objects, including the Database object, to be the Admin user.

# DAO Properties for Security

Jet 3.5, in addition to offering the security features of the Microsoft Access interface, offers the DefaultWorkspaceClone method, the AllPermissions property (for Container and Document objects), and the following DAO properties that allow users to access and manipulate security for Microsoft Access:

■ DBEngine.DefaultPassword

■ DBEngine.DefaultUser

■ DBEngine.SystemDB

■ DBEngine.IniPath

Jet 3.5 also offers the following DAO methods:

■ Database.Newpassword

■ Workspace.OpenDatabase

■ Workspace.CompactDatabase

The dbSecDBAdmin security constant, which you use to specify the new Administer permission for the Database object, is also available with Jet 3.5.

Now let's see how these DAO properties and methods can be used with security in Microsoft Access 97.

## Logging On to the Default Workspace in Code

The DefaultUserName and DefaultPassword properties can be used to log on to the default workspace as a user other than Admin. If these properties are not set, the user must create a Workspace object, using the DBEngine.CreateWorkSpace method to log on, in code, as another person.

■ Use the DefaultPassword property to set the password used by the Microsoft Access Jet database engine when it is initialized. The setting is a String data type that can be up to 14 characters long and can contain any character except ASCII 0. Passwords are case-sensitive. By default, DefaultPassword is set to a zero-length string ("").

■ Use the DefaultUser property to set the user name that is used by the Microsoft Access Jet database engine when it is initialized. The user name is *not* case-sensitive unless you are re-creating it in a different Workgroup information file. By default, DefaultUser is set to "Admin."

When you are coding in Microsoft Access 97, the DefaultPassword and Default-User properties are not applicable. Therefore, they are not useful for Microsoft Access programmers. These properties are useful for other VBA applications, such as Microsoft Excel or Microsoft Visual Basic, that are attempting to access a secured database file.

Suppose you are using another VBA application, such as Microsoft Visual Basic, and want to open a secured Microsoft Access database. To do this, you must ensure that you are logging in to the session of Jet as the appropriate user. Therefore, before using any DAO objects below the DBEngine object, you must set the DefaultUser and DefaultPassword properties appropriately. This will ensure that Jet will log you on to the default workspace as the appropriate user rather than as the Admin user.

In Microsoft Access, these properties have no bearing. However, you do have the ability to create another Workspace object within Microsoft Access to log in as another user, thereby achieving similar functionality. The following code demonstrates:

```
Sub CreateAWorkspace()
    Dim WS As Workspace, DB As Database

    Set WS = DBEngine.CreateWorkspace("MyWorkspace", "John", "")
    Set DB = CurrentDb()
    ...' code to manipulate the database objects as user John
End Sub
```

The advantage of having multiple workspaces is that each workspace defines a session. Each session can establish a security level and can manage transactions independent of other sessions. If you do not need multiple security levels or transaction scopes, there is no need to reference the DBEngine or Workspace object. Microsoft Access will use the default DBEngine.Workspaces object.

## Locating the Current Workgroup Information File

DBEngine.SystemDB points to the location of the current Workgroup information file. DBEngine.IniPath returns the installation-dependent portion of the Registry key location in which can be found some details about the Workgroup information file. For example, the Jet Registry key has an Engines.SystemDB entry with a value of the full file path to the current Workgroup information file. The scope of these settings is limited to the application instance and cannot be changed unless the Microsoft Access application is restarted. Depending on your installation, DBEngine.IniPath might return the Registry entry on the following page.

```
Software\Microsoft\Office\8.0\Jet\3.5
```

DBEngine.SystemDB might return the following Workgroup information file:

```
C:\WINDOWS\SYSTEM\SYSTEM.MDW
```

Microsoft Access preloads this information, so Microsoft Access 97 can use these properties only to return the information. Although these properties are read-only for Microsoft Access, they can be set from other VBA applications that need to access a secured database file. This is because these properties tell Jet where to locate the Workgroup information file, which contains the list of users and groups. If you are accessing a secured database from another VBA application, set the IniPath property first, and then set the DefaultUser and DefaultPassword properties. You need to set them in this order because the latter properties rely on the IniPath property to look up the settings.

## Opening a Database with a Password

The OpenDatabase method of the Workspace object allows you to specify a password as part of the fourth argument:

```
Dim MyDB As Database
Set MyDB = DBEngine(0).OpenDatabase("BIBLIO.MDB ", True, _
    False, ";pwd=password")
```

> **NOTE**  When used on a Database object, the NewPassword method changes the password parameter that appears in the "pwd=..." part of this argument. In other words, the "pwd=" must be preceded by a semicolon: ";pwd=". You must also supply the exclusive and read-only arguments to specify a source string.

For backward compatibility, the password parameter can also be used with the OpenDatabase *function*. Microsoft Access is moving toward an object-oriented technology, so you should use the OpenDatabase *method*.

To change a password for a database, you can call the new NewPassword method on the database object or the enhanced CompactDatabase method on the DBEngine object.

## Using the DefaultWorkspaceClone Method for the Application Object

Use the DefaultWorkspaceClone method to create a new Workspace object without having the user log on again with the same name and password. After all, why not let the method do the work of logging on? The workspace created by the default workspace and DefaultWorkspaceClone method are exactly the same except that the default workspace's Name property is #Default Workspace# and DefaultWorkspaceClone's name property is #CloneAccess#. Here is an example of creating a workspace identical to that of the default workspace:

```
Dim WS As Workspace
Set WS = Application.DefaultWorkspaceClone
```

# Programming Security

Managing security through the interface is a great way to secure your application. In the run-time environment, however, you do not have the ability to work with the interface. By using DAO, you can create your own interface and allow users to change security options.

## Working with Users and Groups

Each user can belong to one or more groups. Users and groups share a common namespace, so you cannot have a group and a user with the same name. With DAO, a Users collection and a Groups collection can be accessed for each Workspace object. The Users collection contains a list of all valid users defined in a Workgroup information file, and the Groups collection contains a list of all valid groups defined in a Workgroup information file. You can enumerate these collections by using the For...Next or For...Each looping structure.

The following example (which can be found in CHAP12.MDB in the CHAP12 subfolder of the folder in which you installed the files from the companion disc) lists all the users defined in whichever Workgroup information file was joined at the start of a session of Microsoft Jet:

```
Sub PrintUsers()
    Dim W As Workspace, U As User
    Set W = DBEngine.Workspaces(0)
    For Each U In W.Users
        Debug.Print U.Name
    Next
End Sub
```

### Changing someone's password

User Bob needs a new password. His old password was "password"; the following code gives him the password "pioneer":

```
Dim U as User
Set U = DbEngine.Workspaces(0).Users("Bob")
U.NewPassword "password", "pioneer"
```

To be able to change Bob's password, of course, the user will have to be logged on as Bob or be a member of the Admins group.

## Adding and removing users and groups

At run time, or after the application has been distributed, the developer might need to add users or groups to the system. It is helpful to add a Site Administrator user to the Admins group so that the developer does not have to maintain the system personally. Managing security, or at least users and groups, can be the responsibility of the Site Administrator user. The following code demonstrates how to add a user to a Workgroup information file:

```
Sub CreateUser()
    Dim UserName As String, UserPID as String, UserPW As String
    Dim W As Workspace, New_User As User
    UserName = "Bob"
    UserPID = "1234"             ' 4-20 chars
    UserPW = "password"          ' <= 14 chars
    Set W = DBEngine.Workspaces(0)
    Set New_User = W.CreateUser(UserName, UserPID, UserPW) '(1)
    W.Users.Append New_User                                '(2)
    New_User.Groups.Append W.CreateGroup("Users")          '(3)
End Sub
```

The important step to note is the addition of the new user to the Users group. By default, a new user will not be added to the Users group automatically if you are creating the user using code, so the user will not belong to any groups. Here are comments on the steps numbered from (1) to (3) in the preceding code:

1. This step creates a newUser object, assigning the name, the PID, and the password to the new user.

2. Appending the New_User object to the Users group in this step actually stores the new information in the Workgroup information file.

3. With this step, you add the Users group to the collection of groups associated with the new user. It is important to do this for consistency within the Microsoft Access security interface, where all users are automatically added to the Users group.

The following code adds a group to a Workgroup information file:

```
Sub CreateGroup()
    Dim GroupName As String, GroupPID As String
    Dim W As Workspace, New_Group As Group
    GroupName = "Finance"
    GroupPID = "1234"
    Set W = DBEngine.Workspaces(0)
    Set New_Group = W.CreateGroup(GroupName, GroupPID)
    ' Add the Finance group to the Groups collection.
    W.Groups.Append New_Group
End Sub
```

Here is an example of how to remove a user from a group:

```
Sub RemoveUserFromGroup(UserName, GroupName)
    Dim GName As String
    Dim U As User
    Set U = DBEngine.Workspaces(0).Users(UserName)
    On Error Resume Next
    GName = U(GroupName).Name    ' separate for error handling.
    If GName = GroupName Then
        U.Groups.Delete GroupName
    Else
        Debug.Print "No user <" & UserName & "> in group <" & _
            GroupName & ">"
    End If
End Sub
```

It may be necessary to find out what groups a user belongs to or to find out which users belong to a particular group. The following code shows all users and the groups to which they belong in the system database:

```
Sub PrintUsersAndGroups()
    Dim W As Workspace, U As User, G As Group
    Set W = DBEngine.Workspaces(0)
    For Each U In W.Users
        Debug.Print U.Name
        For Each G In U.Groups
            Debug.Print "    " & G.Name
        Next
    Next
End Sub
```

You can reverse the order of the loops to show which groups have which users in them.

Here are a few interesting points:

■ If a user or a group is deleted from a Workgroup information file, an object to which that user or group has specific permissions will retain those permissions. If the group or user is ever created again with exactly the same name and PID, those permissions will again be applicable. (The user sees evidence of his or her deletion upon examining the Owner property of the objects, when the Owner name is returned as "unknown.")

■ If you want to find out which users and groups have permissions to an object, you will need to write a small program that iterates through each user and group name, first setting the UserName property and then reading the Permissions property. (See the section below titled "Container objects.")

- Not everyone has permissions to view user and group information, only users in the Admins group can do so. Generally, it is best to be logged on as the system administrator (or someone in the Admins group) if you are modifying security details.

## Container Objects and Document Objects

Each Database object has a single Containers collection of Container objects, which are used in conjunction with Document objects. It is not possible to create or delete Container or Document objects. Container and Document objects are used principally for enumerating all application- and engine-defined objects stored in the database, including those objects that are defined by client applications, and for setting user permissions and ownership, which is done when the Permissions property is set on a Document object or a Container object.

### Container objects

A Container object collects information about the database or about each of its types of objects (all its saved forms, macros, modules, relationships, reports, or tables, including queries). For example, Microsoft Access defines several Container objects: the Form object, the Script (macro) object, the Report object, and the Module object. The Jet 3.5 DBEngine object also defines its own Container objects, such as the Table object and the Relationship object.

The Container object has four major properties of which you should be aware:

**Inherit**   The Inherit property is used in conjunction with new objects only. You use the Inherit property to specify whether a user or a group will have certain permissions to all new objects of a particular type. This property is useful because it allows you to create your objects as you normally do, without having to go back and set or revoke permissions for users and groups.

**Permissions**   The Permissions property is a Long integer value that stores the permissions of a particular Container object.

**Owner**   The Owner property indicates which user is the owner of a Container object.

**UserName**   The UserName property specifies the user or group whose permissions you are setting or checking for the Container object.

The following table shows the names of each Container object, lists its originator, and gives a short description of the object's contents.

| Container Object | Originator | Contents |
|---|---|---|
| Databases | Jet | Saved databases |
| Forms | Microsoft Access | Saved forms |
| Modules | Microsoft Access | Saved modules |
| Relationships | Jet | Saved relationships |
| Reports | Microsoft Access | Saved reports |
| Scripts | Microsoft Access | Saved macros |
| Tables | Jet | Saved tables and queries |

### Document objects

Each Container object has a Documents collection, which contains Document objects that describe instances of the appropriate type. Each Document object includes information about a single instance of that type of object. For example, all the forms in an Access database can be enumerated using the Document collection that is contained in the Forms container. You can grant or revoke security privileges to an object by setting user permissions to its corresponding Document object.

With the exception of the Relationship object, Document objects refer to items displayed in the Database window. The Relationship object corresponds to a saved relationship created with the Relationships command in the Tools menu of the Database window.

The Document object has properties similar to those of the Container object. The most commonly used ones are the Name property, the Permissions property, the Owner property, and the UserName property. The Name property identifies a particular object in the database (for example, a particular Form object). The remaining Document object properties are used as they are for Container objects.

## Using DAO to Set Permissions and to Program Security

You can assign different permissions by setting or resetting specific bits or groups of bits of the Long value in the Permissions property of a Document object or Container object. Typically, you set values by combining predefined constants, using the And and Or operators. The following shared constants are predefined in the Microsoft DAO 3.5 Object Library for all objects other than Tables and Database containers:

- dbSecNoAccess

- dbSecFullAccess

- dbSecDelete

- dbSecReadSec

- dbSecWriteSec

- dbSecWriteOwner

The following descriptions of constants apply to both Container objects and Document objects, except as noted:

- dbSecNoAccess and dbSecFullAccess work as expected—almost! To remove all permissions to a class of objects from a given user or group, set the appropriate Container object's Permissions property to dbSecNoAccess. To grant a given user or group all permissions, set a Document or Container object's Permissions property to dbSecFullAccess. "Full access" means full access to the object itself; it does not grant permission to set permissions. For example, someone with full access to a Table object can edit that object to his or her heart's content, but he or she cannot grant the same full-access permission to someone else or delete the object entirely (although, in the case of a Table object, he or she can delete everything in it, including all the field definitions).

- dbSecDelete represents the specific permission bit associated with deleting a Document object. Although dbSecDelete can be set for a Container object, it has little meaning for the Container object itself, since a Container object cannot be created or deleted. This constant can be useful, however, when combined with the Inherited property of the Container object. (See the "Container objects" section on page 438.)

- dbSecReadSec is the "permission to read" permission. The owner of an object implicitly has this permission.

- dbSecWriteSec is the permission to set permissions. The owner of an object implicitly has this permission so that he or she can always make changes.

- dbSecWriteOwner is the permission to change the owner of an object by setting the Owner property of the appropriate Container object or Document object.

> **NOTE** Always use defined constants, never actual values. Values might change in future releases, but the constants should remain valid.

### The Database object

Every object seems to have its own special permissions, and the Database object is no exception—in fact, the Database object is so special that it has *no* Permissions property at all! Because of some internal details, permissions for the whole database are set via modification of the single document, called MSysDb, found in the Database Container object. The following security constants apply to it and can deny a user permission to open a database at all or just stop him or her from opening a database exclusively:

- dbSecDBAdmin, which gives a user or a group permission to make a database replicable and change the database password

- dbSecDBCreate, which removes a user's permission to create databases and can only be set and removed via code (see below)

- dbSecDBExclusive, which gives a user permission to open a given database exclusively (although it does not imply dbSecDBOpen permissions, which a user or a group that the user belongs to must also have in order to open the database at all)

- dbSecDBOpen, which gives a user permission to open a given database

If you want the Admins group, but not the Users group, to be able to open the database, you can use the following code:

```
Sub DatabasePermissions()
    Dim MyDoc As Document, MyDB As Database
    Set MyDB = DBEngine(0).OpenDatabase("BIBLIO.MDB")
    Set MyDoc = MyDB.Containers("Databases").Documents("MSysDb")
    ' Remove Users group permission to open the database.
    MyDoc.UserName = "Users"
    MyDoc.Permissions = dbSecNoAccess

    ' Give Admins group permission to open the database exclusively.
    MyDoc.UserName = "Admins"
    MyDoc.Permissions = MyDoc.Permissions Or dbSecDBExclusive _
        Or dbSecDBOpen
End Sub
```

Because dbSecDBCreate is applied to an individual user, not to any particular database, this permission is stored in the Workgroup information file. By default, it is available to anyone in the Admins or Users groups, and hence to any user. To remove permission from anyone in the Users group to create databases, you can use the following code:

```
Sub NoUserCreate()
    Dim MyDB As Database, C As Container
    Set MyDB = _
        DBEngine(0).OpenDatabase("C:\WINDOWS\SYSTEM\SYSTEM.MDW")
    Set C = MyDB.Containers("Databases")
    C.UserName = "Users"
    C.Permissions = C.Permissions And Not dbSecDBCreate
End Sub
```

Of course, if a user has dbSecDBCreate permissions because he or she is in another group (such as Admins), that user would still be able to create databases. Note the use of And combined with Not to reset a particular permission bit. This is a useful strategy for retaining whatever permissions a user might already have to an object.

The Databases container has three other Document objects in addition to MSysDb: AccessLayout, SummaryInfo, and UserDefined. For more information on these Document objects, search for "Document" in the Microsoft Access online Help.

## Form, Report, Module, and Script objects

Only three types of permissions make sense for these objects: Read, Write, and Open/Run. Several security constants apply to these objects. These constants are defined in the Microsoft Access 8.0 Object Library, so the naming conventions are a bit different: "ac" stands for Access and "Sec" stands for security, and they are followed by the object that the constant applies to and the permission. Here are the security constants:

- acSecFrmRptReadDef, which is permission to view the Form object or Report object in design mode ("read its definition")

- acSecFrmRptWriteDef, which is permission to make changes to the Form object or Report object in design mode

- acSecFrmRptExecute, which is permission to "run" the Form object or Report object. (Execute permission to a Form object is permission to browse or print it, and Execute permission to a Report object is similar.)

- acSecModReadDef, which is permission to view the Module object in design mode. (This permission is not required for all kinds of access to the object.)

- acSecModWriteDef, which is permission to make changes to the Module object in design mode

- acSecMacExecute, which is permission to run the code in a saved macro (contained in a Script Container object)

- acSecMacReadDef, which is permission to view a saved macro (contained in a Script Container object) in design mode

- acSecMacWriteDef, which is permission to make changes to a saved macro (contained in a Script Container object) in design mode

**NOTE**   All Module object code stored in a database can be executed by anyone, so there is no Open/Run permission to the Module object. It would slow down the execution of VBA code too much to check every function and see whether a given user had

> permission to run it, not to mention the problems this could create with debugging.

The following example grants to a group Execute permissions for a Form object:

```
Sub FormPermissions()
    Dim GroupWithExecute As String
    Dim FormToExecute As String
    Dim MyDB As Database, D As Document
    GroupWithExecute = "Finance"
    FormToExecute = "Customer Orders"
    Set MyDB = DBEngine(0).OpenDatabase("MYDATA.MDB")
    Set D = MyDB.Containers("Forms").Documents(FormToExecute) '(1)
    D.UserName = GroupWithExecute                             '(2)
    D.Permissions = D.Permissions Or acSecFrmRptExecute      '(3)
End Sub
```

Here are comments on the steps numbered from (1) to (3) in the preceding code:

**1.** Specify the document corresponding to the object for which you are setting permissions.

**2.** Set the UserName whose permissions you want to modify—but in this case, the "user" is a group.

**3.** Note the Or in the Execute permission to the Form object, and notice that this permission is specific to Form objects and Report objects.

This example can be used as a template for similar code using Report objects, Module objects, or Script objects (which contain saved macros).

## Tables and queries

Table and Query Document objects are both stored in Tables Container objects, so from this point on the term "table" will denote both Table objects and Query objects. The following security constants, defined in the Microsoft DAO 3.5 Object Library, apply to tables:

- dbSecReadDef, which is permission to read the definition of a table (that is, to see what fields it has)

- dbSecWriteDef, which is permission to modify the definition of a table

- dbSecRetrieveData (commonly called Read permission), which grants permission to read the data in a Table object and is defined to include dbSecReadDef permission. (You could separate the two permissions, but most database software, including Access, requires users to be able to read a table's definition in order to read the table's data. That way, the software knows what fields there are to retrieve.)

- dbSecInsertData (sometimes called Insert or Append permission), which is permission to insert new data rows in a Table object

- dbSecReplaceData (commonly known as Modify permission), which is permission to modify data that is already in a Table object

- dbSecDeleteData, which is permission to delete data rows from a Table object. (Note the subtle but important distinction between dbSecDeleteData and the permission to "zero out" all the fields of a particular row, which is given by dbSecReplaceData.)

You can combine these permissions by using the Or keyword in VBA. For example, to grant someone permission to modify and insert data in a table, the user could set the Permission property as follows:

```
dbSecInsertData Or dbSecReplaceData Or dbSecRetrieveData
```

We include dbSecRetrieveData because most programs, including Access, have to be able to read data before they can update it.

Here is an example of granting a user Read permission to a Table object:

```
Sub TablePermissions()
    Dim UserWithRead As String
    Dim TableToRead As String
    Dim MyDB As Database, D As Document
    UserWithRead = "Bob"
    TableToRead = "Categories"
    Set MyDB = DBEngine(0).OpenDatabase("MYDATA.MDB")
    Set D = MyDB.Containers("Tables").Documents(TableToRead)  '(1)
    D.UserName = UserWithRead                                 '(2)
    D.Permissions = D.Permissions Or dbSecRetrieveData        '(3)
End Sub
```

The sequence of events, numbered from (1) to (3) in the example, is as follows:

1. Specify the document corresponding to the object for which you are setting permissions.

2. Set the user (or group) to be modified.

3. Change the permissions.

Note how the permissions are modified. In this instance, the permissions could simply have been set directly, as shown here:

```
D.Permissions = dbSecRetrieveData
```

If you use Or to modify the existing permissions, you will ensure against the possibility of inadvertently removing other permissions that the user already had.

You can use And to check for existing permissions, as shown in the next example, which shows how to see whether a particular user has explicit Read permission to an object:

```
Sub CheckPermissions()
    ' See if a user has Read permission to a Table object.
    Dim UserToCheck As String
    Dim TableToCheck As String
    Dim MyDB As Database, D As Document
    UserToCheck = "Bob"
    TableToCheck = "Categories"
    Set MyDB = DBEngine(0).OpenDatabase("MYDATA.MDB")
    Set D = MyDB.Containers("Tables").Documents(TableToCheck)  '(1)
    D.UserName = UserToCheck                                   '(2)
    If (D.Permissions And dbSecRetrieveData) > 0 Then         '(3)
        MsgBox UserToCheck & " has RetrieveData permission."
    Else
        MsgBox UserToCheck & " has no RetrieveData permission."
    End If
End Sub
```

The sequence of events, numbered from (1) to (3) in the example, is as follows:

**1.** Specify the document corresponding to the object for which to check permissions.

**2.** Set the user or group to be checked.

**3.** Use the And operator to mask off specific permissions from the set of permissions that are being checked.

In general, the following approach would not work:

```
If D.Permissions = dbSecRetrieveData Then...
```

If the user (or group) had only RetrieveData permissions, this approach would give the correct result, but other bits might also be set, so you must use the And operator.

One more important caveat: the preceding code technique does not take account of whether the user is a member of a group that has Read permission to the Table object. For example, the user might not have explicit Read permission as an individual, but that does not rule out the possibility that some group to which the user belongs *does* have Read permission.

The following code, which shows how to remove all Write Data permissions from a user or a group, removes a user's Write permissions to a Table object:

```
Sub RemoveWritePermissions()
    Dim UserToRemove As String
    Dim TableToRemove As String
    Dim WritePerms As Long
    Dim MyDB As Database, D As Document
    UserToRemove = "Bob"
    TableToRemove = "Categories"
    Set MyDB = DBEngine(0).OpenDatabase("MYDATA.MDB")
    Set D = MyDB.Containers!Tables.Documents(TableToRemove) '(1)
    D.UserName = UserToRemove                               '(2)
    WritePerms = dbSecInsertData Or dbSecReplaceData Or _
        dbSecDeleteData
    D.Permissions = D.Permissions And Not WritePerms       '(3)
End Sub
```

The important steps, numbered from (1) to (3) in the example, are as follows:

**1.** Select the document corresponding to the Table object for which permissions will be revoked.

**2.** Select the user from whom to revoke permissions.

**3.** Revoke all variations of Write permission, including permission to modify data, insert new data, and delete existing rows.

Notice how a group of permissions are removed. To remove just one permission while leaving others intact, do something like this:

```
D.Permissions = D.Permissions And Not dbSecWriteData
```

This has the effect of resetting the bit in question. Sometimes, though, it's just easier to define new permissions. The preceding example, for instance, does not take account of whether the user has WriteDef permission (permission to modify the definition of the table), but removing WriteDef with the preceding technique would also remove ReadDef permission, without which the user cannot read the Table object at all. For the preceding example, it might be easier to assign only Read permission by doing something like this:

```
D.Permissions = dbSecRetrieveData
```

Remember, too, that only the user's explicit permissions are affected. He or she could have other permissions by virtue of being in a group that has them.

### Container objects

Not all the permissions that can be set to a Document object make sense for a Container object. For a Container object, it is useful to set only the following security constants:

- dbSecNoAccess
- dbSecFullAccess
- dbSecDelete
- dbSecReadSec
- dbSecWriteSec
- dbSecWriteOwner
- dbSecCreate

The dbSecCreate constant is a permission that is not used with other objects. Someone with dbSecCreate permission is able to create a new Document object for a Container object. For example, to create a new Table or Query object, you need dbSecCreate permission for the Tables Document object of the Container object.

Although these are the only truly useful permissions to set for a Container object, the Container object's Inherit property allows users to set any other permissions they want. For example, if the user sets the Container object's Inherit property to True and then sets a permission to that Container object, that permission will apply to any subsequently created Document object in the Container object. This is a very convenient way of presetting permissions to an object.

> **NOTE** The Container object's Inherit property cannot be used to set permissions to a Document object that has already been created.

## Creating an .MDE File

An .MDE file is a database whose VBA code is saved in a compiled format that prevents others from being able to view or edit the source code. Creating an .MDE file should be your last step prior to distributing your application. The reason you wait to do this is that once an .MDE file is created, you can't do much editing of database objects.

> **NOTE** Before creating any .MDE files, be sure to make a copy of your original database.

Once you've created the .MDE file, you can no longer modify any modules, forms, or reports. If these objects need to be modified, you must go back to the original copy of the database, make the modifications, and resave the database in an .MDE file format.

To create an .MDE file, follow these steps:

**1.** Close the database.

**2.** Choose Database Utilities from the Tools menu, and select Make MDE File.

**3.** In the Database To Save As MDE dialog box, specify the database you want to save as an .MDE file.

**4.** In the Save MDE As dialog box, specify the new location of the database.

For more information on .MDE files, search Microsoft Access online Help.

TIP   If your only concern is preventing users from viewing code and you're not interested in implementing the full user-level security model, just create and distribute an .MDE file.

## PREVIEW of the next chapter

In the preceding two chapters you were introduced to the Data Access Object (DAO) hierarchy and the different types of security available to Microsoft Access databases. In Chapter 13 you will create a solution database involving a bank automatic teller machine (ATM), applying the DAO and security components you've learned about. The user interface of the ATM will be provided, and you will set up the inner operations of the ATM, such as multiuser functionality, and implement the necessary security.

# 13

# Transaction Processing and Secure Solutions

In the last few chapters, you learned how to use Visual Basic for Applications (VBA) to work with data, handle multiuser situations, and, last but not least, work with the Microsoft Access security model. In this chapter, you will create an application similar to that of a bank automatic teller machine (ATM).

We will cover the following topics in this chapter in the context of the ATM application:

- Completing the application by adding features such as transaction processing

- Implementing Microsoft Access security

- Adding users via VBA code

- Splitting the database

- Distributing the secure solution

- Securing your code

We are by no means trying to write an entire application to simulate the day-to-day activities of a real bank or ATM. Such an endeavor would require several books of information. Instead, we will focus on some key situations involved in programmatic security and transaction processing to help you better understand the relevant issues.

# The Automatic Teller Machine Application

In this application you will look at the workings of a small bank that has a very basic automatic teller machine. The ATM is limited in its abilities and can perform only the following tasks:

- Withdraw $20.00 from a checking or savings account

- Transfer $20.00 from a customer's savings account to his or her checking account

Although setting up such an application may sound simple, many issues are involved. You must implement security and deal with multiuser issues, topics we'll cover later in this chapter. As mentioned in Chapter 12, different types of security options are available in Microsoft Access. In a banking situation such as the one described in this chapter, you will want to implement the most secure option: user-level security.

## CD Starting Point

You will find CHAP13.MDB, the sample database we are using as the basis for this chapter in the \CHAP13\START subfolder of the folder in which you installed the files from the companion CD. In this database, the relationships among the tables are already established, and a few sample forms are provided. Open the database and examine the tables.

## Tables

The database includes three tables: Checking, Members, and Savings. The Members table is the main table and contains information about the bank's customers. It's pretty basic in that it can't handle joint accounts, in which two parties are liable for the same account (for example, spouses who share an account). This Members table has a one-to-one relationship with both the Checking table and the Savings table. Some members listed in this table have only a checking account, some have only a savings account, and some have both checking and savings accounts.

## Queries

The database has only one query, MemberQuery. This query is a simple select query that displays the contents of all three tables with outer joins to show members who have only a checking or savings account in addition to members who have both checking and savings accounts.

## Forms

The ATM application includes three forms. The first form is the ATM form, which is shown in Figure 13-1.

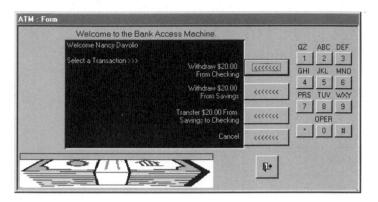

**Figure 13-1.** *The ATM form.*

This ATM form is designed to resemble the screen you would find on any ATM. The main difference here is that a user does not insert a card into the machine but instead enters an account number and a Personal Identification Number (PIN) to gain access to the machine. This is the form on which you will be doing most of your work in the exercises in this chapter. You will need to add functionality to the two Withdraw buttons as well as to the Transfer button. In the exercises in this chapter, you will use transaction processing and implement security so that customers who use the ATM form will have access only to their own personal data.

The next form, which appears in Figure 13-2, is the Bank Manager form. This form is used by the bank manager to add new tellers to the application. New tellers should be added only after security for the database has been implemented.

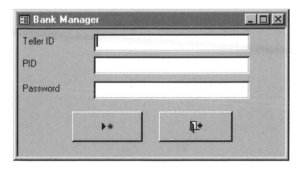

**Figure 13-2.** *The Bank Manager form.*

The last form, shown in Figure 13-3 on the following page, is the Member Administration form the bank tellers use to add new members and accounts.

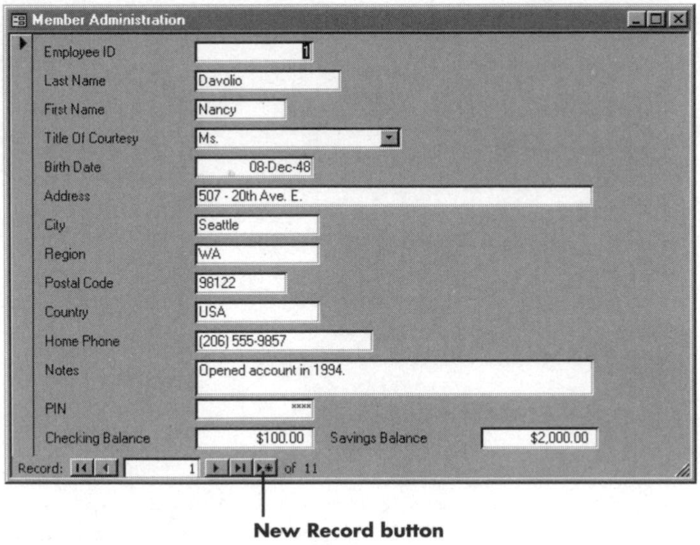

**New Record button**

**Figure 13-3.** *The Member Administration form.*

## Familiarizing Yourself with the Application

Take a few moments to familiarize yourself with the objects included in the database. Next, so that you can understand the tasks that need to be accomplished, try adding a user to the database as if you were a teller at the bank. To do this, open the Member Administration form, click the New Record button as shown in Figure 13-3, and add a user with the following name, address, and PIN:

> Mr. John Doe
> 123 Maple Street
> Nowhere, NA 12345
> PIN = 1234

Let's say that this customer is opening a checking account with $300.00. He is not opening a savings account.

Add yourself as the second user, depositing $100.00 in a savings account and $100.00 in a checking account. Next open the ATM form and enter your account number, which should be 13, and click the button to the left of where you enter your account number. Then enter the PIN number you selected when you entered yourself as the second user, and again click the button to the left of your entry.

The database already has the functionality built into it to make it look as if the ATM form is giving you money. To see how it works, select the Withdraw $20.00 From Checking button. The ATM cash drawer opens. Click the Money pile to remove the money. The drawer closes. Click the Close Form button (the button with the door on it). If you look at your record in the Member Administration form, you'll see that your account balance hasn't been updated.

## Transaction Processing

Now you will need to add functionality to the ATM form in order to update account balances. You will add this functionality to the three buttons shown in Figure 13-4.

**Figure 13-4.** *The ATM screen buttons.*

In this exercise you will add the functionality to the Withdraw $20.00 From Checking button.

To start, open the ATM form in Design view. Right-click the appropriate command button (SB1), and choose Build Event from the shortcut menu. You will see the following procedure:

```
Private Sub SB1_Click()
    open_door
End Sub
```

The open_door sub procedure opens the cash drawer.

In this procedure, you'll need to subtract $20.00 from the account of the user who was granted permission to retrieve the record based on his account number and PIN. You'll have to check the account balance to ensure that the account has $20.00 available and then display a message box with the balance before the withdrawal.

You will use three Access built-in procedures to complete these tasks: BeginTrans, Commit, and Rollback. A recordset is created when the user enters the account number and the PIN. The recordset is named rs and is a global variable defined in Module1. You will need to read a value from this recordset to determine whether the checking account contains at least $20.00. Read the value and store it in a variable. You will also want to disable all the transaction buttons so that they cannot be selected before the first transaction is completed.

Your result should look like the following:

```
Private Sub SB1_Click()
    Dim Current_Checking_Value As Currency
    If rs![checking.amount] >= 20 Then
        DBEngine.Workspaces(0).BeginTrans
        SB4.SetFocus
        SB1.Enabled = False
        SB2.Enabled = False
        SB3.Enabled = False
        Current_Checking_Value = rs![checking.amount]
        With rs
            .Edit
            rs![checking.amount] = rs![checking.amount] - 20
            .Update
        End With
        open_door
        MsgBox "Balance is " & Current_Checking_Value
    Else
        MsgBox "Insufficient Funds or " & _
               "You Do Not Have A Checking Account"
    End If
End Sub
```

The call to BeginTrans in this procedure starts a transaction that will later have to be committed or rolled back. You want to commit this transaction when someone clicks the Money pile to take the money, so you can place the call to Commit in the Click event of the Money pile. You can place the call to Rollback in the Click event of the Cancel button. Change the Money pile procedure first by adding the Commit statement to the last line in the procedure. Also enable the other command buttons in this procedure. The following code shows the result:

```
Private Sub Image57_Click()
    Image57.Visible = False
    Do While Box47.Height <= Box58.Height
        Box47.Height = Box47.Height + 10
        DoEvents
    Loop
    Image57.Visible = True
    DBEngine.Workspaces(0).CommitTrans
    SB1.enabled = True
    SB2.enabled = True
    SB3.enabled = True
End Sub
```

Now add the Rollback statement to the Click event of the Cancel button. You will also have to add an On Error statement in the event that someone clicks Cancel without first creating a transaction. Add the following lines to the end of the SB4_Click procedure:

```
On Error Resume Next
DBEngine.Workspaces(0).Rollback
SB1.Enabled = True
SB2.Enabled = True
SB3.Enabled = True
```

It's time to test the procedure. Using account number 1, whose PIN is 1234, withdraw $20.00 from checking. After completing this transaction, try again. You'll notice that the checking account contains only $80.00, which verifies that the first $20.00 was successfully removed. Now click the Cancel button after selecting the Withdraw button. Go back into the account, and click the Withdraw button again. You'll see that the balance is still $80.00, which verifies that the second transaction was rolled back.

Finally, you must test for multiuser situations. A lock could occur if another user is trying to use the same account at another ATM. (This could happen in a joint account: each user would have his or her own ATM card.) To see this type of locking, do the following:

1. Open the Checking table, and change the balance to $20.00 for Nancy Davolio, who has account number 1.

2. Close the table, and open the ATM form.

3. Enter account number 1 and 1234 for the PIN, and select the Withdraw $20.00 From Checking button.

4. Start a second instance of Microsoft Access from the Start menu, and open the same database you are currently working on.

5. Open the ATM form in the second instance of Access, log on again as account number 1 with PIN 1234, and attempt to withdraw $20.00 from the checking account. You will receive an Access error indicating that the table is locked. Close the second instance of Access.

Now we'll see how to accommodate multiuser situations by trapping the table-locked error. The error handler must reevaluate the checking account balance in case the first user changed the account balance. It can then recursively call the same procedure. Add the following changes to the SB1_Click procedure to implement the error trapping and handling.

```
Private Sub SB1_Click()
    On Error GoTo multiuser1
    Dim Current_Checking_Value As Currency
    Dim Response
    If rs![checking.amount] >= 20 Then
        DBEngine.Workspaces(0).BeginTrans
        SB4.SetFocus
        SB1.Enabled = False
        SB2.Enabled = False
        SB3.Enabled = False
        Current_Checking_Value = rs![checking.amount]
        With rs
            .Edit
            rs![checking.amount] = rs![checking.amount] - 20
            .Update
        End With
        open_door
        MsgBox "Balance is " & Current_Checking_Value
    Else
        MsgBox "Insufficient Funds or " & _
                "You Do Not Have A Checking Account"
    End If
    Exit Sub
multiuser1:
    If Err.Number = 3260 Then
        DBEngine.Workspaces(0).Rollback
        Response = MsgBox("Another ATM is using " & _
            "this account; try again?", vbYesNo)
        If Response = vbYes Then
            rs.Requery
            SB1_Click
        End If
        Exit Sub
    End If
End Sub
```

After completing and saving these changes, repeat steps 1–5 on page 455. You will receive the database locked message box instead of the Access error. Return to the first instance of Access, and click OK in the message box that displays the current balance of the checking account. Commit the transaction by clicking the Money pile. Now go back to the second instance of Access and retry. You will see that your code has correctly handled the two withdrawals because it displays an Insufficient Funds message box. As another experiment, repeat steps 1–5 on page 455, but this time allow the second user to get the funds by canceling the first user's transaction instead of clicking the Money pile.

## Withdraw from Savings

Now that you have successfully withdrawn money from checking accounts, you can copy the code in the SB1_Click procedure to the SB2_Click procedure to withdraw money from savings accounts. Simply modify the code to use the Savings field instead of the Checking field. Pay special attention to field names.

```
Private Sub SB2_Click()
    On Error GoTo multiuser2
    Dim Current_Savings_Value As Currency
    Dim Response
    If rs![savings.amount] >= 20 Then
        DBEngine.Workspaces(0).BeginTrans
        SB4.SetFocus
        SB1.Enabled = False
        SB2.Enabled = False
        SB3.Enabled = False
        Current_Savings_Value = rs![savings.amount]
        With rs
            .Edit
            rs![savings.amount] = rs![savings.amount] - 20
            .Update
        End With
        open_door
        MsgBox "Balance is " & Current_Savings_Value
    Else
        MsgBox "Insufficient Funds or " & _
                "You Do Not Have A Savings Account"
    End If
    Exit Sub
multiuser2:
    If Err.Number = 3260 Then
        DBEngine.Workspaces(0).Rollback
        Response = MsgBox("Another ATM is using " & _
            "this account; try again?", vbYesNo)
        If Response = vbYes Then
            rs.Requery
            SB2_Click ' Make sure you change this line, or you will
                      ' invoke the wrong procedure.
        End If
        Exit Sub
    End If
End Sub
```

## Transfer from Savings to Checking

The procedure for transferring funds from savings to checking is a little bit different from the last two procedures, even though the same concept applies. The code used in the two preceding procedures will serve as a basis for this procedure, so go ahead and copy the code from the SB1_Click procedure to the SB3_Click procedure and make the changes shown in bold below. Your routine will need to do a little more testing to ensure that the customer has both a savings and a checking account. And of course you do not want the cash drawer opened since funds are being transferred but none are being received. So you will place your call to Commit right in the SB3_Click procedure.

```vb
Private Sub SB3_Click()
    On Error GoTo multiuser3
    Dim Current_Checking_Value As Currency
    Dim Current_Savings_Value As Currency
    Dim Response
    If rs![savings.amount] >= 20 And _
        Not IsNull(rs![checking.amount]) Then
        DBEngine.Workspaces(0).BeginTrans
        SB4.SetFocus
        SB1.Enabled = False
        SB2.Enabled = False
        SB3.Enabled = False
        Current_Checking_Value = rs![checking.amount]
        Current_Savings_Value = rs![savings.amount]
        With rs
            .Edit
            rs![savings.amount] = rs![savings.amount] - 20
            rs![checking.amount] = rs![checking.amount] + 20
            .Update
        End With
        DBEngine.Workspaces(0).CommitTrans
        SB1.Enabled = True
        SB2.Enabled = True
        SB3.Enabled = True
    Else
        MsgBox "Insufficient Funds or " & _
                "You Do Not Have Both A Checking " & _
                "And A Savings Account"
    End If
    Exit Sub
multiuser3:
    If Err.Number = 3260 Then
        DBEngine.Workspaces(0).Rollback
        Response = MsgBox("Another ATM is using " & _
            "this account; try again?", vbYesNo)
        If Response = vbYes Then
            rs.Requery
            SB3_Click
```

```
            End If
            Exit Sub
        End If
End Sub
```

In these last few exercises, we have covered some aspects of multiuser and transaction processing. In the next several exercises, we will examine how to implement security on the ATM application you just created.

# Implementing Microsoft Access Security

Our ATM application is rather unsecure. Any user could start the application, open one of the tables, and set the balance in her account to any amount she would like.

The bank in this exercise will have three types of users, each of which will have different levels of security: Bank Managers, Bank Tellers, and Customers. There will also be you the developer, and of course you will have full permission to all objects in the database.

## Back Up Your Database

The first step in adding security to your database is to make a backup of the file that you were using in the preceding exercise.

## Create a Workgroup

In the same folder in which you installed your companion CD files, create a Workgroup information file to be used with this database. This will let you switch back to the default Workgroup (SYSTEM.MDW) when you open files that are not secured.

To create the Workgroup, start Windows Explorer and change to your Windows SYSTEM folder. Double-click the file WRKGADM.EXE, which is the Workgroup Administrator program. Then click the Create button. Add your name and organization. For the Workgroup ID, enter *Chapter13*. Then click the OK button.

Now click the Browse button, and switch to the folder in which the database you've been working with is stored. Enter ATM.MDW as the filename. Click the OK button to change the text box in the Workgroup Information File dialog box to that directory, and then choose OK. You will need to choose OK again to confirm the folder, or choose the Change button to select a different one. A dialog box informing you of a successful creation of the new Workgroup information file will appear. Click OK again. You can now select the Exit button to close the Workgroup Administrator program. When you restart Microsoft Access, you will be joined to the new Workgroup information file.

If you want to rejoin the default SYSTEM.MDW file, restart WRKGADM.EXE, select the Join button, click the Browse button, and change to your Windows SYSTEM folder. Then select the SYSTEM.MDW file. Do not rejoin the SYSTEM.MDW file now, however, because we will be modifying the new Workgroup information file for the remainder of this chapter.

## Restart Microsoft Access

If you had Microsoft Access running when you changed workgroups, you will need to restart it for the change to take effect. This is always the case, whether you have created a new Workgroup or simply joined an existing one, because the location of the SYSTEM.MDW file is stored in the Registry and is read only when a new instance of Access is started.

So now restart Microsoft Access to effect the change. After restarting Access, you must assign a password to the Admin user so that Access will prompt you to log on. At the same time, you can create a new user named Developer, add that user to the Admins group, and remove the Admin user from the Admins group. Then exit and restart Microsoft Access, logging on as the new user (Developer). Set the password for the Developer user as "dev."

**NOTE** Passwords are case-sensitive, so make sure you do not have Caps Lock on when you enter your password. When you are still in the development stage, it's fine to use a short password because you're likely to be starting and restarting Microsoft Access a lot. Just before you ship your application, however, we strongly recommend that you use as long a password as possible. The maximum length is 14 characters. The password can be a combination of strings and numbers, and it is a good idea to use both. This password is the only method you have for protecting your database design.

Open the database you've been working with. Choose Security from the Tools menu, and then select User-Level Security Wizard. When the wizard starts, you'll be prompted to select the objects you want to secure; leave all objects selected, and click OK. You'll now be prompted for the name of the new database. Type *SecurATM.mdb*, and click Save. The last dialog box confirms that security has been implemented on your database. Open the new, secured database.

## Add the Users

Bank Managers will have read/write permissions for all objects. They will not be able to modify any of the objects, however. For example, they cannot open a table in Design view and add a new field. Bank Tellers will have permissions only to open the Member Administration form. They will not be able to open any of the tables directly. In this exercise, however, they will be able to open the query, which includes all the data from the tables. We use this example so that you can see the operation of a query with its Run Permissions property set to Owner's.

In the bank application, several situations will occur in which you will need to decide who has permissions and for what objects and who can perform what actions against various tables. You could add permissions for every user. The easier method, however, is to create groups, assign permissions for each group, and then add users to those groups.

## Create Groups

Create two groups using the group name for the Personal ID (PID); that is, add the group Managers with the PID "Managers" and the group Tellers with the PID "Tellers."

## Set Permissions

The table below displays all the objects in the database and indicates which group gets assigned which permissions. Notice that we did not create a Customers group. All users joined to the Workgroup, by default, will have the permissions defined for the Users group. The Users group will have permissions to open only one object, the ATM form.

Set all of the permissions in the following table.

| Object | Managers | Tellers | Users |
|---|---|---|---|
| Table: Members | Read Design<br>Read, Update, Insert, Delete Data | | |
| Table: Savings | Read Design<br>Read, Update, Insert, Delete Data | | |
| Table: Checking | Read Design<br>Read, Update, Insert, Delete Data | | |
| Query: MemberQuery | Read Design<br>Read, Update, Insert, Delete Data | | |
| Form: ATM | | | Open/Run |
| Form: Member Administration | Open/Run | Open/Run | |
| Form: Bank Manager | Open/Run | | |
| Module: Module1 | None | None | None |

## Assign Users to Groups

In the following sections, we'll see how to add users and assign them to the appropriate groups. In the following table, all users have been assigned to the Users group.

| Group | Managers | Tellers | Users |
|-------|----------|---------|-------|
| **User** | Bob | Mary | Customer |
| | | Kim | |
| | | Andy | |

Create the user Customer with the PID "Customer." You should not assign a password because all customers will use this user account to access the database. Next create the user Bob, and assign him the PID "Bob1." Add Bob as a member of the Managers group.

An application isn't secure until all accounts are assigned a password. Typically, you would generate some random password for each new account and give the password to the user, instructing him or her to change it the first time he or she logs on. You need to log on as the user to assign this initial password. Adding users with this method could become tedious, especially if you have numerous users to add. In the next section, you'll learn how to add users using VBA code, and you'll add all of the tellers to the Tellers group in that fashion.

# Adding Users Using VBA

At times, many users might need to be added to the Workgroup, but you will not necessarily want to do this task as the developer. You will need someone else to administer the Workgroup in your place. The way to allow for such situations is to add these users through code. As we have seen, the bank manager does not have administrator privileges on this database; however, we will use code to let the bank manager log on as a user with the necessary privileges. Because our user Bob is the only user in the Managers group, and only the Managers group has permission to open the Bank Manager form, Bob will be the only user able to execute the code that adds tellers to the Workgroup.

If a new user needed to be added to the Managers group, there would be only two ways to add that user. Either the Developer user would have to add the new user, or you would have to assign Admin permissions to the Managers group and have some member of the Managers group add the user. Giving the Managers group Admin permission would make the database less secure because that would allow any member of the Managers group to modify the database. The easiest and most secure method is to log on a member of the Managers group as the Developer user through code in order to add new users. The code below shows how to add a user to the Tellers group; you could modify this code slightly if you wanted to add users to the Managers group instead of to the Tellers group.

You must add the following code to the Bank Manager form:

```
Private Sub Command4_Click()
    On Error GoTo Err_Command4_Click
    Dim UserName, UserPID, UserPW
    Dim W As Workspace, New_User As User

    UserName = Me![Teller ID]
    UserPID = Me!PID
    UserPW = Me!Password

    DBEngine.SystemDB = "ATM.MDW"

    Set W = CreateWorkspace("TempDeveloperLogin", _
            "Developer", "dev", dbUseJet)
    Workspaces.Append W

    Set New_User = W.CreateUser(UserName)
    New_User.PID = UserPID
    New_User.Password = UserPW
    W.Users.Append New_User

    Set New_User = _
                W.Groups("Users").CreateUser(UserName)
                W.Groups("Users").Users.Append New_User

    Set New_User = _
                W.Groups("Teller").CreateUser(UserName)
                W.Groups("Teller").Users.Append New_User

    MsgBox "User Successfully Added"

    Me![Teller ID] = ""
    Me!PID = ""
    Me!Password = ""

    Exit Sub

Err_Command4_Click:
    MsgBox Err.Description
    Exit Sub
End Sub
```

You have completed the form to enable the bank manager to add tellers to the Workgroup. But before a teller can open the Member Administration form, he or she will need permission to run the query. So open MemberQuery in Design view, click the Properties toolbar button, and change the Run Permissions property to Owner's, as shown in Figure 13-5.

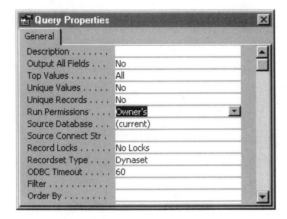

**Figure 13-5.** *The Query Properties sheet.*

Now log on as Bob, and use the Bank Manager form to add the following three tellers.

| Teller ID | PID | Password |
|-----------|---------|----------|
| Mary | Teller1 | Mary |
| Kim | Teller2 | Kim |
| Andy | Teller3 | Andy |

Close the form and restart Microsoft Access, logging on as Developer.

## The Customer

Because security has been implemented on the database, the ATM form will not work—the customer does not have a logon ID. To get around this, simply apply the same concept to the ATM form that we did to the bank manager: have the customer log on through code.

To enable this, you will need to modify the Init_data procedure in Module1 to appear as follows:

```
Sub Init_data()
    Dim dblocation As String
    dblocation = CurrentDb().Name

    DBEngine.SystemDB = "ATM.MDW"

    Set w = CreateWorkspace("TempDeveloperLogin", _
        "Developer", "dev", dbUseJet)
    Workspaces.Append w
    Set db = w.OpenDatabase(dblocation)

    sql = "SELECT Members.[Member ID], Members.PIN, " & _
            "Members.LastName, Members.FirstName, " & _
            "Members.TitleOfCourtesy, Members.BirthDate, " & _
            "Members.Address, Members.City, Members.Region, " & _
            "Members.PostalCode, Members.Country, " & _
            "Members.HomePhone, Members.Notes, Savings.Amount, " & _
            "Checking.Amount " & _
        "FROM (Members LEFT JOIN Checking " & _
            "ON Members.[Member ID] = Checking.[Member ID]) " & _
              "LEFT JOIN Savings " & _
                "ON Members.[Member ID] = Savings.[Member ID] " & _
        "WHERE (Members.[Member ID] = " & _
            [Forms]![atm]![txtAccountNumber] & ") AND " & _
            "(Members.PIN = " & [Forms]![atm]![txtPIN] & ");"

    Set rs = db.OpenRecordset(sql)
End Sub
```

In addition, before executing the code, you will need to add

```
Global w as Workspace
```

to the General Declarations section of Module1.

Close and reopen Access, and log on as one of the tellers. Open the ATM form, and perform a transaction. Enter account number 1 and PIN 1234. Note that, even though this user does not have permissions to the application's tables or query, you can still perform the transaction.

Now that security has been applied to the database, how will the customer access the ATM form? She can simply log on to Access as the Customer user without entering a password.

## Splitting the Database

Now that you have completed the application and secured it, you need to consider how to ensure that your application performs at the highest level possible. In its current state, the database would need to be in a shared folder on a network, and everyone who used it would have to open it from that share point. To avoid this situation, we recommend that you have a Data database with just the data tables and an Application database that contains all the queries, forms, and code and that links to all the tables in the Data database. You can create such a database by hand or by using the Database Splitter wizard. This wizard is very useful, especially if you have a database with many tables and relationships, because it also re-creates all the table relationships for you. In addition, it keeps all the security attributes for you.

## Run the Wizard

In this exercise, you will split the database using the Database Splitter wizard. To do this, follow these steps:

1. Restart Microsoft Access, and log on as the Developer user.

2. Open the SECURATM.MDB file.

3. Choose Add-Ins from the Tools menu, and then select Database Splitter. You will see the dialog box shown here:

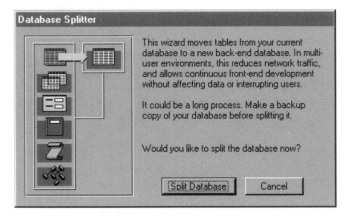

4. Choose the Split Database button.

5. From the Create Back-End Database dialog box, enter *ATMData.mdb* and select the Split button.

6. Select the Tables tab in the Database window to see all of the linked tables.

You have successfully split the database. In the following section, you will learn how to distribute this secure solution.

# Distributing the Secure Solution

Now that you have split your application into Data and Application databases, you will have to load these files on other machines. This brings up an interesting issue: the tables on each user's machine will not be in the folder to which the Database Splitter linked the Data database. In fact, you cannot be sure in which drive or folder the user will place them. First let's simulate the problem.

1. In the directory where you placed the ATMDATA.MDB file, create a new folder named Data.

2. Move (do not copy) the ATMDATA.MDB file to this folder.

3. Now try to open a linked table in the SECURATM.MDB file by double-clicking on it. You will receive an error stating that the .MDB file cannot be found.

In the next section, you will see how to work around this problem, not only when the user first installs the application but also if he or she ever moves the Data database.

# Relinking Tables

In this section you will create the code to relink the tables when a user first installs the application. You will use VBA code to complete this task and to properly apply the security permissions you need to relink the tables. Keep in mind that you need to have Administrator or Owner permission to relink the tables and that you will not be sure which user has just installed the application. The bank manager, a teller, or a customer could have installed it.

## Create a Startup Form

You will first have to have a place from which to execute this code. If you create a startup form for the application, you can execute this code while the startup form is being displayed. A startup form will distract the user while the task of relinking the tables is completed.

Start a second instance of Microsoft Access, and open the SOLUTIONS.MDB file that comes with Microsoft Access. Select Sample Forms from the Select A Category Of Examples list, and then select Startup from the Select An Example list. Click OK. You will be prompted with step-by-step instructions for creating a startup form. Follow the steps to create a startup form in the SECURATM.MDB database.

Once you have created a startup form, you will need to add code in order to relink the tables. The Solutions database that comes with Microsoft Access also has an example that demonstrates how to physically relink tables. To view this example in the Solutions database, select Use Multiple Databases from the Select A Category Of Examples list and then select Link Tables At Startup from the Select An Example list. Click OK, and then choose the Linking Tables At Startup topic in the Show Me help screen.

Read the steps in the Solutions database for relinking the Northwind Traders tables. The easiest way to use this example in your own application is to copy the necessary code from the Solutions database and paste it to your ATM application. After placing the code in the ATM application, you'll need to modify the code so that it corresponds to the ATM application and not to the Northwind Traders application.

The code from the Solutions database example will relink the tables if you are the owner of the database. Keep in mind, however, that the user will not have permission to relink the tables in the ATM database, so your code will need to log on the user as the developer to relink them. You will need to create a new workspace to do this:

```
Set W = CreateWorkspace("TempDeveloperLogin", _
        "Developer", "dev", dbUseJet)
```

After modifying the code, execute it and locate the Data folder in the Open File dialog box. The database will now work as it did when everything was in one folder.

## Securing Your Code

Microsoft Access 97 includes a new feature that allows you to protect your code without having to implement full user-level security: an .MDE file. To show you how an .MDE file works, we'll make one using the Northwind Traders database.

Before making an .MDE file, you should always make a backup of the .MDB file. After you have backed up the Northwind Traders database, open the database. Choose Database Utilities from the Tools menu, and then select Make MDE File. Select a new filename, and click OK. The new file will have an .MDE extension by default. Close the database, and open the new .MDE file. Notice that you can't open any forms, reports, or modules in Design view.

### PREVIEW of the next chapter

In the next two chapters you'll discover how to work with ActiveX Controls and the Internet. We will introduce you to the Internet features of Microsoft Access and show you how to extend your application to the Internet. As the popularity of the Internet continues to grow, your need to develop Internet-aware applications will increase.

# PART

# FOUR

## Using ActiveX and the Internet

# 14

# Using ActiveX with Microsoft Access

As you are well aware, Microsoft Access is an extremely flexible and capable product all by itself. However, other Microsoft products are better suited for particular tasks. For example, Microsoft Word is better than Access for printing form letters. Using Microsoft's ActiveX technology, however, you can enhance the capabilities of Access by drawing on the strengths of other Microsoft products.

ActiveX is Microsoft's name for the technologies that enable product interoperability using the Component Object Model (COM). Previously, this technology was referred to as OLE (Object Linking and Embedding). OLE is now a subset of ActiveX.

The main purpose of ActiveX is to allow applications to interoperate more effectively and seamlessly. Applications such as Word or Microsoft Excel can supply objects to other applications such as Microsoft Access. This capability allows you to create and maintain documents that can include many differently formatted items. In this chapter we will focus on the top-level classes of objects exposed by Microsoft Excel, Word, and Microsoft PowerPoint. We will discuss how to manipulate instances of these classes from within a Microsoft Access database.

**NOTE** In this chapter, "application" generally refers to a Microsoft product. "User interface" means an application that you develop using a Microsoft Office product.

# What Is Automation?

Automation is a feature of ActiveX that enables you to access and manipulate another application's objects from outside that application. The objects that an application exposes are called Automation objects. Different applications expose different objects. Microsoft Excel exposes, for example, worksheet, chart, and cell range objects; Word exposes, for example, document, paragraph, and sentence objects.

Automation objects can be accessed only by using a programming language such as Visual Basic for Applications (VBA). When you develop a user interface that uses Automation, the Automation objects typically are not visible to the user of your interface; they are used mostly to automate repetitive tasks or tasks that don't require user interaction.

When you use an ActiveX control, the application that exposes the Automation object is called the *object* or *server* application, and the application that contains the ActiveX object is called the *container* or *client* application. For example, if you have a Microsoft Excel spreadsheet embedded in a Microsoft Access form, Excel is the server application and Access is the client application.

# Why Use Automation?

Using Automation objects gives you the ability to create applications centered around a particular type of document. That is, you can create a user interface in the application on which your interface depends most heavily but that uses objects from several different applications. This can save you a lot of development time because you won't have to reinvent the wheel to implement a feature that's included only in an application other than the one in which you are creating your user interface. When working with Automation objects, keep in mind the following "rules":

- Automation objects are created and supplied by ActiveX servers (such as Word, Microsoft Excel, PowerPoint, and even Microsoft Access).

- Automation objects must be declared using both information indicating the application to which the Automation object "belongs" and the object's class type.

- An object variable in the client application contains a *reference* to an object, not the object itself.

- When an object variable goes out of scope, the reference to the object is lost, so you can no longer use that variable to manipulate the object.

# How to Automate Applications

Using any VBA application, such as Microsoft Access, you can create Automation objects using one of two functions: CreateObject and GetObject. Although both of these functions will provide a reference to an Automation object, they have some important differences.

## The CreateObject Function

The CreateObject function will create a reference to a new Automation object. This function has one parameter, a character string that indicates the application name as well as the type of object to be created. Some applications, such as Microsoft Excel, support multiple types of objects. For example, to create a new Excel worksheet in Microsoft Access, you could use the following line of code:

```
Dim XL As Object
Set XL = CreateObject("Excel.Sheet")
```

When this line of code is executed, the specified application is started and an object is created. The object is part of the server application. For example, the worksheet is part of Microsoft Excel but may be manipulated via the object variable that references it in the client application. The following code, which will place "Hello World!" in bold in the first row and column of the new worksheet, shows how this works:

```
Dim XL As Object
Set XL = CreateObject("Excel.Sheet")
XL.Cells(1,1).Value = "Hello World!"
XL.Cells(1,1).Font.Bold = True
```

When using Automation, you can hide the manipulation of objects from the user of your interface. Like controls on a form, server applications have properties that control their appearance and environment. To hide a control on a form, you could set the control's Visible property to False. Typically, server applications provide an object named Application that controls the server application's environment. The Application object supports properties and methods native to the server application. The following example builds on the previous lines of code but makes Microsoft Excel visible at the end of the procedure:

```
Sub StartExcel()
    Dim XL As Object
    Set XL = CreateObject("Excel.Sheet")
    XL.Cells(1,1).Value = "Hello World!"
    XL.Cells(1,1).Font.Bold = True
    XL.Application.Visible = True
End Sub
```

## The GetObject Function

Many Automation applications allow you to save objects in a file. For example, Microsoft Excel allows you to save a workbook in a file. You can use the GetObject function to activate an object that has been saved in a file or to reference a server application that may already be running.

The GetObject function has two parameters, the second of which is optional. The first parameter is a character string that indicates the file's name and location. The second parameter is a character string that specifies the class of the object to be activated. The client application identifies both the server application and the object class based on the type of file specified in the first parameter. If the server application supports more than one class, however, you need to specify the class in the second parameter to ensure that the appropriate object is invoked. For example, the following line of code will set a reference to a worksheet in the SALES.XLS sample file:

```
Set XL = GetObject("C:\MSOffice\Excel\Examples\Sales.xls", _
                "Excel.Sheet")
```

Like the CreateObject function, GetObject will start the specified application. It then loads the appropriate file. Once the Automation object is created as an instance of that class, the object variable may be used to manipulate the object's properties or to invoke its methods.

To use an existing instance of a server application, simply omit the first parameter. If the server application is running, the object variable can be used to manipulate the existing instance of the application. If no instance of the server is running, a trappable error will be returned to Microsoft Access. For example, the following code will look for an instance of Microsoft Excel that is already running:

```
Dim XL As Object
Set XL = GetObject(,"Excel.Application")
```

When using Automation, you should try to use the least amount of memory you can so that your application will run as fast as possible. Therefore, you should try using the GetObject function first to see if the server application is already running. As a rule of thumb, you should close a server application that you started; if you used an existing instance, you should leave the application running. The following code shows how to close the Excel.Application automation server:

```
XL.Quit
```

## Object Libraries and References

In the above examples, we declared the object variable to be of type Object. Doing this is similar to using a Variant variable, because a variable of type Object can refer to any type of object at run time. To get better performance at run time, you should always define your variables as a specific type. For example, if you are going to be using Microsoft Excel, you might define your object variable to be of type Excel.Application. To create instances of ActiveX objects, you can also use the New keyword and object libraries rather than the CreateObject or GetObject functions.

An object library contains definitions of all the objects an application exposes, including definitions for all available methods and properties. To provide objects or an object library, applications must be registered in the system Registry. Registration typically occurs when an application is installed or when it is run for the first time. If an application provides an object library, just add a reference to it in the current database. To do so, choose References from the Tools menu while editing a module. The dialog box shown in Figure 14-1 will open.

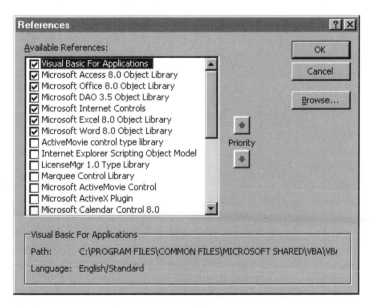

**Figure 14-1.** *The References dialog box.*

Locate the library you need in the dialog box, and select the check box to the left of its name. When referring to an object in code, VBA searches each library selected in the References dialog box in the order the libraries are displayed. If two applications use the same name for an object, VBA uses the definition provided by the library listed higher in the Available References box. To determine the methods and properties of objects stored in a library, use the Object Browser and select that particular library. You can also refer to the library's online Help and documentation.

**TIP**

You can add a reference with VBA by using the following code:

```
References.CreateFromFile(file)
```

Specify the filename and location of the appropriate .DLL file in the file argument. For example, use

C:\Windows\System\MSO97.DLL

to specify the Microsoft Office 8.0 Object Library. You can find out the path and DLL name by selecting the library in the References dialog box. You can check for the success of this code by seeing if the library is selected in the References dialog box.

## The New Keyword

You've already seen the New keyword used to create new instances of Microsoft Access forms and reports. You can also use it to create new instances of Automation objects. Once you add a reference to an object library, you can use the Dim and Set statements together to create a variable that refers to an object in that library. The New keyword is allowed only for objects that are created externally; dependent objects are accessed by using methods on higher-level objects, as discussed later in this chapter. An example of an object created externally would be the Excel Chart object. A dependent object would be a Label object. You could use the New keyword to create an instance of the Chart object, but you could not use it for a Label object because a Label object can't exist without a Chart object. The following code shows how to use the New keyword to create a new instance of a Word Document object after adding a reference to the Microsoft Word 8.0 Object Library:

```
Dim WrdDoc As New Word.Document
```

## The Macro Recorder

Before we jump into using object models, we need to discuss VBA's macro recorder. Microsoft Office 97 is a great suite of products for many reasons, but two big reasons stand out. One, all of the Office applications have moved to a similar interface and have essentially the same format in their object models. This makes it effortless for users to move among applications. The second reason to love Office 97 is that VBA is *everywhere*. VBA is used in all Office applications now, and as a result you need learn only one programming language. For example, if you are currently unfamiliar with the syntax needed to add a slide to your PowerPoint presentation using VBA, have no fear—you can use the macro recorder. The VBA code that the macro recorder produces should be easy for you to understand, even if you have never programmed using PowerPoint.

> **NOTE**  Microsoft Access is the only Office application that does not contain the macro recorder functionality—another great reason for using this book!

Using the macro recorder, you can perform the desired action using the interface and let the macro recorder convert those actions to VBA syntax. For example, if you want to know the VBA syntax needed to place a value into row 1 and column 1 of a Microsoft Excel worksheet, you can take the following steps once the worksheet is open:

1. In Excel, choose Macro from the Tools menu, and then select Record New Macro.

2. In the dialog box that appears, enter any name you want for this macro. The name you give your macro is the name of the VBA procedure that will be created. In this example, something like "NewCellValue" might be appropriate. Once you click OK, the Stop Recording toolbar will appear.

3. Select the cell for which you want to set a value in the worksheet, and then type in the value.

4. Click the Stop Recording button on the Stop Recording toolbar.

To see the resulting VBA syntax, follow these steps:

1. Choose Macro from the Tools menu, and then select Macros.

2. In the dialog box that appears, highlight NewCellValue and click the Edit button.

3. Voilà, the VBA syntax appears.

If you want to automate this application from another, you can simply copy and paste the code with only slight modifications. Keep in mind one thing when doing this: the macro recorder creates VBA code based implicitly on the Application object. Therefore, the syntax you use to manipulate Automation objects must be modified to start explicitly from the Application object. The Application object, which is discussed in the object models below, is the top-level object in all Office application environments.

Now that you know how to use the macro recorder, let's discuss automating some Office applications. We're not going to discuss the entire object hierarchy for each application, however, but just introduce you to various key objects. If we do not show you how to perform a specific task using Automation, don't worry—the macro recorder will give you the syntax.

The following sections describe the primary external objects for most Office 97 applications. For a complete list of externally createable objects, consult VBA Help for the appropriate application.

## Microsoft Excel Objects

Microsoft Excel exposes well over a hundred Automation objects that you can manipulate using VBA. Each of these objects encapsulates some aspect of Excel, such as charting or drawing. This section will focus on the top-level objects and how to create them. The diagram in Figure 14-2 depicts only a portion of the Excel object hierarchy. For a complete view, consult the Excel documentation.

> **NOTE**    As with the DAO hierarchy, all Automation object hierarchies can be traversed by using the dot(.) operator.

Objects in the Microsoft Excel hierarchy, which can be created using either the New keyword or the CreateObject or GetObject functions, are Application, Workbook, and Chart. These objects are the three main objects that will provide you with the means of achieving the results you want when manipulating Excel.

### Microsoft Excel's Application Object

The Application object represents the highest-level object in the Microsoft Excel object hierarchy. The other objects in the hierarchy exist only as subobjects of the Application object. You can use any of the methods discussed previously to create an instance of the Application object. For example, the following code uses the CreateObject function:

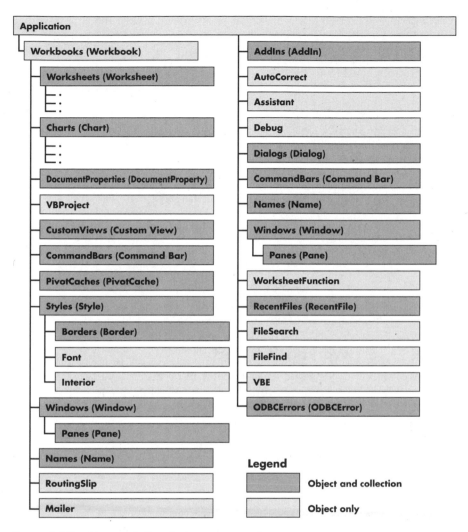

**Figure 14-2.** *Microsoft Excel object hierarchy.*

```
Sub StartExcel()
    Dim XL As Excel.Application
    Set XL = CreateObject("Excel.Application")
    XL.Visible = True
    XL.WorkBooks.Add
End Sub
```

This procedure will create a new instance of Microsoft Excel, make it visible to the user, and create a new workbook. When the procedure ends, you will notice that Excel is still running. With some Automation objects, you release an object variable by setting the variable to Nothing, which closes the object; but with Excel, you must first call the Quit method, as shown here:

```
Sub StartExcel()
    Dim XL As Excel.Application
    Set XL = CreateObject("Excel.Application")
    XL.Visible = True
    XL.WorkBooks.Add
    XL.Quit              ' Close Excel.
    Set XL = Nothing     ' Release object variable.
End Sub
```

> **TIP**  When using a server application that starts up invisibly, as Microsoft Excel does, immediately set its Visible property to True when testing your code. If you do not do so and an error occurs, you could be leaving multiple instances of Microsoft Excel running, which would slow down your system.

## Microsoft Excel's Workbook Object

Using the Workbook object, Microsoft Excel will create a new Workbook object called "Object" that contains worksheets and modules. You can then manipulate any of the objects within the Workbook object by referencing their properties and methods. Although using the Workbook object bypasses the Application object, you can still refer to the Application object, as the following code shows, so that Excel is visible:

```
Sub NewWorkbook()
    Dim XL As Excel.Workbook
    Set XL = CreateObject("Excel.Sheet")
    XL.Application.Visible = True  ' Make Excel Visible.
    XL.ActiveSheet.Cells(1,1).Value = "Hello World!"
End Sub
```

> **NOTE**  When using Excel.Sheet to create an instance of an Excel Sheet object, you must define the object variable to be of type Excel.Workbook because the Excel.Sheet class returns an instance of a Workbook object.

This code creates a new Microsoft Excel workbook and adds the character string "Hello World!" to the first cell in the first worksheet. Once this procedure ends, Excel is closed. If you want to save the workbook, use the SaveAs method of the Workbook object, as in the following code example:

```
Sub NewWorkbook()
    Dim XL As Excel.Workbook
    Set XL = CreateObject("Excel.Sheet")
    XL.Application.Visible = True   ' Make Excel Visible.
    XL.ActiveSheet.Cells(1,1).Value = "Hello World!"
    XL.SaveAs FileName:="C:\My Documents\MyBook.XLS"
End Sub
```

## Microsoft Excel's Chart Object

The Chart object in Microsoft Excel represents a graphical chart as might exist within a workbook or on a worksheet. This object is created externally and is dependent. The following code can be used to create a new chart based on values added to a worksheet:

```
Sub CreateChart()
    Dim XL As New Excel.Application
    Dim XLChart As Excel.Chart
    XL.Visible = True
    XL.Workbooks.Add
    XL.Range("A1").Value = 3
    XL.Range("A2").Value = 2
    XL.Range("A1:A2").Select
    Set XLChart = XL.Charts.Add
    XLChart.Type = xl3DColumn    ' Reference library for value.
End Sub
```

**NOTE**  With Automation objects, you can implicitly reference the default objects in the object hierarchy just as you can with Access's own objects. This is demonstrated in the code above. For example, the line

```
XL.Range("A1").Value = 3
```

could be written explicitly as

```
XL.Workbooks(1).Sheets(1).Range("A1").Value = 3
```

**Executing Microsoft Excel Macros (Procedures)**

When using Automation, each call you make to control an object takes time—time to communicate the request between applications and then time to execute the request. If you are inserting several values or repeating tasks on a worksheet, you should consider using a Microsoft Excel macro because you will increase the performance of your application. To execute the macro, you would simply make one Automation call and Excel will do the rest of the work. For example, suppose the following macro exists in a workbook called MyBook.XLS:

```
Sub ChangeValues()
    For Each c In Worksheets("Sheet1").Range("A1:D10")
        c.Value = Rnd() * 100
    Next c
End Sub
```

To run this macro from Microsoft Access, you would use the following code:

```
Sub RunMacro()
    Dim XL As Excel.Workbook
    Set XL = GetObject("C:\Accsol\Chap14\MyBook.XLS", "Excel.Sheet")
    ' Make Excel Visible.
    XL.Application.Visible = True
    ' Make the Workbook visible.
    XL.Application.Windows("MyBook.XLS").Visible = True
    XL.Application.Run "ChangeValues"
End Sub
```

The end result would be the same if you replaced

```
XL.Application.Run "ChangeValues"
```

with

```
Dim c As Excel.Range
For Each c In XL.Worksheets("Sheet1").Range("A1:d10")
    c.Value = Rnd() * 100
Next c
```

but the performance would be much slower because each iteration of the For...Next loop makes an Automation call to Microsoft Excel.

# Microsoft Word Objects

Microsoft Word 97's object model has changed extensively from previous versions; Word has now become a member of the VBA family. Previously, you could create an instance of only the Word.Basic object. This gave you some flexibility, but you were essentially limited using Automation because it was built on the Word Basic macro language rather than on VBA. The Word object model is shown in Figure 14-3.

**Figure 14-3.** *Microsoft Word object model.*

Objects in the Word hierarchy, which can be created using either the New keyword or the CreateObject or GetObject functions, are Application, Basic, and Document. We will discuss only the Application object here, because using the other two objects does not provide the greatest flexibility. More than likely, you'll use the Document object in conjunction with the GetObject function when opening a specific document. If you want information on these objects, check Microsoft Word VBA Help.

## Word's Application Object

In an effort to standardize object models, Word uses the Application object as its highest-level object in the hierarchy. As with Microsoft Excel, you can use the New keyword or the CreateObject or GetObject functions to obtain a reference to Word. The following function demonstrates how to check whether Word is running and, if so, get a reference to it; if Word is not running, this function starts it:

```
Sub StartWord()
    On Error GoTo Err_StartWord
    Dim wrd As Word.Application, IsRunning As Boolean

    IsRunning = True
    Set wrd = GetObject(, "Word.Application")
    wrd.Visible = True
    ' Perform other tasks.
    ⋮
    If IsRunning = False Then   ' If Word was started, close it.
        wrd.Quit
    End If
    Exit Sub
Err_StartWord:
    If Err.Number = 429 Then    ' Word is not running.
        Set wrd = CreateObject("Word.Application")
        IsRunning = False
        Resume Next
    Else
        MsgBox Err.Number & " " & Err.Description
        Exit Sub
    End If
End Sub
```

Like Microsoft Excel, when the above procedure finishes, Word is left open by default. This is why the variable IsRunning is used. With it, you can keep track of whether the procedure opened Word or whether the procedure was already running. If the procedure opened Word, the Quit method is called and Word shuts down.

## Printing a Word document

Two tasks that are well-suited to using Word as a server application are printing a document and performing a mail merge. Printing a document is very easy in Word using Automation. Just follow these steps:

**1.** Obtain a reference to Word.

**2.** Open the document to print.

**3.** Print the document.

**4.** Exit Word.

The following code demonstrates how to do this:

```
Sub PrintDocument()
    Dim wrd As Word.Application

    Set wrd = Word.Application
    wrd.Visible = True     ' Not necessary
    wrd.Documents.Open FileName:="C:\Accsol\Chap14\TEST.DOC"
    wrd.ActiveDocument.PrintOut
    Do While wrd.BackGroundPrintingStatus <> 0
        DoEvents     ' Let Word print the document.
    Loop
    wrd.Quit
End Sub
```

## Printing a mail merge document

Microsoft Access is a great repository for holding any kind of data you want to store: data about customers, about friends, or about anything else. However, a word processor it is not. But don't worry: Word and Microsoft Access work together to give you the capabilities of a word processor that works with your data. Using Microsoft Access, you can easily create a new mail merge document in Word by clicking the down arrow on the OfficeLinks toolbar button and selecting Merge It With MS Word, which invokes the Word Mail Merge wizard.

Once you have a mail merge document saved in a file, you can open and manipulate it just like any other document in Word. To print a mail merge document from Microsoft Access using Automation, use the following code:

```
Sub PrintMergeDoc()
    Dim wrd As Word.Application
    Dim MyMerge As Word.MailMerge

    Set wrd = Word.Application
    wrd.Visible = True  ' Not necessary, only to show effect
```

*(continued)*

```
    wrd.Documents.Open FileName:="C:\Accsol\Chap14\Merge.doc"
    Set MyMerge = wrd.ActiveDocument.MailMerge
    If MyMerge.State = wdMainAndDataSource Then
        With MyMerge
            .DataSource.FirstRecord = 1
            .DataSource.LastRecord = 2
            .Destination = wdSendToPrinter
            .Execute
        End With
        Do While wrd.BackgroundPrintingStatus <> 0
            DoEvents    ' Let Word print the document.
        Loop
    End If
    wrd.ActiveDocument.Close SaveChanges:=False
    wrd.Quit
End Sub
```

Notice that a separate MailMerge object is created. This is done only to reduce the number of Automation calls Microsoft Access has to make, which increases this procedure's performance. By setting the MailMerge object to a local variable, manipulated using the With...End With construct, the variable MyMerge is evaluated only once. Running the above function will print the results of the merged document.

# Microsoft PowerPoint Objects

Microsoft PowerPoint is the ultimate presentation package. It allows you to create colorful, animated presentations. Each presentation that you create in PowerPoint is based on a set of slides, and you will notice that the object hierarchy, which is shown in Figure 14-4, follows this same paradigm. Using Automation, you are able to manipulate the presentations and slides using code in the same way you manipulate the slides in PowerPoint.

The Application object in the PowerPoint hierarchy is the only object that can be created using the New keyword or the CreateObject or GetObject functions.

## PowerPoint's Application Object

Again, the Application object is the top-level object. Accessing this object gives you the capability to open presentations, manipulate the environment, and even run slide shows. The following code uses the Application object to open a presentation and run it.

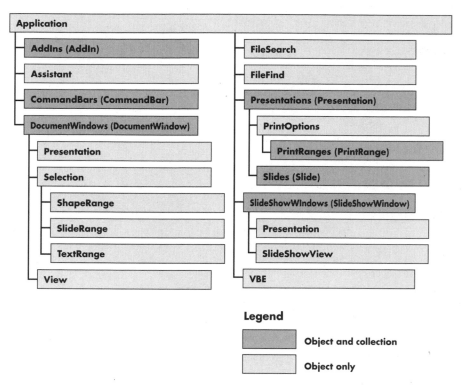

**Legend**

|  | Object and collection |
|--|----------------------|
|  | Object only |

**Figure 14-4.** *Microsoft PowerPoint object model.*

```
Sub StartPPoint()
    Dim ppt As PowerPoint.Application

    Set ppt = CreateObject("PowerPoint.Application")
    ppt.Visible = True
    ppt.Presentations.Open Filename:="C:\Accsol\Chap14\TEST.PPT"
    ppt.ActivePresentation.SlideShowSettings.Run
End Sub
```

Fortunately, when the above procedure has finished, the slide show is still running full screen. If you are using Automation from Microsoft Access to PowerPoint and you are manipulating a presentation, you might want to exit PowerPoint before leaving your function. You do this in the same way as with the other object models: by using the Quit method of the Application object.

### Adding a new slide to a presentation

The following procedure demonstrates how to add a slide to a presentation using data from a Microsoft Access database.

```
Sub CreateASlide()
    Dim ppt As PowerPoint.Application
    Dim db As Database, rs As Recordset
    Dim Msg As String, i As Integer

    Set db = CurrentDb
    Set rs = db.OpenRecordset _
        ("Ten Most Expensive Products", dbOpenSnapshot)
    ' Move to the first record.
    rs.MoveFirst
    ' Start a new instance of PowerPoint.
    Set ppt = CreateObject("PowerPoint.Application")
    ppt.Visible = True
    ' Open a presentation.
    ppt.Presentations.Open Filename:="C:\Accsol\Chap14\TEST.PPT"
    ' Add a new slide to the presentation.
    ppt.ActivePresentation.Slides.Add _
        Index:=2, Layout:=ppLayoutText
    ' Change the slide view so that
    ' the new slide can be selected.
    With ppt.ActiveWindow
        .ViewType = ppViewSlideSorter
        .Presentation.Slides.Range(Array(2)).Select
        .ViewType = ppViewSlide
    End With
    ' Modify the title and text of the new slide.
    With ppt.ActiveWindow
        .Selection.SlideRange.Shapes("Rectangle 2").Select
        .Selection.TextRange.Text = _
            "Our Three Most Expensive Products"
        .Selection.SlideRange.Shapes("Rectangle 3").Select
        For i = 1 To 3
            Msg = Msg & rs(0) & Chr(9) & rs(1) & vbCr
            rs.MoveNext
        Next i
        .Selection.TextRange.Text = Msg
    End With
    rs.Close    ' Close the recordset.
    db.Close    ' Close the database.
    ppt.ActivePresentation.Save   ' Save the presentation.
    ppt.Quit                      ' Close PowerPoint.
End Sub
```

# Microsoft Access Objects

To automate common database tasks, Microsoft Access can be driven from any Automation controlling application, including Microsoft Excel, Microsoft Visual Basic, and Word. This means that if you build an application based on a product other than Microsoft Access, you can still take advantage of Microsoft Access's impressive functionality such as the Access reporting facility. The Microsoft Access object model is shown in Figure 14-5.

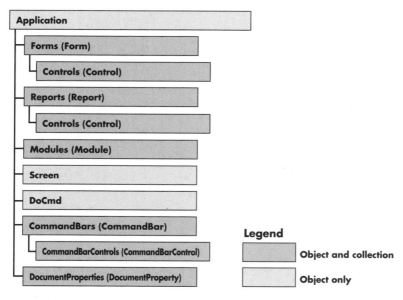

**Figure 14-5.** *Microsoft Access object model.*

Microsoft Access exposes only one external object, the Application object. To control Microsoft Access via Automation, you can create an instance of the Application object and manipulate it by accessing its properties and methods.

> **NOTE** Although Microsoft Access can be an ActiveX client (an ActiveX controlling application) and an ActiveX server application, it cannot be used as an embedded object within another application. For example, a Microsoft Access database cannot be embedded into an ActiveX client such as Microsoft Excel.

## Microsoft Access's Application Object

To create an instance of Microsoft Access using code, an application can call CreateObject or GetObject or use the New keyword, with Access.Application as the class name. One benefit Microsoft Access offers that other Office applications do not is a great report generator. For example, users often want to print the contents of a table. This can be done from within Microsoft Access or by using Access as a server application.

### Printing a Microsoft Access report

To use Microsoft Access as a server application to print a report, open any Automation controller application. As an example, let's do it in Microsoft Excel. In a new module in Excel, add a reference to the Microsoft Access 8.0 Object Library. Add the following function to the module, but wait to run it until after you've added another routine to the Northwind Traders sample database:

```
Sub StartAccess()
    Dim objAccess As Access.Application
    Dim strPath As String
    Set objAccess = CreateObject("Access.Application")

    With objAccess
        .Visible = True
        ' Get the path and name of the database.
        strPath = .SysCmd(acSysCmdAccessDir) & _
            "Samples\Northwind.mdb"
        .OpenCurrentDatabase FilePath:=strPath
        .Application.Run _
            "Northwind.PrintReport", "Catalog", False
    End With
End Sub
```

> **NOTE** The first argument after the Run method refers to the Project-Name. The ProjectName property defaults to the name of the database, but you can set it using the Advanced tab of the Options dialog box.

To print a specific report using VBA in Access, you need to use the OpenReport method of the DoCmd object. The above procedure executes a sub procedure called PrintReport within the database rather than calling the OpenReport method directly. Taking this approach allows you the flexibility of specifying the report name and print mode (whether to send the output to the printer or preview the output on the screen) so that you don't have to change your code if you want to print a different report. The procedure in Microsoft Access would look like the following, which we added to the Northwind Traders database:

```
Sub PrintReport(strRptName As String, bPrint As Boolean)
    On Error GoTo Err_PrintReport
```

```
        If bPrint Then
            DoCmd.OpenReport strRptName, acNormal
        Else
            DoCmd.OpenReport strRptName, acPreview
        End If
        Exit Sub

Err_PrintReport:
        MsgBox "Error printing report " & strRptName
        Exit Sub
End Sub
```

## Automation Error Handling

With the increase in interoperability between products, it is critical that you know how to trap and handle errors coming from Automation objects. In applications that use one or more Automation objects, being able to determine where an error occurs and what exactly is causing it is a necessity for developers. Microsoft Access 97 allows you to evaluate Automation errors at a more specific level than in earlier versions. VBA now enables a server application to return error information specific to that application. Two types of errors can be returned by Automation objects:

- The error returned by the server application as defined by the server

- The error defined by VBA in Microsoft Access to which the error returned by the server is mapped

To determine whether an error is specific to the object's application or is returned by VBA, you can use the predefined VBA constant vbObjectError. This constant is defined in the VBA object library. Server applications add this constant to their errors before returning the error to the client application. This fact helps you in two ways:

- Subtracting vbObjectError from Err.Number will indicate the error as defined by the server application.

- If subtracting the vbObjectError from Err.Number results in a number outside the range 0–65535, the error is a VBA error.

To demonstrate, let's assume that an error number 2007 is generated within Microsoft Excel, the server application. The client application, Microsoft Access, may already have an error number 2007 defined, which would cause confusion. Because Excel is being used as a server application, it adds vbObjectError to

2007 and returns the result to the client application. Microsoft Access receives an error number that you can use to evaluate the valid Excel error without having conflicts with the native Microsoft Access errors. The following code sample shows how to determine whether an error is coming from a server application or from VBA:

```
' Remove the constant added by the server application.
MyError = Err.Number - vbObjectError
' Is the result in the range 0-65535?
If MyError > 0 And MyError < 65535 Then
    Msg = "The object you accessed assigned this number to " & _
          "the error: " & MyError & ". The originator of " & _
          "the error was: " & Err.Source & ". Press F1 to " & _
          "see the originating application's help topic."
Else        ' It is a VBA error.
    Msg = "This error " & Err.Number & " is a VBA error. " & _
          "Press Help button or F1 for VBA Help topic on " & _
          "this error."
End If

MsgBox Msg, , "Object Error", Err.HelpFile, Err.HelpContext
```

## Manipulating ActiveX Objects in Forms

Until now, we have discussed manipulating ActiveX objects outside of the client application by using the CreateObject and GetObject functions as well as the references to those objects via their libraries. Using these functions either creates a new instance of an application or uses an existing instance of it.

What about the ActiveX objects that are embedded in or linked to a Microsoft Access form? Believe it or not, you can use the Automation knowledge you now have to manipulate the ActiveX objects on your form.

Using the Unbound Object Frame control on the Microsoft Access toolbox, you can place a new Microsoft Excel worksheet onto a Microsoft Access form. Excel opens in its own window, in which you can add information to the workbook. Closing Excel shows a portion of the workbook on the Microsoft Access form. This portion, or portal, allows you to double-click the workbook to edit it in place. However, be sure to set the Enabled property of the Unbound Object Frame to True and the Locked property to No if you want to be able to double-click to the object to edit it at run time.

Once the object exists on the form, you can also use Automation to manipulate that object. The syntax you use is the same as all the examples you've seen so far in this chapter, with the exception of how you refer to the object. Because the object is already created on the form, there is no need to use the CreateObject or GetObject functions. To reference the ActiveX object, refer to the name of the form, the name of the control, and the control's Object property, and then to any Automation call you want to make. The following code uses this syntax to add text to a cell in a workbook, MyWkBook, which is embedded on a form using an Unbound Object Frame:

```
Forms("Form1").MyWkBook.Object.ActiveSheet.Cells(1,1).Value = _
    "Hello World!"
```

## **PREVIEW** of the next chapter

In this chapter you were introduced to portions of the ActiveX Controls, in particular, Automation. The next chapter will focus on the Internet and how you can use Microsoft Access to create robust Internet and intranet applications. Chapter 15 will also discuss some Internet and intranet features such as hyperlinks, which you can use to create integrated Microsoft Office applications. We will also introduce the Microsoft Web Browser ActiveX control, which will open the door for you to use ActiveX controls in your applications.

# 15

## Accessing the World Wide Web

We have all been hearing about the Information Superhighway—the Internet. This chapter will focus on how you can use Microsoft Access both to view and to create content for the Internet and for intranets. Before we dive into how Microsoft Access can help you create Internet-aware applications, let's briefly discuss what the Internet is and how it compares to intranets.

### The Internet and Intranets

The Internet was first conceived in the early 1960s and was originally intended for communication within the Defense Department. Universities were quick to adopt this technology; academics and researchers used it to discuss research projects and to communicate with each other. In its infancy, the Internet was not often used by corporations or by individuals outside of academia—hard as it may be to believe now, remember that personal computers were not a part of most business organizations or private homes until the 1980s. In the early 1990s, the ability to combine words, pictures, and sounds on Web pages turned on the corporate world to this new medium. The Internet was becoming a popular means of communicating among businesses, customers, and individuals because of the increased presence of personal computers. Currently, people throughout the world make travel arrangements, communicate, exchange information, do research, and even telecommute over the Internet.

The Internet is changing the way we do business. Its technologies—Hypertext Markup Language (HTML) and Hypertext Transfer Protocol (HTTP)—are finding their way into the corporate world. Intranets, which are networks within organizations, use Internet technologies to give the organization's members or employees easier access to much more information than was available through more traditional channels. Such capabilities can boost a company's competitive advantage in many ways, including helping to get information to customers more quickly and efficiently. When creating your Microsoft Access applications, don't neglect the Internet or intranets if you know these technologies will be available to your users. In the remainder of this chapter, we will be exploring how easy it is to integrate these concepts into your applications.

## Using the Microsoft Office Web Toolbar

The Microsoft Office Web toolbar is available in all Office 97 applications. You can use this toolbar to move among objects in the Office 97 products as well as to explore information on the Internet and any intranets. The Web toolbar can be visible all the time within your application, and there is even an option to make it the only visible toolbar. Using the Web toolbar, you can easily open and explore Web pages—because the options available on this toolbar directly manipulate Microsoft Internet Explorer. This toolbar is shown in Figure 15-1. In the following sections, we'll examine each control on the Office Web toolbar.

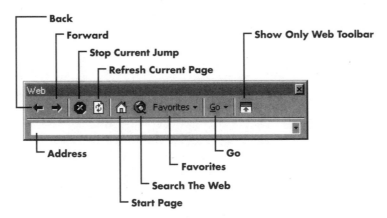

**Figure 15-1.** *Microsoft Office Web toolbar.*

### Address control

The Address control allows you to enter a valid address to open a file, document, or object resource, or you can select one of the Web sites you have previously visited or objects you have previously opened from the drop-down list.

### Back and Forward buttons

Use the Back and Forward buttons to move through any resources opened by an address or by a hyperlink. The Back button takes you to previous resources you visited. The Forward button returns you to resources you left using the Back button.

### Stop Current Jump and Refresh Current Page buttons

If you are in the middle of loading a resource and want to stop the process, just click the Stop Current Jump button on the Web toolbar. The Refresh Current Page button reloads the current resource, refreshing any information that has changed since the last time you opened that resource. If you press the Stop Current Jump button in the middle of a refresh, the refresh will stop.

### Start Page and Search The Web buttons

The Start Page button will take you to your home page. This is the default page you see when starting Internet Explorer. The Search The Web button is your default link to an external Internet search engine page; from a good search page, you can find almost anything on the Internet.

### Favorites drop-down menu

The Favorites control allows you to add hyperlinks to your Favorites folder and then to access them conveniently. The hyperlinks listed on this menu are in the Favorites folder on your hard drive. You don't have to worry about writing down your favorite Web page addresses if you save them in your Favorites folder. To do so, choose Add To Favorites from this menu while viewing the page or object whose address you want to save.

### Go drop-down menu

The Go control allows you to browse for other resources. Selecting an item from the Go drop-down menu will move the browser to that hyperlink address; the result is the same as entering the URL (Uniform Resource Locator) in the address box. From this drop-down menu, you can also access the objects you have opened during this session of Microsoft Access. You can also set your start page and search page to the currently opened resource by selecting the Set Start Page or Set Search Page options from the Go drop-down menu.

### Show Only Web Toolbar button

The Show Only Web Toolbar button does just what its names suggests: it shows only the Web toolbar and hides all other toolbars. If only the Web toolbar is visible, clicking this button shows any toolbars that were previously hidden.

## Microsoft on the Web

All Microsoft Office applications have a convenient way for you to find out the latest information from Microsoft. Choose Microsoft On The Web from the Help menu, as shown in Figure 15-2. Look at all the information at your fingertips!

- Choose Free Stuff and find out about cool things you can get from Microsoft for free.

- Pick Product News and get the latest information on the Microsoft product you are using.

- Select Developer Forum and see information about development topics on line.

- Choose Frequently Asked Questions and get answers to some of the burning questions you have about Microsoft Access.

- Select Online Support to get extensive information about troubleshooting.

Try cruising around these options, and see what you can find. Figure 15-2 shows you what options are available.

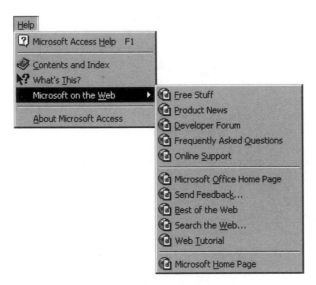

**Figure 15-2.** *Microsoft On The Web options.*

# Hyperlinks

Hyperlinks simplify getting around on and retrieving information from the Internet and from intranets. You can simply click a specified link rather than having to remember a URL address. Microsoft Access makes it easy for you to incorporate hyperlinks into your applications. So what kinds of hyperlinks can you create? Because the hyperlinks you create are dependent on the protocols available, to answer that question we'll first need to look at the various types of Internet URL protocols, which are shown in the following table.

## INTERNET URL PROTOCOLS

| Protocol Name | Prefix | Functionality |
| --- | --- | --- |
| Hypertext Transfer Protocol | http:// | Allows you to access Web pages from a Web server on the World Wide Web. Such a page can contain information ranging from plain text to graphics and multimedia. |
| Universal Naming Convention | \\ | Allows you to refer to a file without having to specify a drive letter. |
| File Transfer Protocol | ftp:// | Allows you to copy and move files between computers via the Internet. |
| Gopher protocol | gopher:// | Allows you to access information on a Gopher server. |
| WAIS protocol | wais:// | Allows you to access information on a Wide Area Information Server. |
| File protocol | file:// | Allows you to open a file on a local hard drive or on a computer network. |
| Hypertext Transfer Protocol with Privacy | https:// | Allows you to create an HTTP connection using Secure Sockets Layer data encryption. |
| MailTo protocol | mailto:emailname-@domainname | Allows you to send an e-mail message to a specific Internet e-mail address. |
| Microsoft Network protocol | msn:// | Allows you to access information at a specific location on The Microsoft Network. |
| News protocol | news:newsgroup-name | Allows you to access a specific Usenet newsgroup. |
| Network News Transfer Protocol | nntp:// | Same as News Protocol except that you can use the two-slashes format. |
| Musical Instrument Digital Interface (MIDI) protocol | mid:// | Allows you to play MIDI files. |
| CompuServe® Dialer (CID) protocol | cid:// | Allows you to access information on the Internet through CompuServe's online service. |
| Prospero protocol | Prospero:// | Allows you to access information on the Prospero file system. |
| Telnet protocol | telnet:// | Allows you to launch the telnet terminal-emulation program to issue commands to a remote UNIX server. |
| Rlogin protocol | rlogin:// | Allows you to launch the Rlogin terminal-emulation program. |
| TN3270 protocol | tn3270:// | Allows you to launch the TN3270 terminal-emulation program. |
| RealAudio protocol | pnm:// | Allows you to play RealAudio media from a RealAudio server. |
| Microsoft Media Server protocol | mms:// | Allows you to play Microsoft Media multimedia from an MMS Server. |

You can also create hyperlinks to Microsoft Access objects as well as to objects in any of the other Office 97 products, such as Microsoft PowerPoint slides or Microsoft Word documents. In fact, you can create a hyperlink to any object or to any file with a file extension that has an association in the Registry. For example, you could create a hyperlink to a bitmap file such as "C:\WINDOWS\-BUBBLES.BMP." When you click the hyperlink text, the application associated with that file type will automatically launch. You can also create a hyperlink to an executable file, so that the application will automatically launch when the hyperlink is clicked.

## Hyperlink Data Type

Microsoft Access 97 has a data type called Hyperlink that allows you to store a hyperlink in a table. Using this data type, you can simply click the hyperlink text to see the information at that address. To store a hyperlink in a table, you must first create a field with a data type of Hyperlink, as shown in Figure 15-3.

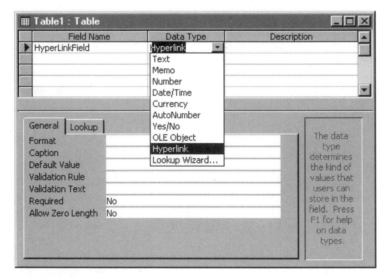

**Figure 15-3.** *Hyperlink data type.*

**NOTE**   To Microsoft Jet, the Microsoft Access Hyperlink data type is stored as a memo field.

You can also create a Hyperlink column in Datasheet view of a table by choosing Hyperlink Column from the Insert menu.

As mentioned earlier, you can create many types of hyperlinks. Figure 15-4 shows some examples of stored hyperlinks.

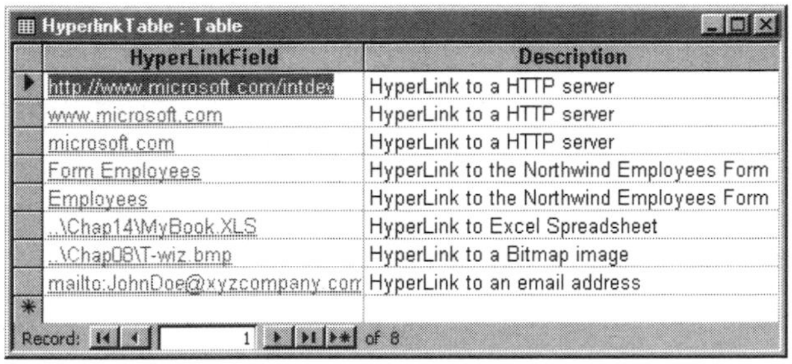


| HyperLinkField | Description |
|---|---|
| http://www.microsoft.com/intde | HyperLink to a HTTP server |
| www.microsoft.com | HyperLink to a HTTP server |
| microsoft.com | HyperLink to a HTTP server |
| Form Employees | HyperLink to the Northwind Employees Form |
| Employees | HyperLink to the Northwind Employees Form |
| ..\Chap14\MyBook.XLS | HyperLink to Excel Spreadsheet |
| ..\Chap08\T-wiz.bmp | HyperLink to a Bitmap image |
| mailto:JohnDoe@xyzcompany.com | HyperLink to an email address |

**Figure 15-4.** *Examples of stored hyperlinks.*

When a hyperlink is stored in a table, it is made up of three parts separated by pound signs (#). When you enter data in a Hyperlink field, you must use the pound sign to separate the different parts of the hyperlink. (Later in this chapter, you will see Microsoft Access do this for you when adding hyperlinks to other objects in your database.) The three parts of a hyperlink are the display text, address, and subaddress. If you wanted to use all three parts when storing a URL, the string would look like this:

```
Display text#Address#Subaddress
```

The following table describes the parts of a hyperlink.

**PARTS OF A HYPERLINK**

| *Hyperlink Part* | *Description* |
|---|---|
| Display text | This text, which is displayed to the user, describes what the hyperlink will do. This field is optional. |
| Address | The address specifies the path to a designated object, document, Web page, URL, or UNC location. This field is required unless you want to create a hyperlink to a Microsoft Access object in the currently open database. |
| Subaddress | This designates a specific location within the object pointed to by the address. It could include a form within a Microsoft Access database, a range of cells in a Microsoft Excel workbook, a bookmark within a Word document, a slide number within a PowerPoint presentation, a name tag within an HTML document, and so on. This field is optional. |

When displaying hyperlinks, Microsoft Access uses the following rules:

- If there is display text, only the display text will be shown.
- If there is no display text, only the address will be shown.
- If there is no display text or address, the subaddress will be shown.

Therefore, in Microsoft Access a hyperlink to www.microsoft.com could be shown in the following ways, depending on whether the hyperlink includes display text:

| Actual Hyperlink Stored | Hyperlink Displayed |
|---|---|
| Microsoft Home Page#http://www.microsoft.com# | Microsoft Home Page |
| #http://www.microsoft.com# | http://www.micro-soft.com |

> **TIP**    When you have display text and you want to see the entire hyperlink as it is stored in the hyperlink field, tab to the hyperlink field and press F2 or right-click on the hyperlink field and select Hyperlink from the shortcut menu, then select Edit Hyperlink.

You can always tell if your cursor is over a hyperlink in Access because the cursor changes to an upward-pointing hand whenever it's over a hyperlink. Also, the color of the hyperlink changes once you have visited the resource. By default, hyperlinks you have not visited are blue and those you have visited are purple. To change these default colors, choose Options from the Tools menu. In the Options dialog box, click the Hyperlinks/HTML tab, as shown in Figure 15-5, and set the Hyperlink Color and the Followed Hyperlink Color.

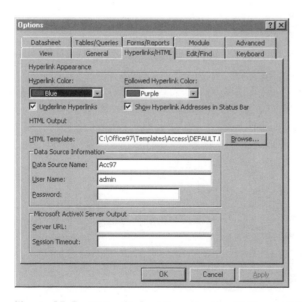

**Figure 15-5.** *Hyperlink options in the Options dialog box.*

## Adding a hyperlink to a field

You can add a hyperlink to a Hyperlink field in the following ways:

- Type the hyperlink directly into the Hyperlink field.
- Choose Hyperlink from the Insert menu, as shown here.

- Select the Insert Hyperlink button on the Table Datasheet toolbar, as shown here:

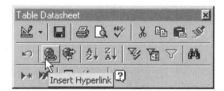

- Use code. We will discuss how to do this later in the chapter.

When you select Hyperlink from the Insert menu or click the Insert Hyperlink button, the Insert Hyperlink dialog box shown in Figure 15-6 will open.

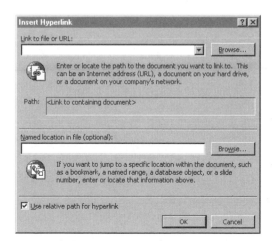

**Figure 15-6.** *Insert Hyperlink dialog box.*

The Insert Hyperlink dialog box includes the following elements:

- The Link To File Or URL combo box contains the address information.

- The Named Location In File (Optional) combo box contains the sub-address information.

- The Use Relative Path For Hyperlink check box, when checked, indicates that the path to which the hyperlink points will be interpreted relative to the path of the database. If this check box is unchecked, an absolute path will be stored in the hyperlink. Unchecking this option is useful only if you know that the file to which the hyperlink points will never change physical locations.

> **NOTE**  You cannot set the display text using the Insert Hyperlink dialog box. You must edit the display text directly in the hyperlink field or on the Hyperlink shortcut menu after it has been created.

By default, the Link To File Or URL combo box refers to the current database or path. If you are going to be adding a lot of hyperlinks from one particular database or path, you can enter a Hyperlink Base address in the database properties sheet. This address will be added to the beginning of relative hyperlink addresses. To set a base address for all hyperlinks, choose Database Properties from the File menu. You will then see the database properties sheet shown in Figure 15-7. Enter the base address in the Hyperlink Base text box.

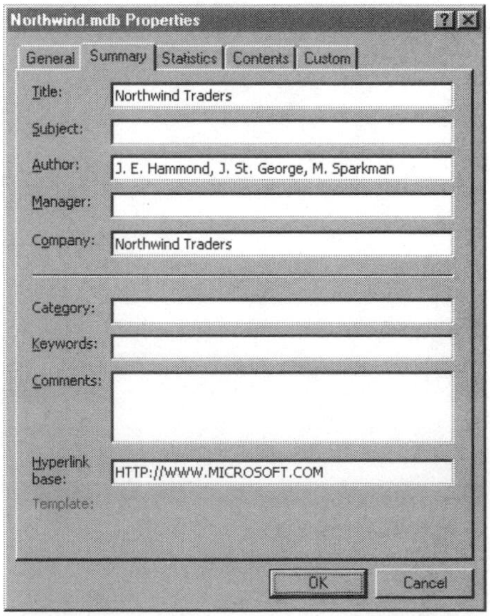

**Figure 15-7.** *Hyperlink base address for a database.*

Once you have created a hyperlink, you launch it by clicking the hyperlink. To further manipulate the hyperlink, you can right-click the hyperlink field and then select Hyperlink to display its shortcut menu, as shown in Figure 15-8.

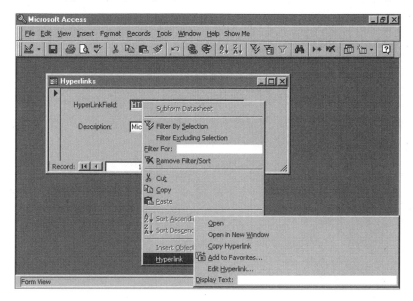

**Figure 15-8.** *Hyperlink field shortcut menu.*

From the hyperlink shortcut menu, you can choose any of the options listed in the following table.

### HYPERLINK SHORTCUT MENU OPTIONS

| Options | Description |
|---|---|
| Open | Opens the hyperlink. |
| Open in New Window | Opens the hyperlink in a new application window. |
| Copy Hyperlink | Copies hyperlink information to be pasted as a hyperlink in another location. |
| Add to Favorites | Adds the hyperlink to your Favorites folder. |
| Edit Hyperlink | Brings up the Edit Hyperlink dialog box, which is the same as the Insert Hyperlink dialog box. |
| Display Text | Shows the display text for the hyperlink. You can edit the display text in the text box on the shortcut menu. |

## Linking Within Microsoft Access

With Microsoft Access you can create hyperlinks to any objects in the Database. The hyperlink will open each object in its default view. To create a hyperlink for a Microsoft Access object in the current database, you can use the following hyperlink format:

```
DisplayText##SubAddress
```

Notice that when you are referring to a Microsoft Access object in the current database, you do not need the address portion of the hyperlink. Therefore, you could create the following hyperlink to open the Employees form:

```
Open Employees Form##Employees
```

If you do not add display text, the hyperlink above would have the following syntax stored:

```
##Employees
```

Because objects within Microsoft Access share the same name space, if you just type the name of an object, such as Employees, Microsoft Access will look for an object with that name in the following order: form, report, table/query, macro, and finally, module. If two different objects, such as a form and a report, have the same name, you must prepend an object identifier to distinguish which type of object you are referring to. An object identifier is simply the name of the type of object, followed by a space. You could rewrite the preceding example using an object identifier as follows:

```
##Form Employees
```

If you want to reference a database object that does not exist in the current database, you must use the address portion of the hyperlink to identify the other database location, as shown here:

```
Open Other Form#C:\Databases\MyMDB.MDB#Form MainForm
```

> **NOTE**  When you click on a hyperlink to another database, the hyperlink will launch a new instance of Microsoft Access and open the database, running the AutoExec and AutoKeys macros and the Startup properties. If the hyperlink points to a specific object, that object is then opened.

The above example uses an absolute path. If you were to use a relative path, it would look something like the following if the current database is in the C:\Databases folder and the database you are referencing is in the C:\Testing folder:

```
Open Other Form#..\Testing\MyMDB.MDB#Form MainForm
```

Hyperlinks are not stored only in hyperlink fields in a table. They can also be added to unbound controls such as labels, images, and command buttons, all of which have HyperlinkAddress and HyperlinkSubAddress properties. (Use the Caption property as the "display text" for command bars and labels. With images, the image acts as the "display text".) You can either set these properties manually or use the Insert Hyperlink dialog box while in Design view of a form.

**NOTE** When the user clicks a command button that has a hyperlink, the hyperlink is launched and the OnClick event is invoked.

## Linking to Microsoft Office 97 Applications

To link to other Microsoft Office 97 applications, you use the same syntax you use to create any other hyperlink. For example, you can store the following portions of the hyperlink syntax in a hyperlink field:

```
Display text#Address#SubAddress
```

**NOTE** Microsoft Access relies on file association and other Registry entries to know how to link to other Office files and start their associated applications.

The address specifies the Office 97 file you want to link to. The subaddress can be a specific location within the file that you want to have the focus. The following table lists some examples of hyperlinks you can create within Office 97 applications.

| HyperLink | Description |
| --- | --- |
| Accounting Sheet#\\Server\Share\- My Documents\accounts.xls# | Launches a Microsoft Excel workbook |
| Accounting Sheet#\\Server\Share\- My Documents\accounts.xls#- Sheet2!A4:D10 | Launches a Microsoft Excel workbook file and places the cursor at a range of cells (A4:D10) on a specific sheet (Sheet2) within the workbook |
| Accounting Sheet#\\Server\Share\- My Documents\accounts.xls#- SelectedFigures | Launches a Microsoft Excel workbook file and places the cursor at a named range of cells (Selected Figures) within the workbook |
| Business Letter#C:\My Documents\- BL.doc# | Launches a Word file |
| Business Letter#C:\My Documents\- BL.doc#Bookmark Signature | Launches a Word file and places the cursor at a bookmark (Bookmark Signature) designating the location of the signature part of the document |
| Sales Presentation#C:\My Documents\Sales.ppt# | Launches a PowerPoint presentation |
| Sales Presentation#C:\My Documents\Sales.ppt#35 | Launches a PowerPoint presentation and opens a specific slide (slide number 35) |

When moving among Microsoft Office applications using hyperlinks, you can use the Back and Forward buttons on the Office Web toolbar in each application to return to the application and the object from which it was originally launched.

If you click a hyperlink for Word, Excel, or PowerPoint, that application will be launched only if it is not currently open. Otherwise, clicking the hyperlink will use the current instance of that application.

## Linking to the Internet and to Intranets

To link to Internet file types on the Internet or on your company's intranet, you can create hyperlinks that allow you to move among those resources (URL addresses). For example, you can store the following portions of the hyperlink syntax in a hyperlink field.

```
Display text#Address#Subaddress
```

The address must use a valid Internet protocol as well as the correct Internet server address (the domain name used to uniquely identify the server on the Internet or intranet) and subsequent path to the actual file or resource on that server. The address uses the following syntax:

```
Internet protocol://serveraddress/path-to-resource
```

For example, to make a hyperlink to the Microsoft Web page, you could use the following syntax:

```
GoTo Microsoft Web Page#http://www.microsoft.com#
```

You do not need to include the path-to-resource portion if the Internet server has a default path.

To go to Microsoft's Internet Center on www.microsoft.com, you can use the following syntax to include that specific page:

```
MS Internet Center#http://www.microsoft.com/internet/#
```

The subaddress, if used, can refer to a name tag in the HTML (Hypertext Markup Language) document. Specifying a subaddress is useful if you have an extremely long HTML page. You might have an HTML page with a series of hyperlinks at the top of the page that allow you to go directly to specified topics farther down the page without having to scroll through the entire page. As an example, the following HTML reference allows the user to skip down to phone number listings for names that begin with P:

```
<a href="PhoneList.HTML#P">P Names</a>
```

The name tag itself would then be coded in HTML as follows:

```
<A NAME="P">Names Beginning With P</a>
```

In Microsoft Access the entire hyperlink to get you directly to the names beginning with the letter *P* on the PhoneList.HTML page would be stored as follows:

```
Display text#http://serveraddress/PhoneList.HTML/#P
```

## Using Office Applications to Create Hyperlinks to Microsoft Access

You can create hyperlinks from other Office 97 applications to a Microsoft Access database as well as to specific objects within that database. Keep in mind the point we mentioned earlier: if you create a hyperlink just to the database file itself, the hyperlink will launch Microsoft Access and open the database running the AutoExec and AutoKeys macros and the Startup properties. If a specific object is selected, that object will be opened after the macros and properties just mentioned are run. Database objects will be opened in their default view.

To create a hyperlink to Microsoft Access from another Office 97 application, in Word, Microsoft Excel, or PowerPoint, choose Insert Hyperlink from the Insert menu or click the Insert Hyperlink toolbar button. This will bring up the Insert Hyperlink dialog box, just as it does in Microsoft Access.

> **NOTE** If the hyperlink refers to a Microsoft Access Database that is already open, it will use that instance of Microsoft Access and will not rerun the AutoExec and AutoKeys macros and Startup properties. If Microsoft Access is not running, or is running with a different database open, a new instance of Microsoft Access will be launched.

## Manipulating Hyperlinks Using VBA Code

Whatever you can do with hyperlinks through the user interface you can also do via VBA code. This includes both setting hyperlink properties and following hyperlinks.

### Modifying hyperlink properties using VBA code

Hyperlinks have the properties listed in the table on the next page.

| Properties | Description |
|---|---|
| HyperlinkAddress | Use this property to read or change the address portion of a hyperlink. |
| HyperlinkSubAddress | Use this property to read or change the sub-address portion of a hyperlink. |
| Hyperlink | Use this property to return a reference to a control's Hyperlink object. |

These properties are available only to the non-data-aware controls, such as command buttons, labels, and the image control. To set the "display text" of a command button or label, use the Caption property. For the image control, the picture acts as the "display text". The following code examples demonstrate how to write code for each of these non-data-aware controls.

This code changes a label's hyperlink to open the Employees form in the current database:

```
' Change the "display text" for the hyperlink.
Forms![My Form]!lblLink.Caption = "Open the Employees Form"
' Clear the address.
Forms![My Form]!lblLink.HyperlinkAddress = ""
' Set the subaddress.
Forms![My Form]!lblLink.HyperlinkSubAddress = "Form Employees"
```

This code changes the hyperlink of a command button to open www.microsoft.com:

```
' Change the "display text" for the hyperlink.
Forms![My Form]!cmdLink.Caption = "Go to Microsoft"
' Set the address.
Forms![My Form]!cmdLink.HyperlinkAddress = _
    "http://www.microsoft.com"
' Clear the subaddress.
Forms![My Form]!cmdLink.HyperlinkSubAddress = ""
```

This code changes the hyperlink of an image control to open a Word document at the BM1 bookmark:

```
' Change the "display text" (a picture) for the hyperlink.
Forms![My Form]!imgLink.Picture = "Books.BMP"
' Set the address.
Forms![My Form]!imgLink.HyperlinkAddress = _
    "C:\My Documents\Library.DOC"
' Set the subaddress.
Forms![My Form]!imgLink.HyperlinkSubAddress = "BM1"
```

Once you click a hyperlink, its color will change to indicate that it has been visited. If you don't want a particular hyperlink to change color, you can override this feature by setting the Fore-Color property. The image control does not have this feature because it does not display any text.

You must use the Hyperlink property if you want to reference a Hyperlink object's properties in code for a command button, label, or image control. You can even reference a text box bound to a hyperlink field on a form, which you cannot do using the HyperlinkAddress and HyperlinkSubAddress properties. The following code shows how to use the Hyperlink property to set the address and subaddress of a label:

```
' Declare the Control object variable as type Label.
Dim ctl As Label
' Declare a Hyperlink object variable.
Dim hlk As Hyperlink

Set ctl = Forms![My Form]!lblLink
Set hlk = ctl.Hyperlink

' Set the Address and SubAddress properties of the
' Hyperlink object.
hlk.Address = ""
hlk.SubAddress = "Report Catalog"
```

Because there is no DisplayText property, you must still use the Caption property of the control itself, except for the image control, which uses a picture, and for a text box, which has no Caption property. For a command button, a label, or an image control, the Address and SubAddress properties of the Hyperlink object are read/write. With text boxes, however, they are read only.

To read and write to a hyperlink field in a table or query, you can create a Recordset object and change or return the value of the hyperlink as shown here:

```
Sub ChangeHyperlink()
    Dim rs As Recordset
    Set rs = CurrentDb.OpenRecordset("HyperlinkTable")

    rs.MoveFirst
    ' Print the value of the hyperlink in the Debug window.
    Debug.Print rs!HyperLinkField

    ' Change the value of the hyperlink.
    rs.Edit
```

*(continued)*

```
    rs!HyperLinkField = _
        "Goto Microsoft#http://www.microsoft.com#"
    rs.Update

    ' Display the new value of the hyperlink in the Debug window.
    Debug.Print rs!HyperLinkField

    rs.Close
End Sub
```

In the Immediate pane of the Debug window, you will see the following results:

```
#http://www.microsoft.com/intdev#
Goto Microsoft#http://www.microsoft.com#
```

Keep in mind that you have to use the complete hyperlink syntax, including the appropriate pound signs (#), when editing or changing a hyperlink.

To parse out and return the different portions of the hyperlink, you can use the HyperlinkPart function. This function provides read-only information. It cannot be used to change a specific portion of a hyperlink. This function has one required argument: Hyperlink. Because the hyperlink is made up of several parts, the HyperlinkPart function has one optional argument, Part, which is used to distinguish and subsequently return a specific portion of the hyperlink.

**Hyperlink**   This argument represents the hyperlink information stored in the hyperlink field of a table that can be accessed via a Recordset object, query, or text box bound to a hyperlink field on a form.

**Part**   This argument is used to parse out and return a specific portion of the hyperlink:

- *acDisplayedValue (value = 0)* returns the underlined text displayed in the hyperlink field. This is the default value for this argument.

- *acDisplayText (value = 1)* returns the display text portion of the hyperlink.

- *acAddress (value = 2)* returns the address portion of the hyperlink.

- *acSubAddress (value = 3)* returns the subaddress portion of the hyperlink.

If you specify acDisplayedValue, the function returns whatever portion of the hyperlink is displayed in the hyperlink field. For example, if the hyperlink has a display text portion, the HyperlinkPart function will return the display text. If the hyperlink does not have a display text portion but does have an address, the HyperlinkPart function will return the address. If the hyperlink does not have a display text or an address portion, the HyperlinkPart function will return the subaddress.

**NOTE** If you are going to use the HyperlinkPart function in a query, you must use the actual value instead of the intrinsic constants for the Part argument.

To return the individual portions of a hyperlink stored in a hyperlink field, you can create a Recordset object and return the values of the hyperlink as shown here:

```
Sub GetPartOfHyperlink()
    Dim rs As Recordset
    Set rs = CurrentDb.OpenRecordset("HyperlinkTable")

    rs.MoveFirst
    ' Print the value of the hyperlink
    ' in the Debug window.
    Debug.Print rs!HyperLinkField

    ' Print the displayed value of the hyperlink
    ' in the Debug window.
    Debug.Print HyperlinkPart(rs!HyperLinkField, acDisplayedValue)

    ' Print the display text portion of the hyperlink
    ' in the Debug window.
    Debug.Print HyperlinkPart(rs!HyperLinkField, acDisplayText)

    ' Print the address portion of the hyperlink
    ' in the Debug window.
    Debug.Print HyperlinkPart(rs!HyperLinkField, acAddress)

    ' Print the subaddress portion of the hyperlink
    ' in the Debug window.
    Debug.Print HyperlinkPart(rs!HyperLinkField, acSubAddress)

    rs.Close
End Sub
```

In the Immediate pane of the Debug window, you will see the following results:

```
Goto Microsoft#http://www.microsoft.com#
Goto Microsoft
Goto Microsoft
http://www.microsoft.com
```

To change a specific portion of a hyperlink in a hyperlink field in a table, you can create a Recordset object, parse out the parts of the hyperlink, and then update the hyperlink, as shown on the following page.

```
Sub NewAddress(Address As String)
    Dim rs As Recordset
    Dim DT As String, SubAdd As String

    Set rs = CurrentDb.OpenRecordset("HyperlinkTable")
    rs.MoveFirst

    ' Print the value of the hyperlink in the Debug window.
    Debug.Print rs!HyperlinkField

    ' Store the display text and subaddress information.
    DT = HyperlinkPart(rs!HyperlinkField, acDisplayText)
    SubAdd = HyperlinkPart(rs!HyperlinkField, acSubAddress)

    ' Change the address portion of the hyperlink.
    rs.Edit
    ' Bring the portions back together, making sure to include
    ' the appropriate pound sign (#) placeholders.
    rs!HyperlinkField = DT & "#" & Address & "#" & SubAdd
    rs.Update

    ' Print the value of the hyperlink in the Debug window.
    Debug.Print rs!HyperlinkField

    rs.Close

End Sub
```

If you pass in the address http://www.msn.com, you will see the following results in the Immediate pane of the Debug window:

```
Goto Microsoft#http://www.microsoft.com#
Goto Microsoft#http://www.msn.com#
```

Remember that you can also use the HyperlinkPart function to return portions of a hyperlink stored in a text box bound to a hyperlink field on a form. The following code returns the displayed value of the hyperlink:

```
Dim strDV As String
strDV = HyperlinkPart(Forms![My Form]![HyperlinkField])
```

**Changing the Hyperlink Base Database property**    You can also use code to create or change the Hyperlink Base property on the database properties sheet, as shown here:

```
Sub ChangeDatabaseHyperlink(NewValue As String)
    Dim db As Database
    Dim doc As Document
```

```
      Dim prop As Property
      Dim flag As Boolean

      flag = False
      Set db = CurrentDb

      ' Set the Document object variable to the SummaryInfo document.
      Set doc = db.Containers("Databases").Documents("SummaryInfo")

      ' Check to see whether the SummaryInfo's Hyperlink Base
      ' property exists.
      For Each prop In doc.Properties
          ' If the Hyperlink Base property exists, set the
          ' flag to True.
          If prop.Name = "hyperlink base" Then flag = True
      Next

      If flag = True Then
          ' If the Hyperlink Base property does exist,
          ' assign it the new value.
          doc.Properties("hyperlink base") = NewValue
      Else
          ' If the Hyperlink Base property does not exist,
          ' append it to the SummaryInfo's Properties collection
          ' using the new value.
          doc.Properties.Append _
              doc.CreateProperty("hyperlink base", dbText, NewValue)
      End If
End Sub
```

## Following hyperlinks using VBA code

Now that you can create and modify your hyperlinks, let's use code to open the resources they refer to. You can do this by using either the Follow or the FollowHyperlink methods.

**Follow**   You can use this method to "click" on a hyperlink. Use it for command buttons, labels, image controls, and text boxes that are bound to hyperlink fields.

The Follow method has these optional arguments:

- **newwindow** If this value is set to True, the document referred to in the hyperlink will be opened in a new window (for example, an additional instance of Microsoft Internet Explorer will be created). The default is False, which opens the document in the current window.

- **addhistory** If this value is set to True, the hyperlink will be added to the History folder; a False value will not add it there. The default is True.

- **extrainfo** Use this argument if you need additional information (such as coordinates of an image map on an HTML Web page) to get to a hyperlink resource.

- **method** This argument indicates how the extrainfo argument is attached. It can be one of the following constants:

  - **MsoMethodGet** The extrainfo argument is appended to the hyperlink address and can be only a string. This is the default value.

  - **MsoMethodPost** The extrainfo argument is posted, or sent to the new address, either as a string or as an array of type Byte. This method is usually used with HTML form objects.

- **headerinfo** Use this argument to provide header information (information specific to the hyperlink document). The default for this is a zero-length string.

With the Follow method, you do not have to know or reference the address or subaddress portion of the hyperlink; you just refer to the control's Hyperlink property on the form that contains the hyperlink. The following example launches the hyperlink of a label on a form.

```
Forms![My Form]!lblLink.HyperLink.Follow
```

> **NOTE**  You cannot use the Follow method on a hyperlink field in a Recordset object.

**FollowHyperlink**  If you do not have a control that contains a specific hyperlink you need to launch, use the FollowHyperlink method of the Application object in Microsoft Access. This method allows you to provide a hyperlink address and subaddress via an unbound text box, an input box, or a variable in code.

The FollowHyperlink method has these arguments, all of which are optional except Address:

- **address** This string value supplies the address portion of the hyperlink.

- **subaddress** This string value supplies the subaddress portion of the hyperlink.

- **newwindow** As with the Follow method, if this value is set to True, the document referred to in the hyperlink will be opened in a new window. The default is False, which opens the document in the current window.

- **addhistory** If this value is set to True, the hyperlink will be added to the History folder; a False value will not add it there. The default is True.

- **extrainfo** Use this argument if you need additional information to get to a hyperlink resource.

- **method** This argument indicates how the extrainfo argument is attached by using one of the following constants:

  - **MsoMethodGet** The extrainfo argument is appended to the hyperlink address and can be only a string. This is the default value.

  - **MsoMethodPost** The extrainfo argument is posted, either as a string or as an array of type Byte.

- **headerinfo** Use this argument to provide header information. The default for this is a zero-length string.

The following example launches the Employees form in the current database. The Address argument is required, so you must use CurrentDB.Name to get the Address of the current database.

```
Application.FollowHyperlink Address = _
    CurrentDB.Name, SubAddress = "Form Employees"
```

You can implicitly reference the Application object, as shown here:

```
FollowHyperlink Address = CurrentDB.Name, _
    SubAddress = "Form Employees"
```

You can also use the FollowHyperlink method in conjunction with the HyperlinkPart function to launch hyperlinks from a hyperlink field in a Recordset object. You use the HyperlinkPart function to parse out the necessary address and subaddress information, as shown here:

```
Sub GoToHyperlink()
    Dim rs As Recordset
    Set rs = CurrentDb.OpenRecordset("HyperlinkTable")
    rs.MoveFirst

    ' Launch the hyperlink stored in the hyperlink field
    ' of the first record in the recordset.
    FollowHyperlink _
        Address:=HyperlinkPart(rs!HyperlinkField, acAddress), _
        SubAddress:=HyperlinkPart(rs!HyperlinkField, acSubAddress)
End Sub
```

### Adding a hyperlink to your Favorites folder using VBA code

If you want to add a hyperlink to your Favorites folder, use the AddToFavorites method of the Hyperlink object. You can use this method to add to the Favorites folder a hyperlink address specified in a command button, a label, an image control, or a text box bound to a hyperlink field.

The following code adds to the Favorites folder a hyperlink from a text box bound to a hyperlink field on a form. You must use the Hyperlink property to call this method.

```
Forms![My Form]!txtHyperlink.Hyperlink.AddToFavorites
```

> **TIP** If you are using hyperlinks from a Recordset object or any other hyperlink that is not bound to a control, you can still use the AddToFavorites method to add those hyperlinks to your Favorites folder. Simply create a label on a form that will be open at the time you will want to add such a hyperlink. Set the label's Visible property to False, and then set the label's Caption property for the display text, its HyperlinkAddress property for the address, and its HyperlinkSubAddress property for the subaddress. Then use the label to add the hyperlink to your Favorites folder.

## The Microsoft Web Browser Control

Installed with Microsoft Internet Explorer versions 3.0 and later is the Microsoft Web Browser control. This control allows you to put the power of Internet Explorer in your Microsoft Access forms. The Web Browser control provides a "window" (the Explorer window) and the associated properties, events, and methods that allow you to manipulate it. Because the Web Browser control is an ActiveX control, it can be used inside Microsoft Access forms to view Web pages and other documents. And because the Web Browser control is installed as part of Internet Explorer, it has almost the same capabilities that Internet Explorer does.

To use the Web Browser control in a Microsoft Access form, follow these steps:

**1.** In Design view, choose ActiveX Control from the Insert menu.

**2.** In the list box that appears, select Microsoft Web Browser Control, and click OK.

The control is inserted on your form just as any other control, as shown in Figure 15-9. Notice that the control is blank at design time; it will remain blank until its Navigate method is invoked with a URL address to go to.

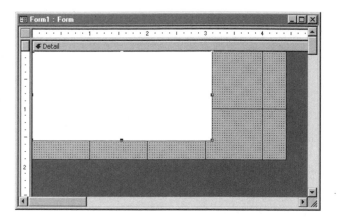

**Figure 15-9.** *The Microsoft Web Browser control.*

Internet Explorer must be installed on your machine for you to use this control. You can install Internet Explorer from the \Valu-Pack\IExplore folder on the Microsoft Office CD-ROM or from http://www.microsoft.com/ie/download if you prefer to install from the Web.

To see the Web Browser control's properties, methods, and events, you must use the Object Browser after first setting a reference to the Microsoft Internet Controls object library. To set this reference, open a module, choose References from the Tools menu, and select the Microsoft Internet Controls check box in the Available References box.

The Web Browser control has the following properties. (Not all the properties are listed here.)

- **Busy** allows you to see if something is still in progress.

- **LocationName** contains the user-friendly name of the URL currently being viewed.

- **LocationURL** contains the URL address for the page currently being viewed.

The Web Browser control has the following methods (though not all methods are given here):

- **GoBack** goes to the previous item in the history list.

- **GoForward** goes to the next item in the history list.

- **GoHome** goes to your start page.

- **GoSearch** goes to your search page.

- **Navigate** goes to a specific URL address.

- **Refresh** refreshes the current page.

- **Stop** stops loading the current page.

The Web Browser control has the following events. (Not all events are listed here.)

- **BeforeNavigate** is fired before a new hyperlink is opened.

- **DownloadBegin** is fired when the downloading of a page begins.

- **DownloadComplete** is fired when the downloading of a page is completed.

- **FrameBeforeNavigate** is fired when a new hyperlink is being opened in a frame.

- **FrameNavigateComplete** is fired after a new hyperlink is loaded into a frame.

- **FrameNewWindow** is fired when a new window should be created.

- **NavigateComplete** is fired when a new hyperlink is being opened.

- **NewWindow** is fired when a new window needs to be created.

- **ProgressChange** is fired when download progress is updated.

- **PropertyChange** is fired when a property of the control changes.

- **StatusTextChange** is fired when the text on the status bar changes.

- **TitleChange** is fired when the document title has changed.

- **WindowActivate** is fired when the window is activated.

- **WindowMove** is fired when the window has been moved.

- **WindowResize** is fired when the window has been resized.

Using the above properties, methods, and events, you can create a truly interactive application without ever leaving Microsoft Access. In the next section, you'll do just that, putting it all together in a Microsoft Access form.

## Using the Web Browser Control in an Application

As mentioned previously, just about anything that Internet Explorer can display, the Web Browser control can display. (For exceptions, see Chapter 21 of *Building*

*Applications with Microsoft Access.* To view this online book, open the file DEFAULT.HTM in the \ValuPack\Access\BldApps folder of your Microsoft Office CD-ROM.) Using a Microsoft Access form, you will create a browser that can be used within your application.

First you'll need to create a new blank form. Then add the Microsoft Web Browser control to the form. Size the form so that most of the contents of a Web page can be seen, and size the control to be the same size as the form. Set the Name property of the control to WebBrowser1.

The form should be interactive, allowing the user to enter a file name or Web address. In the form's header, place a text box named "txtAddress" and four command buttons to accomplish the following tasks: Go Back, Go Forward, Home, and Print. Name the command buttons cmdGoBack, cmdGoForward, cmdHome, and cmdPrint, respectively. The form should look like the one in Figure 15-10.

**Figure 15-10.** *Microsoft Access form with Web Browser control.*

When the form is loaded, a default page should be displayed in the Web Browser control. Otherwise, the form will appear empty. In the Load event of the form, place the following code, which will display Microsoft's home page:

```
Private Sub Form_Load()
    Me!txtAddress = "www.microsoft.com"
    Me!WebBrowser1.Navigate Me!txtAddress
End Sub
```

In the command buttons, place the necessary code to call the appropriate method. The procedures should resemble the code on the following page.

```
Private Sub cmdGoBack_Click()
    ' In case there is nowhere to go back to
    On Error Resume Next
    Me!WebBrowser1.GoBack
End Sub

Private Sub cmdGoForward_Click()
    ' In case there is nowhere to go forward to
    On Error Resume Next
    Me!WebBrowser1.GoForward
End Sub

Private Sub cmdHome_Click()
    Me!WebBrowser1.GoHome
End Sub

Private Sub cmdPrint_Click()
    WebBrowser1.SetFocus
    ' Simulate pressing Ctrl+p
    SendKeys "^(p) {ENTER}", True
End Sub
```

The Web Browser component of Internet Explorer 3.0 does not support a Print method. You can still print the contents of the Web Browser control using the method shown above, which simply sets the focus to the Web Browser control and sends a key combination of Ctrl-p to the keyboard buffer. Doing this will open the Print dialog box, allowing the contents of the Web Browser control to be sent to the printer.

To make this form truly interactive, the text box should allow the user to enter any valid document or Web address and have it displayed in the Web Browser control. The appropriate time to go to that address is while processing the AfterUpdate event of the text box. Going to the address at that time ensures that the code will run only if the user changes something in the text box. Keep in mind that a change to the text box includes removing all text from the text box, so error handling should be included, as the following code demonstrates:

```
Private Sub txtAddress_AfterUpdate()
    On Error Resume Next
    If Len(Me!txtAddress) > 0 Then
        Me!WebBrowser1.Navigate Me!txtAddress
    End If
End Sub
```

Now run the form. In the text box, try entering an Internet address, such as www.msn.com. Also try entering the name of a Microsoft Office document on your machine, say, C:\Program Files\Microsoft Office\Office\Samples\Products.doc. This will display the Word document in your Microsoft Access form.

Given the properties, methods, and events supported by the Web Browser control, you could add many other features to the form you just created. For example, you could add the capability to store a user's favorite links in a Microsoft Access table. You could also add search capabilities to the form so that users could search for items on the Internet. To see an example of these items, open the Developer Solutions sample application (SOLUTIONS.MDB) located in the Samples subfolder of your Office folder.

# Automating Microsoft Internet Explorer

Using the Microsoft Web Browser control, you have seen some of the features of Microsoft Internet Explorer. Now let's explore how you can use Automation with the application you just created. Internet Explorer exposes only one Automation object that you can manipulate using VBA. In this section, we'll focus on the Application object—its properties and methods and how to create it.

The Application object is the only object in the Internet Explorer hierarchy that can be created using the New keyword or the CreateObject or GetObject functions. For a complete list of the objects that you can use in Automation or from within your HTML pages using scripting, consult the ActiveX SDK documentation available on http://www.microsoft.com/intdev.

## The Application Object in Internet Explorer

The Application object represents the highest-level object in the Internet Explorer object hierarchy. The other objects in the hierarchy exist only as subobjects of the Application object. You can use any of the methods we discussed in Chapter 14 to create an instance of the Application object, as shown here:

```
Sub StartIE()
    Dim IE As Object
    Set IE = CreateObject("InternetExplorer.Application")
    IE.Navigate "www.microsoft.com/intdev"
    Do While IE.Busy
        DoEvents   ' Let Windows handle other applications.
    Loop
    IE.Visible = True ' Show Internet Explorer after page is loaded.
End Sub
```

**NOTE**  Because no object library is supplied with Internet Explorer, you must declare your variables to be of type Object.

The procedure on the previous page will create a new instance of Internet Explorer, make it visible to the user, and move to the given URL address. When the procedure ends, you will notice that Internet Explorer is still running. With some Automation objects, setting the variable to Nothing closes the object; with Internet Explorer, however, you must first call the Quit method.

The Application object has the following properties that allow you to manipulate Internet Explorer (not all are included in this list):

- **Busy** returns a Boolean value indicating whether Internet Explorer is currently loading a page.

- **FullScreen** returns or sets whether Internet Explorer is maximized.

- **Height** returns or sets the height of the Internet Explorer window.

- **Left** returns or sets the location of the left border of the Internet Explorer window.

- **LocationName** returns the name of the current page.

- **LocationURL** returns the URL address of the current page.

- **StatusBar** returns or sets a Boolean value indicating whether the status bar in the Internet Explorer window is visible.

- **StatusText** returns or sets the text in the status bar.

- **Top** returns or sets the location of the top border of the Internet Explorer window.

- **Type** returns the type of browser being used.

- **Width** returns or sets the width of the Internet Explorer window.

- **Visible** returns or sets a Boolean value indicating whether the Internet Explorer window is visible.

The Internet Explorer Application object has the following methods. (Not all methods are listed here.)

- **GoBack** moves you back to the previous page in the history list.

- **GoForward** moves you to the next page in the history list.

- **GoHome** moves you to your start page.

- **GoSearch** moves you to your search page.

- **Navigate** moves you to a specific URL address.

- **Refresh** refreshes the current page.

- **Stop** stops the current page from loading.

- **Quit** exits the Internet Explorer.

Although the Internet Explorer object model is limited compared to Office applications, you do have the same basic abilities to manipulate the browser using VBA instead of working through the interface.

# Creating Web Pages from Database Objects

Microsoft Access is a powerful database application that gives you access to the Internet and intranets. You also have the capability to easily format your data to be put on the Internet or on an intranet. Simply tell Microsoft Access to save an object as an HTML document, and Access will create the necessary HTML files for you.

An HTML file is a text file that allows you to format text for display on a browser and to create hyperlinks to other documents. HTML is a platform-independent language with which you can achieve some sophisticated results. We're not going to cover HTML here. However, you can find many books on working with HTML that will teach you how to code your own Web pages from scratch.

Using Microsoft Access to export your database objects, you do not have to worry too much about the HTML language—Microsoft Access takes care of it for you. When Microsoft Access database objects are exported, they will create either a static or a dynamic Web page.

## Static Web Pages

A static Web page is a page that will show a representation of the data at the time it was saved, similar to a snapshot-type recordset in DAO. Changes to the data in the database are not reflected in the Web page. To incorporate the updates into the Web page, you would have to re-create the page. You can use Microsoft Access tables, queries, forms, and reports to create a static Web page.

> **NOTE** OLE objects cannot be saved to a Web page.

To create a static Web page, follow these steps:

1. In the Database window, click the table, query, form, or report you want to save as a Web page.

2. Choose Save As/Export from the File menu.

3. In the Save As dialog box, select To An External File Or Database, and then click OK.

**4.** In the Save As Type drop-down list on the Save *Object* In dialog box, select HTML Documents, as shown below. The Save Formatted check box allows you to preserve any formatting of the data. For example, data that is formatted as currency in your database will include the "$" in the Web page representation if this box is checked. The Autostart check box allows you to open the Web page in your browser immediately after it is created. Click the Export button.

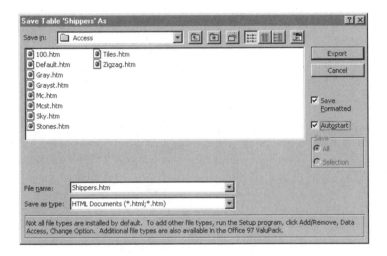

When you save a form or report as HTML, if you want Microsoft Access to merge an HTML template with the new HTML document, you can specify this template in the HTML Output Options dialog box, which will be displayed after you click the Export buttons.

> **NOTE** You can also use the Publish To The Web Wizard to create static Web pages. We will discuss how this wizard works later in the chapter.

> **NOTE** If you do not have the HTML Documents file type available in the Save As dialog box, run the Setup program again for Microsoft Office. In the Setup program, click the Add/Remove button, select the Data Access item, and click the Change Option button. Then select the Database Drivers item, and click the Change Options button. Select the Text And HTML Driver item. Click the OK button and then the Continue button to install the new component.

When you save any Microsoft Access table, query, or form as an HTML document, the resulting page will appear as similar as possible to the original data representation. If you want to save a Microsoft Access report as a static Web page, be aware that one page will be created for each page of output the report generates. This happens because you are electing to have a static display of your data on the Web. When these pages are created, Microsoft Access will create the appropriate hyperlinks on the page so that you can move from one page to another without having to know the names of the pages.

If you want to modify how the output looks, you can specify an HTML template. A sample HTML template is shown below. It simply defines placeholders for Microsoft Access information, including tags to the next and last page. The parts of this template that are of interest to Microsoft Access are the information for AccessTemplate_Title, which is the place to put the name of the object you are exporting; the information for AccessTemplate_Body, which is a placeholder for the data of the object being exported; and the first page, previous page, next page, and text page tags, which tell Access to create links among the various pages.

```
<HTML>

<TITLE><!--ACCESSTEMPLATE_TITLE--></TITLE>

<BODY BGCOLOR="#FFFFFF">

<!--ACCESSTEMPLATE_BODY-->

</BODY>

<BR><BR>

<A HREF = "<!--AccessTemplate_FirstPage-->">First</A>
<A HREF = "<!--AccessTemplate_PreviousPage-->">Previous</A>
<A HREF = "<!--AccessTemplate_NextPage-->">Next</A>
<A HREF = "<!--AccessTemplate_LastPage-->">Last</A>

</HTML>
```

For information on using an HTML template, see Chapter 21 of *Building Applications with Microsoft Access*, an online book that comes with the Microsoft Office CD-ROM. The Microsoft Access online help topic titled "About HTML template files" gives a full listing of the HTML template tokens that Access understands.

## Dynamic Web Pages

A dynamic Web page is a page that shows a representation of the data as it exists in the table at the time the page is being viewed, similar to a dynaset-type recordset in DAO. Dynamic Web pages provide viewers with up-to-date information.

You can export Microsoft Access tables, queries, and forms to create a dynamic Web page. Because this data is "live," an HTML file by itself cannot be used. In addition to the HTML file, an IDC and HTX file are created. The IDC file uses a predefined data source to open a database and query for requested information. The HTX file is used to format the resulting data into a Web page for the user.

> **NOTE** After building a dynamic Web page, you must store it on a machine that is running Microsoft Internet Information Server, because the server itself will query the database for the requested information.

To create a data source, follow these steps:

1. Open the Windows Control Panel and double-click the 32bit ODBC icon.

2. To create a System DSN, which is a data source that all Internet Information Server HTX/IDC files can use, click the System DSN tab; you will see the following dialog box:

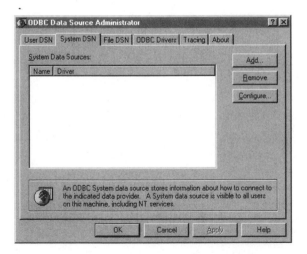

3. Choose the Add button, and then choose Microsoft Access Driver (*.mdb) in the dialog box. This specifies which ODBC driver you will be using to access the data. After clicking the Finish button, the following dialog box allows you to specify the database-specific information:

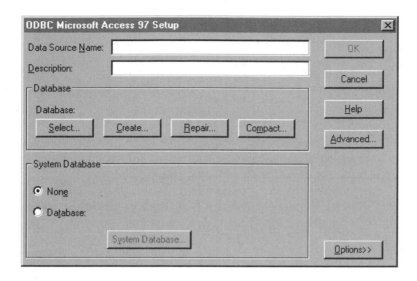

4. You can enter any data source name. This name is what you will refer to when creating your dynamic Web pages. Click the Select button, and choose the Microsoft Access database from which you want to extract information. Click OK in the Select Database dialog box, then click OK in the ODBC Microsoft Access 97 Setup dialog box. Then click OK in the ODBC Data Source Administrator dialog box.

Once a data source exists, you can create your dynamic Web page. Just follow these steps:

1. In the Database window in Microsoft Access, click the table, query, or form you want to present in a dynamic Web page.

2. Choose Save As/Export from the File menu.

3. In the Save As dialog box, select To An External File Or Database, and then click OK.

4. In the Save As Type drop-down list on the Save *Object* In dialog box, click Microsoft IIS 1-2. Click the Export button.

5. In the HTX/IDC Output Options dialog box, shown on the next page, you can specify the data source name that will be used to query the database; a user name and a password, if it is required to open the database; and an HTML template, if you want Microsoft Access to merge one with the HTX file. Click OK.

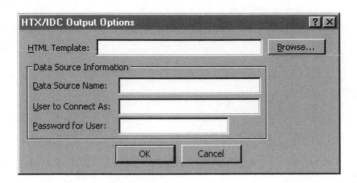

Using the above process to export the Shippers table in the CHAP15.MDB database will produce the following IDC and HTX files:

### SHIPPERS.IDC

```
Datasource:Acc97
Template:Shippers.htx
SQLStatement:SELECT * FROM [Shippers]
Password:
Username:
```

### SHIPPERS.HTX

```
<HTML>
<TITLE>Shippers</TITLE>
<BODY BGCOLOR="#FFFFFF">
<TABLE BORDER=1 BGCOLOR=#ffffff CELLSPACING=0><FONT FACE="Arial"
COLOR=#000000><CAPTION><B>Shippers</B></CAPTION>
<THEAD>
<TR>
<TH BGCOLOR=#c0c0c0 BORDERCOLOR=#000000 ><FONT SIZE=2 FACE="Arial"
COLOR=#000000>Shipper ID</FONT></TH>
<TH BGCOLOR=#c0c0c0 BORDERCOLOR=#000000 ><FONT SIZE=2 FACE="Arial"
COLOR=#000000>Company Name</FONT></TH>
<TH BGCOLOR=#c0c0c0 BORDERCOLOR=#000000 ><FONT SIZE=2 FACE="Arial"
COLOR=#000000>Phone</FONT></TH>
</TR>
</THEAD>
<TBODY>
<%BeginDetail%>
<TR VALIGN=TOP>
<TD BORDERCOLOR=#c0c0c0  ALIGN=RIGHT><FONT SIZE=2 FACE="Arial"
COLOR=#000000><%ShipperID%><BR></FONT></TD>
<TD BORDERCOLOR=#c0c0c0 ><FONT SIZE=2 FACE="Arial"
COLOR=#000000><%CompanyName%><BR></FONT></TD>
<TD BORDERCOLOR=#c0c0c0 ><FONT SIZE=2 FACE="Arial"
COLOR=#000000><%Phone%><BR></FONT></TD>
```

```
</TR>
<%EndDetail%>
</TBODY>
<TFOOT></TFOOT>
</TABLE>

</BODY>

<BR><BR>

</HTML>
```

As you can see from the preceding files, the IDC file is querying the data source on the server for the information from the Shippers table. The resulting information is then formatted according to the HTX file, which is simply an HTML template file that formats the data in a tabular format.

### Creating Active Server pages

Active Server pages are Web pages that use scripting, a language understood by Internet Information Server, in this case to extract data from a database and display it on a Web page. Active Server pages can be used only with Microsoft Information Internet Server 3.0 or later. Starting with Microsoft Internet Information Server 3.0, the type of browser you are using does not matter when it comes to Active Server pages. Internet Information Server 3.0 includes the core objects and basic components Web developers need to get up-and-running quickly. These include database access, state management, form processing, file access, dynamic billboards, browser capability determination, and a content linking component that specifies previous and next links.

What does this mean to Microsoft Access developers? Microsoft Access developers can now put their forms on the Web. If you have a form that shows in single Form view, such as the Customers form in the Northwind Traders database, you can export it as an Active Server page. This will allow users to view the page almost exactly as you designed it in Microsoft Access and look at the underlying data as it concurrently exists in the database! To create an Active Server page, follow these steps:

1. In the Database window, click the table, query, or form you want to make available as an ActiveX Server page.

2. Choose Save As/Export from the File menu.

3. In the Save As dialog box, select To An External File Or Database, and then click OK.

4. In the Save As Type drop-down list on the Save *Object* In dialog box, select Microsoft Active Server Pages. Click the Export button.

**5.** In the Microsoft Active Server Pages, Output Options dialog box, shown below, you can specify the data source name that will be used to query the database; a user name and a password, if required to open the database; an HTML template, if you want Microsoft Access to merge one with the HTX file; the URL for the server where the Active Server page will reside; and the Session Timeout setting, which determines how long a connection to the server is maintained after the user stops working with the Active Server page. Click OK.

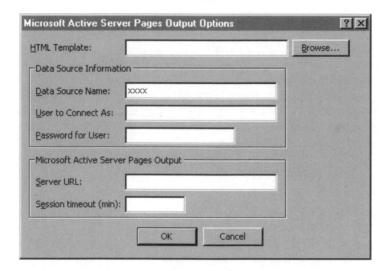

The forms you create in Microsoft Access are not guaranteed to look *exactly* the same on the Web. Not all controls available in Microsoft Access can be used in the contents of a Web page. The controls in Microsoft Access that are not supported in Active Server pages are Tab, Rectangle, Line, Page Break, Unbound Object Frame, Bound Object Frame, Image, and the background of a form when set with the Picture property. Other controls will look as they did in Microsoft Access, but because the underlying code in them is not added to the page they will not function in the same way. Once the HTML page is generated, you do have the ability to add scripting to the control's events, however.

> **NOTE**  You can add code to your Active Server pages by using an ActiveX scripting language such as VBScript. You can obtain more information on this language at
>
> http://www.microsoft.com/intdev

## Importing HTML Tables

In Microsoft Access 97 you have the ability to import and link HTML tables into your database. When you link to an HTML table, Microsoft Access stores the HTML table in your Windows cache folder and builds a table from the cached data so that connection time to the page is minimal. Because of this, however, the information that comes back from a linked HTML table is always read-only.

Tables that exist in HTML pages can also be imported into your Microsoft Access database. To import or link to an HTML table, follow these steps:

**1.** Choose Get External Data from the File menu, and then select Import.

**2.** In the Files Of Type drop-down list, select HTML Documents.

**3.** Specify the file to import by selecting it in the dialog box or typing a valid URL address in the File Name text box.

**4.** Click the Import button.

Microsoft Access starts a wizard that will walk you through the process of creating a new table in your database with the data from the HTML table.

Because tables in HTML pages can include items besides text, you can't always import the tables successfully in Microsoft Access. The HTML tags that are supported when importing HTML tables follow:

| HTML Tag | Description |
| --- | --- |
| `<TABLE>...</TABLE>` | Specifies the beginning and end of the table |
| `<TH...>...</TH>` | Specifies table header cells |
| `<TR...>...</TR>` | Specifies a row in a table |
| `<TD...>...</TD>` | Specifies table data cells |
| `<CAPTION...>...</CAPTION>` | Specifies the table's caption, usually at the beginning or end of the table |

For more information on the supported tags and various HTML table syntax that may be used, see Chapter 21 of *Building Applications in Microsoft Access*.

## Creating a Web Representation of Your Database

Microsoft Access 97 also provides a wizard that can publish your database to the Web. With this wizard you can create any type of Web page discussed in this chapter: static, dynamic, or Active Server. To start the wizard, choose Save As HTML from the File menu. You will then be presented with the dialog box shown in Figure 15-11 on the following page.

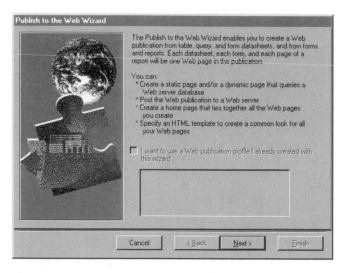

**Figure 15-11.** *Page 1 of the Publish To The Web Wizard.*

This first dialog box allows you to select any profile that you have previously created through the wizard. If this is your first time running the wizard, there won't be anything for you to select in the first screen. Click the Next button, which displays page 2 of the wizard (Figure 15-12). On this screen you can select multiple objects in the database.

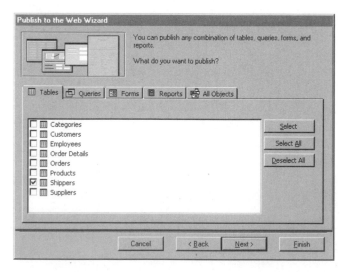

**Figure 15-12.** *Page 2 of the Publish To The Web Wizard.*

Page 3 of the Publish To The Web Wizard (Figure 15-13) allows you to select any HTML document template from which to create your new Web pages. Notice that you also have the option of selecting a different template for any object.

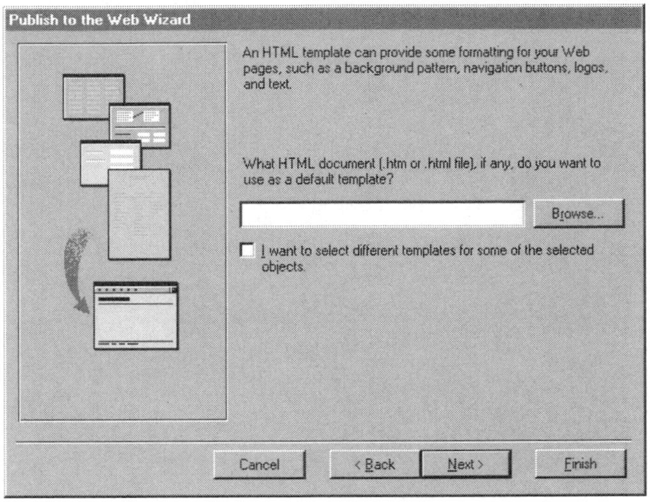

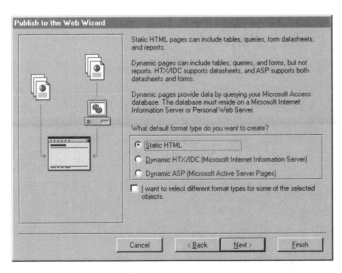

**Figure 15-13.** *Page 3 of the Publish To The Web Wizard.*

Now you can select the type of Web page or pages that you would like to create: static, dynamic, or Active Server. You may elect to create a different type of page for any object. (See Figure 15-14.)

**Figure 15-14.** *Page 4 of the Publish To The Web Wizard.*

If you chose either dynamic or Active Server pages in page 4, the page shown in Figure 15-15 will appear. This page will allow you to enter the data source information so that the appropriate IDC or ASP file can be created. You can also enter the Server URL and Session_Timeout properties if the type of page you are creating is an Active Server page.

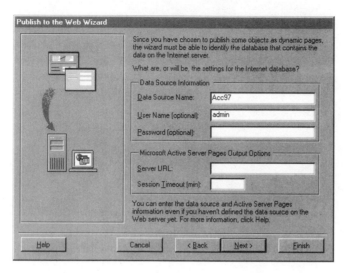

**Figure 15-15.** *Page 5 of the Publish To The Web Wizard.*

The dialog box shown in Figure 15-16 will appear next, regardless of the type of Web pages you chose. Select a location to save the Web pages.

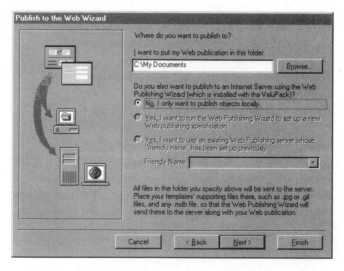

**Figure 15-16.** *Page 6 of the Publish To The Web Wizard.*

The next page of the Publish To The Web Wizard (Figure 15-17) gives you the ability to create a home page. A home page will provide hyperlinks to the other pages that you create. If you do not elect to do this, you will have to create a Web page manually to link the other pages together.

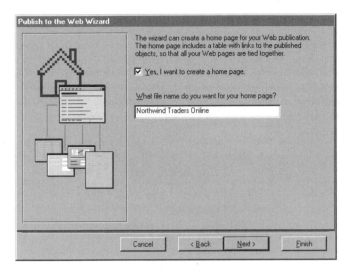

**Figure 15-17.** *Page 7 of the Publish To The Web Wizard.*

The final page of the wizard (Figure 15-18) allows you to save your responses to the wizard in a Web publication profile. If you do so, whenever you run this wizard again, you can choose the profile in the first page of the wizard. Choosing a profile pre-sets all the choices in the wizard, but you still have the option of changing any choices on any page of the wizard.

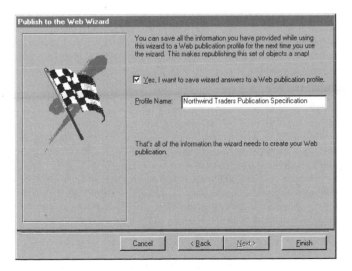

**Figure 15-18.** *Page 8 of the Publish To The Web Wizard.*

As you can see, the Publish To The Web Wizard makes creating an online representation of your database quick and easy.

## SUMMARY

Now that you know about the Internet features Microsoft Access 97 has to offer, be sure to use them in your applications. The era of the Internet is just beginning—the more you use the Internet and become familiar with its workings, the easier it will be to integrate your Microsoft Access applications with it.

Microsoft Access is a very powerful database application that allows you to create both simple and complex solutions. We hope this book has not only introduced you to the world of VBA but has also shown you how to use this powerful programming language to extend the feature set of Microsoft Access.

# PART

# FIVE

## Appendixes

# Using Dynamic-Link Libraries (DLLs)

One major advantage to writing Microsoft Windows applications is that much of the code and functionality is already provided for you, often through dynamic-link libraries (DLLs). As a developer, you will want to use this built-in functionality in your applications for several reasons:

■ The interface among Windows applications is uniform, so learning to use new Windows applications is easier for users. If your application is easy to use, more people will adopt it.

■ DLLs can perform tasks that are not possible from within Microsoft Access. For example, say that you want to determine the amount of free disk space, the directory in which a user installed Windows, or the name of the user currently logged on to the network. You can find out all of this information by using DLLs.

■ DLLs improve your application's performance. DLLs are generally written in C or C++, and depending on the functionality of the DLL, performance can be much faster than if it were written in Microsoft Visual Basic. Complex calculations that might not even be possible in Visual Basic can be written using DLLs.

■ You can update a DLL without having to modify your application. If you are calling a procedure in a DLL and a newer version of the DLL is installed, your application receives those enhancements automatically.

■ If you have a set of procedures that you commonly use (for example, some mathematical calculation procedures) and they compile to approximately 45 KB, when you link this file into your other applications you add 45 KB of overhead to each application. By creating this set of procedures as a DLL, you'll allow all of the applications to share the

DLL procedures so that they are linked dynamically when an application needs them.

The many DLLs that exist as part of the Windows family of operating systems will provide you with numerous options for using built-in code. Even if you've never created or called a DLL before, the information provided in this appendix will give you insight into the functionality of Microsoft Access and the Microsoft Windows 95 operating system.

In this appendix we have provided cross references to the C source code for the examples on the companion CD. We in no way intend to teach you C; however, after calling the DLL and viewing the C code, you'll have a much better understanding of what is taking place in the DLL. If you intend to write DLLs in C, these samples will be a very valuable resource and you can use many of them as a starting point.

If you do not have a C compiler, you can find the DLL that all of the examples in this appendix call on the CD that accompanies this book. Simply copy ACC-DEVHB.DLL to your \Windows\System directory. If you do have a C compiler, you can modify and compile the code provided.

## What Is a DLL?

Simply put, a DLL is a group of procedures. Think of a DLL as a module in Microsoft Access, with the procedures in a DLL equating to the procedures within the module. Dynamic-link libraries are the key components of the Microsoft Windows operating system. There are hundreds of procedures you can call from a vast assortment of DLLs. Some of these procedures interact with the user interface, and others perform system-level actions. The procedures in the DLLs that come with Windows are more commonly referred to as the Windows API (Application Programmer's Interface).

> **NOTE** Because DLLs are generally written in C or C++, you have to be proficient in at least one of these languages in order to create complex DLLs. You can also create DLLs in Fortran or Pascal.

## What DLLs Can You Call?

The following DLLs comprise the main Windows libraries:

- Kernel32.dll
- User32.dll
- Gdi32.dll
- AdvApi32.dll

We will examine each of these DLLs in addition to some DLLs relating to multimedia and telephone usage in more detail in the "Core Windows DLLs" section later in this appendix.

If you intend to use DLLs or the Windows API from Microsoft, you'll have to get the documentation required to use these procedures properly. Here is a partial list of where you can obtain the documentation for the Windows API:

- Microsoft Win32 Software Development Kit

- Microsoft Developer Studio

- The Microsoft Developer's Network

- The Microsoft Knowledge Base

For more information on any of these products, search Microsoft's Web site at http://www.microsoft.com.

You have literally hundreds of APIs to choose from. Some APIs are provided with various software development kits. Many third-party DLLs are also available. When using non-Microsoft DLLs, be sure to get the documentation you need from the vendor.

## What DLLs Can't You Call?

Microsoft Access 97 is a 32-bit application and runs only under Microsoft's 32-bit family of operating systems, which includes Windows 95 and Microsoft Windows NT 3.51 or higher. As a rule, you can't under any circumstances call 16-bit DLLs from within Microsoft Access 97—you'll receive a run-time error if you attempt to do so.

More important, you can't call a procedure within a DLL unless you have the proper Declare statement. In addition, the procedure in the DLL must be defined as exported so that it can be called from another application. You might not be able to call some functionality within a particular DLL because the developer decided not to make it available.

## How Do You Use a DLL?

Using a DLL from within Microsoft Access involves four steps.

### Step 1: Save Your Work!

Have you ever experienced a general protection fault or application error while working with the Microsoft Windows operating systems? It might have resulted from an improper call to a DLL. If you get such an error when working with DLLs, you might not have a chance to save your work. Depending on the type of error, Microsoft Access might shut down completely, and all of the work you've done up to that point could be lost. So to avoid frustration and wasted effort, don't forget to save your work.

## Step 2: Declare the DLL Procedure

You must declare the DLL procedure before you can call it. If you declare a DLL procedure in a module, it is Public by default and can be called by code anywhere in your application. You must declare the DLL procedure in the Declarations section of the code module. Here is a sample declaration:

```
Declare Function IsIconic Lib "user32" _
    (ByVal hwnd As Long) As Long
```

If you declare a DLL procedure in a class module, you must declare it as Private. Declare statements within a class module cannot be Public. The following code shows a sample declaration of a function called IsIconic using the Private keyword:

```
Private Declare Function IsIconic Lib "user32" _
    (ByVal hwnd As Long) As Long
```

How do you figure out the details of how the procedure should be declared? Included with the Microsoft Office Developer Edition is the API Viewer, API-LOAD.EXE. This application has one form, shown in Figure A-1, that allows you to select any Windows API function and copy it to the clipboard so that you can simply paste the Declare statement into your Microsoft Access application.

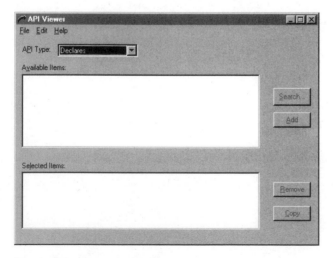

**Figure A-1.** *Win32 API Viewer.*

To see the list of Win32 API functions, choose Load Text File from the File menu, select Win32api.txt, and click OK. You will then be prompted to convert this file to a database. If you want to convert the file, go ahead. This will decrease load time in the future but is not required. Look for the IsIconic API in the Available Items list box. Double-click IsIconic, and it will appear in the Selected Item text box. Click the Copy button. This Declare statement is now in the clipboard. You can open the module of your choice within Microsoft Access and choose Paste from the Edit menu. Although the IsIconic Declare statement may seem straightforward, you will see later in this appendix that declarations for DLL procedures can be fairly complex.

## Step 3: Call the Procedure

The function IsIconic determines whether a window is minimized. The function will return 1 if the form is minimized and 0 if it is in any other state. By searching in the Win32 SDK, you can determine the return values for the IsIconic function as well as for all of the Win32 APIs.

Now that the procedure has been declared, you can call the IsIconic function just as you would call any other function in any other procedure in Microsoft Access. If this were a sub procedure, you would call it just as you would any other sub procedure in Microsoft Access. In fact, after you declare your procedure you will see the ScreenTip for the procedure, as shown in Figure A-2, when typing in the function name.

```
lResult = IsIconic(
          IsIconic(ByVal hwnd As Long) As Long
```

**Figure A-2.** *ScreenTip for the IsIconic procedure.*

## Step 4: Save Your Work!

Sound familiar? The final step is the same as the first one: **save your work**! Microsoft Access can't verify that you are passing correct values to a DLL procedure. If you pass incorrect values, your application might crash. We can't stress this point enough: save your work often when you're working with DLLs.

# How Do You Create a DLL?

Although you can create DLLs in several languages, in C or C++ you will need the following files in order to create even the simplest DLL:

- A C file (*.CPP), which will contain the source code

- A mak file (*.MAK), which will contain a list of files necessary to compile and link your DLL

■ A def file (*.DEF), which will hold the export information so that VBA can find the procedures within the DLL

The examples shown here were created using Microsoft Visual C++ 4.2, but you could use any C++ compiler. We're not going to teach you C++ or how to use a C++ compiler. Use your favorite C++ compiler to create a DLL project that includes the following .CPP file. The procedure in this sample file will add two numbers passed to the DLL and return the sum.

```
short _stdcall AddTwoNumbers(short x,short y)
{
    short sum;

    // Add the values
    sum = x + y;
    // return the result
    return (sum);
}
```

Save the file as MYDLL.CPP.

**NOTE**    Notice that the _stdcall keyword is used prior to the function name. This keyword is required for Win32 functions that will be called from any VBA application.

Now you'll need to create the definition file (.DEF), which permits the DLL procedure to be identified by Microsoft Access and any other VBA application. The .CPP file at this point would compile and create the DLL, but you couldn't call it from Microsoft Access. Enter the following information into the .DEF file.

```
LIBRARY MYDLL
EXPORTS
    AddTwoNumbers @1
```

The first line identifies the name of the library this .DEF file will be associated with. The second line allows you to identify which functions can be called by other applications. The @1 after the name of the function defines the ordinal number that can be used to call the function. (For more information on using the ordinal number from Microsoft Access, see page 550.) Save the file as MYDLL-.DEF, and add it to the project.

You have now created all the files required to build the DLL and can compile it. Congratulations! You've just created a DLL!

## Calling the DLL from Microsoft Access

Now you need to know how to call your DLL from Microsoft Access. First open a database and create a new module. Then declare the procedure in the General Declarations section as follows:

```
Declare Function AddTwoNumbers Lib _
    "c:\msdev\projects\mydll\debug\mydll.dll" _
    (ByVal X As Integer, ByVal Y As Integer) As Integer
```

Of course, you'll need to change the path of the DLL to the project directory where you created the DLL.

If you do not have a compiler and would like to declare the procedure using the DLL from the companion CD, declare it as shown here after copying the DLL to your \Windows\System directory.

```
Declare Function AddTwoNumbers Lib "accdevhb.dll" _
    (ByVal X As Integer, ByVal Y As Integer) As Integer
```

You'll notice that the arguments in Microsoft Access are defined as type Integer, whereas in the DLL they were defined as type short. You must define arguments and return values appropriately, or Access will misinterpret the results of the DLL procedure; you could even receive a general protection fault when calling the procedure.

Once the procedure is declared, create a new sub procedure in the same module. In the following sub procedure, you will create three variables—two for the two integers you are passing and one for the values you are returning.

```
Sub CallAddTwoNumbers()
    ' Dimension the variables.
    Dim intX As Integer, intY As Integer
    Dim intRetVal As Integer

    intX = 1
    intY = 2
    intRetVal = AddTwoNumbers(intX, intY)
    MsgBox intRetVal
End Sub
```

Run the procedure to see the results. The sum of the two integers, 3, should appear in the message box.

If you want to learn more about the C++ side of creating DLLs, refer to the Microsoft Press book *Programming Windows 95* by Charles Petzold.

# DLLs in Detail

In the following sections you will discover the in-depth details of declaring DLLs and the parameters that are passed to them.

## Declaring a DLL Procedure

Declaring is a crucial part of calling DLLs. It is within the Declare statement that you provide Microsoft Access all the information about the DLL. This information includes the procedure's name and type, the DLL's location, the types of arguments the procedure accepts, and the return value's data type if the procedure is a function.

To declare a DLL procedure, you place a Declare statement in the Declarations section of a module. If two DLLs provide procedures that use the same name, you can declare only one of them. If you declare a DLL procedure in a standard module, it is Public by default and can be called by code anywhere in your application. To declare a DLL procedure in the Declarations section of a class module, you must include the Private keyword in the declaration.

Like Microsoft Access, DLLs have two main types of procedures: sub procedures and function procedures.

> **NOTE**
> If you have a DLL function procedure and you want to ignore the return value, you can declare it as a sub procedure in Microsoft Access.

### Sub procedures

Sub procedures perform tasks without returning values. You use the following syntax to declare sub procedures:

```
Declare Sub publicname Lib "libname" _
    [Alias "alias"] _
    [([[ByVal] variable [As type] _
    [,[ByVal] variable [As type]]...])]
```

This example uses an actual API:

```
Declare Sub ClientToScreen Lib "user32" _
    (ByVal.hWnd As Long, lpPoint As POINT)
```

### Function procedures

Function procedures return values. And because function procedures return a value, you need to specify the data type of the returned value at the end of the Declare statement. Here is the syntax for function procedures:

```
Declare Function publicname Lib "libname" _
    [Alias "alias"] _
    [([[ByVal] variable [As type] _
    [,[ByVal] variable [As type]]...])] As Type
```

An example using an actual API follows:

```
Declare Function IsIconic Lib "user32" _
    (ByVal hwnd As Long) As Long
```

> **WARNING** The procedure names that you declare are case-sensitive. If you declare the function "IsIconic" as "isiconic," you will receive run-time error 453: "Can't find DLL entry point isiconic in User32.dll." If no path is included in the library name, Microsoft Access searches the local directory, the Windows directory, the Windows System subdirectory, and finally any directories specified in the Path statement.

### Specifying the library name

Just as you name your modules in Microsoft Access, Declare statements tell Microsoft Access the name and location of the DLL. DLLs in the Windows System directory will be found even if you do not specify the directory. Because the Windows directory is in your Path statement, Microsoft Access will search the \System subdirectory for the DLL. A DLL does not have to be placed in the Windows System directory, however. If you do not place it there, you must specify the complete path to the file, as shown in the following Declare statement:

```
Declare Function AddTwoNumbers Lib _
    "c:\msdev\projects\accdevhb\debug\accdevhb.dll" _
    (ByVal X As Integer, ByVal Y As Integer) As Integer
```

## Using the Alias Keyword

To change the name of a given procedure to something more meaningful to you, you can use the Alias keyword in the Declare statement. The name of the procedure within the DLL—not your more meaningful name—follows the Alias keyword. For example, to rename the IsIconic function IsFormMinimized, you would declare the procedure as shown here:

```
Declare Function IsFormMinimized Lib "user32" _
    Alias "IsIconic" (ByVal hwnd As Long) As Long
```

> **NOTE** Library names and Alias arguments must have quotation marks.

You can also use the Alias keyword to change a function name that does not comply with Microsoft Access naming conventions. For example, a DLL created in C++ could have characters in procedure names that are not valid in Microsoft Access.

In addition, some procedures in DLLs might have the same name as procedures in Microsoft Access or they might have illegal names, so you must rename any such procedures to ensure that the procedure that gets called is the one you want. For example, the _lopen API procedure conflicts with the Microsoft Access function naming convention. To use this procedure, you must alias the procedure name as shown here:

```
Declare Function lopen Lib "kernel32" Alias "_lopen" _
    (Byval strPathName as String, ByVal lReadWrite as Long) _
    As Long
```

### Ordinal references

Some DLL procedures can be identified by a number known as an ordinal value. If you want to use the ordinal value from within Microsoft Access, you must use the Alias keyword. The ordinal number is the number designated in the EXPORTS section of the definition file.

The hardest part of using an ordinal number is finding it, especially if you did not create the DLL. You'll need to refer to the documentation to obtain this number or use a utility such as DUMPBIN, which comes with Microsoft Visual C++. To use this number, you alias it in your Declare statement by placing the pound symbol (#) followed by the actual number. For example, the library Kernel32 has a function GetStartupInfo, for which the ordinal number is 276. The following Declare statement shows how to declare this procedure using just the ordinal number:

```
Declare Sub GetStartupInfo Lib "kernel32" Alias _
    "#276" (lpStartupInfo As STARTUPINFO)
```

You call this procedure in the same way you would call any other procedure you declare. You will want to alias the ordinal number with a descriptive name similar to GetStartupInfo in the above Declare statement.

## Using the ByRef and ByVal Keywords

You use the ByRef and ByVal keywords to indicate how you want to pass variables. When you use the ByRef keyword to pass an argument by reference, the address of the original variable is passed to the procedure. If the procedure changes the value of the variable, the original variable is modified. You can also specify ByRef when you invoke the procedure, as shown here:

```
IsIconic(ByRef Form1.hwnd)
```

**NOTE** By default, VBA passes all arguments by reference. Other than for documentation purposes, you don't need to include the ByRef keyword to have a variable passed by reference.

When you pass an argument by value, using the ByVal keyword, a copy of the contents of the argument is passed to the procedure. If the procedure changes the value of the argument, the original variable is not affected. To pass an argument by value, place the ByVal keyword in front of the argument declaration in the Declare statement.

Many DLL procedures expect an argument to be passed by value. This means that they expect the actual value instead of its memory location. Refer to the documentation for the particular API you are calling to find out if a particular argument must be passed a certain way.

## Passing Data to DLLs

When items are passed to DLLs, some data types must be passed a specific way. In this section we'll look at some VBA data types and explain how to pass them to DLL procedures.

Microsoft Access VBA affords developers a wide variety of data types: variable-length strings, currency, objects, and user-defined types, to name just a few. In some of these data types, however, properties and objects might not be supported by the procedures within a DLL. You might need to convert the data type. The following table lists some data types and their C and VBA equivalents.

| C Argument Declaration | VBA Argument Declaration | What You Can Pass to the Procedure |
| --- | --- | --- |
| Pointer to a string (LPSTR) | ByVal *variable* As String | Any String or Variant variable |
| char | ByVal *variable* As Byte | Any expression that evaluates to a Byte |
| int | ByVal *variable* As Long | Any expression that evaluates to a Long |
| short | ByVal *variable* As Integer | Any expression that evaluates to an Integer |
| Windows handle (hWnd, hDC, hMenu) | ByVal *variable* As Long | Any expression that evaluates to a Long |

### Numerical values

You pass numerical data types such as Byte, Long, and Double to a DLL in the same way that you pass them to a procedure in Microsoft Access. The declaration must indicate the proper type. Remember to use the correct type, because the data types in C++ are not necessarily the same as those in VBA. For example, both C++ and VBA have an integer data type. However, in C++ an integer equates to 4 bytes, and in VBA to 2 bytes.

## The As Any keyword

Some DLL procedures can accept more than one type of data for the same argument. This means that the DLL has been developed to handle various data types and will treat them appropriately. To pass more than one type of data, declare the argument with the As Any keyword as shown here:

```
Declare Function FindWindow Lib "user32" Alias _
    "FindWindowA" (ByVal lpClassName As Any, _
    ByVal lpWindowName As Any) As Long
```

You may be asking yourself, "Since As Any is so flexible, why not just use it for everything?" Sorry, you can't. Some DLL procedures expect certain data types; if you pass an incorrect data type, your application might crash. So be certain the DLL truly can expect any data type before using the As Any keyword.

## Variants

Passing an argument of the Variant data type is very similar to passing a variant data type within VBA. There are very few limitations with passing variants because they can be passed either by reference or by value.

The Variant data type in C is actually a type of structure. The first element of the structure indicates the variable's data type. You can compare this value to the constants defined in the VarType structure. The next three elements of the structure are reserved for internal use by the type, and the last is a union. Here is the actual C++ type definition:

```
typedef struct tagVARIANT  {
    VARTYPE vt;
    unsigned short wReserved1;
    unsigned short wReserved2;
    unsigned short wReserved3;
    union {
        unsigned char      bVal;        /* VT_UI1     */
        short              iVal;        /* VT_I2      */
        long               lVal;        /* VT_I4      */
        float              fltVal;      /* VT_R4      */
        double             dblVal;      /* VT_R8      */
        VARIANT_BOOL       bool;        /* VT_BOOL    */
        SCODE              scode;       /* VT_ERROR   */
        CY                 cyVal;       /* VT_CY      */
        DATE               date;        /* VT_DATE    */
        BSTR               bstrVal;     /* VT_BSTR    */
        Iunknown    FAR* punkVal;       /* VT_UNKNOWN */
```

```
    Idispatch    FAR* pdispVal;     /* VT_DISPATCH    */
    SAFEARRAY    FAR* parray;       /* VT_ARRAY|*        */
    unsigned char FAR *pbVal;       /* VT_BYREF|VT_UI1  */
    short        FAR* piVal;        /* VT_BYREF|VT_I2   */
    long         FAR* plVal;        /* VT_BYREF|VT_I4   */
    float        FAR* pfltVal;      /* VT_BYREF|VT_R4   */
    double       FAR* pdblVal;      /* VT_BYREF|VT_R8   */
    VARIANT_BOOL FAR* pbool;        /* VT_BYREF|VT_BOOL */
    SCODE        FAR* pscode;       /* VT_BYREF|VT_ERROR */
    CY           FAR* pcyVal;       /* VT_BYREF|VT_CY   */
    DATE         FAR* pdate;        /* VT_BYREF|VT_DATE */
    BSTR         FAR* pbstrVal;     /* VT_BYREF|VT_BSTR */
    IUnknown     FAR* FAR* ppunkVal; /* VT_BYREF|VT_UNKNOWN */
    IDispatch    FAR* FAR* ppdispVal;/* VT_BYREF|VT_DISPATCH*/
    SAFEARRAY    FAR* FAR* parray;  /* VT_ARRAY|*      */
    VARIANT      FAR* pvarVal;      /* VT_BYREF|VT_VARIANT */
    void         FAR* byref;        /* Generic ByRef */
    };
};
```

Now let's put this to work. Microsoft Access includes a procedure called VarType that determines the data type of a variable. The following table shows just a partial list of the constants and return values of the VarType function.

| Constant | Value | Description |
|---|---|---|
| vbInteger | 2 | Integer |
| vbDouble | 5 | Double-precision, floating-point number |
| vbCurrency | 6 | Currency value |
| vbString | 8 | String |
| vbObject | 9 | Object |
| vbBoolean | 11 | Boolean value |

The C++ function MyVarType in the ACCDEVHB.CPP file on the companion CD simulates the VarType procedure. This function accepts a variant passed by value and returns the data type of the variant just as the VarType procedure does.

To use this function in Microsoft Access, you need to declare the procedure in the General Declarations section of a module in the following way. Keep in mind that if the DLL is not in your path the Lib should point to the location of the DLL.

```
Declare Function MyVarType Lib "accdevhb.dll" _
    (ByVal v As Variant) As Integer
```

A sample procedure, MyVarTypeProc, that calls the procedure from within Microsoft Access is included in the DLLs.MDB database on the companion CD.

## Strings

The String data type differs from a numerical data type because a string in VBA is actually a BSTR in C++. A BSTR is similar to a pointer to the address of a variable. It does not contain the actual value but rather a reference to the location of the data in memory. Strings in VBA start with a header that contains information used internally by VBA and are null-terminated, which means that the string ends in a null character (an ANSI 0). By default, strings are of variable length in VBA. You can, however, create strings of fixed length, as you will see later in this section.

By default, a VBA string argument, or BSTR, is passed by reference. This means that a pointer to the BSTR is passed, so the DLL procedure receives the address of the address of the data.

The UpperCaseByRef procedure in the ACCDEVHB.CPP file and the PassString-ByRef procedure in the DLLs.MDB database on the companion CD demonstrate how to pass strings by reference. Be careful when passing strings. If you fail to initialize the variable before passing it, you will pass a Null value to the procedure and may get unpredictable results. Null is not the same as "" and is discussed in the "Null" section in this appendix.

The UpperCaseByVal procedure in the ACCDEVHB.CPP file and the PassString-ByVal procedure in the DLLs.MDB database on the companion CD demonstrate how to pass strings by value. If you run this procedure, you will see that it achieves the same results as the PassStringByRef procedure. Although you explicitly pass the string variable by value, the DLL is still able to modify it. This is because the String data type in VBA is most similar in C++ to a BSTR, which contains the address of the actual string data. Therefore, when passing strings by reference or by value, a DLL will still be able to modify them. The String data type is the only data type in VBA for which this is true.

## LPSTR strings

The procedures in some DLLs recognize LPSTR strings, which are pointers to standard null-terminated C++ strings that have no header. The API can modify the string passed to the DLL rather than return a string. For example, the Get-WindowsDirectory API per the Win32 SDK documentation indicates the argument as an LPSTR:

```
UINT GetWindowsDirectory(
    LPTSTR  lpBuffer,       // address of buffer for Windows
                            // directory
    UINT    uSize           // size of directory buffer
    );
```

However, if the changed data is longer than the original string, the procedure simply writes beyond the end of the string, potentially corrupting other data.

For example, the GetWindowsDirectory procedure modifies the string for the path to the Windows directory. The way to call this procedure is to make the modified string a specified length and prefill it with null characters.

```
Declare Function GetWindowsDirectory Lib "kernel32" Alias _
    "GetWindowsDirectoryA" (ByVal lpBuffer As String, _
    ByVal nSize As Long) As Long
Sub WhereisWindows()
    Dim sWinDir As String
    Dim lLen As Long

    sWinDir = String(255, 0)  ' String length 255 with 0's
    lLen = GetWindowsDirectory(sWinDir, Len(sWinDir))
    sWinDir = left(sWinDir, lLen)
    sWinDir = sWinDir + "\"
    MsgBox "Windows is in " + sWinDir
End Sub
```

If you run the above procedure, the directory in which Windows is running is displayed.

### Null

What is null? Null is an unknown value. As mentioned earlier, it is *not* the same as "". You will often have to pass a null value to a DLL. Because null is an unknown, you will have to declare the argument with As String or As Any. Declaring the argument As String allows you to use the VBA constant vbNullString.

The keyword Null in VBA is not the same as what a C++ DLL expects. Therefore, you will need to pass a null value in a slightly different format. You can pass a null value to a DLL in two ways. The first way is to pass 0& when the argument is defined using As Any. The second is to pass the constant vbNull-String when the argument is defined As String. For example, the FindWindow procedure accepts two string arguments, so you declare it as follows:

```
Private Declare Function FindWindow Lib "User32" _
    Alias "FindWindowA" (ByVal Class As String, _
    ByVal Cap As String) As Integer
```

**NOTE** When working with the Win32 APIs, you may notice that some procedure names end in the letter *A* or *W*. These letters designate whether you are calling the ANSI or Unicode version of the

API, respectively. For more information on the differences between the two, search under "Unicode" in the Visual C++ documentation.

However, FindWindow also accepts a null pointer for either or both of its arguments. Passing a zero-length string ("") does not work; this passes a pointer to a zero-length string, not a null pointer. Instead, you should use the VBA constant vbNullString. The following VBA example demonstrates:

```
Sub FindAccessWindow()
    Dim iReturnVal As Integer

    iReturnVal = FindWindow(vbNullString, "Microsoft Access")
    MsgBox iReturnVal
End Sub
```

## Arrays

You have the ability to pass many different array types to a DLL. C++ has a data type named SAFEARRAY that allows VBA applications to pass arrays to DLLs. When working with arrays, you can pass either the entire array or just one of the array elements. You can pass individual elements of an array in the same way you pass any variable that has the same type as the base type of the array. You can pass an entire array by passing the first element of the array.

The procedure accepting the array must be able to handle an entire array. If it does not, you must pass one element at a time. Just like the Variant data type, the SAFEARRAY is a structure in C++.

The procedure AverageArray in the ACCDEVHB.CPP file on the companion CD for this book determines the upper and lower bounds of an array and then loops through the array producing the sum of the elements in the array. The Average-OfElements procedure in the DLLs.MDB database demonstrates how to pass an entire array.

**Using arrays of strings**    String arrays have the same ability as any other array. Working with an array of strings is not uncommon, especially in a database product. You may want to pass an array of data extracted from a table within your database. One of the great benefits of SAFEARRAYs is that they can contain elements of any allowable type, including BSTRs. If your DLL is written to use SAFEARRAYs, you can take advantage of passing these various data types. Otherwise, you'll be limited to numerical data.

The ArrayOfStrings procedure in the ACCDEVHB.CPP file and the BytesInString procedure in the DLLs.MDB demonstrate the versatility of SAFEARRAYs.

## User-defined types

Some DLL procedures may require you to pass a user-defined type (UDT). In the C++ programming language, UDTs are more commonly referred to as structures. VBA gives you the ability to pass either an entire UDT or any single element within a UDT. For example, the following code shows a UDT named Employee defined in the General Declarations section of a module:

```
Type Employee
    dHireDate As Date
    dblSalary As Double
    iAge As Integer
    strName As String * 25
End Type
```

> **NOTE** Declaring a variable as String * *length* tells Access that the variable is a fixed-length string.

If this data type is to be passed to a DLL, it is imperative that the type defined in VBA and the structure in C++ are the same size—element by element. In C++ the same type definition would appear as here:

```
#define MAXSIZE 26
typedef struct
{
    double    dblDate;
    double    dblSalary;
    short     iAge;
    char      strName[MAXSIZE];
} Employee;
```

To pass the entire UDT, pass by reference a variable of type Employee. User-defined types must be passed by reference. You can also return a UDT from a DLL procedure. The ModifyUDT procedure in the ACCDEVHB.DLL file and the PassUDT_toDLL procedure in the DLLs.MDB database on the companion CD demonstrate how to pass a UDT to a DLL procedure.

## Objects

In Microsoft Access 97 you can pass and return objects to and from a procedure. When doing so, you are actually passing a pointer to an OLE interface. Microsoft has devised a specification indicating what an object must support if it can be manipulated using Automation. Because this is a standard, you can be sure that any object that supports Automation, whether created by you or someone else, will work the same from any Windows application.

The procedure GetObj in the ACCDEVHB.CPP file on the companion CD accepts an object passed by reference and a string passed by value. The string, indicates the name of a method that belongs to the object and that GetObj is to invoke. The class module Class1 in the DLLs.MDB database contains a simple public sub procedure, the Clear method, as shown here:

```
Public Sub Clear()
    MsgBox "In the Clear Method"
End Sub
```

The PassObject procedure in the standard module named ACCDEVHB And Other Procedures in the same database demonstrates how to invoke this method by passing an object of type Class1 to the GetObj DLL procedure.

### Properties and handles

Much of your programming in VBA is done through the setting of properties. Properties can be passed to a DLL as long as the argument is declared as ByVal. One of the most common properties to pass to a DLL is a handle to an object. In the Windows environment, all windows have a unique handle, called an hWnd in C. Many Windows APIs that manipulate or check the state of a window require an hWnd as a parameter. All DLL procedures that expect a handle will have to have an argument declared as Long, and your Microsoft Access procedure will have to pass the handle by value.

Use the hWnd property of a form to pass the form's handle. You can open the Form1 and Use IsIconic forms in the DLLs.MDB database to see how to call a DLL procedure that requires a window handle.

In addition to the hWnd property of a form, Access also provides the hWnd-AccessApp property of the application object, which returns a handle to the Microsoft Access window. To use this property, refer to it as follows:

```
Application.hWndAccessApp
```

## Core Windows DLLs

In this section we'll cover the main Windows DLLs in more detail.

### Kernel32

The Kernel32.Dll includes many procedures related to system-level tasks, such as copying and moving files and opening communications ports. At some point you might need to determine which operating system a user is running. To do this, you can simply call the GetVersionEx function. This function accepts a UDT named OSVERSIONINFO as one of its arguments; this type definition can be retrieved from the API Viewer.

The OSVERSIONINFO data structure contains operating system version information, including:

- **dwMajorVersion** identifies the major version number of the operating system. For example, the major version number of Windows NT 3.5 is 3.

- **dwMinorVersion** identifies the minor version number of the operating system. For example, the minor version number of Windows NT 3.5 is 5.

- **dwBuildNumber** identifies the build number of the operating system in the low-order word. (The high-order word contains the major and minor version numbers.)

- **dwPlatformId** identifies the platform supported by the operating system. This member can have one of the following values:

| Value | Platform |
|---|---|
| VER_PLATFORM_WIN32_WINDOWS | Windows 95 |
| VER_PLATFORM_WIN32_NT | Windows NT |

The WhatOS procedure in the DLLs.MDB database on the companion CD shows you how to use the GetVersionEx function to determine the operating system currently being run.

> **NOTE** You need to change the OSVERSIONINFO argument from ByVal to ByRef in the GetVersionEx declaration statement provided by the Win32 API Viewer.

## User32

The User32.dll contains many functions related to user tasks, such as creating windows, testing to see whether a form is minimized, selecting an object, and shutting down Windows. For example, the GetSystemMetrics function retrieves various system metrics and system configuration settings. The table on the following page is a partial list of values that can be used by the GetSystemMetrics API.

| Value | Meaning |
| --- | --- |
| SM_CMOUSEBUTTONS | Number of buttons on mouse, or zero if no mouse is installed. |
| SM_CXFULLSCREEN, SM_CYFULLSCREEN | Width and height of the client area for a full-screen window. |
| SM_CXHTHUMB | Width, in pixels, of the thumb box in a horizontal scrollbar. |
| SM_CXMIN, SM_CYMIN | Minimum width and height, in pixels, of a window. |
| SM_CXSCREEN, SM_CYSCREEN | Width and height, in pixels, of the screen. |
| SM_CXSIZE, SM_CYSIZE | Width and height, in pixels, of a button in a window's caption or title bar. |
| SM_CYCAPTION | Height, in pixels, of the normal caption area. |
| SM_CYMENU | Height, in pixels, of a single-line menu bar. |
| SM_CYVTHUMB | Height, in pixels, of the thumb box in a vertical scrollbar. |
| SM_DEBUG | TRUE, or nonzero, if the debugging version of USER.EXE is installed; FALSE, or zero, otherwise. |
| SM_MOUSEPRESENT | TRUE, or nonzero, if a mouse is installed; FALSE, or zero, otherwise. |
| SM_CLEANBOOT | Windows 95 only: Value that specifies how the system was started. |
| SM_CMETRICS | Windows 95 only: Number of system metrics and flags. |
| SM_CYMINIMIZED | Windows 95 only: Dimensions, in pixels, of a normal minimized window. |
| SM_CYSMCAPTION | Windows 95 only: Height, in pixels, of a small caption. |
| SM_MIDEASTENABLED | Windows 95 only: TRUE if the system is enabled for Hebrew/Arabic languages. |
| SM_NETWORK | Windows 95 only: The least significant bit is set if a network is present; otherwise, it is cleared. |
| SM_SECURE | Windows 95 only: TRUE if security is present; FALSE otherwise. |
| SM_SLOWMACHINE | Windows 95 only: TRUE if the computer has a low-end (slow) processor; FALSE otherwise. |

The GetMouse_ScreenInfo procedure in the DLLs.MDB database on the companion CD shows how to use the GetSysMetrics API to get information on the size of the screen and number of mouse buttons.

## GDI

The Gdi32.dll includes many functions related to graphical appearance, such as fonts, text color, and bitmaps. The PrintScrn procedure in the DLLs.MDB database on the companion CD demonstrates how to capture a Microsoft Access screen and place it on the clipboard using the GDI APIs.

## ADVAPI32

The AdvApi32.dll contains many procedures related to security. These procedures are necessary to perform such tasks as shutting down or rebooting the system through code. The ADVAPI32-LogOff/Shutdown module in the DLLs-.MDB database on the companion CD contains procedures that show you how to use code to log off, shut down, and reboot your computer from Microsoft Access.

## WINMM

The Winmm.dll contains many functions that are related to multimedia, such as playing a wave file or a midi file. Using these procedures, you can turn your Microsoft Access applications into multimedia applications. The Multimedia-PlayWAV module in the DLLs.MDB database on the companion CD includes a procedure that uses the sndPlaySound API to play a WAV file.

## TAPI

The TAPI32.dll includes many procedures related to the telephone. The TAPI-PhoneDialer module in the DLLs.MDB database on the companion CD demonstrates how to use the tapiRequestMakeCall API to dial the telephone.

As you can see, the possibilities are limitless as to what your Microsoft Access application can do when using DLLs. We highly recommend looking at the Windows SDK or at the Visual C++ online documentation for more information on the functions described here and other APIs that make up the Windows operating systems.

# B

# Creating Windows Help Files

Useful and informative Help files make it easier for users to understand your application and work with it more efficiently. Just as important, professional-quality Help files enhance the value of your application. You'd be wise to make sure that your application's Help files are an integral part of your development process and not just tacked on as an afterthought.

The first step in creating Help files is to determine the topics you want to include and the best place to cover them in your application. To give you a better sense of the big picture of your planned Help system, try creating a flowchart of it to make sure that the content of your files is complete and that their arrangement makes sense and is easy to use.

In this appendix we're going to briefly introduce you to the components that make up a good Help system, discuss some of the tools you can use to create Microsoft Windows Help files, and look at some files you can use to access the full capabilities of the Windows Help system. We're also going to walk you through creating a sample Help project file. Even better, on the companion CD that comes with this book, you'll find complete and detailed instructions on how to create a Windows Help file system. This "tutorial" includes simple, straightforward examples. We created the examples from scratch rather than using the graphical user interface of the Microsoft Help Workshop that ships with the Office 97 Developer Edition because we wanted you to understand the fundamental issues involved in structuring Help files from the ground up. Once you know the rudiments of creating a Help system, you'll be able to use the Microsoft Help Workshop to create your Help file system much more quickly.

**TIP** You'll find more information about the Microsoft Help Workshop and how to build custom Help files in the Help Author's Guide (HCW.HLP) that ships with the Office 97 Developer Edition.

Here's a preview of the topics you'll find in the HELP.DOC file on the companion CD:

- Creating Help topics
- Keyword search for Help topics
- Help topic titles
- Topic IDs
- Hot spots: definitions, jumps, jumps to secondary windows, graphics
- Browse sequences
- Help macros
- Graphics
- Nonscrolling regions
- Pointing to additional Help topics
- Creating hot spots in nonscrolling regions
- Custom menus
- Custom buttons
- Enhanced keyword searches
- Creating contents files
- Calling dynamic-link libraries (DLLs)
- Adding multimedia to your Help files

## What Is a Windows Help File System?

Okay, let's start at the very beginning. In a nutshell, a Windows Help file system consists of Help files that provide online information about your application.

## What Is a Windows Help File?

And just what is a Windows Help file? A Windows Help file can be a combination of text and graphics (multimedia) divided into logical sections, or topics. Users can search through these topics by clicking hot spots, using keyword searches, or browsing through the topics.

## What Are the Help Compiler Tools?

The files listed in the following table ship with the Office 97 Developer Edition and comprise one set of tools that can be used to create a Windows Help file.

| Program | Filename | Description |
|---------|----------|-------------|
| Windows 95 Help Compiler | HCW.EXE | Microsoft Help Workshop (Graphical User Interface); translates a Help project file (.RTF) into a Help file (.HLP) |
| Windows 95 Help Compiler | HCRTF.EXE | Command line version of HCW.EXE; translates a Help project file (.RTF) into a Help file (.HLP) |
| Hotspot Editor | SHED.EXE | Puts Help jumps in pictures |
| Multi-Resolution Bitmap Compiler | MRBC.EXE | Combines bitmaps for different screen resolutions into one file; WINHELP picks the best bitmap; runs from a DOS prompt |

In this appendix and in the tutorial on the companion CD, you will be using the command line version of the Windows 95 Help Compiler (HCRTF.EXE) to learn about Help file basics and the graphical user interface of the Windows 95 Help Compiler (HCW.EXE) to organize and manage your Help file projects.

# Which Files Does Windows 95 Help Use?

The files listed in the following table can be used to access the full capabilities of the Windows 95 Help system. These files are examined in greater detail on the companion CD.

| File Type (extension) | Description | Comments |
|-----------------------|-------------|----------|
| HLP | Help file | Final Help file accessed by the user; generated and shipped by the developer |
| HPJ | Help project file (.HPJ) | Resource file used to help generate the final Help file; needed only for generating the Help file |
| RTF | Rich Text Format file | Contains the Help file topic information the user reads when viewing a Help file; needed only for generating the Help file in conjunction with the .HPJ |
| CNT | Contents file | Hierarchical table of contents for the topics contained in the Help file; created and shipped by the developer |
| GID | Contents database file | Hidden configuration file automatically generated by WinHelp when the user first opens the Help file; contains information about the Help file |
| FTS | Full-Text Search (index) file | Automatically generated by WinHelp when the user first opens the Help file's Find tab; contains information that allows the user to search the entire contents of the Help file |
| FTG | Full-Text Search (group) file | Automatically generated by WinHelp when the user first opens the Help file's Find tab; contains information about full-text search on multiple files |

TIP For the sake of simplicity when you're first learning how to create Help files, keep all of the component files you'll need in the same directory. You'll avoid file-referencing problems if you keep them together. Once you're comfortable with the process, you can begin to break out your different files into logical folders or locations. The graphical user interface of the Microsoft Help Workshop (HCW.EXE) is an excellent tool for this type of organization.

NOTE You can also use the methods presented in this appendix to create Help files for Microsoft Windows NT.

## More About the Help Project File (.HPJ)

The Help project file (.HPJ) contains all the information the Help compiler needs to combine .RTF files and other elements into a Help file. Among other information, the Help project file alerts the compiler to the following:

- Where to find the files used to build the Help file
- Which custom elements (including menus, buttons, and windows) are added to the Help file
- Which custom DLLs (if any) are used with the Help file
- Which options to include during the build process

You can use any text editor to create the Help project file. You must, however, save the file as unformatted text. The Help project file contains up to nine sections, each of which provides information for the Help compiler to follow at compile time. The table on the facing page describes each section that can be included in the Help project file.

NOTE The order in which these sections appear in the Help project file is relatively unimportant except for the [ALIAS] section, which must precede the [MAP] section.

## Creating a Sample Help Project File

Now that you know what sections comprise an .HPJ file, you are ready to create a sample one. Your sample Help file will use the following sections: [OPTIONS], [CONFIG], [BITMAPS], [FILES], and [WINDOWS]. Your sample Help project file will look like the code on the facing page. The sections are broken apart to make it easier for you to understand what each item in the section is doing.

| Section | Description |
|---|---|
| [OPTIONS] | Specifies what options (e.g., compression, error logging, copyright information) will be used when the Help file is compiled. |
| [ALIAS] | Allows multiple topic IDs to refer to one topic. |
| [BAGGAGE] | Lists files stored within the Help file after compilation. (This can make for a rather large Help file.) |
| [BITMAPS] | Lists bitmap type files to be included in the building of the Help file not already specified by the ROOT or BMROOT options in the [OPTIONS] section. |
| [BUILDTAGS] | Allows you to create different builds of your Help files by including or excluding topics. |
| [CONFIG] | Allows you to register WinHelp macros, custom menus, and custom buttons to be run when the Help file is opened. (You can even register custom DLLs to be called from within the Help file as macros.) |
| [CONFIG:$n$] | Lists all the macros that will be run when a particular window type defined in the [WINDOWS] section is opened. |
| [FILES] | Lists .RTF source files included in the build. Multiple .RTF files can contain Help topics to be compiled into one Help file. This is a required section. |
| [MACROS] | Allows you to automatically run a macro when a keyword has been selected by the user in the index. |
| [MAP] | Allows you to create context-sensitive Help by assigning topic IDs to context numbers that can be referenced from within your application such as Microsoft Access. |
| [WINDOWS] | Defines size, position, and colors of various windows. |

```
[OPTIONS]
TITLE = Application Help Title
COPYRIGHT = Application Copyright Info in About Dialog
COMPRESS=12 Hall Zeck
LCID=0x409 0x0 0x0 ;English (United States)
ERRORLOG = MyHelp.ERR
BMROOT = C:\TEST
ROOT = C:\TEST
```

This sample [OPTIONS] section indicates the following information to the Help compiler:

- The title bar of the Help file will display "Application Help Title."

- The copyright information will be displayed in the About dialog box of the Help file.

- Compression will be used during this build.

- Default language will be used when compiling the Help file.

- Error messages during the build will be saved in the file MYHELP.ERR.

- The directory where the WinHelp application will look for bitmap files specified by reference in the .RTF file is designated by the BMROOT option. This is used in conjunction with the [BITMAPS] section.

- The directory used to locate topic and data files listed in the Help project file is designated by the ROOT option.

> **NOTE**  When you compile a Help file, it will automatically use the name of the .HPJ file to generate the name of the .HLP file. If you want to specify a different name for the Help file, add HLP=YourName-Here.HLP in the [OPTIONS] section of the .HPJ file.

This sample [FILES] section indicates all of the .RTF files being used by this Help file:

```
[FILES]
MyHelp.RTF
```

This sample [BITMAPS] section indicates a graphic file that will be used and compiled into the Help file:

```
[BITMAPS]
Help.SHG
```

This sample [CONFIG] section indicates that the browse buttons will be available on the toolbar of the Help file:

```
[CONFIG]
BrowseButtons()
```

This sample [WINDOWS] section indicates the names of all windows and specifies the title and color of each:

```
[WINDOWS]
Main = , (0,0,1023,1023),,(255,255,255),(255,255,255)
Sec_Win = "This is the Secondary Window Caption",
(222,206,725,486),,(255,255,255),(192,192,192),1
```

That wasn't so hard, was it? This is just a taste of what you'll find on the companion CD.

## How Do I Select an Authoring Tool?

Another decision you'll have to make once you're ready to start creating your Windows Help file is which authoring tool to use. Because Help files are authored in a word processor, you have many options. The only requirement for the authoring tool is that it must support the Rich Text Format (.RTF) file format and custom footnotes. This requirement makes Microsoft Word an excellent choice.

To help you create Windows Help files even faster in Microsoft Word, try using the Word template called HelpTmpl.DOT on the companion CD. This file contains macros you can use to make formatting the Help topic file easy.

## What's Next?

Now it's time to take off the training wheels. Take some time to look through the HELP.DOC file on creating custom Help files that's included on the companion CD. After you've mastered the information there, it won't be long before you're writing Help files like the pros!

And since it never hurts to get a second opinion, here is another Microsoft Press book that contains information on writing Help files that you can use with your Microsoft Access applications: *Microsoft Windows 95 Help Authoring Kit*.

# INDEX

An *italic* page-number reference indicates a figure or table.

## Special Characters

& (ampersand)
    for concatenating strings, 17, 41–42, 69, *69*, 370–71
    for setting shortcut keys, 153, 175, 176
' (apostrophe) for comments, 16
* (asterisk)
    multiplication operator, *41*
    in SQL statements, 394
\ (backslash) rounding operator, *41*
[] (brackets)
    for optional arguments, 43
    for surrounding class names with spaces, 226
^ (caret) exponentiation operator, *41*
: (colon) for separating statements, 16
...(ellipsis) as a visual cue for buttons, 159
= (equal sign)
    for calling functions, 28, *29*
    relational operator, *41*, 374
>= (greater than or equal to) relational operator, *41*, 374
> (greater than) relational operator, *41*, 374
<= (less than or equal to) relational operator, *41*, 374
< (less than) relational operator, *41*, 374
– (minus sign) subtraction operator, *41*
<> (not equal to) relational operator, *41*
+ (plus sign) addition operator, *41*

\# (pound sign)
    for concatenating date/time values, 371
    for separating hyperlink parts, 501
? (question mark) as shorthand for Print, 93
; (semicolon) for terminating SQL statements, 394
/ (slash) division operator, *41*
_ (underscore)
    for event procedure names, 194
    for line continuation, 17

## A

AbsolutePosition property, 368
accelerator (access, shortcut) keys, 153, *153*, 174–76, *175, 176*
Access. *See Microsoft Access entries*
access (accelerator, shortcut) keys, 153, *153*, 174–76, *175, 176*
ActionControl property, 264
action queries, 396–97
Activate event, 199–200
activating forms, 141
ActiveControl property, 205
active form, 141
Active Server pages, 531–32
ActiveX controls, 150, 161–62, 471. *See also* Automation objects
ActiveX objects, 381–83
Add-In database splitter, 384, 466, *466*
AddItem method, 262, *263*
addition (+) operator, *41*
Add method, 238–39, 249–53, *250, 252,* 258–59, 262, 266

The manuscript for this book was prepared using Microsoft Word for Windows 95 and submitted to Microsoft Press in electronic form. Galleys were prepared using Microsoft Word for Windows 95. Pages were composed by Microsoft Press using Adobe PageMaker 6.01, with text type in Garamond and display type in Futura Medium Bold. Composed pages were delivered to the printer as electronic pre-press files.

*Cover Graphic Designer*
**Robin Hjellen**

*Cover Illustrator*
**George Abe, Landor Associates**

*Interior Graphic Designer*
**Kim Eggleston**

*Interior Illustrator*
**Travis Beaven**

*Principal Compositor*
**Barb Runyan**

*Principal Proofreader/Copy Editor*
**Roger LeBlanc**

*Indexer*
**Hugh Maddocks**

**Tim O'Brien** has been a professional in the computer industry for almost 10 years; however, he started programming in BASIC in 1981. Until recently the majority of his programming experience has been focused in database development. Prior to Microsoft, he was the Director of Computer Services for the Economic Development Commission of Mid-Florida and a Programmer/Analyst for Martin Marietta's Information Systems division, where he specialized in Clipper Summer '87, UNIX, and Visual Basic programming. Tim became a Microsoft Certified professional in 1992 and continues to hold certifications in Microsoft Access as well as being a Microsoft Certified Trainer in Access and Visual Basic. During his career at Microsoft he has had the opportunity to work on the Access Electronic Services team, develop the original Microsoft Access Security Wizard, participate in the development of the Survey Application, and be an Access Trainer/Subject Matter Expert for Microsoft Education Services, where he created courseware and trained Microsoft Solution Providers worldwide. Tim is currently a Strategic Account Engineer in Developer Support, where he specializes in OLE programming. Tim can be reached at Tim_OBrien@msn.com.

**Steven J. Pogge**, a Microsoft Certified Solutions Developer and Microsoft Certified Systems Engineer, grew up in sunny Orlando, Florida. He attended the University of Central Florida, where he received a B.S. in Political Science with a focus in International Law and Relations. He also received an M.A. in Applied Economics, with a focus in International Economics and Finance. Prior to

Microsoft, Steve developed XBase database applications for the Economic Development Commission of Mid-Florida and Lockheed-Martin. Steve is currently a Technical Account Manager for Microsoft's Corporate and ISV Premier customers. Before coming to his current position, Steve was a World Wide Training Specialist, designing and developing courseware for Microsoft Access. He also delivered these courses to support engineers and third-party vendors worldwide. Steve is a Floridian currently residing in Charlotte, North Carolina. He can be reached at Spogge@Microsoft.com.

**Geoffrey E. White**, a Microsoft Certified Solutions Developer, grew up in Yardley, Pennsylvania, and attended Seton Hall University, where he received a B.S. in Management Information Systems with a minor in German. Immediately out of school, he worked at Fox Software supporting the Fox family of database products. He came to Microsoft one month later when Microsoft acquired Fox Software. Geoff is currently a Microsoft Consultant specializing in Application Development in the Internet/Intranet and Client/Server arenas. Prior to his current position, Geoff was a Strategic Account Engineer supporting Microsoft's ISV customers; he was also a training specialist and participated in the course design of the Access Basic Programming, Access Developer's Toolkit, Visual FoxPro, and Visual Basic support courses. He has also delivered these database and programming courses to support engineers and third-party vendors worldwide. Geoff currently resides in Charlotte, North Carolina, with his wife, Michele, and dog, Amber. He can be reached at GeoffW@Microsoft.com.

# Tap the **power** *of the*

## *Microsoft®* **Excel 97** *Object Model*

## *and* **Visual Basic®** *for Applications.*

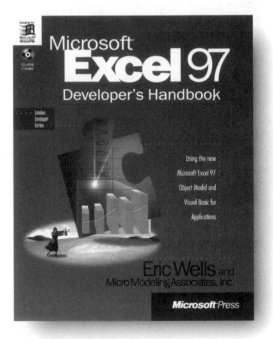

**Microsoft® Excel 97**
Developer's Handbook

Using the new
Microsoft Excel 97
Object Model and
Visual Basic for
Applications

**Eric Wells** and
Micro Modeling Associates, Inc.

**Microsoft** Press

**M**icrosoft Excel is a powerful development tool—and now it features important new Internet and intranet capabilities. That and much more is covered in the third edition of this classic one-volume reference for application programmers. The enclosed CD includes source code, files, utilities, and example applications. Get this valuable book. And get the most from Microsoft Excel 97.

| | |
|---|---|
| **U.S.A.** | **$39.99** |
| U.K. | £37.49 [V.A.T. included] |
| Canada | $53.99 |
| ISBN 1-57231-359-5 | |

**Microsoft®** Press

# The most *popular* office suite —*and the* *top* development platform.

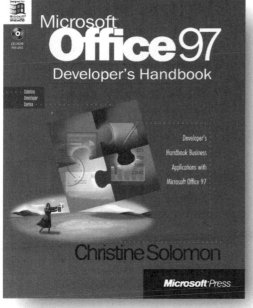

**Microsoft Office 97 Developer's Handbook**
Christine Solomon
*Microsoft* Press

**I**n this thoroughly revised edition, well-known author and experienced consultant Christine Solomon shows systems professionals and developers how to automate and re-engineer a wide assortment of businesses on the powerful Microsoft® Office 97 platform. You'll find plenty of information on new features and technologies. And everything is clarified with detailed explanations, sample applications, anecdotes, examples, and case studies. Plus, the enclosed CD-ROM contains source code and files for sample applications. Get MICROSOFT OFFICE 97 DEVELOPER'S HANDBOOK. And find out why Microsoft Office 97 is a whole new development.

| | |
|---|---|
| **U.S.A.** | **$39.99** |
| U.K. | £37.49 [V.A.T. included] |
| Canada | $53.99 |
| ISBN 1-57231-440-0 | |

*Microsoft* Press

**IMPORTANT—READ CAREFULLY BEFORE OPENING SOFTWARE PACKET(S).** By opening the sealed packet(s) containing the software, you indicate your acceptance of the following Microsoft License Agreement.

# *MICROSOFT LICENSE AGREEMENT*

(Book Companion CD)

This is a legal agreement between you (either an individual or an entity) and Microsoft Corporation. By opening the sealed software packet(s) you are agreeing to be bound by the terms of this agreement. If you do not agree to the terms of this agreement, promptly return the unopened software packet(s) and any accompanying written materials to the place you obtained them for a full refund.

## MICROSOFT SOFTWARE LICENSE

**1. GRANT OF LICENSE.** Microsoft grants to you the right to use one copy of the Microsoft software program included with this book (the "SOFTWARE") on a single terminal connected to a single computer. The SOFTWARE is in "use" on a computer when it is loaded into the temporary memory (i.e., RAM) or installed into the permanent memory (e.g., hard disk, CD-ROM, or other storage device) of that computer. You may not network the SOFTWARE or otherwise use it on more than one computer or computer terminal at the same time.

**2. COPYRIGHT.** The SOFTWARE is owned by Microsoft or its suppliers and is protected by United States copyright laws and international treaty provisions. Therefore, you must treat the SOFTWARE like any other copyrighted material (e.g., a book or musical recording) except that you may either (a) make one copy of the SOFTWARE solely for backup or archival purposes, or (b) transfer the SOFTWARE to a single hard disk provided you keep the original solely for backup or archival purposes. You may not copy the written materials accompanying the SOFTWARE.

**3. OTHER RESTRICTIONS.** You may not rent or lease the SOFTWARE, but you may transfer the SOFTWARE and accompanying written materials on a permanent basis provided you retain no copies and the recipient agrees to the terms of this Agreement. You may not reverse engineer, decompile, or disassemble the SOFTWARE. If the SOFTWARE is an update or has been updated, any transfer must include the most recent update and all prior versions.

**4. DUAL MEDIA SOFTWARE.** If the SOFTWARE package contains more than one kind of disk (3.5", 5.25", and CD-ROM), then you may use only the disks appropriate for your single-user computer. You may not use the other disks on another computer or loan, rent, lease, or transfer them to another user except as part of the permanent transfer (as provided above) of all SOFTWARE and written materials.

**5. SAMPLE CODE.** If the SOFTWARE includes Sample Code, then Microsoft grants you a royalty-free right to reproduce and distribute the sample code of the SOFTWARE provided that you: (a) distribute the sample code only in conjunction with and as a part of your software product; (b) do not use Microsoft's or its authors' names, logos, or trademarks to market your software product; (c) include the copyright notice that appears on the SOFTWARE on your product label and as a part of the sign-on message for your software product; and (d) agree to indemnify, hold harmless, and defend Microsoft and its authors from and against any claims or lawsuits, including attorneys' fees, that arise or result from the use or distribution of your software product.

## DISCLAIMER OF WARRANTY

**The SOFTWARE (including instructions for its use) is provided "AS IS" WITHOUT WARRANTY OF ANY KIND. MICROSOFT FURTHER DISCLAIMS ALL IMPLIED WARRANTIES INCLUDING WITHOUT LIMITATION ANY IMPLIED WARRANTIES OF MERCHANTABILITY OR OF FITNESS FOR A PARTICULAR PURPOSE. THE ENTIRE RISK ARISING OUT OF THE USE OR PERFORMANCE OF THE SOFTWARE AND DOCUMENTATION REMAINS WITH YOU.**

**IN NO EVENT SHALL MICROSOFT, ITS AUTHORS, OR ANYONE ELSE INVOLVED IN THE CREATION, PRODUCTION, OR DELIVERY OF THE SOFTWARE BE LIABLE FOR ANY DAMAGES WHATSOEVER (INCLUDING, WITHOUT LIMITATION, DAMAGES FOR LOSS OF BUSINESS PROFITS, BUSINESS INTERRUPTION, LOSS OF BUSINESS INFORMATION, OR OTHER PECUNIARY LOSS) ARISING OUT OF THE USE OF OR INABILITY TO USE THE SOFTWARE OR DOCUMENTATION, EVEN IF MICROSOFT HAS BEEN ADVISED OF THE POSSIBILITY OF SUCH DAMAGES. BECAUSE SOME STATES/COUNTRIES DO NOT ALLOW THE EXCLUSION OR LIMITATION OF LIABILITY FOR CONSEQUENTIAL OR INCIDENTAL DAMAGES, THE ABOVE LIMITATION MAY NOT APPLY TO YOU.**

## U.S. GOVERNMENT RESTRICTED RIGHTS

The SOFTWARE and documentation are provided with RESTRICTED RIGHTS. Use, duplication, or disclosure by the Government is subject to restrictions as set forth in subparagraph (c)(1)(ii) of The Rights in Technical Data and Computer Software clause at DFARS 252.227-7013 or subparagraphs (c)(1) and (2) of the Commercial Computer Software — Restricted Rights 48 CFR 52.227-19, as applicable. Manufacturer is Microsoft Corporation, One Microsoft Way, Redmond, WA 98052-6399.

If you acquired this product in the United States, this Agreement is governed by the laws of the State of Washington. Should you have any questions concerning this Agreement, or if you desire to contact Microsoft Press for any reason, please write: Microsoft Press, One Microsoft Way, Redmond, WA 98052-6399.

# Register Today!

### Return this
### *Microsoft® Access 97 Developer's Handbook*
### registration card for
### a Microsoft Press® catalog

U.S. and Canada addresses only. Fill in information below and mail postage-free. Please mail only the bottom half of this page.

1-57231-358-7A  **MICROSOFT® ACCESS 97**  *Owner Registration Card*
**DEVELOPER'S HANDBOOK**

_____

NAME

_____

INSTITUTION OR COMPANY NAME

_____

ADDRESS

_____

_____

CITY                                             STATE          ZIP

# **Microsoft**®*Press*
## *Quality Computer Books*

For a free catalog of
Microsoft Press® products, call
## **1-800-MSPRESS**

## **BUSINESS REPLY MAIL**
FIRST-CLASS MAIL    PERMIT NO. 53    BOTHELL, WA

POSTAGE WILL BE PAID BY ADDRESSEE

**MICROSOFT PRESS REGISTRATION**
MICROSOFT® ACCESS 97
DEVELOPER'S HANDBOOK
PO BOX 3019
BOTHELL  WA    98041-9946